# CONTRACT FARMING AND THE STATE

# CONTRACT FARMING AND THE STATE

## Experiences of Thailand and India

Sukhpal Singh

Publications

KALPAZ PUBLICATIONS

DELHI - 110 052

Contract Farming and the State: Experiences of Thailand and India
Rs. 890

ISBN : 81-7835-511-6



Published in 2006 in India by
Kalpaz Publications
C-30, Satyawati Nagar,
Delhi-110 052
Email : kalpaz@hotmail.com

*Lasertype Setting by*: Tact Computer Graphics, Delhi
*Printed at*: Salasar Imaging System, Delhi

*Dedicated to the memory of*

*My uncle S. Hardit Singh*
*and My father S. Mota Singh*
*who kenw the value of education*

# Contents

# Preface

The policies of liberaliztion and globalisation of agriculture have made inroads into the developing Asia during the 1990s. The pressures of increasing competition and demanding markets, besides global and local regulations, are forcing the agribusiness firms and farmers to explore and adopt new ways of working together. The liberaliztion of industrial sector has had effects on the farming sector in terms of entry and interest of agribusiness firms into the farm sector directly or indirectly in India. One such effect has been the introduction of contract farming in India in a very formal sense as a part of policy framework for agricultural development. Contract farming which involves contractual relations between agribusiness processing and/or marketing firms and farmers has been subjected to serious scholarly analysis in the context of African and Latin American countries where it was introduced much earlier (in the 1970s) and has been found to be reponsible for many undesirable developmental effects. In India, the studies are being undertaken only now. Fortunately, Thailand has had a very extensive and intensive experience with contract farming focusing so far and examines its relevance for small farmer dominated Indian agricultural sector and suffests ways and means of leveraging contract farming for agricultural development focusing on the role of the Indian state and the civil society.

Many friends and well wishers helped me in this project conducted in Thailand as an ASIA Fellow of the Asian Scholarship Foundation (ASF) of the Institute of International Education (IIE), Washington, with time and language constraints, and in the Indian Punjab. It may not be possible to thank them all but still a modest attempt has been made below:

**I am grateful to:**

Mr. Kowit Sittiyos, Sales/Export Executive, and Mr. Wasuthorn Sriwanawong, Factory Manager, KC Chiang Mai

Food Processing CO. Ltd. and Mr. Chawala Wongyai, Agro-Supply Manager and Mr. Sujai Pudnhoi, Assistant Agro-supply Manager of Frito Lay, Thailand (FLT), for time and information about their companies' operations; Ms. Velavidi K, Manager, San Sai Potato Growers' Co-operative Ltd. for sharing her co-operative's business operations and dealings with the FLT; Khun Roj Burusratanabhand, President, River Kwai International Food Industry Co. Ltd. for time for interview and frank answers through many e-mails; Khun Pattaphong Iamsuro; Managing Director, BJC Foods for agreeing to supply information about his company's operations and Mr. Sunchai Choongan, Agronomy Director for actually providing all the informationl; and all the farmers and the middlemen for sparing time and answering never ending questions in a foreign language.

Mr. Jirasak of Department of Agricultural Extension (DOAE) for providing papers on contract farming training provided by his Department; Mrs. Wanna Issariyanukula of Office of Agricultural Economics (OAE) for providing a data source and introducing to the DOAE.

Dr. Aree Wiboonpoongse of Multiple Cropping Centre (MCC), Chiang Mai University (CMU) for sending her work on contract farming by e-mail; Dr. Songsak Sriboonchitta of School of Economics, CMU; Mr. Kusol Thong-ngam of MCC, CMU for providing contact information on companies in CM; and Dr. Paiboon Suthasupa and Mr. Songwood P of Chiang Mai for helping in primary data collection at the company and the farmer level in terms of interpretation and logistics.

Mr. Pienlert Wongpiromsarn of Bank of Agriculture and Agricultural Co-operatives (BAAC) for interview and information; Dr. Prayong Netayarak of Faculty of Economics, Thammasat University for providing his report on sugar sector in Thailand; Dr. Somporn Isvilanonda of Dept. of Agril. and Resource Economics, Faculty of Economics, Kasetsart University for providing some useful papers; Anoop Sukumaran, Ranee Hasarungse, and Chanida C Bamford of the Focus on the Global South, Bangkok for discussion and general goodwill; and the National Economic and Social Development Board (NESDB) for sparing copies of national economic and social development plans.

Friends at Chulalongkorn University: Dr. Sompop Manarungsan of Faculty of Economics for providing many leads on the sources of information and discussing the topic at length; Dr. Kitti Limsakul of Faculty of Economics and Policy Advisor to the Prime Minister as my host; Dr. Suthiphand Chirathivat, Dean, Faculty of Economics, for general co-operation during my stay at the Department; Dr. Sitanon Jesdapipat, Director, Centre for Ecological Economics, Faculty of Economics, for providing a paper of his; Ms. Bulanchai of the Dean's Office and Ms. Witchuda Poonsawat of Dr. Kitti Limsakul's office at Faculty of Economics for their kindness and ever ready attitude to help me in logistics and paper work; and Dr. Banjob Bannaruji of the Department of Eastern Languages, Faculty of Arts for his caring attitude and friendship, and some help with language.

Libraries: Chulaongkorn University Main library, and the Thailand Information Centre (TIC), and Economics and Political Science faculties' libraries, the Thammasat University main library and the economics library, the Kasetsart Universtiy library, the Asian Institute of Technology library and the Thailand Development Research Institute library.

Friends: Dr. Uma Rani of GIDR, Dr. Lakhwinder Singh (also an ASIA fellow from the same cohort), and Dr. Peter Rosset of the Food First, for sending very relevant papers from abroad (Japan, South Korea, and USA repectively).

The Asian Scholarship Foundation (ASF, earlier Asia Fellows Program (AFP)) for offering me this fellowship, particularly Dr. L Salvador, Ms. Somkamol C, and Ms. Sasithara S for their co-operation and encouragement before and during my stay in Thailand; the National Research Council of Thailand, in particular Mr. Warapan Wicharn, for permitting me to conduct research in Thailand and fieldwork for it in Chiang Mai province.

Dr. Shashi Ranjan Pandey and Dr. Souvanic Roy, ASIA fellows, for general help, and company during the fellowship period; and Ms. Natcha Klanniem, Training Officer, The Co-operative League of Thailand, and personal friend for her Thai hospitality.

In India, the studies on contract farming in Punjab were made possible by the information provided by all the companies and the contract growers especially Dr. Aneesh Chawla of Pepsi Foods Ltd. Channo, Mr. H C Bahl and Dr. O P Thakur of HLL Ltd., Zahura, Mr. Nijjer and Dr. SK Mishra of Nijjer Agro Foods Ltd., Jandiala and Mr. Manjit Singh and Mr. Satnam Singh of Markfed Canneries Jalandhar.

I am extremely grateful to my family, especially Sukhi (my wife) and Paras (our daughter) for giving me company in Thailand and for their cheerfulness all the time during the stay overseas and making it worthwhile.

I am also thankful to the editors of the EPW, Mumbai, the IJAM, Nagpur, the Co-operative Perspective, Pune, and the co-ordinator of the Gatekeeper Series, IIED, London for permitting me to use my papers on contract farming published by them (chapters 11, 12, 13, and 14 respectively). All these publications have been duly acknowledged at the beginning of the respective chapters. I hope the book will be useful for various stakeholders in contract farming i.e. policy makers, academics, agribusiness firms, farmers, farmer bodies, development agencies and NGOs to understand and make use of contract farming for agricultural development and to managing it for the benefit of all involved.

*Sukhpal Singh*

# 1
# Introduction

## Concept of Contract Farming

Contract farming can be defined as a system for the production and supply of agricultural and horticultural produce under forward contracts, the essence of such arrangements being a commitment to provide an agricultural commodity of a type, at a particular time and price, and in the quantity required by a known buyer. In fact, contract farming can be described as a halfway house between independent farm production and corporate/captive farming. It basically involves four things - pre-agreed price, quality, quantity or acreage (minimum/maximum) and time. From a developmental interventionist point of view, it is a situation in which the relationship between agribusiness firms and farmers takes the form of an expert endowing the apprentice with resources, knowledge, and skills. Alternatively, it is a case of bringing the market to the producers which is then navigated by agribusiness firms (Christensen, 1992).

The contracts could be of three types: (i) procurement contracts under which only sale and purchase conditions are specified; (ii) partial contracts wherein only some inputs are supplied by the contracting firm and produce is bought at pre-agreed prices; and (iii) total contracts under which the contracting firm supplies and manages all the inputs on the farm and the farmer is just a supplier of land and labour. The relevance and importance of each type varies with the product and over time (Hill and Ingersent, 1982; Baumann, 2000; Eaton and Shepherd, 2001). Whereas the first type is generally referred to as marketing contracts, the other two are types of production contracts (Scott, 1984; Welsh, 1997). However, there is a systematic link between product and factor markets under the contract arrangement as contracts require definite quality of produce and, therefore, specific inputs (Scott, 1984; Little and Watts, 1994). Also, different types of production contracts allocate production and market risks, between the producer and the processor, in different ways.

Contract farming is also practised by governmental and semi-governmental agencies in many countries, in different commodity sectors like tea production in Kenya, tobacco and livestock in Thailand, rubber in Malaysia, palm oil in the Philippines, and seed in India (Nanda, 1995; Shiva and Crompton, 1998). The contracts also differ in their nature and effect due to the variations in the nature of crops, contracting agencies, farmers, crop technology, and the context in which they are practised.

## Logic of Contract Farming

Contract farming emerged as an important phenomenon in the developed countries of the West during the 1950s and 60s due to various reasons discussed later in this section. By 1980, about one-third of the total farm output in the United States was produced under contract and in many other sectors like poultry meat, milk and certain vegetables, as much as 100 per cent of the production was under contracts (Winson, 1990; Little and Watts, 1994). In the developing countries, the system of contract farming was brought in by the Multi-National Corporations during the late 1970s and early 1980s. Even in the island of Tasmania in Australia, by the mid-1990s, 95 per cent of the potato production was under contracts compared to almost nil in the 1950s (Fulton and Clark, 1996). There are several reasons for the increasing sophistication in the production, marketing and distribution of agricultural products. First, modern advances in technology have made it feasible for agricultural products to be produced to 'specification' and preserved as fresh. Second, the optimum scale of operations has been increasing, especially in processing and distribution. Third, new selling methods have emerged emphasising a brand image based on consistent quality.

While part of the impetus for these changes in the production/marketing system for agricultural products comes from the supply side wherein processors and distributors see a larger volume/throughput of branded products as a means of adding to their profits, another part comes from the demand side where, due to rising incomes, consumers are becoming increasingly discriminating in their tastes, especially about the timing of production and marketing, and the quality of products. Moreover, increased sophistication in consumer demand gives an added impetus to the search for ways of improving the co-ordination of production, processing and distribution, especially with respect to timing and quality control (Hill and Ingersent, 1982). In fact, the value addition is increasingly taking place in the upstream stages of the agribusiness chain, as the downstream stages have been more or less exhausted so far as quality and value of the products are concerned. Whereas upstream stages refer to primary production and processing part of the agribusiness chain, the downstream stages comprise of higher level processing, manufacturing, and marketing.

For different reasons, both farmers and processors/ distributors of farm products may prefer contracts to complete vertical integration. A contract reduces price risk for a farmer and can be terminated at reasonably short notice. Also, contractual arrangements are attractive to farmers seeking additional sources of capital to expand their businesses and a more certain price by shifting part of the risk of adverse price movement to the buyer (Hill and Ingersent, 1982). Contracts can be source of new technology for farmers as generally new crops with modern technology or existing crops with new seeds and other inputs are promoted under such arrangements. On the other hand, food processors can minimise their overhead costs per unit of production by operating their plants at or near full capacity. They, therefore, need assured and stable supplies of raw materials from farms. In procuring the supplies, the prime requirements of the agribusiness firm are that each supplier must be in a position to guarantee a large volume, continuity of supply and a standardised quality. To the extent that these requirements cannot be met by purchasing through traditional open market channels, more direct links with large producers and producers' organisations are built up. The contracts are more flexible in the face of market uncertainty, make smaller demands on scarce capital resources and impose less burden on management (Buch-Hansen and Marcussen, 1982). They also overcome land constraint for corporate firms, reduce production risk, and are politically more acceptable than corporate farming (Hill and Ingersent, 1982; Eaton and Shepherd, 2001). Contracting can give a positive image to the company as it may be perceived as progressive especially if it works with small farmers, and help it get access to state or donor funds (Baumann, 2000). By contracting, a firm even makes use of state funds indirectly, through land and agricultural production, which are directed at farmers by development agencies (Clapp, 1988).

Therefore, improvement in quality and timely delivery of products for consumers is not the only advantage of contract farming, the processors gain from the reduction in processing costs and business uncertainties, and the farmers can avoid the financial risk involved in price fluctuations in the open market, and gain access to better production methods. At the macro economic level, contracting can help to remove market imperfections in produce, capital, land and labour markets, and can help in better co-ordination of local production activities as it often involves initial investment in processing, extension etc. (Grosh, 1994). From an institutional economics perspective, contract farming could be looked upon as a way of creating positive externalities which can result in overall rural development. In other words, can contract farming help people other than those who have direct stakes and pay for it? The logic for contract farming, thus, could also come from the creation of these externalities, if they are created better by these firms than by the open market or the state. Contracting can lead to more employment opportunities for farm and non-farm labour as generally it deals with labour intensive high value crops requiring labour for harvesting, grading, and packaging at the farm level, and in processing, transportation, packaging and marketing at the post-farm stage, reducing the seasonality of employment and giving higher wages through competition in the labour market. There can also be larger developmental effects from the improvement in infrastructure and other amenities due to contracting and general expansion of demand due to higher incomes under contracting (Haque and Birthal, 1998). Thus, contract farming figures as an institutional arrangement for agricultural development in the fields of inputs, product exchange, and product upgrading, the last referring to research and innovations (Christensen, 1992). Thus, state can play an important role in making contract farming meaningful for rural development by creating incentives and disincentives for agribusiness firms in terms of allowing or not allowing captive farming, investing directly or through joint ventures for contracting, provision of infrastructure, and regulation and enforcement of contracts (Grosh, 1994).

However, a political economy view of contracting rejects these benefits to consumers and farmers and argues that contracts develop only when there is diminished role of the state in agriculture, increased specialisation of agricultural production processes, and the agricultural markets for farm produce or credit become less competitive or inefficient. In fact, it argues that contract production is one mode of capitalist penetration of agriculture for capital accumulation and exploitation of the farming sector. This even leads to processes of 'self-exploitation' of farmers, and companies gain indirect control of land. The political economy approach rejects the various rationale of contracting like perishability of produce, specialisation of a crop, capital intensity of production etc., as it is the social relations of production which determine these aspects of the production system. It argues that product differentiation and monopolistic tendencies cause contracting (Wilson, 1986). Thus, though there are many benefits of contract production for farmers, what happens when yields stagnate, costs rise and there are open market gluts?

## Understanding Contracts and Growers

Since the system of contract farming has its influences on the local and regional economy, it is likely that all producers and organisations have to recognise the intervention of such a system and bear the consequences. Even for individual farmers, it is not the contract per se but the relationship it represents which is crucial as the divergence between the two may prove crucial in determining the development of contract farming as an institution (Clapp, 1988). Further, the context of the contract can make a huge difference as there are many actors and factors in the environment which influence its working and outcome, and lead to a culture of contracting which is location and community specific. The way farmers perceive contract farming i.e. define their relationship with companies, differs in each cultural context (Asano-Tamanoi, 1988; White, 1997). In fact, there is so much diversity in the type of firms, farmers, nature of contracts, crops, and socio-economic environment that it is better to focus on a specific situation than on the generic institution of contract farming (Little, 1994). And, there are others who argue that contract farming should be viewed as a cultural and historical phenomenon rather than as an imposed legal category of relationships, as these contexts determine the response of the farmers to the new arrangement (Asano-Tamanoi, 1988). Since contract farming also leads to changes in the way agricultural production, processing and marketing are organised (White, 1997), it is important to understand its practice and dynamics.

## Nature of Contracts

A review of evidence reveals that farming contracts are generally oral or unwritten. If written, they are in non-local language, and are quite loose in their specifications. For example, seed companies in India do not have written contracts and do not even guarantee a price, though farmers are assured of a profit in terms of seeds being bought at a rate higher than the market price of the grain. Some of them do not even assure of the purchase of seed (Shiva and Crompton, 1998). Only a delivery slip or a credit/seed/seedling slip is the proof of the contract a grower has. The contracts are heavily biased against the growers. The company's obligations are not specified. The contracting agencies end up rejecting low quality produce without any compensation to the grower, and the defaulters are expelled from future contracts. Firms favour large farmers for various reasons (discussed later) and large farmers too become dependent on these firms due to the large volumes of produce they grow (CDC, 1989; Little and Watts, 1994).

The plantation contracts are much more stringent as the quality standards are tough, companies control plantations, and a very early advance notice (3 years) is necessary to withdraw from contracting for both the parties. The company can refuse to procure produce and the growers are not even allowed to grow food crops (Sachikoyne, 1989; Porter and Phillips-Howard, 1995). Generally, a grower's fixed price is the price formula followed in most contracts, but there are other possibilities like processor's fixed price, sharing of profits between firm and farmer, and administered prices which are rarely practised in contract situations. Each method has its limitations and strengths (CDC, 1989; Little and Watts, 1994).

## Nature of Contract Growers

Contract farming may involve both medium or large capitalist farmers relying on wage labour, and small peasant producers who depend to an extent on family labour, and even the landless who lease land for contract production as was the case in Thailand (USAID 1994). However, the agribusiness corporations tend to prefer large farmers for contract farming because of their capacity to produce better quality crops due to efficient and business-oriented farming methods. Also, large volumes of produce reduce the cost of collection for the firm. Moreover, large producers provide services like transport and storage (Wilson, 1986). This trend was observed in Australia where the MNCs started working only with large producers and rationalised the numbers of growers as soon as the government withdrew from the contract regulation. Also, the companies resorted to growers' groups and group contracts to reduce farmers' freedom to hold multiple contracts which were prevalent earlier (Burch and Pritchard, 1996). As a result of the contract farming system, the number of potato growers declined from 7000 in 1950s to just 550 in the 1990s (Fulton and Clark, 1996). Similarly, in the Indian Punjab, more than one-third of Pepsi's contract growers had more than 10 acres each under tomato cultivation. In a state like Punjab, that is known for small holdings, this kind of commitment of large acreage is possible only for large farmers (Sharma, 1995). This means that the small farmers are excluded from the benefits of such arrangements (Baumann, 2000).

Small farmers are picked up by firms only when the area is dominated by small farmers, or there is government directive to do so, or they are found to be low cost producers in particular area and crop (CDC, 1989). Further, firms may work with small farmers to make use of the state support (financial and technical) to these producers under various development programmes (Glover and Kusterer, 1990). Companies often engage local procurement agents, and NGOs and state agencies as intermediaries to procure and to enforce contracts respectively (Clapp 1988; USAID, 1994).

# 2

# Practice of Contract Farming: An International Review

Though there are many studies which report the success of contract system in countries like Thailand, Taiwan, Canada, and Australia (Benziger, 1996, Winson, 1990, Miller, 1996, Rickson and Burch, 1996), there are many others which point to equally strong failures of the arrangement (Glover and Kusterer, 1990, Korovkin, 1992, Little and Watts, 1994, Morvaridi, 1995, and Porter and Phillips-Howard, 1997). The studies on the effects of contract farming can be grouped into three broad categories; (a) agribusiness management approach which looks at contract only as a management tool and a strategy to overcome procurement and related business problems (e.g. Williams and Karen, 1985); (b) project evaluation approach which views it as a project and evaluates it in terms of tangible development objectives of the project like income, employment, and technology transfer (e.g. Glover and Kusterer, 1990); and (c) political economy approach which goes beyond tangible outcomes and looks at the contracting system's effects on production and social relations (e.g. Feder, 1976; Wilson, 1986; Watts, 1992).

## Firms and Contract Growers

According to many project evaluations, the farmers agreed that contracting helped them improve farming, gave moıe reliable incomes, generated employment especially for women, provided new skills in farming, helped do away with the patron-client relationship between large and small producers, and got them better help in farming (Glover and Kusterer, 1990, USAID, 1994; Dunham, 1995; Porter and Phillips-Howard, 1995; Fulton and Clark, 1996). Farmers were also found to switch between companies for deliveries under contract as well as to default on produce delivery and the relevant use of inputs supplied by the firm (Christensen, 1992; USAID, 1994). However, farmers generally find that the contract firms provide poor extension service, over price their services, pass on the risk to the producers, offer low prices for the produce, delay payments, and do not explain the pricing method (Grosh, 1994; Glover and Kusterer, 1990). On the other hand, companies face problems of extra-contractual marketing and diversion of inputs to non-contract crops (Eaton and Shepherd, 2001). But, most problems result not due to the terms of the contract which are written, but due to the contingent nature of the contract and the manipulations by both sides (Baumann, 2000).

The major problems contract growers face in the developing countries are: biased contracts, different contracts for different classes of farmers, tying up of contracts, penalties for involuntary non-compliance, bribes by company officials, manipulation of inspection standards by companies, burden of costs due to any calamity put on producers only, poor technical assistance, late payments, out-right cheating in accounts, indebtedness to companies, and monopoly behaviour by companies (Glover, 1987; Singh, 2000; Eaton and Shepherd, 2001). In some areas like Africa, the farmers faced problems of bribing by company officials, manipulation of inspection standards by companies, tying of one contract to another, and outright cheating in accounts (Little and Watts, 1994; Porter and Phillips-Howard, 1997). On a larger level, farmers felt that they had little bargaining power as compared to the company which they perceived benefited more than the farmers in the contracting process, and that they became dependent on the firms for credit and other inputs (Burch et al, 1996; Glover and Kusterer, 1990). A significant proportion of contract growers in Australia also felt that companies gained more than the farmers, but that they were generally fair in their dealings with farmers (Fulton and Clark, 1996).

There is generally a monopsony of a processing firm in a given area and the contracts are one-sided i.e. they favour the firm and their enforcement on farmers is carried out very strictly (Grosh, 1994). Further, firms backtrack in times of surplus produce and do not compensate the farmers for losses due to natural calamities (Collins, 1993). Contracting alters the relationship between the producers and the firms to the disadvantage of the farmers. Also, there are generally more fluctuations in incomes over time under a contract (Dunham, 1995). Finally, how can a contract between a processor and a farmer be equitable, when the two are not equal entities? The terms of the contract are usually anti-farmer, the market choices are limited, and contracting tends to reinforce itself (Wilson, 1986).

Though contracts lead to an increase in income and employment initially, they may not be sustainable and may prove costly in terms of use of local resources in the presence of instability in international markets, for which the produce is meant, and due to the way the contracts are practised in a given context (Dunham, 1993; Jaffee, 1994; Little, 1994; Dunham, 1995; Torres, 1997). In case of Australia, the firms used local resources for global competition and it was doubtful whether they would continue to procure them locally. They did not show any concern for the local economy, which was perceived as a route to access Asian markets (Burch and Pritchard, 1996). The agribusiness firms also tend to practice "agribusiness normalisation" over time which means that they reduce prices and other benefits offered to the growers with which they commence operations, when the procurement base is created and there are enough farmers to procure from (Glover and Ghee, 1992; Burch, 1996). Further, the contracting farmers are exposed to the adverse impact of misjudgement of market requirements by the firms, and other policy decisions (Hill and Ingersent, 1982; Little and Watts, 1994; Torres, 1997).

The growth of contracting might also so reduce the volume of trading in the open market to an extent that prices may no longer reflect overall market conditions. In other words, the open market may become so narrow that prices cease to be truly representative of the total market situation, and the contracting farmer would no longer have a reliable benchmark for judging the fairness of his contract price. Nevertheless, there are others who suggest that effective competition in agricultural marketing may not be reduced by contractual arrangements provided firms are competing with each other for the contracts with adequately informed producers (Hill and Ingersent, 1982). Also, due to their unequal bargaining power vis-a-vis large buyers or suppliers, contracting farmers may not be able to negotiate a 'fair' contract price. However, wherever there have been collective responses to contracting situations through co-operatives or farmers' groups, the farmers have managed their relationship with companies well, as in Japan. These collective responses were rooted in the cultural and historical contexts (Asano-Tamanoi, 1988). Finally, contractor monopsony and profit maximisation often combined with a powerful contract can have serious repercussions for small contract farmers (Baumann, 2000).

The efficiency and equity implications of contracting is an important economic issue as it creates asymmetries of both types - static as well as dynamic. The static asymmetries are created by the monopsony of the firm, and incomplete contract specifications. Crop specific access to inputs leads to allocational inefficiencies and reduce grower income, thus creating inequity. On the other hand, dynamic asymmetries in the production contracting arrangement like quality control exercised by the processor, transfer of skills to growers, and relative bargaining power of the growers lead to very uncertain or unfavourable outcomes for efficiency and equity depending on the local context of the participating growers, the processor, and the markets (Scott, 1984).

Contract farming also tends to exclude small farmers. In fact, the eligibility criteria for participation in CF projects/schemes like irrigated land, suitable land, land near main road, literacy level of the farmer are themselves discriminatory in terms of who can be a contract grower. In fact, in contract farming everywhere, private agribusiness firms have less interest and ability to deal with small scale farmers on an individual basis (Hazell, 2005).

Contracting also leads to monocropping which in turn leads to deskilling of farmers and labour over time as they no longer grow other crops, or the same crop with different local techniques (Clapp, 1988). The companies tend to prefer monocropping as it is necessary to meet processing unit needs, gives better control over farmers and is easy to manage. For the farmer, however, this reduces the efficiency of his other crop initiatives, reduces food availability, leads to duplication of input services as he has to approach another source for procuring inputs for the non-contracted crops, increases farmer risk, leads to under-utilisation of his labour time as each crop has only certain periods of work requirement, and increases chances and implications of the misuse of cash crop money (CDC, 1989).

While little has been written about the relations between agribusiness corporations and capitalist farmers, the impact of contract farming on the Latin American peasantry is widely discussed in the literature. It is frequently argued that agribusiness in general and contract farming in particular reinforces the trend toward proletarianisation of the peasantry (Korovkin, 1992). It is agreed, however, that contract farming leads to proletarianisation of an incomplete or impure character. To reduce their production costs, transnational corporations and capitalist farmers rely on seasonal rather than stable labour. As a result, a majority of workers employed in agribusiness are either semi-proletarianised peasants or pauperised labourers - the rural semi and sub-proletariat with little or no land and no stable jobs (Payer, 1980; Clapp, 1988; Little and Watts, 1994).

It is also argued that in the case of peasant contract farming, the trend towards proletarianisation appears in a disguised form, whereby peasant producers preserve their access to land but lose their productive autonomy to agricorporations. Clapp calls them "piece-workers with their own tools for the job" (Clapp, 1988). The loss of autonomy is especially pronounced when contract farmers incur heavy debts from the corporations. Such arguments can be questioned on the basis of evidence concerning the differentiation and disintegration, rather than overall proletarianisation, of Latin American peasants. While a majority of impoverished peasants become progressively proletarianised, a wealthy minority develops into commercial producers (Clapp, 1988). This process can eventually result in the disintegration of the peasantry, whereby poor peasants lose all their links with land while rich peasants develop into peasant capitalists (prosperous small farmers who combine family and wage labour). Some of them may further evolve into full-fledged capitalist producers.

It seems plausible that contract farming, especially if supported by state development agencies, reinforces the trend towards differentiation and disintegration of the peasantry, offering rich peasants an opportunity to incorporate modern technologies, augment their assets and increase reliance on wage labour while at the same time accelerating the transformation of poor peasants into a rural semi-and sub-proletariat (Korovkin, 1992; Wilson, 1986; Burch, 1996). There are others who argue on the basis of their studies of the Kenyan agricultural economy that contract farming, per se, does not create a class of rural accumulators as household production is sustained only at a subsistence level, and does not lead to proletarianisation and food insecurity, though capitalist relations of production do develop in contracting contexts, and a rural bourgeoisie emerges. But, other pressures from the world economy, however, might lead to the implications of contracting pointed out by the dependency school (Buch-Hansen and Marcussen, 1982; Currie and Ray, 1986). Also, the exercise of control over production and procurement by the contracting firm may not be easy and feasible in all situations (Jaffee, 1994).

### Food Production, Availability, and Security

The effect of contracting on non-contract farmers and the surrounding areas may not be always positive. Therefore, contracting needs to be examined in its totality as what is favourable for the contracting firms and farmers may harm other actors and sectors of the local economy (Little and Watts, 1994; Porter and Phillips-Howard, 1995). It is argued by some that contract production tends to shift the production in favour of export-oriented and cash crops at the cost of basic food crops. This may lead to higher prices for food commodities and products, especially for non-contract farmers and the labour households who do not benefit from contracting in terms of higher incomes. Even regional differentiation tends to increase as the firms choose relatively developed areas for contracting (Shiva, 1991; Little and Watts, 1994).

### Effect on Environment

The contracting firms tend to aggravate the environmental crisis as most of the contracts are short term (one or two crop cycles) and the firms tend to move on to new growers and lands after exhausting the natural potential of the local resources, particularly land and water, or when productivity declines due to some other reason (Morvaridi, 1995; Torres, 1997). The over-exploitation of groundwater, salination of soils, decline in soil fertility, and pollution are examples of environmental degradation due to contract farming (Siddiqui, 1998; Rickson and Burch, 1996; USAID, 1994). The firms do not pay heed as the costs of such effects are externalised so far as the firm is concerned.

### Social and Economic Differentiation

Contract farming may lead to changes in social relations of production, both in terms of relations between farmers and between farmers and companies. The loss of independence, if it exists at all, suffered by the farmer and the dominance of local production systems by an outside firm may be counted as a social cost. The contract growers, in Australia, agreed that field officers exercised significant influence on farmer decisions which were of tactical nature and more day to day decisions like use of inputs and timing of harvest of the crop. Also, farmers become dependent on companies for financial requirements due to the use of high cost inputs (Fulton and Clark, 1996). Further, it is feared that by favouring the large-scale farmer, who is better able to meet the exacting requirements of producing to contract specification, contracting may encourage a socially undesirable 'dual' agricultural development (Grosh, 1994; Sachikoyne 1989; Little and Watts, 1994; Dunham, 1995).

The agribusiness companies may follow different contract methods for different types of farmers for the production of the same crop. The bigger farmers have contracts which provide for an advance assessment of produce, and fixing of and payments of price, as against the small and/or poor farmers from whom the firm picks up only a part of the produce which meets quality standards (Morvaridi, 1995; Grosh, 1994). This socio-economic divide between the contracting and non-contracting farmers can be deepened further (Glover and Kusterer, 1990). Even the wage rate for the landless workers may be lowered over time due to contracting as workers from outside may in-migrate and the out-migration may stop. This can further accentuate the disparity between the landed and the landless (Little and Watts, 1994).

Korovkin (1992) found that agribusiness expansion in Chile involved not only transnational but also powerful domestic corporations. It gave rise to an alliance consisting of multinational and domestic agricorporations, the state, and capitalist fruit growers. Largely because of state efforts, small growers of fruits, were included into this alliance as minor and subordinate partners. Despite the conflicts and tensions between peasant capitalists on the one hand and fruit corporations and state agencies on the other, they all appeared to have a common stake in the expansion of fruit exports, as well as in the preservation of low agricultural wages - an indispensable condition for this expansion. If small fruit, farmers formed part of the agribusiness alliance, seasonal workers paid the price for the fruit export expansion.

### Gender Issues

The gender effects of contract farming is an important area of enquiry. Gender, like class, is a relational concept. In the same way, as class implies a relationship between labour and capital, gender implies a relationship between women and men. Therefore, gender is not 'only about women', but refers to structural relations between men and women which involve state, economy and society and institutions therein. Further, gender is not a homogeneous category. It is internally differentiated by many factors like class, caste, education, age, etc. (Panda, 2001). Also, gender needs of women can be put into two categories – practical and strategic. The former refer to material conditions of women and are short term in nature, like seeking improvement in the working conditions for women. The latter (strategic) deal with gender hierarchies and other mechanisms of subordination and are long term in nature (Panda, 2000; Ahmed, 2001).

Women have increasingly been employed in agribusiness for their supposedly feminine skills and nimble fingers to undertake delicate work. For example, in Mexico, the growth of agribusiness led to highly seasonal work, in farms and factories, with low wages. Most of the women hired were young, new comers to employment and from small villages. In this gender change in employment profile, the men were the losers. Further, most of the women employed were mainly trimmers, sorters, and packagers in freezing and canning factories (Young, 1993). But, these are not natural or innate skills. They are more based on social skilling embedded during the upbringing of girls to undertake household duties as part of their socially defined subordinate position within the society. In fact, the expanding employment of women in agribusiness has many parallels with female employment in industry where women are preferred for their so-called nimble fingers, and their work is insecure, lowly paid, and flexible. In agribusiness, some of these aspects are the result of the nature of production in the sector which is characterized by seasonality, mono-cultivation and natural risk (Collins, 1993; Barrientos et. al., 1999). Contracting not only displaces local farm workers, but at the same time, those in work have to deal with insecure work and poor working conditions as was the case in Mexico (Barron and Rello, 2000).

Though, in many cases, rural women working in processing plants and related activities reported that the employment under contract production had given them self-esteem, self-confidence and the power to influence decisions within the household (Glover and Kusterer, 1990; USAID 1994; Dunham, 1995; Porter and Phillips-Howard, 1995; Torres, 1997), contract farming does lead to gender inequalities both in the quantity as well as quality of work. The women or children not only end up working longer hours in the field, as they provide efficient and cheap labour (Collins, 1993), but also the burden of off-farm work falls on them due to the occupation of men with contract production (Porter and Phillips-Howard, 1997).

The gender relations within the farming households are affected by tension over the contribution by women to contract production, and negotiation by women for share in the contract income (Carney, 1988). This, in turn, affects productivity of the farm as fields tend to be neglected and these disputes, being private family matters, are difficult to resolve. But, it is important to recognise that the impact on women is class differentiated. There have been instances of collective action by women's groups for control over contract production and income (Buloh and Sorensen, 1993).

But, such studies on contract farm labour households are yet to be seen. As members of the wage labour force, women are affected by shift in employment opportunities resulting from direct and indirect agribusiness hiring. But, the employment in contract farms is temporary and sporadic. Since there is a close connection between contract system and gender, it affects gender division of labour and gender relations of production. There is gendering of tasks in the fields which means pruning, spraying, thinning, pinching out, tying and harvesting in grape cultivation being reserved for women, and it extends even to the processing sector. Activities like grape cleaning, wrapping and selection are exclusively reserved for women (Torres, 1997; Barrientos et. al., 1999). There have been only two recent studies on the gender aspects of contract farm labour in India which explore the nature of work and exploitation of women and children in cotton seed production farms under contracts to national and multinational seed companies (Ramamurthy, 2000; Venkateshwarlu and Corta, 2001).

### Contracting and Local Organisations and Institutions

Contract farming may have profound organisational implications. Historically, peasants in the Latin American, Asian, and African countries have relied for their survival on communal arrangements which spun off various forms of communal organisations. These organisations regulated the management of local resources (natural pastures, woods, and water for irrigation) and defended their members' interests against outsiders. The growth of contract farming leading to commercialised and sophisticated export agriculture undermines the communal arrangements, giving rise to new forms of mass-based rural organisations: labour unions among agricultural workers, on the one hand, and associations defending the commercial interests of small agricultural producers, on the other (Clapp, 1988). Little is known, however, about the relationship between the new and old organisations, as well as their impact on the differentiation and disintegration of the peasantry. Do the communal organisations in fact wither away as a result of agribusiness expansion? Or do they adjust to the new economic realities? (Korovkin, 1992).

The growing importance of contract farming has serious implications for agribusiness co-operatives, which have been practising some form of contract procurement in the past, simply because they are producer-owned organisations. They will now have to compete with agribusiness organisations to sustain producer members by providing competitive price and other incentives. This will require more efficient functioning of the co-operatives. In Australia, the lack of financial support to co-operatives by the state and competition from MNCs and other local agribusiness firms under a deregulated environment led to the closing of some co-operative processing plants and a change in organisation in others (Burch and Pritchard, 1996).

Also, an agribusiness firm generally does not encourage co-operative formation and expansion in its area of operation as it may become a competitor in the long term and spoil the procurement base of the firm (Wilson, 1986). This happened in the case of a Unilever subsidiary in Cameroon wherein when farmers tried to organise a co-operative to strengthen their bargaining power, the company refused to procure the produce, thus wasting the farmers' crop. This was despite the fact that the co-operative was dominated by large farmers. Finally, the co-operative failed. However, it is seen that a para-statal may encourage co-operatives and if that happens, then they do succeed as well, as happened in Kenya in the case of tea (Konings, 1998). But, the success of the contract system per se in the case of Kenya was the result of the coming together of the state, donors and transnational capital, favourable market conditions, access to capital, and a relatively decentralised management system (Little and Watts, 1994). The other tools of mitigating loss of control used by farmers in the developed world have been the petitioning of the state for intervention to regulate the contracts, the formation of producer bargaining units, and the formation of farmers' markets (Welsh, 1997). However, a difficulty in collective action arises due to the heterogeneity of farmers and the conflict between self-interest and collective interest. Each farmer views his relationship with the company as an individualised one (Rickson and Burch, 1996). In Sudan, where co-operatives dealt with contracting firms, the farmers put self-interest before the collective interest and the agribusiness project was a failure (Kontos, 1990).

The above review of literature reveals that in the context of the African, Latin American and a few Asian countries including India, contract farming has led to many ill-effects in the spheres of livelihoods of producers, community organisations and other institutions, environment and gender. These studies point out that though the contract system leads to better incomes and employment in the beginning, the relations between firms and farmers worsen overtime and the system results in ecological and economic degradation of local production systems. Most of the studies which are in the context of relatively less developed regions find contracts inequitable, short-term, and ambiguous. The above discussion suggests that it is not the contract per se which is harmful as a system but how it is practised in a given context.

## References

Ahmed, S.: *Engendering Organisational Practice: The Case of Utthan*, IRMA Working Paper No.156, Institute of Rural Management (IRMA), Anand, March, 2001.

Asano-Tamanoi, M: "Farmers, Industries, and the State: The Culture of Contract Farming in Spain and Japan", *Comparative Studies in Society and History*, 30(3), 1988.

Barrientos, S., A. Bee, A. Matear and I. Vogel: *Women and Agribusiness – Working Miracles in the Chillean Fruit Export Sector*, Macmillan, London, 1999.

Barron, M. A. and F. Rello (2000): "The impact of the tomato agroindustry on the rural poor in Mexico", *Agricultural Economics*, 23(3), 289-297.

Baumann, P.: *Equity and Efficiency in Contract Farming Schemes: The Experience of Agricultural Tree Crops*, ODI Working paper No. 139, ODI, London, October, 2000.

Burch, D.: "Globalized agriculture and agri-food restructuring in southeast Asia: The Thai experience" in D Burch, R E Rickson and G Lawrence (eds.): *Globalisation and Agri-Food Restructuring – Perspectives from the Australasia Region*, Avebury, Brookfield (USA), 1996.

Burch, D. and B. Pritchard: "The uneasy transition to globalisation: Restructuring of the Australian tomato processing industry" in D Burch, R E Rickson and G Lawrence (eds.): *Globalisation and Agri-Food Restructuring – Perspectives from the Australasia Region,* Avebury, Brookfield (USA), 1996.

Burch, D., R. E. Rickson and G. Lawrence (eds.): *Globalisation and Agri-Food Restructuring – Perspectives from the Australasia Region,* Avebury, Brookfield (USA), 1996.

Christensen, S. R.: *Between the Farmer and the State: Towards A Policy Analysis of the Role of Agribusiness in Thai Agriculture*, Thailand Development Research Institute (TDRI) Background Report to the 1992 Conference on Thailand's Economic Structure: Towards Balanced Development?, Chon Buri, Thailand, 1992.

Collins, J. L. (1993): "Gender, Contracts and Wage Work: Agricultural Restructuring in Brazil's Sao Francisco Valley", *Development and Change*, 24(1), 53-82.

Currie, K. and L. Ray: "On the class location of contract farmers in the Kenyan economy", *Economy and Society*, 15(4), 1986.

Dunham, D.: "Crop Diversification and Export Growth: Dynamics of Change in the Sri Lankan Peasant Sector", *Development and Change*, 24(4|), October, 1993.

Dunham, D.: *Contract Farming and Export Horticulture: Can Agribusiness revitalise the Peasant Sector in Sri Lanka?* , IPS Agricultural Policy Series No. 3, Institute of Policy Studies, Colombo, Feb. 1995.

Eaton, C. and A. W. Shepherd: *Contract farming – Partnerships for growth*, FAO, Rome, 2001.

Feder, E.: "Agribusiness in Underdeveloped Agricultures: Harvard Business School Myths and Reality", *Economic and Political Weekly*, 11(29), July 17, 1976.

Glover, D. and K. Kusterer (eds.):_*Small Farmer, Big Business - Contract Farming and Rural Development,* Macmillan, London, 1990.

Glover, D. and L.T. Ghee (eds.): *Contract Farming in Southeast Asia-Three Country Studies,* University of Malaya, Kuala Lumpur, 1992.

Hazell, P B R (2005): "Is there a future for small farms?", in D Colman and N Vink (eds.): *Reshaping Agriculture's Contributions to Society*, Proceedings of the 25th Intl. Conference of Agricultural Economists (ICAE), August, 16-22, Blackwell, USA, 93-101.

Hill, B. E. and K. A. Ingersent: *The Economic Analysis of Agriculture*, Heinemann, London, 1982.

Jaffee, S. M.: "Contract Farming in the Shadow of Competitive Markets: The Experience of Kenyan Horticulture", in Peter D Little and Michael J Watts (eds.): *Living Under Contract - Contract Farming and Agrarian Transformation in Sub-Saharan Africa*, The University of Wisconsin Press, Madison, 1994.

Kontos, S.: "Farmers and The Failure of Agribusiness in Sudan", *Middle East Journal*, 44 (4), Autumn 1990.

Korovkin, T.: "Peasants, Grapes, and Corporations - The Growth of Contract farming in a Chilean Community", *The Journal of Peasant Studies*, 19 (2), January 1992.

Little, P.D.: "Contract Farming and the Development Question" in Peter D Little and Michael J Watts (eds.): *Living Under Contract - Contract Farming and Agrarian Transformation in Sub-Saharan Africa*, The University of Wisconsin Press, Madison, 1994.

Miller, L.: "Contract farming under globally-oriented and locally-emergent agribusiness in Tasmania" in D Burch, R E Rickson and G Lawrence (eds.): *Globalisation and Agri-Food Restructuring – Perspectives from the Australasia Region*, Avebury, Brookfield (USA), 1996.

Morvaridi, B.: "Contract Farming and Environmental Risk - The Case of Cyprus", The *Journal of Peasant Studies*, 23 (1), October 1995.

Nanda, M.: "Transnationalisation of Third World State and Undoing of Green Revolution", *Economic and Political Weekly*, 30(4), January 28, 1995.

Panda, S. M.: *Women's Empowerment Through NGO Interventions: A Framework for Assessment*, IRMA Working Paper No.145, Institute of Rural Management (IRMA), Anand, April, 2000.

Panda, S. M.: *A Framework for Assessing Gender Sensitivity in Forest Management Policy and Practices,* IRMA Working Paper No.158, Institute of Rural Management (IRMA), Anand, March, 2001.

Payer, C.: "The World Bank and the Small Farmer", *Monthly Review*, 32 (6), Nov. 1980.

Porter, G. and K. Phillips-Howard: "Farmers, Labourers and the Company: Exploring Relationships on a Transkei Contract Farming Schemes", *The Journal of Development Studies*, 32 (1), October 1995.

Porter, G. and K. Phillips-Howard: "Comparing Contracts: An Evaluation of Contract Farming Schemes in Africa", *World Development*, 25 (2), 1997.

*Ramamurthy, P: "The Cotton Commodity Chain, Women, Work and Agency in India and Japan: The Case for Feminist Agro-Food Systems Research",* World Development, *28(3), 2000.*

Rickson, R.E. and D. Burch: "Contract farming in organisational agriculture: The effects upon farmers and the environment" in D Burch, R E Rickson and G Lawrence (eds.): *Globalisation and Agri-Food Restructuring – Perspectives from the Australasia Region*, Avebury, Brookfield (USA), 1996.

Sachikoyne, L.M.: *The State and Agribusiness in Zimbabwe: Plantations and Contract Farming,* Leeds Southern African Studies No. 13, African Studies Unit, Department of Politics, University of Leads, Aug. 1989.

Shiva, V.: *The Violence of the Green Revolution: Third World Agriculture, Ecology and Politics,* Zed Books, London, 1991.

Siddiqui, K.: "Agricultural Exports, Poverty and Ecological Crisis – Case Study of Central American Countries", *Economic and Political Weekly*, 33(39), Sept.26-Oct.2, 1998.

Torres, G.: *The Force of Irony: Power in the Everyday Life of Mexican Tomato Workers,* Berg, Oxford, 1997.

USAID (United States Agency for International Development): *Assessment of Contract Farming in Lam Nam Oon, Thailand,* Centre for Development Information and Evaluation, USAID working paper No. 193, USAID and the The Royal Thai Government, April 1994.

*Venkateshwarlu, D. and L.D. Corta: "Transformations in the Age and Gender of Unfree Workers on Hybrid Cottonseed Farms in Andhra Pradesh",* The Journal of Peasant Studies, *28(3), April, 2001.*

Williams, S. and R. Karen: *Agribusiness and the Small Scale Farmer: A Dynamic Partnership for Development,* Westview Press, London, 1985.

Young, L. W.: "Labour Demand and Agroindustrial Development: The Evidence from Mexico", *The Journal of Development Studies*, 30(1), October, 1993.

# 3
# Contact Farming in Thailand: A Review

Thailand has an area of 513115 square kms. which is 11.46% of the total area of the south-east Asia. Its population of 61.1 million accounted for 12.2% of the total in the region and it had 12% of the region's agricultural population as well, in 1998. One-fourth of the total land area of Thailand is forest area. About 58% of the economically active population and 50.5 of the total population was engaged in agriculture in 1998 but only about 16 of GDP came from primary sector with secondary and tertiary sectors contributing 36% and 48 % respectively. This is the lowest in the region after Singapore. The female participation rate was 66 per cent in general and the trade to GDP ratio was as high as 91 per cent in 1997. Thailand accounts for 24% of the region's total GNP, and in terms of Purchasing Power Parity (PPP) based wealth per person, it was next only to Singapore and Malaysia in 1997 (Hill, 2002). Only 20% of Thailand's farmland was irrigated in 1991 with maximum in the central region (45%) and minimum in north-eastern region (8%). The northern region had 24% of its farm lands irrigated and the southern about 16% (Paopongsakorn et al, 1995). On an average, a farmer in Thailand cultivates about 3.5 hectares of land (Saenjan, 1998). Major problems of Thai agriculture in the 1990s have been shortage of water and labour and inefficient use of inputs, especially pesticides (Poapongsakorn et al, 1998).

Recent studies of boom and bust in growth in Thailand economy show that during the boom, absolute poverty fell dramatically but relative inequality increased. The 1997 crisis led to poor becoming worse off in an absolute sense but proportionately less so than the rich, leading to reduced inequality (Warr, 2000; Kakwani and Pernia, 2000). During the 1990s (1987-

1998), a village level study showed, area under non-rice crops also grew significantly, especially in central and north-east regions though double cropping of rice also increased (Isvilanonda et al, 2000). This study concludes, " Farmers are also allocating resources to grow more profitable upland and horticultural crops". But, this cropping pattern shift has led to other consequences as the authors state "Income inequality has grown substantially due to the increasing share of non-rice crops and a highly unequal distribution of income from this source. The number of poor has declined despite of the growing inequality in the distribution of income because the growth in per capita income has been impressive. The intensity and severity of poverty has, however, increased" (Isvilanonda et al, 2000, p. 4649).

Thailand has traditionally been an agricultural country and a major food exporter. It was in the 1990s that agricultural products which occupied the top positions in exports despite declining share of agriculture in GDP, lost ground to industrial products. But, still Thailand is one of the few countries in the Asia Pacific region that has the capacity to produce more food than it consumes (Canadian Embassy in Bangkok, 2000). Thailand is one of the world's leading producers and exporters of processed food products and is home to more than 7,000 food processing units. About 50% of its processed food output is exported. Within last two decades, it has become one of the few net producers in the world of a wide range of agricultural and fishery products, the second most significant food exporter in Asia, after China, the number one Asian exporter of processed food, the world's top exporter of frozen shrimp and canned pineapple, pineapple juice and concentrates, and frozen chicken, the second largest exporter of all types of sea food, one of the top five global exporters of rice and sugar, and one of the main exporters of baby corn and tropical fruits to various parts of the world (Subhapholsiri, 2000).

## Contract Farming in Thailand

Contract farming system emerged more than three decades ago, to begin with, in poultry, sugarcane, tobacco, pineapple and vegetables. In poultry, the system of contracting was put in place by the Charoen Pokphand (CP) group first of all in the early 1970s and they introduced wage and price guarantee contracts for growers in 1976. The CP group also tried contract faming in shrimp production through independent growers and co-operatives in the mid 1980s, with support from the BAAC but, since farmers were opposed to the fixed price contracts, the co-operatives broke down. Thus, CP no longer practices contract farming system in shrimp and procures from open auctions markets and from its own farms (Goss et. al, 2000). The CP group also tried contract farming in rice in the early 1980s and then again in 1986, failing both the times (Christensen, 1992). BAAC had supported projects in contract farming in early 1980s in crops of pineapple and oil palm as well (CUSRI, 1984). During the mid 1980s, many NGOs in north-east Thailand promoted contract farming of organic rice supported by European NGOs under fair-trade networks (Setboonsarng, et al, 2005).

By the early 1990s, contract farming was in place in the following crops/commodities in Thailand: poultry, dairying, palm oil, pineapple, tobacco, sugarcane, kenaf, asparagus, maize, maize seed, castor oil, eucalyptus, baby corn, cashew nuts, sun flower, bamboo, barley, sea shrimp, cotton, tomato, tomato seed, rubber, gherkins, peas, string beans, silk worms, swine, asparagus, bamboo shoots, ginger, mushroom and fragrant rice (Kusakabe and Higuchi, 1992; Paopongsakorn, et al, 1995; Goss and Burch, 2001). Contract farming has been so popular in Thailand that even the Royal Project Food Processing Section has adopted it as a central hub in its operations (IMC, 1996, p. 35).

By the late 1990s, almost 100% of commercial production of poultry in the country, especially that meant for frozen chicken exports, was under some form of contract (Burch, 1994; Tisdell et al, 1998). Later, it expanded to vegetable seeds and crops like tomato (Saenjan, 1998) and by the early 1990s, production of canned bay corn, bamboo shoots, and tomatoes, and various fruits was largely under contracts (Burch, 1994).

By 2002, it was estimated that there were 10,000 contract potato growers, 16-17,000 contract sweet corn growers, 20, 000 contract chicken growers (CP alone 12, 000), 10, 000 contract swine growers (CP alone 5,000), 20, 000 contract rice growers (CP alone 10, 000), 2,50,000 contract sugarcane growers with 46 sugar mills, 50, 000 contract vegetable growers, 20,000 contract vegetable soyabean growers and 10,000 contract eggplant growers in Thailand (author's own estimate based on field interaction). The major success has been in sunflower, wheat, barley, hybrid sorghum, cashew nuts, fast-growing trees, sugar, silk worms, bamboo shoots, ginger, mushroom, okra, mango, basmati rice, jasmine rice, organic rice, fragrant rice, prawn/sea shrimp, duck, chicken, swine, Japanese cucumber, hybrid maize seed, vegetable seed, potato, vegetable soybean, baby corn, sweet corn, gherkins, peas, string beans, dairy milk and new kinds of vegetables for frozen industry. On the other hand, major contracting failures happened in asparagus, bamboo for paper pulp, pineapple, oil palm, tomato and cotton.

There have been many studies of contract farming in the north-east region (Songmuang, 1984; Volden, 1994; Benziger, 1996; and Rosset et al, 1999) and in the central and southern region (CUSRI, 1984; Nundhapana, 1985; Manarungsan and Suwanjindar, 1992; Kusakabe and Higuchi, 1992; Padmanabha, 1995; and Naritoom, 2000; Setboonsarng, et al, 2005).

## Contract Farming in North East Thailand

An early 1980s study of tobacco contract farming system in the north-east region of Thailand (Songmuang, 1984) revealed that in this pioneer contract crop, the growers were either working for Thailand Tobacco Monopoly or with private companies like the Adams International who were permitted by the government to operate in the area. The study found that contracts of the two companies were similar in that they specified quantity, quality, price and extension support to be given by the company. Companies also provided inputs on credit and bought the produce which grower was supposed to sell only to the company. But, the interest charged on input credit was higher in the case of private company, though in both cases input loan repayments were made in terms of company deducting from final payment to the growers for their produce. An estimation of allocative efficiency showed that growers for private companies were using inputs more efficiently, though their returns were lower than those of the Thailand Tobacco Monopoly growers. But, there was scope in both cases to increase growers' net income by reducing labour input, especially hired one, and choosing more suitable lands and increasing chemical input use. Another study (Turton, 1987) also documented the experience of tobacco growers with Adams International in this area in terms of monopolization of input sales and produce purchase by the company, manipulation of grading, lowering of prices, use of agents and opposition to farmer organization, besides its operations leading to use of harmful chemicals and child labour in tobacco farms, and landless being excluded from contracting. Similar were the grower experiences in sugar in this region wherein first the company lured the farmers into sugarcane cultivation and then started manipulating the contracts in terms of lowering prices, not accepting entire produce, too many delayed deliveries from farmers at factory, deductions from payments, delayed payments, exclusion of small producers after some time, and use of quota men for procurement, besides retrenching poor performing quota men themselves later on. As a result, many farmers became indebted to company and lost their land.

An early 1990s study of contract farming in maize by the Thailand's largest agribusiness group (Charoen Pokphand or in short CP) in a north-eastern province (Loei) revealed that it was part of four sector co-operation plan implementation in which BAAC recruited the contract growers, provided credit, distributed CP produced and supplied inputs to the growers, and handled most of the paper work involved and covered the administrative costs. Ministry of Agriculture (MOA), together with CP, ran the extension service. The other so-called partners were contract growers (Volden, 1994). Further, in this project, farmers were not restricted in terms of whom they sell their produce, or how much is to be sold to CP. The company did not buy directly from farmers, but from middlemen. Even the guaranteed price was more to act as a price support against the market price as it was always below the market price. Based on a survey of 286 contract, non-contract, and previous contract growers, it was revealed that the Contract Farmers' group was made up of mostly medium farmers. The average holdings of contract and previous contract growers were 46 rai and that of non-contract growers only 37 rai which was close to the average in the study area. Only $1/5^{th}$ of the contract growers were small as they owned 29 rai or less or just equal to or less than the average holding of the north-east. The farmers only valued guaranteed price in the contract farming system as market was never a problem as was not credit. But, they were highly dissatisfied with prices set by the middlemen.

The system of contracting led to higher input use on contract farms as against on other farms which the study claims was a deliberate strategy of the company to increase its product (agricultural inputs) sales. Further, the new inputs use led to decline in labour use on farms. In terms of economics of contract crop, the cost of production was higher on contract crops and net returns more or less same as in non-contract crops, despite the fact that their yields were higher than those of the non-contract and the previous contract growers by 33%. But still, majority of the contract growers were satisfied with yields and most of them had positive attitude towards contract farming and the company, BAAC and other government agencies involved as they perceived them to be trustworthy. However, the proportion of those satisfied with yields was lower among non-contract and previous contract growers though they also had positive opinion about contract farming. There was no indication that contract farming was leading to economic differentiation within the community.

The study concluded that it was basically the CP strategy to convert contract farming into a national policy so that it could make the public sector bear most of the expenses involved in running the project of contract farming (p. 18). The main beneficiary of the project was CP as it could avoid all the risk by making public sector (BAAC) bear all the risk of lending money to growers and could meet its business objectives of getting assured supply of desired quality and quantity raw material and assured market for its products i.e seeds and other inputs. Though company claimed that its seeds and technology had reduced risk of cropping, but that no insurance company was willing to enter this project spoke of the risks involved (p. 23).

Another early 1990s study (Benziger, 1996) of the contract farming system in the north-east region (Sakon Nakhon province) has a highly positive opinion about contract farming role as it revealed that the area under contracts went up substantially compared to those under traditional system and average revenues per rai were much higher (4-5 times) than those under traditional cropping, though it was more so only in a few crops like tomato and cantaloupe seed production which the author does not recognize. In fact, the author compares contract farming system with traditional interlinked (interlocked) factor markets represented by the relationship between a landlord and the tenant which were considered exploitative, and emphasises that the company-farmer relationship under contracting is better and more desirable as it has the positive aspects of assured market, risk coverage, and one-stop input supply.Therefore, it is argued that it (contract farming) should be replicated, though it is acknowledged that it can lead to socio-economic differentiation. It is further concluded that this successful transition to high value crops was possible as state could rope in private business interest that had resources and access to international markets which does matter for success of any market-oriented project.

This project (Lam Nam Oon) is considered the most successful in contract farming in Thailand and has been studied and analysed by others as well (Paopongsakorn et al, 1995; Falvey, 2000). The project was jointly launched by a private tomato paste manufacturing firm and the BAAC. The firm provided inputs and assured produce purchase (from allocated 1-5 rai acreage under contract) with a price guarantee and the BAAC offered the loans (3000 baht per rai of tomato) which were to be recovered by the firm when farmers delivered produce to the company. The contracts were signed between firm and farmers in the presence of the Royal Irrigation Department staff (RID had started the irrigation project (LNO) in the area and the contract farming project is now known by this project name), and the agricultural extension officer at the district level as witnesses. Both parties were to pay penalties for defaulting on contract. The local headmen acted as middlemen between the company and farmers and were paid 80 baht per tonne of tomato delivered, as commission. The farmers selected by company personnel and local headman for the project were put into groups of about 50 each under each local headman or middleman. The project was successful as it co-ordinated production schedule with irrigation schedule from the RID for the area, farmers were well aware of the concept of contract farming for more than a decade, there was facilitation and monitoring of contracts by government agencies though the contracts were voluntary, there was good extension and monitoring of production by the company staff, besides availability of irrigation facility and good infrastructure in the area in general (Paopongsakorn et al, 1995).

Contract farming of seed was another important high value enterprise introduced in the north-east in the mid 1980s. In 1992, there were at least eight companies with international links operating in the region working with more than 5000 growers who grew 0.25 to one rai each of tomato, chili, watermelon or cantaloupe seeds (Suphanchaimat, 1998). In a study of contract farming of tomato see and processing tomato producers with average contracting experience of 5 and 7 years respectively in

Isaan in north east Thailand in the mid 1990s, Rosset et al (1999) revealed that 75% of the seed producers contracted with two seed companies, and contract farming, whether for seed or fruit production, was the primary source of income for 80% of them. Those involved in tomato seed production devoted an average of 0.39 rai for this and derived a net income of 17,000 baht from tomato seeds production, on the average. Growers of processing tomatoes devoted seven times more land, an average of 2.72 rai, to this much simpler and more extensive form of tomato cultivation. Their net incomes were higher, averaging 30,000 baht.

For those farmers producing tomato seed, 69% of the total income came from contract farming, and 69% of them had grown cantaloupe for seed and 26% tomatoes for processing. All other farming, including rice production, accounted for just under 25% of total income. Overall, more than 85% of the tomato seed farmers reported that they felt wealthier than in the past. As for plans related to future planting of tomatoes for seeds, 49% had a plan to increase the area currently devoted to seed production, while 11% wanted to decrease it. 29% reported that they would leave it the same. Processing tomato growers earned 63% of their total income from contract farming, with 24% coming from all other farming. 84% of them reported feeling wealthier than before. Only 38% wanted to increase the area devoted to tomatoes, while 49% had plans to keep it unchanged.

More than 97% of seed producers received inputs from the contracting buyer, and the same percentage reported that credit or advances were conditional upon using pesticides in the production process. While growers belonged to village associations and groups were well organized around many local issues, the vast majority of contracted seed producers (94%) negotiated the terms of their contracts as individuals. But, only 33% of processing tomato growers received inputs from the buyer, while 55% received credit from cooperative banks and only 65% of their credit was conditional upon use of pesticides. Unlike their seed producing counterparts, only 51% negotiated their contracts alone while 41% did so as part of a village group or cooperative.

A majority of those involved in seed production belonged to the smallest farm size category of 10 rai or less. The average area devoted to seed production in this category was quite small (0.28 rai), a testament to the labor-intensive nature of the work involved. Processing tomatoes, on the other hand, were more evenly distributed across farm sizes. Surprisingly, farmers in the largest size category devoted the least land to processing tomatoes. But, the seed producers in the smallest farm size category had the highest average yields, as well as high prices paid for their seeds. The higher yields are probably associated with the greater attention given to production by smaller producers. Higher prices are usually associated with degree of difficulty associated with the labor process, which can vary even within tomatoes, depending upon the seed variety being produced. This same group of producers reported the highest percentage of total income (72%) being generated by contract farming, and the lowest percentage (20) derived from all other farming, including rice production. In the case of processing tomatoes, it was the second from the smallest size category which reported the highest yields, and it was the largest farmers who received the highest price. The was more in accordance with reports on contract farming prices elsewhere in the world, where the larger volume offered and stronger negotiating power reported by larger growers translates into a price premium. In the case of tomato seeds, there was a strong diseconomy of scale due to the intricate labor involved, while in processing tomatoes a more typical marketing economy of scale seemed to act (Rosset et al, 1999, pp. 86-88). The default, and therefore, farmer attrition rate was 12% every year in seed production and there were no price incentives for more production (p. 86).

So far as participation of landless households in contract farming is concerned, it was found that, on the average, 19.5% of all villagers participating in contract farming of some kind were landless, but in seed contracting villages, 23.6% of those involved in contract farming were landless. Further, 96% of the landless farmers contracted with companies during the dry season to produce a crop of some kind. The study reports that peasants involved in contract farming in northeast Thailand appeared to be reaping a number of economic benefits. Substantial quantities of cash were flowing into the villages involved, with new pickup trucks, communal projects, and private building efforts in evidence which has been reported by other studies of contract farming in the region as well (Dolinsky, 1991). But, there was also higher level of indebtedness of the farmers as crops were capital intensive. Although banks were more willing to lend to farmers who joined with a company in a contract faming project, growers involved in seed production relied heavily upon the companies, with which they contracted, to provide credits. These took the form of cash advances and/or agrochemical inputs. More than 95% of the contract seed growers identified the companies as the source of credit and less than 6% made use of private banks, in contrast to the processing tomato growers who relied much more on bank credit.

Most local firms continue to have production arrangements with foreign interests, with Taiwanese firms playing a major role. Thus, there is a strong presence of foreign capital in the hybrid seed business of northeast Thailand, the activities of which are colored by the unusual demands of the production. But, already by 1995, thee were reports which pointed to the eventual migration of hybrid seed production and tomato processing to China, where costs of production are significantly less than that in northeast Thailand. Due to the inexperienced labor force and corruption involved in export licensing and other government controls, however, only selective migration was occurring. Newer, more popular varieties of tomato seeds were staying in northeast Thailand. Production of older varieties, as well as that of easier-to-produce seeds such as melon was moving to China and Vietnam. At the other extreme, Thai production of tomato paste produced for export is controlled almost exclusively by domestic capital, with little international intra-firm integration, and reflects a relatively low degree of contractual intensity with farmers. Again, lower production costs in China act to attract regular, non-specialized, paste production. As work force knowledge, experience, and discipline deepen, the eventual migration of all tomato paste, and perhaps even the high-end, difficult tomato seed, production to China was expected (Rosset et. al, 1999). Another study (Makarbhirom, 1997 analysed the organzation and peformance of contract tree farming by phoneix pulp and paper company in Khankaen prouince and found that its contract was quite detailed both for encalyptus and bamboo. It report farmer defaults in delivery of trees and the future of CTF was reported to be uncertain.

Based on a 2003 data set provided by the MOAC which covered 140 organic rice contract growers and 137 conventional rice non-contract growers in three provinces, Setboonsarng et al (2005) find that organic rice contract growers fared better on profitability as well as efficiency of rice production and they had higher area under rice.

### Contract Farming in Central and Southern Thailand

An early 1980s study of contract farming of pineapple and oil palm (CUSRI, 1984) found that there were both individual as well as group contracts prevalent in oil palm where group sale was more common. BAAC was found supporting these contracting projects with loans to growers against contracts. Similarly, in pineapple, firms were buying directly from growers as well as from merchants, with the latter preferred as it was less uncertain compared to the growers. Some of the canneries even attempted their own production, but could not sustain due to high costs and lack of experience in farming.

Another study for the early 1980s on swine production contracting, which was initiated by the CP group in 1977 first of all, due to high cost of its in-house production, in central Thailand provinces found three systems of contracting in the industry - agricultural village program, swine raising promotion, and contracted customer promotion (Nundhapana, 1985). It focused on determining the factors in the existence of different systems in the same industry, and returns to farmers under different systems and reasons thereof. It was found that agricultural village raisers were landless farmers and only contributed labour on company provided farms. On the other hand, swine raising promotion farmers were different from the contracted customer promotion farmers in that they had land, but lacked the capital to run the business of swine raising and, therefore, worked with companies in their contract production program. The contracted customer farmers were dependent on firms only for the sale of their produce as they had only sales contract with them. Between the two wage contract programs (agricultural village and swine raising promotion), contracts differed in transaction costs and distribution of risks of activity, besides endowment of the growers. The agricultural village project had high negotiation costs and high investment risk involved for the contractor. On the other hand, swine raising promotion project had high enforcement costs. But, in contracted customer promotion system, the contractor had no control on production as against in other two systems where exercise of control was substantial. Further, piece rate system of wages was found to be more prevalent in feeder pig production as against the time rate system in finishing hog production.

An early 1990s study of practice of contracting in four major crops/commodities (broiler chickens, pineapple, oil palm and asparagus) of the central and southern regions (Manarungsan and Suwanjindar, 1992), locating the contract farming system in the government policies, found that contracting was predominant in broiler meat, to the extent of 70% of exported chicken meat being produced under contracts, though with a tendency to go towards direct corporate farming due to export market quality conditions, and in asparagus to some extent which was introduced to the Thai farmers first time in 1973 under the Royal Project. But, most of the exported produce in palm oil, and pineapple came from open market production and whatever contract farming existed in these crops, was more of contract procurement, with no supply of inputs or credit. In pineapple, for example, the local firms only provided minimum price guarantees and no inputs or credit and obtained only a part of their raw material procurement through contracts. The firm would pay market price if it was more than the minimum price. But, an MNC never really got into contract farming. Wherever firms provided inputs on credit and technical support to contract growers, they faced farmer default on delivery and lost recovery of input cost many times. Therefore, many firms also used other channels of raw material procurement like middlemen, and co-operatives.

In terms of type of farmers for contract farming, broiler chicken companies preferred large landholders for guaranteed price contracts and small farmers for wage contracts. But, there was no such preference seen in choosing farmers for palm oil or pineapple contract farming. But, in asparagus, due to its labour intensive nature, small farmers with high family labour availability were preferred. In terms of performance, 'agribusiness normalisation' had already set in, in broiler chicken contract farming and therefore, farmers' returns were dropping later on. But, this was one commodity in which farmers enjoyed access to input supply by the firm including to credit from banks, guaranteed by the firm, which was totally absent in other crops. Payments were much faster in field crops, and took 2-6 weeks in broiler chicken contracts. The shifting cost for broiler farmers was high due to the intensity of relationship in terms of input supply and output collection frequently. On the other hand, in other crops, firms and farmers both frequently shifted their sources of purchase/sale among contract farmers/companies, open market and middlemen. In fact, in broiler contract farming as well as other crops, firms frequently discouraged farmer organisation for better bargaining or better management and did not want to purchase from co-operatives of farmers in general. It is concluded that true contract farming did not exist in pineapple, palm oil and asparagus crops (Manarungsan and Suwanjindar, 1992).

Another interesting study of contract farming in Kanchanaburi province of central Thailand in the early 1990s examined the discontinuing behaviour of contract farmers in cotton crop where the company had to finally withdraw from contracting (Kusakabe and Higuchi, 1992). By understanding why farmers discontinued contracting, it was possible to know the shortcomings and impact of the contract system as it (discontinuance) also affects other farmers' adoption behaviour. This kind of analysis helped understand innovation adoption process as well. This examination could throw light on suitability of contract crop, performance of the contracting company, and aspects of farmer decision making process. It was found that there were three types of contract farmers - continuers, discontinuers, and rejecters. Farmers joined the scheme for good service and convenience, high cotton price, good advice on crop, and cheap inputs. They were continuing for reasons of higher price and good crop extension. Those who quit did so for reasons of giving up the crop itself, harmful pesticide impact, and no major benefit of crop. Those who rejected contracting, to begin with itself, did so for not knowing about it or dealing with the co-operative body or the merchant besides not being eligible or being afraid of indebtedness which contracting was thought to lead to. Almost all of the continuing farmers (90-97% across aspects of buying or selling to the company) bought their inputs (all) and sold output to the company only, and most of them were willing to continue with the firm with cotton production. On the other hand, company withdrew for reasons of farmer default on quantity and quality, poor extension, existence of merchants in the area as competitors, physical distance from the factory for farmers, and recruitment of the contract growers by company in one general meeting with the help of government extension officer without much care and planning. It was found that contracting benefited only not-so rich, not-so poor farmers and could not help really poor farmers.

Another study of contract farming in the central Thailand province of Chachoeng Sao assessed its economic impact on the farmers with a survey of farmers in six crops/commodities ranging from pineapple, cashew nuts, and eucalyptus (>50% of total surveyed being in these crops and with only three companies) to ducks and chickens (Padmanabha, 1995). Most of the farmers were large or medium land holders and had a fairly long experience in contracting which were production contracts in all crops except sugar where it was only sales contract, with no input supply. Also, both direct and middlemen contracts as well as written and oral contracts were prevalent. The contracting was being carried out with the active support of the BAAC and the MOAC. In most cases, though buying price was set in advance, the actual price paid at harvest was more of a market price and the contract prices were generally lower than the market prices. Though payments were generally made within two weeks after delivery, in sugarcane and poultry, it was delayed many times. Surprisingly, 1/3 of the farmers were willing to sell outside the contract if got better prices which reflects the low intensity relationship between companies and farmers. In terms of overall impact of contracting, it led to new crops, higher cost of production, new sources of credit like BAAC, commercial banks and companies, availability of new inputs, higher labour requirements, external control of production process, and reduced role of traders and middlemen in farming at the farmer level. Most of the problems farmers faced in contracting were production related like disease/pest attack, poor quality inputs or non-availability of inputs and credit at reasonable rate of interest, and high cost of production which is more to do with firms' extension support. The end result was that whereas some farmers became dependent on firms, others could gain and grow independent, thus contract farming led to a differential impact. The study recommended government monitoring of the contract farming practice, making written contracts must, and organising of farmers into groups for better bargaining with firm, to make it fair for both the parties so that it could lead to farmer development as well. A study of contract tree farming by three companies (Agroline, sain and thai playwood) in this region examined the contract and there implication for contract growing tree. (Makarabhirom 1997) It found the contract to be sample, long duration and compainen were heighly involued in these Projects.

A recent study of group contract farming of asparagus in Nakhon Pathom province of central Thailand (Naritoom, 2000) mentions 5 such groups working with 5 different companies with a total membership of 385 and 685 hectares under asparagus in mid 1990s. The first group organised in 1989 had only 47 members who planted 32 hectares for a Japanese company (Thai-Topy Co.) under contract. Then, every year a new group started working with a new company but there were strong differences of prices and quality standards across companies and even within the same company and group, prices for different grades of asparagus varied from 45 baht/kg. for A1 grade to only 20 bah/kg. for grade C. By 1998, there were only two companies and some village middlemen working with 4 groups whose membership was 514, varying from 77 to 234 across groups. Further, each group had members growing very many other crops as well. But, asparagus was still the most profitable crop followed by baby corn.

## References

Benziger, Vincent (1996): "Small Fields, Big Money: Two Successful Programs in Helping Small Farmers Make the Transition to High Value-Added Crops", *World Development*, 24(11), 1681-1693.

Canadian Embassy in Bangkok (2000): The Market for Imported Food Ingredients in Thailand (http://ats.adr.ca/public/htmldocs/e3021.htm.) (7/12/2001).

Christensen, Scott (1992): "The Public Policy Process and Political Change in Thailand: A Summary of Observations" , *TDRI Quarterly Review*, 7(1), March, pp. 21-26.

**Christensen, Scott R (1992):** Between the Farmer and the State: Toward a Policy Analysis of the Role of Agribusiness in Thai Agriculture, **Background Report to the 1992 Year-End Conference on 'Thailand's Economic Structure: Towards Balanced Development?', Chonburi, Thailand, December 12-13.**

**Dolinsky, D J (1991):** Contract Farming at Lam Nam Oon: An Operational Model for Rural Development, **Thailand Development Research Institute (TDRI), Bangkok.**

EU (The European Union) and MOAC (The Ministry of Agriculture and Co-operatives) (n.d.): *Working with Farmers in North East Thailand – an integrated programme of five rural development projects*. The EU and The MOAC.

Falvey, L (2000): *Thai Agriculture – Golden Cradle of Millennia*, Kasetsart University Press, Bangkok.

Goss, Jasper, D Burch and R E Rickson (2000): "Agri-Food Restructuring and Third World Transnationals: Thailand, the CP Group and the Global Shrimp Industry", *World Development*, 28(3), pp. 513-530.

Goss, Jasper, and David Burch (2001):"From Agricultural modernization to agri-food globalisation: the waning of national development in Thailand", *Third World Quarterly*, 22(6), pp. 969-986.

Hill, Ronald (2002): *Southeast Asia – People, Land and Economy*, Allen & Unwin, Crow's Nest, NSW (Australia).

Isvilanonda, Somporn, Alia Ahmed and Mahabub Hossain (2000): "Recent Changes in Thailand's Rural Economy – Evidence from Six Villages", *Economic and Political Weekly*, 35(52-53), June 5, pp.4644-4649.

**IMC (Industrial Management Co. Ltd) (1996)**: Agro-industry for the Development of Small Farmers: A Case Study of the Royal Project Food Processing Section, **prepared for the FAO, November.**

Kakwani, Nanak and E M Pernia (2000): "What is Pro-poor Growth?", *Asian Development Review,* 18(1), pp.1-16.

Kusakabe, K and Y Higuchi (1992): *A Case Study of Discontinuance: Cotton Contract Farming in Kanchanaburi Province*, Thailand, HSD Monograph No. 24, Division of Human Settlements Development (HSD), Asian Institute of Technology (AIT), Bangkok.

Makarabhirom P (1997): A study on Contract Tree Farming in Thailand, Ph.D. Thes is University of Tsukuba, Japan.

Manarungsan, Sompop, and Suebskun Suwanjidar (1992): "Contract Farming and Outgrower Schemes in Thailand" in David Glover and Lim Teck Ghee (eds.): *Contract Farming in Southeast Asia- Three Country Studies*, Institute of Advanced Studies, University of Malaya, Kuala Lumpur, Malaysia, pp. 10-70.

**Naritoom, Chatcharee (2000): "Contract Farming in Central Plain: a case study of asparagus grower groups in Nakhon Pathom Province", in** Proceedings of the International Conference: The Chao Phraya Delta – Historical Development, Dynamics and Challenges of Thailand's Rice Bowl, Vol. 2, **December 12-15, Kasetsart University, Bangkok.**

**Nundhapana, P (1985):** Contractual Arrangements in Swine Production Industry in Thailand, **Master of Economics Thesis, Faculty of Economics, Thammasat University, Bangkok.**

**Padmanabha, T V Anantha (1995):** Economic Impact of Contract Farming on Farmers: A Case of Changwat Chachoeng Sao, Thailand, **M. Sc. Thesis, Asian Institute of Technology (AIT), Bangkok. August.**

Poapongsakorn, Nipon, Martin Ruhs, and Sumana Tangjitwisuth (1998): "Problems and Outlook of Agriculture in Thailand", *TDRI Quarterly Review,* 13(2), June, pp. 3-14.

**Rosset, Peter, Robert Rice, and Michael Watts (1999): "Thailand**

**and the World Tomato: Globalization, New Agricultural Countries (NACs) and the Agrarian Question",** ***International Journal of Sociology of Agriculture and Food*****, Vol. 8, pp. 71-94.**

**Saenjan, Veerapong (1998): "Future Prospect of Small and Medium Size Agribusiness in Thailand", in** Proceedings of the second international seminar on development of agribusiness and its impact on agricultural production in south-east Asia **(Dabia II), October 15-20, 1997, Faculty of Agriculture, Khon Kaen University, pp.159-180.**

**Songmuang, A (1984):** Tobacco Contract Farming System: A Case Study in the Northeast Region of Thailand, **M.S (Agril. Eco.) Thesis, Graduate School, Kasetsart University, Bangkok.**

Subhapholsiri, S (2000): Thailand's Food Industry Small but E-volving. http://www.foodmarketexchange.com/datacenter/industry/article/idf_o13_01.htm (30/10/01).

**Suphanchaimat, Nongluck (1998):"Agriculture and Agribusiness under Economic Transformation in Thailand", in** Proceedings of the second international seminar on development of agribusiness and its impact on agricultural production in south-east Asia **(Dabia II), October 15-20, 1997, Faculty of Agriculture, Khon Kaen University, pp.75-89.**

**Thavornyutikarn, Supruet (1998):** Restructuring the Revenue-Sharing System in the Thai Sugar-cane and Sugar Industry, **M. Sc. Economics Dissertation, University of Warwick, Coventry (UK), September.**

Tisdell, Clem, Tatjana Kehren and Thomas Murphy (1998):"The Pig and Poultry Industries in Thailand: Development, Trade and Commerce", *Sasin Journal of Management,* 4(1), pp.1-18.

Trebuil, Guy (1995): "Pioneer Agriculture, Green Revolution, and Environmental Degradation in Thailand" in Jonathan Rigg (ed.): *Counting the Costs: Economic Growth and Environmental Change in Thailand,* Institute of South-East Asian Studies, Pasir Panjag, Singapore, pp. 67-89.

Turton, Andrew (1987): *Production, Power and Participation in Rural Thailand – Experiences of Poor Farmers' Groups*, UNRISD, Geneva.

Volden, M (1994): Contract Farming of maize in north-east Thailand, in Jan Hesselberg (ed): *Agriculture and Food Systems, Fertility and Urban Economy*, Department of Human Geography, University of Oslo, pp. 17-24.

Warr, Peter G (2000): "Is growth good for the poor? Thailand's boom and bust", *International Journal of Social Economics*, 27(7-10), 2000, pp. 862-877.

# 4

# Context, Objectives and Scope of the Study

Contract farming has emerged as an important mode of procurement of raw materials by agribusiness firms in many developing countries due to the developments in the field of marketing, food habits, technology, and agriculture in the new economic environment. Contract farming, essentially, is an arrangement between the primary producer/s and the agribusiness firm in order to procure certain pre-agreed, quantity and quality of produce at a particular price and time. It can only be a pure procurement transaction or can extend into supply of inputs or even beyond. This is happening as good quality, timely, and cost effective sufficient raw material is a pre-requisite for any successful agribusiness firm, whether operating in the domestic or international market. As a part of the internationalisation process in agriculture which involves globalisation of production, capital and trade, contract farming encompasses all the three dimensions through intervention in input supply and production decisions, supply of capital and finance, and global sourcing of agro-products. In fact, it is nothing but extension of the phenomenon of global sourcing wherein a firm can produce any thing anywhere, by sourcing inputs from anywhere, to be sold in any market in the world.

It is argued that agribusiness growth leads to big jumps in incomes and employment in agriculturally backward regions and brings a break from low levels of productivity and instability in production, thus putting the local economy on a dynamic path of growth and development. This is possible not only because of the technological and capital resources of these firms, but also because of the international character of processes of agribusiness which gives access to international markets. The agribusiness firms take risk by undertaking new projects in processing and marketing and provide a stream of cash flow to the local economy. This brings not only benefits to the local economy but also helps earn foreign exchange (Williams and Karen, 1985; Leisinger, 1987; Benziger, 1996). However, it is important to recognise the role of the state in encouraging or discouraging the agribusiness firms and in protecting the producers in contract situations (Asano-Tamanoi, 1988; Christensen, 1992; Grosh, 1994; Benziger, 1996). And, there is a need to look at the potential role of agribusiness more specifically for different commodity sectors and regions, not as a blanket solution as there are certain sectors which may require a more effective public sector or state intervention especially in technology and institutional innovations, instead of a private agribusiness effort (Christensen, 1992).

### Context of the Study

A review of literature reveals that in the context of the African and the Latin American countries, contract farming has led to many ill-effects in the spheres of livelihoods of producers, community organisations and other institutions, environment, and gender (Porter and Phillips-Howard 1997, Burch et al 1996, Morvaridi 1995, Watts 1992, Korovkin 1992, and Glover and Kusterer 1990).

These studies point out that though the contract system leads to better incomes and employment in the beginning, the relations between firms and farmers worsen overtime and the system results in ecological and economic degradation of local production systems. Most of the studies which are in the context of relatively less developed regions find contracts inequitable, short-term, and ambiguous. This study examines the various aspects of the contract farming system in two Asian countries - Thailand and India , with a view to locate its dynamics and draw inferences for its practice in newly emerging contract farming candidate countries in the region where contracting has now emerged as an important intervention in the farm sector in the presence of liberalisation and globalisation policies.

### Why Thailand?

1. In the case of Thailand, there is some evidence to believe that contract farming has been implemented and managed

differently which has resulted in better overall agricultural growth, and developmental effects through shift to high value crops; as well as better farmer level performance (Burch, 1996; Benziger, 1996). Thailand is known to have moved from primary commodity export oriented farming to value added agro exports as part of deliberate state strategies of interventionist type which resulted in mobilisation of local capital and farmer involvement through contract farming and incentives for agro processing. The end result is that the country has been able to perform well in agro exports and still avoid problem of import dependence for food unlike many other countries of the south. Though contracting is not totally harmless, there are many policy lessons which can be learnt from this experience by countries like India.

2. "Of all the countries in Asia, Thailand probably has the most extensive experience with contract farming, in the widest range of crops.." (Glover, in Glover and Ghee, 1992, p. 4).
3. There has been deliberate state intervention for promotion of contract farming under 4-sector plan since the $6^{th}$ plan, as Glover notes "Contract farming is a key element of the Thai government's development plan, reflecting a strategy of 'private-led integrated agricultural development'" (Glover in Glover and Ghee, 1992, p. 4), but not adequate analysis of the role of the state in contract farming has been attempted so far, as Burch (1994) points out "This issue (the role of the state in promoting contract farming) is seldom analysed in a literature which usually focuses on the relationship between the agribusiness companies, the main proponents of contract farming, and those farmers who produce commodities under contract" (p. 163).
4. Thailand is one of the newly agro-industrialising countries (NACs) in the region and still agricultural in nature.
5. There has been 'state mediation' of contract situations of which Abbott (1993) writes in the context of monopolisation of contract production by MNCs that "Mediation by a government department, as in Taiwan and Thailand, may be needed for equitable pricing and quality determination" (p. 73).

6. Finally, many recent studies recommend replication of contract farming projects (Benziger, 1996). A recent exposition on development drawing on rural development projects in India and Thailand states "A clear vision for rural development in Thailand has emerged which emphasizes: (among other things) - A rural development partnership that involves local communities, non-government organizations (NGOs), government, private sector and academic institutions" (Epstein and Jezeph, 2001, p. 1449). But, it is argued by others that the contract farming system has not operated well due to the default by farmers or companies and many companies are withdrawing altogether or reducing their dependence on contract procurement to address problems of quality and general control. Some others had to even close their operations altogether due to raw material supply problems. Even the prevailing contract farming system in north-east region is 'loose' and creates many practical problems (Saenjan, 1998, p. 162 & 166). Though contracting is said to promote adoption of new inputs and to cut brokerage and marketing costs, but, because contracts are binding, the farmer loses, for example, when the weather is unfavourable or when the free market offers higher price (Christensen, 1992). A FAO report on the Royal Project (IMC, 1996) also states "However, this method (contract farming) has not yet been successfully implemented by the industries in general. Only in a few cases in Thialand has contract farming been implemented smoothly and successfully" (p. 14). In such a scenario, it is important to understand the nature and impact of contracting in the country, especially in crops like vegetables that are new candidates for contract farming.

### Why India?

India is a relatively new entrant to the field of contract farming so far as perishables are concerned. It has had contract farming of seed for more than three decades now which was undertaken by both state seed agencies as well as private companies. More recently, due to the opening up of the Indian economy in general and agricultural economy in particular, many agencies have got into contract farming arrangements. Financial and extension agencies have also started involving themselves into contract farming arrangements in a big way. Most of all, the Government of India has amended the Agricultural Produce Market Committee (APMC) Act in 2003 making contract farming legal and had earlier announced several measures to promote contract farming right from the 9th Plan. This is being followed by the state governments also now which are promoting contract farming to resolve problems of sustainability of farming by attempting diversification of crop patterns, technologies and markets. In this context, it is important to compare and contrast Indian approach and experience of contract farming with that of Thailand which has been the pioneer in Asia and is known for the role of the state in such an initiative for agricultural development.

## Objectives

1. An exhaustive review of literature on contact farming practice in Thailand to raise issues of research;
2. To explore and analyse the nature of contracts across types of farmers and companies in Thailand and India in terms of specific provisions and their implications;
3. To study the farmer and the firm perceptions of the working of the contract system and problems, if any; in Thailand and India;
4. To examine the role of the state and its mode of participation in the contract system promotion, and its monitoring in Thailand and India;
5. To examine the effect of contract system on the local economy and the sustainability of the contract system in Thailand and India.
6. To examine the Indian experience so far from the perspective of the small farmer and draw comparisons with and lesson from the Thai experience in this regard.

## Scope and Methodology

The Thai contract farming study has been conducted in the context of Chiang Mai province in north Thailand. There are some studies on this aspect of the agrarian economy of the country which have been used to identify the issues and the background (Christensen, 1992; Glover and Ghee, 1992; USAID, 1994; Benziger, 1996; and Burch, 1996). This province has seen contracting in high value fruit and vegetable crops like potato which is relevant for comparison with the Indian situation and other Asian situations. This study looks at the practice and performance of contract farming in Thailand to draw lessons for the emerging scenario in the Indian agribusiness. It supplements the existing literature with the help of more secondary research and two case studies of such arrangements in Thailand. The first objective is met by procuring the contracts of the various companies which are analysed on various aspects. For the second objective, some case studies of firms and farmers have been undertaken based on interviews with contract farmers in Thailand and discussions with the state agency officials and company officials in different types of companies - multinational and domestic - in the field of vegetable processing. The third objective is attended to more by way of discussions and interviews with various stakeholders in the system. The study attempts to draw some inferences about the ways in which contracts can be used as more equitable and effective means of sustainable development of the local areas without compromising food security and other concerns in India. The case studies have been carried out in the districts of San Sai, Doi Saket and Mae Rim for potato and Mea Wang and Sanpatong districts for sweet corn, with company officials, brokers and farmers.

The study of Indian experience in contract farming is based on the author's own studies in Punjab across four crops and studies of other scholars conducted in recent years in other parts of India across crops and regions.

## References

Abbott, J (1993): "Marketing, the Rural Poor and Sustainability" in John Abbott (ed.): *Agricultural and Food Marketing in Developing Countries – Selected Readings*, CAB International, Wallingford (Oxon, UK).

Epstein, T C and D Jezeph (2001): "Development – There is Another Way: A Rural Urban Partnership Development Paradigm", *World Development*, 29(8), August, pp. 1443-1454.

Glover D and Ken Kusterer (eds.) (1990) :*Small Farmers, Big Business-Contract Farming and Rural Development*, St. Martin, NY.

Korovkin, T (1992): "Peasants, Grapes, and Corporations - The Growth of Contract farming in a Chilean Community", *The Journal of Peasant Studies*, 19 (2), January.

Leisinger, K M (1987): "Multinational companies and agricultural development - A case study of 'Taona Zina' in Madagascar", *Food Policy*, August.

Watts, Michael (1992): "Peasants and Flexible Accumulation in the Third World - Producing under Contract", *Economic and Political Weekly*, 27 (30).

# 5
# Contract Farming in North Thailand

## Chiang Mai Province

Chiang Mai is one of the 76 provinces of Thailand and about 700-year-old city, about 700 kms. north of Bangkok, located in the fertile chiang mai valley at 310 meter above sea level. It has 27 districts and its main crops are longon, rice, onion and potato. Chiang Mai accounted for more than 90% of onion production of Thailand with the highest yield per rai in 2000-01. The average size of holding here is only 9.8 rai which is the lowest in the country. In fact, the north region itself has the second lowest average size of holdings (23.1 rai) after south (22.3 rai), the national average being 24.4 rai. Even the provinces neighbouring Chiang Mai (Lamphang and Lamphun) have very small holdings on the average (11.38 rai and 11.13 rai respectively (OAE, 2001). The region is known for vegetable cultivation in the country which has grown in area and production over the years (Tables 1 and 2). The royal project foundation had 3000 farmer involued in vegetable production across five province of northern Thailand producing 140 kind of vegetable rops in 2004 (Jayamangkla, 2006): The region is also known for orgainic or perticade free vegetable prodution nine recently where NGOS and prevati agencies work many with growen to produce and market orgainic vegetables (Kramoletal, 2006).

Contract farming is so popular here that even in a crop like rice, a significant proportion is contract farmed (a Japanese variety which is used for making Japanese rice wine). Many farmers no longer produce rice for home consumption and buy rice from the market for their own consumption (Rigg and Nattapoolwat, 2001).

There have been relatively few studies of contract farming in the north (Laramee, 1975; Ekachai, 1990; and Garforth, 1993) as it was a latecomer to the system of contracting and also did not attract attention until the 1990s when the practice and effects of contracting became too common. Even recent studies (Ornberg, 1996 & 1999; Wiboonpongse et al, 1998; and Hassarungsee, 1998 & 2000) focus mainly on potato and baby corn though contracting is in place in most of the vegetable crops since the early 1990s.

**Table 1**

**Main crop area, production and yields, 1987–1997**

| *Crop* | *Year* | | | | | *Percent change 1987–97* |
|---|---|---|---|---|---|---|
| | *1987* | *1994* | *1995* | *1996* | *1997* | |
| **Cereal Crops** | | | | | | |
| Area (1000 ha) | 10673 | 10515 | 10446 | 11694 | 11505 | - 0.1 |
| Yield (kg/ha) | 2006 | 2410 | 2527 | 2293 | 2268 | 1.5 |
| Production (1000 t) | 21414 | 25339 | 26398 | 26808 | 26097 | 1.3 |
| **Roots and Tubers** | | | | | | |
| Area (1000 ha) | 1393 | 1403 | 1281 | 1285 | 1220 | - 2.1 |
| Yield (kg/ha) | 14205 | 13103 | 13737 | 14240 | 14931 | - 0.2 |
| Production (1000 t) | 19784 | 18377 | 17592 | 18292 | 18210 | - 2.3 |
| **Pulses** | | | | | | |
| Area (1000 ha) | 593 | 450 | 448 | 458 | 452 | - 4.0 |
| Yield (kg/ha) | 721 | 847 | 803 | 737 | 753 | - 0.1 |
| Production (1000 t) | 427 | 381 | 359 | 338 | 341 | - 3.8 |
| **Fruits** | | | | | | |
| Area (1000 ha) | NA | NA | NA | NA | 3 359 | NA |
| Yield (kg/ha) | NA | NA | NA | NA | 2 125 | NA |

| | | | | | | |
|---|---|---|---|---|---|---|
| Production (1000 t) | 5 693 | 7 343 | 7 133 | 7 231 | 7 139 | 2.4 |
| **Vegetables*** | | | | | | |
| Area (1000 ha) | 187 | 373 | 353 | 515 | 479 | 3.3 |
| Yield (kg/ha) | 9 464 | 8 638 | 10 997 | 9 318 | 10 707 | 0.4 |
| Production (1000 t) | 1 770 | 3 222 | 3 882 | 4 799 | 5 129 | 2.1 |

*Source:* FAO, 1998. * DOAE calculated statistics,

*Source*: www.fao.org/docrep/004/ac145e/ac 145e 03.html

**Table 2**

**Regional production and per capita supply of vegetables, 1998**

| *Region* | *Overall production (tons)* | *Overall vegetable production per capita (kg)* | *Fresh market production (tons)* | *Fresh market vegetable production per capita (kg)* |
|---|---|---|---|---|
| Central | 325 533 | 26.99 | 262 892 | 21.80 |
| North | 2 130 940 | 176.26 | 1 491 446 | 123.36 |
| East | 331 193 | 81.57 | 270 539 | 66.64 |
| Northeast | 1 232 251 | 58.40 | 805 725 | 38.19 |
| West | 1 085 928 | 304.50 | 684 060 | 192.15 |
| South | 268 446 | 33.76 | 149 443 | 18.80 |
| *Total* | 5 374 291 | | 3 664 105 | |
| *Average* | | 88.36 | | 60.25 |

*Source*: Centre for Agricultural Information, 1996.

*Source*: www.fao.org/docrep/004/ac145e/ac 145e 03.html

A very early study of tobacco contract farming in Chiang Mai province (NESDB, 1968) revealed that tobacco prices were found to be low by growers, and income from tobacco production lower than that from other crops. They also faced delayed payment and inadequate and inefficient input supply by Thailand Tobacco Monopoly (referred to in Songmuang, 1984). Though this region has had long experience with contract farming in state controlled tobacco crop, vegetable contracting started in 1973 with a Thai-Israel joint venture company starting operations in the area by forming a separate company called Thai Farming Limited (part of the larger Lanna Food Complex) that was to handle only raw material production and supply for the group's other three companies which were into freezing, canning and dehydrating of vegetables respectively. It had its own plantations as well as contract farming operations (Wiboonpoongse et. al, 1998; Laramee, 1975). Operating in Chiang Mai and Lamphun provinces, though based at Lamphun, it had to manage its own land as well as contract production, though initially it had to rely on contract production as its own lands were not yet ready for farming. It advertised its contract program and enlisted farmers for seven crops though mainly in sweet corn, tomato, onions, and bushbeans; and written contracts were signed with farmer groups, co-operatives or farmer associations and individual farmers in four districts. Besides seeds (free for first year) and technical help, it even tried to procure credit for farmers on low interest rate. Even landless could be contract growers provided they had right to use the land. The contracts placed all responsibility for farmer compliance on the farmer representatives. Rest of the contract was like any typical contract found even today in Thailand except that the company promised to pay cash to the farmers if crop failed due to natural calamity. Further, the contracts were direct and arbitration was by a committee which had, besides company and farmer representatives, a District Agricultural Extension Officer and another person from the NADC (Northern Agricultural Development Centre) as members (Laramee, 1975).

Laramee points out that despite this meticulous planning and very attractive package, almost everything went wrong on the ground right from farmer recruitment and selection, which was very lax and casual, to delivery of inputs including seedlings, and farm and crop monitoring, harvesting and payments for deliveries. On the part of the company, the reasons for failure were lack of proper feasibility study, funds and staff and a lack of co-ordination with the government. The farmers also never really behaved like partners with the company. Later, the company decided to work only with registered farmers' groups and in direct contracts with them, revised the terms of the contract, removed government representatives from arbitration committee, and promised only possible things to farmers, but still performance was no better (Laramee, 1975).

In a journalistic study conducted in the late 1980s, Ekachai (1990) brings out the impact of contract farming in crops like tobacco and baby corn in north Thailand. She reports from first hand farmer accounts the mechanical processes involved in contract production of crops like baby corn where harvesting was to be done everyday without fail and even whole families were not able to cope with contract crop work, but returns were not any better, though it was the best so far of the various cash crops the farmers had tried. She also reports on how a contract company after making promises of buying string beans just disappeared from the scene. The contracts in bay corn were indirect and verbal through the local middlemen who further subcontracted to locals in each village. Though baby corn was still going strong in the area, farmers were not sure for how long this was to continue as it was totally dependent on companies, and the farmers did not have many choices as the average landholding in the village was just one rai. Therefore, they could not grow only rice for one season and survive without cash crops.

A study on rural people's organisations and agricultural extension in upper north Thailand in early 1990s also reports briefly that rice and vegetable marketing companies and a brewery were having their own farmer groups to practice contract farming wherein they provided inputs, credit and advice to farmers as part of a contract to supply farm produce to the company in each case (Garforth, 1993). Due to the climatic suitability of the northern region for vegetable crops, contract farming has picked up more recently in this region. In 1984, there were only 10 fruit and vegetable processing companies in this area. This increased to 100 in 1994 with 36 of them located in Chiang Mai province alone, another 16 in Tak, and 10 and 9 each in neighboring provinces of Lampang and Lampoon. Most of them were canneries (Wiboonpoongse et al, 1998).

## Practice and Impact of Contract Farming in Chiang Mai Province

A study of 239 farmers in various crops i.e. hybrid maize seed, tomato, potato, vegetable soyabean and Japanese cucumber in 1995 revealed that contracts varied from verbal agreements to formal written and from only marketing arrangements to complete control contracts. In fact, in tomato, there were three type of marketing systems prevalent which varied from only middlemen between company and farmers without any contract with anyone, to middlemen with written contract with firms and informal contract with farmers, to middlemen with informal contract with both the parties, with seed and fertiliser supply being there as part of the agreement in both the latter cases. But, there was no price guarantee for farmers in these contracts. Produce was bought at open market prices and in some cases, farmers were allowed to sell 20% of the total produce in the open market if they found them higher than company prices. The open market type of procurement by the middlemen and then sale to any processing firm was the most common arrangement in the area (Hod district) which accounted for 80 per cent of the tomato acreage of the province. The second system of formal contract with company and informal one with farmers by middlemen was more common in Chomthong district but accounted for only about 6% of total tomato production of the province. The third system of only verbal contracts with both sides by middlemen was more common in Sai Sai district where farmers were not allowed to sell outside and companies were not obliged to buy all produce and that is why, a\ lot of farmers here eventually abandoned tomato farming under contracts and shifted to other crops like potato (Wiboonpoongse et al, 1998). The contract systems of other crops i.e. vegetable soyabean, cucumber and maize seed were found to be more precise and strict.

Farmers mainly took up contracting due to assured market and stable price under contracts, and supply of inputs to some extent. The contract crops also gave them higher returns compared with those under market based alternatives. They had been working under contracts on the average for five years in case of primary crops and four years in case of secondary crops. Surprisingly, potato and tomato farmers did not desire to expand acreage under contract production unlike their counterparts in soyabean, maize seed and cucumber, though all of the farmers had only about 2/3rd of desired acreage under contract. Most of them were happy with input supply and it was only in potato and tomato that farmers had frequently changed contracting firms. Their major demand from the firms in general was higher produce prices, with those in seed production also asking for better quality seed and lower produce rejection, and lower input cost in case of soyabean. Though farmers contracted for reliable income, their net returns under contracts in tomato and potato were lower than those of the non-contract growers most of the time during the mid eighties to the early nineties. However, they enjoyed lower variability in returns in case of potato but higher in case of tomato than their non-contract counterparts.

In terms of production and allocative efficiencies, contracting was found to be more efficient, and even the market for tomatoes was made more efficient as processing varieties finally ended up in the local market for fresh tomatoes due to their abundance (Wiboonpoongse, et al, 1998).

Another recent study in Chiang Mai province reports that in 1983, in Tambon Maeta of Maeta district, 1000 households, or 80% of total, grew baby corn under contract. In 1998, there were 14 representatives of contracting companies to buy baby corn from small growers. These representatives/brokers/ collectors/middlemen supplied seed and other inputs to the contract growers and bought back baby corn at a guaranteed price for the companies and paid after deducting seed and other inputs costs. So far as change in crop economics is concerned, it was revealed that in 1983, baby corn could be harvested only twice a year compared to the six times in 1998 as baby corn requires 45 days to grow and 15 days to harvest per crop cycle now, but still the earnings (650 baht per rai) were enough at that time compared to now for meeting various expenses. This is so as the expenses have gone up to make grow the corn fast and also because the smaller the size of corn, which is preferred by the companies, the less output per rai it means for the farmer, though price does not vary much due to size. But, farmers continue with this crop as it has guaranteed price and input support on credit (Hassarungsee, 1998). A revisit to the same area revealed lower contract prices and higher input costs in baby corn and therefore, growing indebtedness of the growers to the BAAC. It was also reported that many farmers were withdrawing from baby corn contract farming system (Hassarungsee, 2000).

Based on a 2003 data set provided by the MOAC which covered 83 organic rice contract growers and 85 conventional rice non-contract growers in two provinces of North Thailand, another recent study (Setboonsarng, et al, 2005) finds that organic rice contract growers fared better on profitability as well as efficiency of rice production and they had higher area under rice, higher ownership of land, higher presence in rice farming more so fragrant rice, and higher percentage of agricultural income from rice farming compared with their non-contract rice counterparts.

## Potato Contract Farming in North Thailand

North Thailand has traditionally been a major production center for potatoes. In the 1970s and 1980s, it accounted for as much as 80% of total potato production and of area under potato in the country (Scott, 1987) and now it accounts for as much as 100% of the country's total potato production. Within north region, Chiang Mai and Tak are noted for potato production accounting for 53% and 37% respectively, together making for 90% of total potato production in Thailand (OAE, 2001). In fact, in the upper north, farmers take two crops of potato in a year compared with only one crop in the lower region. Within Chiang Mai province, San Sai district where the PGC is located is known for potato production and farmers in this area grow 3–4 different crops every year. In 1994-95, 80–90% of the farmers grew potatoes in this district. In adjoining Mae Taeng district, about 20% of the farmers grew potatoes in 1994-95. Contract farming of potatoes on a larger scale started in San Sai in 1988 (Ornberg, 1996). Further, potato growers are small with 5 rai of owned land or 7 rai with leased in land and grew 3-4 crops a year practicing intensive farming. Companies also work with leasee farmers without much hesitation (Ornberg, 1999).

The Thai companies dominated the domestic production and market for potato snacks through the 1990s, but increased internationalization has occurred recently as FLT (a PepsiCo subsidiary) has expanded the production for export and is also trying to monopolize domestic production (Ornberg, 1999).

A mid 1980s study reports contracting in potato by a Bangkok based company which supplied seed, fertilisers and pesticides to 280 low land and 80 highland farmers through its representatives. It also maintained a rural assembly centre (grading and packing shed) near Fang. Lowland contract growers brought their produce to the packing shed themselves whereas highland growers through a rural assembler. Payment was made after produce was graded and shipped to Bangkok factory of the company, within 15 days usually. Sometimes, the produce from low land was used (60-70%) as seed for highland farmers, by the company in early 1980s (Scott, 1987). The bulk of all potatoes are produced in the lowlands of the Chiang Mai valley during the dry season (November to March) from imported seed, but some of the small tubers from this yield are sold to highland farmers to be used for commercial production. Yields in the highlands are lower, but on the other hand, the price of these potatoes is usually high at harvest time since potatoes, at that time, are in short supply. Some of the highland crop is also sold back as third generation seed for an early crop in the lowlands (Ornberg, 1999, p. 4).

### Development of the Potato Growers' Co-operative

The Potato Growers' Co-operative in Chinag Mai - the only one of its kind in Thailand - was in 1997 an organization with 4666 members. Farmers are individual members; hence there may be more than one co-operative member in the household. The co-operative has evolved gradually over many years, from out of a number of small farmer-groups. One of them has its origin in Huay Kew village in San Sai district, where in 1965 a group of eight potatoes. They had all been growing tobacco, peanuts and soybean before, but and extension officer suggested that they should try a new crop. The farmers got a fifty kg. potato seed from the extension office, together with some advice on how to cultivate the new crop. the first yield was a good ton potatoes per rai and the farmers sold the potatoes for 2.5 baht per kg. In Ban Klang Phattana, a nearby village, one farmer had started to grow potatoes already in 1962, and even though he was not very successful in cultivating the new crop, more farmers followed in the coming years. Tobacco used to be the dominant crop in the village, but the price was low and a lot of firewood had to be used for curing, hence many farmers were looking for a new crop to replace tobacco as a second crop after rice. Potato cultivation became increasingly popular in the Chiang Mai valley and in 1982 the potato farmer-groups in Huay Kew village and Ban Klang Phattana-together with other groups from San Sai, Mae Taeng, Mae Rim, Fang, and Chi Prakarn districts-decided to join in a larger organization (Ornberg, 1999, p. 6).

The Potato Growers' Co-operative has widened its activities over the years, becoming more like a multi-purpose co-operative, and is also becoming more involved in the contract farming system. The leading committee has also managed to put a stop to corrupt behaviour among the top layer of the co-operative's members (Ornberg, 1999, p. 13).

Chiang Mai Potato Growers' Cooperative Limited emerged in 1985 from grouping of 1,400 potato farmers in 5 districts in Chiang Mai Province – San Sai, Mae Taeng, Mae Rim, Fang and Chai Prakan – with the objective of a joint effort to counter potato oversupply. As grouping was made without legal support, the farmers couldn't enter any legal deeds, thus posing administration restrictions. And there was no specific government agency to supervise or support. With recommendations from the Chiang Mai Provincial Agricultural Office, the potato farmers registered their grouping as Chiang Mai Potato Growers' Group. However, the group's activities were still limited within sub-district. The group then applied for registration as a cooperative and registration as a cooperative was made on April 7, 1987 as Chiang Mai Potato Growers' Cooperative Limited. Potato farmers and non-members applied for membership of the cooperative. The number of members rose to 4,665.

On October 6, 1997, cooperative members from Fang and Chai Prakan Districts broke up to set up their own cooperative since they were quite far away from Chiang Mai Potato Growers' Cooperative Limited, inconvenient for them to coordinate with the cooperative. Some 1,033 members from the two districts then resigned from Chiang Mai Potato Growers' Cooperative Limited but the two cooperatives reached an agreement that they would work together in the import of reproducible potatoes for consumption as fresh potatoes according to the ratio of members as of the separation date (source: co-operative provided note in Thai).

## Present Status

Today, Chiang Mai Potato Growers' Cooperative Limited has 3,617 members from three districts – San Sai, Mae Taeng, and Mae Rim. These members cultivate about 3000 rai of potato every season, a member growing about 2 rai of potato on the average. It has been selling to Frito Lay under contract for the lat 4-5 years (*added by self from interview with manager*).

In terms of the cooperative administration, the cooperative currently has 14 Directors and 11 staff members and employees. The cooperative is currently located at No. 121/1, Village No. 3, Mae Faek Mai Sub-district, San Sai District, Chiang Mai Province. Its objectives are to promote stable and sustainable career development of members through cooperative strategies; to engage in cooperative business, e.g. procuring and selling inputs, produce collection, credit and service businesses for the optimum benefits of members; to promote potato production and marketing development; and to provide training for the benefits of members.

### Its Business is Composed of

1. Procuring and selling products to members
   - procuring quality reproducible potatoes from domestic and overseas sources to sell to members according to the quota allocated to meet market demand

- procuring farming materials and equipment, e.g. fertilizers, insecticides, and other farming equipment to sell to members at fair prices
- procuring fuel and lubricant oils to sell to members and the public

2. Credit business
   - Offering credit to members through a loan agreement. But the loan will be offered in the form of fertilizers, insecticides and agricultural materials.
3. Produce collection
   - Collecting and compiling farm produce, e.g. Atlantic potatoes (processing variety) from members and other farmers in the area to hand over to Frito Lay (Thailand) Co., Ltd.
4. Service business
   - Offering weighing services with the cooperative's weighing tools
   - Offering produce depositing in the cooperative's cold storage (as given in the note provided by the co-operative's manager).

## References


Ekachai, Sanitsuda (1990): *Behind the Smile: Voices of Thailand*, The Post Publishing Co. and Thai Development Support Committee, Bangkok.

**Hassarungsee, Ranee (1998):** Field Study Report on the Impact of Economic Crisis on the Villagers, **Focus on the Global South, CUŞRI, Bangkok (mimeograph obtained during personal meeting), February.**

**Hassarungsee, Ranee (2000):** Field Study Report: Impact of Economic Crisis on Villagers, **Focus on the Global South, CUSRI, Bangkok (mimeograph obtained during personal meeting).**

**Garforth, Chris (1993):** "Rural People's Organisations and Agricultural Extension in the Upper North of Thailand: Who Benefits?", **paper at the 5th International Conference on Thai Studies, held at SOAS, London, pp. 25.**

Jayamangkala N (2006) : Vegetable supply chain Management. The Royal Project Foundation "Thailand" in P.J. Batt (ed.): **Proceedings of the first international symponumin improving the performance of supply chain in transational economies, Acta Horti culture,** 699, ISHS, Belgium, Ph. 43- 45.

Kramol, P. K. Thang-ngam, P. Gypmantarsiri and W. P. Davies (2006): Challenges in Developing pesticide free and organic vegetable market and farming system for smallholder Farmers in North Thailand", in P. J. Batt (e.d): same as in Jayamanykale N. pp. 243-251.

Laramee, Peter S (1975): "Problems of Small Farmers under Contract Marketing with special reference to A Case in Chiang Mai Province, Thailand", *Economic Bulletin for Asia And the Pacific*, 26(2/3), Sept.-Dec., pp. 43-57.

**National Economic and Social Development Board (1968): Report on Thailand Tobacco Production and Trading in Provinces of the Northern Region (mimeograph in Thai) referred to in Songmuang, A (1984):** Tobacco Contract Farming System: A Case Study in the Northeast Region of Thailand, **M.S (Agril. Eco.) Thesis, Graduate School, Kasetsart University, Bangkok.**

OAE (Office of Agricultural Economics) (2001): *Agricultural Statistics of Thailand – Crop Year 2000-2001*, Centre for Agricultural Information, OAE, Ministry of Agriculture and Co-operatives (MOAC), Bangkok.

**Ornberg, L (1996): "Farmers' Choice in a Society under Transition: Contract Farming of Potatoes as an Alternative for Farmers in the Chiang Mai Region of Northern Thailand", in** Proceedings of the 6th International Conference on Thai Studies, Theme 1: Globalisation- Impact on and Coping Strategies in Thai Society, **held in Chiang Mai, October 14-17, pp.16.**

Ornberg, L (1999): "Potato Farmers' Organisation in Thailand: A Discussion on the Prerequisites of the Formation and Survival of Farmer Organisations", paper resented at the 7th International Conference on Thai Studies held in Amsterdam, July 4-8, pp.15.

Rigg, Jonathan and Sakunee Nattapoolwat (2001): "Embracing the Global in Thailand: Activism and Pragmatism in an Era of Deagrarianization", *World Development,* 29(6), pp.945-960.

Scott, G J (1987): *Marketing Thailand's Potatoes- Present patterns and future prospects,* Potatoes in Food Systems Research Series Report No. 3, International Potato Center, Lima (Peru) pp. 65.

Setboonsarng, S, P Leung and J Cai (2005): *Contract Farming and Poverty Reduction: A case of Organic Rice Contract farming in Thailand*, Asian Development Bank Institute (ADBI), Tokyo, November.

Wiboonpoongse Aree, Songsak Sriboonchitta, Phrek Gypmantasiri and Kusol Thong-ngam (1998): "The Roles of Contract Farming in Agricultural Transformation in Thailand", *J. ISSAAS*, Vol. 4, pp.74-97.

# 6
# Contract Farming in Potato– Two Case Studies*

## Frito-Lay Thailand Ltd.– A Profile

Frito Lay Thailand (FLT) is a fully owned subsidiary of Frito Lay Company which itself is a subsidiary of PepsiCo Inc. Starting with a humble beginning in 1932 in Texas, Frito Lay had annual revenue of 11 billion US $ in 1998 with employee strength of 37,392. With more than 200 brands, including ten of the largest selling snack brands in the U.S., Frito Lay is the leader in the snack market worldwide. It merged with Pepsi Cola Company in 1965 to make PepsiCo, Inc. with Frito-Lay and Pepsi Cola becoming separate operating divisions. In 1996, it combined its domestic and international operations into a unified company called Frito Lay Company and in 1998, it increased its presence in Latin America with a joint venture with Savoy (Vault.Com- career guide to marketing and brand management, 1998).

## FLT Operations:

FLT operates in 20 districts across five provinces of the country. It has been operating in Thailand since 1994. It procures only potato crop under contract farming and processes 180 tons of potato chip per day during the peak 6 months and about 100-120 tons per day during the rest of the year. It works with a total of 3000 farmers in Thailand and about 1700 of them are in Chiang Mai (CM) province alone. It started with 500 farmers and 3000 rai and had reached a maximum of 5000 farmers in 1998. The average farm size of a FLT contract grower in CM is about 10 rai and the company contracted potato acreage, on the

* Parts of this chapter published in this form of a paper in Economic and political weekly 40 (53), December 31, 2005.

average, 2 rai per grower. In CM province, the main districts of FLT contract operations in terms of number of growers are San Sai (800) and Fang (600). The main reason for the company to go in for contracting is the assured supply of raw material of desired quality of processing variety. About 90% of its procurement is from contracting and 10% from other companies like CMFF, Tek Thai and Sai Thon. The entire produce is meant for catering to Thailand chips market.

## FLT Contract Farming System

The company has direct contracts with individual farmers though there are some group contracts as well. It did not acknowledge the presence of brokers or middlemen in its operations but they are very much there like for any other company practicing contract farming in Thailand, as discussed later in this section. The contracts are seasonal and the company provides seeds, fertilizer and pesticides on credit, which accounts for 70 per cent of total farming cost, and it purchases potato crop of specified quality at 8 baht per kg. The contracts cover quantity or acreage, quality, price (8 baht per kg.) and monitoring of the crop by the company. The payment is made in cash within 2 weeks and there is no incentive for better quality produce. There is no crop insurance so far. The farmers have to transport the produce to the factory but company pays transport cost on per kg. basis. The contracts have land collateral on the basis of which the loans of inputs are given. The company has about 40 extension staff to work with contract growers. The farmer grading is based on 1) potato yield from the last two/three crops and 2) farmer good practices (FGP) which are determined by the FLT agronomist who looks after production.

The quality related rejection rate is about 5% and there is lower price for poor quality produce. The farmer default rate is about 40 percent, with 20% not supplying at all and another 20% supplying less than committed quantity. The company blacklists the farmers who default, gives them another chance if default is due to genuine reasons, and tries to see how the farmer can improve yield and quality and avoid all the risk such that he gets good profit from potato business. The farmer retention rate is about 60%.

The crop failure is caused by three main reasons: (1) farmers' practices such as poor land and seedling preparation, poor irrigation management; (2) disease and insect/pest attacks such as Bacterial wilt, Late blight, Nematode and Cutworm; and (3) weather factors like heavy rain, too hot or too cold weather or flood. The company compensates only partially depending on each case.

## FLT Brokers

FLT also works with brokers who work with small farmers. Mr. Bunsi is one such person. He belongs to Chedee Mak Khua village in Mai Faek Mai tambon in San Sai district of CM. He is high school literate and has been working as a broker for potato for FLT, and for sweet corn for River Kwai International (RKI, another company studied here for sweet corn contracting). He was the president of the Potato Growers' Co-operative (PGC) until last year. He does brokering for FLT with 100 farmers. FLT pays him one baht per kg of potato delivered as commission. FLT took him and another employee of the PGC when he was the president of the PGC to Netherlands to show him the potato farms and systems. The contracts with other farmers working under him are made in the presence of the FLT extension workers. He has been contracting with this firm for the last two years. Earlier, he worked with Siam and BJF for 5 years, thus totaling 7 years. As a broker, he supplies seeds to other farmers growing for FLT under him which are provided to him by the company. Sometimes extension workers of the DOAE also attend contract grower-company meetings as seeds of potato are imported. The broker says he has never failed to meet contract terms so far and has never sold outside the contract.

This farmer-broker was contacted by the company to begin with and now he can grow this crop without contract but will face marketing problem in the absence of the contract from the company and, therefore, practically can not grow this crop without contract. He is of the view that contracting gives better and stable income and even better farming skills. He does not see any problem in contracting with company and rates its performance very good. He thinks that contracts are different for different types of farmers and company has introduced new potato varieties in the area. So far as role of government is concerned, he says that district agricultural office already monitors contract farming system in the area.

As a contract grower, he owns 12 rai and leases another 20 rai from large farmers for potato and corn cultivation besides paddy in San Sai and Mae Tang districts. Leased land is for potato only and at the rate of 1600 baht per rai. He takes three crops in a year starting with potato for 5 months, then corn for 3 months, and finally, paddy for 4 months (June–Sept.). He grows 12 rai of potato for selling to FLT beside brokering for it. As a farmer, the FLT supplies him 150 kg. seed per rai at the rate of 4500 baht which is 30 baht per kg. on credit upto harvest time. He has written seasonal contract with company (Oct.- Feb.). He supplies 80 percent to FLT and 20 per cent in the open market. After potato, he grows sweet corn on this 12 rai owned land (March to May) for RKI under contract which he has been doing for 3 years. He is a broker for RKI as well. He did not grow for RKI once due to problem on the company's side.

The contracts are Procurement and Input (P&I) contracts. But, except seed, all input needs of the farmers are met by the potato co-operative which also has a contract with FLT for supply of potatoes (discussed separately later in this section). FLT does not recommend any other inputs as such, according to Mr. Bunsi, the broker.

Though potato is not new crop for this region and its farmers, but its production has almost tripled in the last 7 years according to the broker - from 3000 tonnes to10,000 tonnes per season. Potato yield per rai is 4 tonnes and it gives 32,000 baht under contract. The working capital cost is about 18,000 baht and net income of the grower about 14, 000 baht. More important is the stability of the income which was highly uncertain earlier. There have been problems of lower yield and lower quality due to pest attack and disease or natural calamity but company waived only seed cost in such situations. Even when market prices are higher than contract prices, the company sticks to its prices.

### Berli Jucker Foods Limited– A Profile

Berli Jucker Foods (BJF) is a 100% owned subsidiary of Berli Jucker Public Limited Company (PLC) in Thailand. Berli Jucker first came to Thailand, as a Swiss trading firm handling imports and exports, in 1882. Berli Jucker got its present name in 1924 and was turned into a PLC in 1968. It was one of the first seven companies to be registered on the Stock Exchange of Thailand in 1975. In 1998, it was 70% owned by First Pacific, a Hongkong based Multi-National Company (MNC) operating in 50 countries, and about 95% of its business was in Thailand.

In 2001, TCC Holding took over majority share holding of the company (Bangkok Post, 1998; Bangkok Post, September 27, 2002, p. 5, company advertisement).

Berli Jucker group's total sales in 2002 were around 11,500 million baht of which consumer products sales accounted for about one third. BJF markets and distributes potato chips and other snack foods under the brand names of Party, Tasto, Campus, Bitee and Dandy. It is one of the four major companies of the group. Its sales registered a 33% increase in 2000 with Tasto brand enjoying 55% volume increase. But, after that, sales dipped and company is now focusing on improved agronomy program to boost raw material (potato) supply (source: website of the company). Its processing capacity at present is 2000 tonnes of potatoes per month.

## BJF Operations

BJF has been contract farming since it established potato chip business in 1995. At first, it started contact farming in San Sai (200), Maerim (40), and Hod (40) districts of CM province with a total of 280 farmers. In 2002, BJF has potato contract farming with 3050 farmers for rainy and winter seasons together. Now, besides San Sai (300), Fang (250), Doi Saket (250), Chomthong (250), Prow (600), and Maejham (100) districts of CM, where it has 1750 growers in all, it also operates in Pobpra and Maesod districts of Tak province (50), Thoeng (100), Kuntan(100), and Viangpapound (150) districts of Chiang Rai, Tounghuchang district of Lumpoon province (300), Chaehum district of Lumpang (400), Pangkoon (200) and Bangmoung (1) districts of Sakoonakorn province, and Saka district (1) of Noungkai. The other two major centers besides CM, therefore, are Lampang and Lamphun provinces.

## BJF Contract Farming System

BJF has both direct contract system with farmers as well as broker system accounting for 75% and 25 % respectively. It has no co-operatives or farmer groups for potato supply. Other companies which contract with BJF are ATC and TPM. These Thai companies get potatoes produced, and supply them to BJF.

BJF provides potato seeds (100-200 kg per rai at 27-30 bath per kg), fertilizers and chemicals to direct contract farmers and a guaranteed price of 7-8 bath per kg. at field. To the broker, it provides potato seed and a guaranteed price of 8-9 bath per kg. at field. BJF buys potato from contract farmers and brokers as per the specifications in agreement which are: minimum tuber size of 4.5-cm diameter, maximum 2% of total external defect, free from soil, etc. Average planted area under potato for each farmer is 2 rai in winter season and 10 rai in rainy season. BJF does not pay any compensation to the growers for crop failure.

In 2001, BJF supplied 5000 kg. of seed through one broker (Mr. Pinich) at the rate of 30 baht per kg Output of potato per rai is 2.5 - 4 tonnes and 100 kg seed is needed for one rai, the cost of which (3000 baht) is deducted on delivery of produce to the company. The contract terms include price, quality, and timing of harvesting and delivery of produce besides monitoring of crop by the firm. The price is same (7 baht per kg) for all growers. Quality is measured in terms of three grades but price is same for all grades. There is no incentive for better quality but low quality or rejected produce is bought at 3 baht per kg. The company also recommends input brands to be used by contract growers. Company picks up produce from the collection point. The payment is made though bank account. The company waives input loan if there is serious crop failure, but no compensation is given for lower yield. It is only responsible for seed failure. But, there have been no major crop failures in the past.

Previously, BJF had a high default rate of 25% but now, default rate has come down as the defaulters are booked in the record system of the company for inputs recovery and then in next season, BJF deducts those debts from each farmer. Strategies to reduce default include setting up of permanent farmer member or VIP farmer groups, focus on farmer visits and education of farmers, and cooperation with local and international experts.

### BJF Broker

Mr. Pinich is a broker for BJF and also He is a primary school literate and lives in Pa Mae Dang village of Papong tambon in Doi Saket district. He has 130 farmers under him as subgrowers whose contract acreage under potato varies from 2-20 rai. Almost 60 per cent of these growers plant only 2 or 3 rai each under contract, another 15 per cent 4 rai each and only a few (two each) 10 and 20 rai each. Rest of the farmers grow potato in acreage ranging from 5 to 8 rai each. He maintains a list of BJF growers working under him which contains names, code number, seed quantity supplied, seed price, and assured contract price, besides bank account number or house number or ID card copy given or not, as evidence for each farmer. The company takes a copy of any of these documents. He monitors these growers though they are contracted by the company. He has a written seasonal (3 month (Dec.- Feb.)) contract with the company and maintains a copy of it. Earlier, he worked for Siam Co. for 5 years, and since last year, he is with BJF. He was chosen by the company for his experience with Siam earlier, and honesty. As a broker, he gets a commission of 10 stang (0.10 baht) per kg. of produce delivered as his monitoring charges. In this district (Doi Saket), he is the only broker for the company though his neighbour is working for another company (FLT) in the same crop (potato). He is working mainly for commission he gets for brokering with farmers on behalf of the company.

As a farmer, grows 5 rai potato for BJF under contract in leased land which has been leased at 400 baht per rai for 3 month potato season. He also grows watermelon and cucumber for open market.

The crop is new for this district for all farmers who have grown it only since 4-5 years. The benefits of contracting are not only better and more stable income but also better quality seeds. He says he has always met the terms of the contract and has never sold outside. He rates company performance as very good and had no problems with it but wants the price to be more flexible and competitive with other companies and with the open market. The government extension officials and workers attend company and contract growers' meeting and also the award functions organised by the company.

## Why Contracting in Potato

The companies have four alternatives to ensure a supply of potatoes for production: to buy it on the open market, to import fresh potatoes, to have their own plantations, or to use contract farmers. Potatoes suitable for processing is not available on the open market in Thailand, partly because there is practically no alternative market for it, hence it would be risky for the farmers to grow it without a contract, and partly because the growers' only way to obtain seed is through the companies.

The allowed import quota of fresh potatoes (at a low tariff) is too small to be of any significance for the companies. Over the quota, there is a tariff of 139% CIF. Since potato tubers are bulky and perishable it is doubtful whether import for production could be a realistic alternative for the companies, even without tariffs. Acquiring plantations is, under the present circumstances, not considered by the companies to be a realistic alternative, as land prices in the areas suitable for potato production are too high. Plantations might be a future option for the companies, if new knowledge about varieties and production techniques makes it possible to grow potatoes on a large scale in the highlands during the rainy season. Some of the large companies already have trial cultivations in the highlands, on their own land or with the help of contract farmers. Either they buy land to cultivate themselves, or they sign contract with hill-tribe farmers. Land prices are lower in the highlands (in Tak province, for example), and with machines, it would be possible to make production cheap and efficient. Nevertheless, with the varieties used presently, it is difficult to grow good quality potatoes during the rainy season. Tubers are more sensitive to disease and the sugar-content tends to be too high for processing. Transportation could also be hindered by flooded roads. For the time being, all companies use contract farmers for the bulk of their supply of potatoes. With the help of contract farmers, it is possible for the companies to grow potatoes in the areas that are the most suitable for the cultivation of potatoes. Small-scale farming is also apt for potatoes, since it is a crop that needs careful attention. Potatoes have been grown for a long time in San Sai, a fact that decreases the companies' costs of educating farmers. The use of freeholders for contract farming has been found to bring about lower costs for supervision than to have wage labourers on plantations. On the other hand, it is possible to make large-scale production more efficient with the help of machines. To supervise contract farmers is not cheap either, but the companies have good help from the existing farmer-groups and from some of the most qualified farmers (Ornberg, 1996, pp. 8-9).

## Company Strategies in Potato Contracting

"Each company has a different strategy to control the farmers, to make them grow a high quality crop and to make them sell it back to the company and not to anyone else. NS Farm (or United Foods) rely on social control within the group of farmers. If one farmer breaks the contract or delivers potatoes of low quality, it affects the group as a whole. A group leader for NS Farm expressed concern about the difficulty of controlling the group. As all potatoes are mixed together, there is no control of the quality of each farmer's yield. The company grades the potatoes and pays to the group leader who then distributes the money among the farmers. Cheating occurs, but no farmer growing for NS Farm has ever been excluded from the group. Companies using brokers have to rely on the broker's ability to control the farmer and the brokers' role is more important than the group leader's as the farmers are spread over many villages and cannot control each other" (Ornberg, 1996, p.10).

In terms of guaranteed price of the yield, there is not much difference between the companies, and even if they try to attract the farmers by different means, all companies tend to be similar in the end. One company pays for ungraded potatoes, another offers cheaper seed (price per kg varies from 25 to 38 baht per kg), and others give machines to the farmer-group and contribute to its credit fund. When one company gives an advantage to the farmers, the others have to follow if they want to keep their farmers in San Sai. Spunta, that is the variety grown for fresh consumption, is not really suitable for processing, but at times of short supply of the other varieties, some companies have used it anyway (Ornberg, 1996, p. 11).

### BJF Farmers

In Pa Mae Dang village of Papong tambon in Doi Saket district, farmers contracting for BJF are only primary literate. One of them owns 8 rai land. He sells to company through broker and has only oral contract with him. He has been contracting for 2 years like this under a seasonal (3 month) contract and grows 2 rai under contract. It gives 4 tonnes produce. In other seasons, he grows cucumber, watermelon and rice in this and other land. The contract is P & I contract as company supplies seed through broker at 30 baht per kg. on credit to be recovered from sale of produce. For 2 rai, he gets 200 kg. seed for 6000 baht. So far as training or extension is concerned, general meetings by extension staff are held in the beginning of potato season.

The contracts specify acreage, quality, price, timing of sowing and delivery and monitoring of the crop by the firm. Contract terms are same for all farmers of the company. Price is 7 baht per kg. of potato. This farmer also takes bank loan with land collateral. Company recommends input type and brand to be used in contracted crop and takes the produce from farm at its own cost. So far as rejection of produce is concerned, last year, out of total of 4000 kgs., only 120 kgs. was rejected and later bought at lower price of 3 baht per kg. It is about 3 percent rejection rate. There are three grades of potato –A, B, and C. If produce is really low quality, farmers sell it in the open market. About half of the revenue from contract potato goes for input cost, leaving only half as profit. There have been no major instances of crop failures in past. The market price has been only marginally above contract price in the past.

This farmer was contacted by broker and agreed to grow potato as it gives reliable and better income. But, he can't grow his crop without contract as there will be no seed availability without company. But, he wants to continue next year as well. He faces no problem under contract and rates company performance as very good. The government extension staff attend contract grower and company meetings and are useful for general extension service.

The second farmer also has 2 rai under potato contract for BJF. He does not own any land and has leased land for contract production at the rate of 500 baht per rai per season from landlord who has 15 rai of land. This leased land is part of family leased land (a total of 7 rai). He has been contract producing for 3 years including earlier for Siam and now for BJF. He has same terms and conditions as in the above case and works through broker. He gets about 4000 kg. potato from 2 rai which gives him 28,000 baht. About half of it is input cost and the net profit is about 12,000 baht per season. He is happy with the company system, has had no problems and rates company performance as very good.

The third farmer is also a primary (6th) literate and sharecrops 6 rai for a big landlord (50 rai) of which 4 rai is for contract production of potato for BJF through broker under oral contract with him. He too has been contracting for 3 years under a seasonal contract of three months. Besides potato, he grows corn and rice. He also gets seed from company and pays for them at harvest time. His terms are also the same but next year, he is planning to grow for FLT as advised by his village leader.

His produce has never been rejected but his yield has been declining year after year. About 10% produce is lost in the field. There have been no major instances of crop failure in the past. He started contracting as broker contracted him first and it gives him better and reliable income. He cannot grow this crop if there is no contracting by companies. He too faces no problem in contracting and rates company performance as very good. He finds that company has introduced better yielding variety seeds in the area.

These farmers have never sold outside the contract. The crop is new for them and their area as earlier they grew tobacco for a company and soyabean for open market.

In summary, potato contract growers are only primary literate on the average and own small holdings and some are even landless who lease in land for contract production. They work with brokers of the company generally and have only oral seasonal contracts. They grow only 2-3 rai under contract and grow other crops, like corn, onion and rice, in other seasons. Potato is somewhat new crop for them though not for the area as there has been large production of fresh potato in this region. They get only seed from companies through broker and pay for them at the time of produce delivery to the company. Contract terms are same for all growers and these growers have an experience of 2-3 years with present companies. They also borrow from banks for their input needs. Companies recommend only input types for contracted crop and not brands of inputs. They have not faced any situation of crop failure so far under contracting. Produce rejection is not very large and rejected produce is bought at lower price. The market price has been only marginally above contract price. They contract for better and more reliable income. They cannot grow without contract as they will have no access to seed of processing variety. They rate contracting performance as very good and want to continue contracting with companies.

### Problems in Potato Contracting and Future of Contracting

As per FLT, the problems in contracting are lower yields, defaults, and competition from other potato companies like BJF, Unichamp which also contract with farmers in this area in large numbers. The company does not see any problem with the government in its operations and finds government extension staff useful for its farmers and estimates that the Bank for Agriculture and Agricultural Co-operatives (BAAC) loans are reaching about 10% of its contract growers. So far as future of contracting is concerned, the company representative interviewed (Agro-supply Manager) felt that it shall continue only in special crops which have special processing needs for the market.

On the other hand, BJF perceive that at present, farmers face high cost of imported potato seeds, variable or uncertain climate, and not much support from state agencies as problems. The role of state agencies is that they are involved in the process of import of seeds, and development of new varieties - both processing and table potato. But, now they are more helpful to private sector than in the past, and encourage activities like demonstration farming. Expansion of contract farming to new areas does not need any permission from the state. BJF feels that growers don't get loan from the BAAC due to company contract, and that brokers and cooperatives provide all inputs.

The future of potato or vegetable contract supply in Thailand, according to the BJF agronomy director, will be:

(a) Private sector looking for import of seeds material from overseas because of better quality, price, and security of supply.

(b) State agencies encouraging development and improvement programs in basic agricultural science and disseminating updated information on globalization (product, price, quality) to growers.

(c) Private sector will focus on contracting with high potential growers only.

## Problems in Sustaining Potato Success in San Sai

The growing market for potato snacks has favoured the farmers in San Sai, at least in the short term - they have the possibility to choose among many companies, and can negotiate more favourable conditions in the contract. Still, farmers in San Sai may not keep their dominant position as potato farmers forever as there is a risk that they will lose their advantages in dealing with the companies if it is possible to expand the area for potatoes. For the time being, the area suitable for cultivation is limited but, as discussed earlier, all companies are trying to expand the area to the highlands ornberg, 1999, (p.11). Potato growers in San Sai are not only facing competition from farmers in other areas, soil degradation has also made it harder and more expensive to grow high quality potatoes in this district. In the long run, it will be necessary to use more organic fertiliser (instead of chemical), to maintain and improve the structure of the soil. Nevertheless, farmers in San Sai have the comparative advantage of being skilful growers Ornberg, 1999, p. 12).

### Present and Future of Potato Contracting

Most of the farmers were happy with contracting as Ornberg also reports: "Nevertheless, most interviewed farmers are happy with the contract farming agreement, as it gives them a reasonable and relatively stable income, but they are not alien to the idea of changing the crop if a better alternative shows up. Companies state that they will continue to get the bulk of their supply from contract farmers, but improved possibilities of growing high-quality potatoes in areas where land is cheaper may make them change their minds" (Ornberg, 1996, p.14). She further adds: "It would be rather naïve to suggest contract farming of potatoes as a solution for all farmers in the Northern region, or even to conclude that contract farming of potatoes will remain the most important activity in San Sai district. Even if the market for potato snacks continues to expand, which it probably will, preconditions for the contract farming system may change (Ornberg, 1996, p.15).

### Effect of Potato Contracting on Local Economy

The brokers and growers for both the companies are of the opinion that potato contracting has no adverse effect on food production as it is grown in a different season and is not a substitute crop to other crops. Wage rate and lease rates have also not been affected by contracting as potato is only one of the three crops in a year and there is mutual exchange of labour in the village.

## References

Bangkok Post (1998): *The World in Thailand - Focus on Foreign Investment*, November.

Chunhawong, Kitti (n.d.): "Problems, obstacles and solutions to buying farm produce", a note obtained from the Department of Agricultural Extension, MOAC, The Royal Thai Government on the topic, (translated from Thai, original note in Thai), River Kwai International Food Industry Co., Ltd. Bangkok.

Shigetomi, Shin'ichi (1998): *Co-operation and Community in Rural Thailand – An Organisational Analysis of Participatory Rural Development*, IDE Occasional Paper Series no. 35, Institute of Developing Economies (IDE), Tokyo.

# 7

# Contract Farming in Sweet Corn: Two Case Studies*

## Maize and Sweet Corn Sector

In 2000, Thailand produced 4.4 million tonnes of maize from an area of 7.5 million rai, with an average yield of 582 kgs. per rai which was lower than the world average, but much higher than that in India (283), Mexico (347) and Brazil and South Africa (438). In terms of regional distribution of maize production, in 2000-01, the northern region accounted for 50% of total followed by the central and north-east regions with 25% each. Within the northern region, maize is widely distributed across many provinces (OAE, 2001).

## River Kwai International Food Industry Company Ltd.– A Profile

RKI is a subsidiary of Agripure Holdings PLC which is listed on the Stock Exchange of Thailand. Its equity ownership is 49% foreign, 41% with the Thai partners, and 10% with public as shares. The president of RKI is also the CEO of Agripure Holdings PLC.

Founded in 1986 with a factory in Kanchanaburi to produce canned fruit and vegetable products, RKI decided to focus on sweet corn in 1993, and today, is the leader among sweet corn products manufacturers as it accounts for 40 per cent of Thailand's canned sweet corn production, and over 95% of its sweet corn production is exported. In 1999, USDA estimated that RKI was producing 60% of Thailand's total canned sweet corn (RKI website). It produces canned super sweet corn, and kernel and cream style with production capacity of 1,00,000 tonnes of raw material annually and is the largest canned sweet corn producer in Thailand. It exports to more than 50 countries

* Parts of this chapter published in this form of a paper in Economic and political weekly 40 (53), December 31, 2005.

across the globe. In addition, it also produces sterilized corn, and sweet corn drinks. It capitalized on the year around production of sweet corn in Thailand as against only for 2 months in other countries like the USA or in Europe. For the last 3 years, the company is also into fresh vegetable production for export markets which are chemical free and organic produce and is planning to enter frozen vegetable business as well.

It has a subsidiary called Sweet Corn Products Ltd. which gets seeds produced under contracts with about 50 farmers for distribution among sweet corn crop contract farmers. It obtains parent seeds from Sweet Seed Co. Ltd. owned by the country's leading sweet corn seed breeder, Dr. Taweesak Pulam. The commercial seed produced by contract growers in two crops annually are then sorted and dried and distributed to contract growers all over the country. It also has its own farms for technology experimentation and dissemination of new technology. It has leased in about 1000 rai on a long term basis of which 600 rai is used for sweet corn production through agents who work on these farms for the company and produce about 150 mt sweet corn annually. The remaining land is used for fresh vegetable production.

## RKI Operations

It has 100 middlemen who work with individual farmers for the company, each one working with about 50, thus making a total of 5000 farmers under sub-contract to the company and cultivating about 30,000 rai of sweet corn in all. One such person is Mr. Bunsi who also works for FLT in potato. His contract with RKI is for 12 rai and he is also a broker for it. His sub-growers here are same farmers who grow potato i.e. 100 farmers. The price per kg. is 3.75 baht and he is happy with RKI performance and has had no problem with them so far.

On an average, a grower cultivates 6 rai of sweet corn under contract. Its main areas for contract production are: Kanchanaburi and Pitich in central Thailand and, Chiang Mai, Chiang Rai, and Petchaborn, in north Thailand. The contract crop has a cycle of 90 days and thus 2-3 crops are taken in a year. The company also works with three agricultural co-operatives in the north region under verbal contracts now, as trust has been established between company and the co-operatives. Earlier, four years ago, when they started first time, they had written contracts for one year with the company.

## RKI Contract Farming System

The company has mostly contracts with middlemen and only 10% procurement is through direct contracts with individual farmers. The contracts, which are in local language and a variant of those recommended by the Department of Internal Trade in 1999 and adopted by the company in 2000, specify various aspects of the deal like price, quantity, quality, delivery schedule, and penalty clause. In fact, RKI is one of the couple of companies (the other one being Wae Ta Foods) which have started using the DIT contract. The other contracting companies have not used the DIT contract which is more fair for both parties and, as this causes trouble for the broker whose income becomes known to government through this agreement which tells his volume of business and thus, he can be taxed. In fact, some brokers do business worth tens of millions of baht each every year. That is why payment for produce is also made directly into the individual farmers' accounts as broker may again face tax liability if it is sent to his account alone.

In fact, one of the former managers of the company is so appreciative of the standard agreement that he says "Today, there is a good and fair contract for both parties, a "standard contract" designed by the Department of Internal Trade, but not widely used. The standard contract features standard sales terms, quality, delivery schedule, quantity, prices of produce to be bought by the factory, terms of payment for each delivery, force majeure if unable to make a delivery, penalties to the farmers and factory that fail to comply with the contract and how to handle a dispute. A dispute determination committee, mostly made up of government officials, will determine a dispute and its decision will be considered final. This is an effective solution to the farm produce buying problems......... A standard contract agreement designed by the Department of Internal Trade and featuring penalties for both parties can be used to avoid problems of buying farm produce by the food processing plants."(Chunhawong, n d.).

Whereas middlemen contracts are written and formal, the individual contracts are verbal and only with the knowledge of the extension officers of the government. The company only supplies seed through broker on credit till harvest. A broker has to collect inputs from the company office in his area. In case of crop failure, company replaces seeds and in case of disease or pest attack, it gives discounted rate of sprayers. The seed cost is 450 baht (one kg.) per rai and sweet corn price is 2.5 baht per kg. for farmers and 3.0-3.2 baht per kg. for broker which includes his 'management fees'. The broker maintains a list of growers for the company and keeps copies of their ID card or land documents as evidence. In rainy season, prices are higher (by 0.5 baht per kg) as it is risky to grow crop at that time. The company has an extension staff of 10 who work with brokers of the company to advise farmers on crop practices. Farmers are encouraged to form groups for working with company, though company contracts mostly with brokers.

Default rate for middlemen is about 10% which is acceptable to the company and it replaces the same with new middlemen every year who are totally new people or those working for other companies. In fact, it grades middlemen as A, B, C, and D with the last being the worst and deleted for next season generally, and A grade ones being rewarded with free seed and so on. About 30% of its brokers are A grade, 50% B grade and about 10% C grade like the D grade ones. Another local competitor of the company (Wae Ta Foods) works more through freelance brokers.

In 1993, all of the company's contracts were directly with farmers and now only 10% are so. It explains this move away from direct contracts in terms of extension costs associated with individual farmer level contracts. Also, since crop is not very complicated to grow, a broker can do the job of monitoring farmers. Further, since final product quality does not depend too much on farm crop quality as on factory level aspects, it is not required to work directly with farmers.

Though no permission is required to start contract farming in any province, the company, to build farmer confidence, takes the help of the provincial agricultural office when contacting farmers for the first time. The company acknowledges the support given by the Ministry of Agriculture and Agricultural Co-operatives (MOAC) through its Department of Agricultural Extension (DOAE) and that by the BAAC of the Ministry of Finance (MOF) (it mentions this on its website as well). In fact, this company is the only one which recognizes the role of the state agencies in its operations. It recognizes the role of state agencies as follows: One, the extension department sometimes promotes production of sweet corn by buying seed from company and selling to farmers at subsidised price. About 10% of company's farmers are those who get this seed supply. Two, BAAC provides concessional credit to groups of farmers who work with company, this or any other. The company gives a commitment to BAAC for buying these groups' produce and this works as guarantee for loan. About 10% of company's growers make use of this credit facility. There are 100 such groups working under contracts with company in sweet corn and each group has about 20 members who grow only once crop annually. These groups are more in new areas of company's operations where procurement base is still small. In fact, under the four-sector plan, companies can request such special assistance of extension and credit from government in specific crops and areas for their operations when budgeting is done for such programs every year.

Due to increasing pressure for quality and traceability of produce, the company is planning to lease 300-1000 rai plots of land on long term basis, and finally, about a total of 10,000 rai land for its own production under the care of brokers who will manage labour and other inputs on this land where landless farmers will work for incentives for quality and quantity of output. Another reason for attempting this is that, in Thailand, lease rates are very low (300-500 baht per rai per year). Also, company can use its own production power to bargain better with contract growers and suppliers. Initially, the aim is to supply 15% of procurement through this system, and finally 50% of total requirement of raw material. The government is in favour of this project as it will help export competitiveness and landless rural people. The company's 600 rai plots (two, of 300 rai each) earlier under this system are doing well in Kanchanaburi province where factory is located. The new plots will also be in this area.

### KC Chiang Mai Food Processing Company Limited– A Profile

KC, set up in 1992 under the BOI privilege program (tax exemptions) and a 100% Thai company, is in the business of canning various fruits and vegetables. It has a registered capital of 50 million baht. Sweet corn processing into canned sweet kernel corn accounts for 90 per cent of its total business. The other seasonal products processed are baby corn, tomato, longan, mushroom and lychee. It was initially set up in 1988 and has now a second plant set up in 1992. Its processing capacity is 20,000 tonnes per year and employs 300 workers. The sweet corn products are canned sweet corn, creamy corn, and corn kernel, and are sold under the brand name of KC as well as to other brands in bulk.

### KC Operations

It works with a total of 1000 growers directly or indirectly. These farmers are mainly in the districts of Sanpathong (500) and MaeTeng, Mae Rim and Doi Saket (500) in CM province. The contracts are written and in local (thai) language. These are annual contracts and involve 3-4 crop cycles of corn as it is a 75-day crop. The contracted area per grower is, on the average, 10 rai. Harvesting is done after 60 days of sowing.

### KC Contract Farming System

The company supplies only seeds and agrees to buy sweetcorn at pre -agreed price and of specified quality. The price is 3 baht per kg. And farmer brings produce to the factory at his cost. Quality means not too large or too small size corn but medium size length. Also, it should be soft, not dry. It checks quality by sugar content test (no. of bricks) also. Payments for delivered produce are made within 15 days after deducting seed cost.

The company has five extension workers. The default rate is about 20%. Farmers tend to sell out when open market price is about double that of contract price. The defaulters are blacklisted and the retention rate is about 80%. Small growers defect more to open market as they have small quantities. On the other hand, large growers and brokers defect more between companies and some times have multiple contracts. A large grower or broker can be so large that he conducts 2 million baht worth business per month in sweet corn. Low quality produce is rejected by the company which is sold in the open market by the farmers. In case of crop failure, only seed cost is waived. The competition in sweet corn is from Riverkwai and Vita. These three companies account for 80% of sweetcorn products production in Thailand.

KC has three types of farmers as contractors. One, the large farmers who are only 4 in number and work as brokers for the company. They further contract with 100 or more farmers each, with maximum being 500 in one case. They contract for 150-200 rai of corn and supply 300-500 tonnes per month. Two, medium farmers who are 15 in number and grow 10-30 rais each and supply 15-45 tonnes per month. Three, there are about 20 small farmers who directly supply about 15 tonnes each and grow about < 10 rai each. Intially there were more direct contracts with growers (100%), but now it is only 30%. The company claims that contracts terms are same for all growers. KC also works with about 20 tomato growers who grow 5-40 rai each under contract and price of tomato is 2 baht per kg. An average grower supplies about 100-200 tonnes of tomato per season. Tomato contract is annual and it is grown only once a year. Tomato contracting has been practiced by the company since 1988.

### KC Brokers

Mr. Siridak, one of the typical KC brokers, is a grower and a broker for KC. He belongs to Pateaw village in Don Pao tambon in Mae Wang district. He was the first grower for the company in the village and then became broker also. He has a KC ID card and is a sweet corn representative of the company in the area. He is primary literate and owns 5 rai land. He also leases in 6 rai and thus has a total of 11 rai cultivated. His leased land belongs to his parents who take rice share as a rent from him (1/3 of total rice produce from 6 rai).

He monitors 100 farmers with 500 rai sweet corn for KC. He has only oral contract with other sub-growers. The broker commission per kg. is 0.3 baht and he gets 0.1 baht per kg. of sweet corn for transport cost. He has not been able to meet contract terms as broker sometimes but as a farmer, he has always met the terms. If supply is less, company gives better price. He has two more sub-contractors who help him monitor farmers and he pays them 0.05-0.1 baht per kg. as commission. He maintains a list of growers for KC.

is own contract, as a farmer, with the company is also more of an oral one as he has only the seed supply slip as evidence of contract. The contract is seasonal (for 75 days). He has been working for KC for 6 years. He has all 11 rai under sweet corn and delivery of produce is under monthly contract. He has to follow all farm practices suggested by the company. The seed credit is for 90 days and it is signed by both (farmer and company) in the presence of witnesses. It is just one page document and has seed quantity, price and total cost of seed supplied specified on it. He also contracts with another company for onion. In this area, onion is major crop, not sweet corn. Rice is grown as food crop besides onion and sweet corn. There is an onion growers' co-operative in this area which supplies most of the inputs.

Corn yield per rai is 2.5 tonnes when it is grown after onion and only a tonne if grown in other seasons. The seeds cost is 500 baht per kg per rai. An 800 gram pack is for 470 baht. First seedlings are made and then transplanted if grown after onion. In other seasons, it can be sown directly. The quality, which is in terms of size and color, is better if grown after onion. He gets about 3-4000 baht per rai if sweet corn is grown after onion and much less otherwise.

Price is 3 baht per kg. of sweet corn. The company recommends only type of inputs, not brands. Transport of produce is farmer/broker responsibility but company pays for it. Only about 5-10% of total produce delivered is rejected, and payment is by cheque to both farmers as well as broker. It is not possible to grow sweet corn without contract as there is no open market. He has not faced any crop failures and therefore, no action from the company, of any kind. Contracting gives him better and reliable income and he grows and works for company as it is located nearby. He has not faced any problems with company and rates its performance as good. But, he wants more regular payments and better delivery system for his produce in terms of company taking it every time without fail. But, he finds this company better than others.

### KC Farmers

Mr. Ruan is a primary literate of Namton village in Wankard tambon of Mae Wong district. He owns one rai land and leases another rai. He grows 2 rai under sweet corn and the leased rai is from a small farmer. Besides corn, he grows onion and rice. He has been working for KC through broker for the last 4 years. He changed company with the same broker due to delayed payments but the alternative had the same problem. He has never changed the broker. He gets 2.6 baht per kg. of sweet corn delivered under contract to broker which is an oral contract for 70 days (season).

The company supplies only seed through broker. The contract terms include price, quantity, quality and timing and monitoring of the crop by the company. Rejection on quality grounds is about 5%. The company also recommends other input types, not brands. Farmer directly or through broker has to transport the produce to the factory. Payment is made through broker within 1-1.5 months. There are 5-6 brokers in the area who work for different companies. The crop is new for farmers in this region. This crop is more remunerative than rice with an yield of about 2.5 tonnes per rai. But, it is less remunerative than onion. There have been no major problems of crop failure in the past. The farmer was contacted first by the broker. The farmer cannot grow this crop without contract as there will be marketing problem. Major reasons for growing the crop are better and reliable income and new crop skills gained. Only problem is delayed payment. Otherwise company performance is OK.

In the second case as well, the farmer (Yung) is primary literate from the same village and owns 2.5 rai, all of which is used for sweet corn production under contract through the broker. He has been contracting for 3 years with a different broker. He has been to KC factory only once. He too has faced no problems with contracting and rates KC performance as good. The company replaces seed if not good quality. He has changed broker almost every year as the earlier ones could not supply seed. The prices are same for all types of farmers.

The third KC farmer (Intha) is also a primary literate from Village No. 4 in Vankard tambon of Mae Wong district. He owns one rai and leases 3 rai at 1000 baht per rai for season. He works for KC through broker and has only oral contract with him. He has been working for 3 years under contract with same broker and grows one rai of sweet corn under contract. The other crops grown are rice and onion. He sells onion to local onion co-operative which is in the business of exporting them.

The seed cost per rai is about 500 baht and the seed rate per rai is about 1 kg. The seed is supplied by the company through broker. The contract specifies price, quantity, quality, timing, delivery and monitoring of crop. The price is 2.6 baht per kg. of sweet corn and he has to pay from this for transport cost of produce to the factory. The seeds sown are transplanted after one week. This farmer uses broker for transport of produce to the factory. He delivers only in one go and gets paid in 15 days. He has never sold outside the contract. He gets about 5000 baht per rai after meeting input cost. He has never faced crop failure in the past. There is no incentive for better quality and price is more like market price outside. For him, the crop is new like most other farmers in this region. He was contacted by the company for contract production initially. He cannot grow this crop without contract as there will be marketing problem. Due to better and reliable income, he wants to continue contracting in future and has faced no problem in this system so far. He rates company performance as good. The farmers feel that the government should monitor contracts for seed quality and payment schedule. They also want better price and faster payment.

In summary, the sweet corn growers under contract to the companies are generally primary literate and marginal or small landholders or even landless who grow corn under contract, in leased in land. They grow 2-4 rai under contract and have been working with present companies for 3-4 years on the average, through brokers. Other crops of the farmers are rice and onion. They are more loyal to brokers than to companies as they change companies when brokers change the companies. They have only oral contracts with brokers. Though the crop is new for them, they have not faced crop failure so far. They have faced no problems under contracts and rate company performance as good or very good. Due to better and more reliable income, they want to continue contracting. But, without contract, they cannot think of growing the crop as they will face marketing problem. The farmers feel that the government should monitor contracts for seed quality and payment schedule. They also want better price and faster payment.

## Effect of Sweet Corn Contracting on Local Economy

The brokers and farmers revealed that there is no impact of sweet corn contract production on lease rates or on food production. The lease cost per rai is about 1000 baht for a season (3 months) which is not affected much by contract system. There has been no impact of corn on food supply as it is not a substitute crop for rice. Labour is also not a problem as there is practice of exchange of labour in the village. That there has been and still is a widespread practice of labour exchange in rural Thailand, including in the north,where farm holdings are very small, is well documented in a recent study by Shigetomi (1998). But, labour becomes a problem during harvest time as there is competition from longan harvesting and rice transplantation and one rai harvest costs 500 baht.

# 8
# Nature of Contracts

The contracts are mostly one-sided i.e. pro-company in case of most of the companies as will be clear from the following paragraphs:

## Potrate Contracts

### FLT contract (Appendix 8.1 and 8.2)

"**Section 5.** The farmer agrees to pay for the reproducible potatoes and potato production facilities procured by the company on the date the company buys the produce from the farmer or in ....... days from the date the company delivers the reproducible potatoes and/or potato production facilities to the farmer, whichever comes first. When the farmer sells the produce to the company, the company will deduct the cost of reproducible potatoes and potato production facilities from the produce price payable to the farmer. If the produce price is less than the cost of reproducible potatoes and potato production facilities, the farmer shall pay the missing cost of reproducible potatoes and potato production facilities to the company in 15 days upon receiving a notice from the company. Late payment will be subject to a fine of ....... percent or Bt........ (...............) per day on the amount due."

"**Section 10.** The farmer agrees to sell the produce grown from the company's reproducible potatoes to the company only. If the farmer distributes, sells, transfers or does anything with the produce grown from the company's reproducible potatoes to other persons, the farmer agrees to compensate the company at ...... times of the value of produce so distributed, sold or transferred to other persons."

But, no liability for company for not buying produce is specified. It is only stated that

"**Section 11.** In case a party breaks a section in the Agreement, the other party is entitled to cancel the Agreement and demand compensation for damage at the actual cost of damage."

## Appendix 2

The farmer agrees to let the company fix the quantity and price of each item of production facilities."

In its agreement with the potato growers' co-operative (Appendix 8.2), it is stated in Additional Agreement, which is part of the agreement, that

"the farmer agrees to sell all his/her produce to the company and not sell his/her produce to another person or farmer in order to sell it to the company and not accept produce of other persons to sell to the company in the name of the farmer. If the farmer does any of the above, the farmer is well aware that he/she shall be held liable to civil and criminal charges and the farmer agrees to let the company take possession of potatoes that another person consigns to him/her in his/her name without payment for those potatoes."

It means proxy buying or selling is prohibited under the agreement and is to be penalized. But, what about company using middlemen to procure potatoes and to sell seeds?

### BJC Foods (Appendix 8.3)

"**Section 6.** If the reproducible potatoes that the farmer receives from the company to cultivate are damaged due to the farmer's defects and/or faults to the point that there is no produce, hereinafter called, potatoes to be delivered to the company, the farmer shall be responsible for compensation to the company equivalent to cost of reproducible potatoes that the farmer receives from the company."

"**Section 11.** The farmer shall not distribute, sell or transfer or does anything with potatoes grown from the company's reproducible potatoes to anyone. Such act is an offense against civil and criminal law.

If the farmer does as mentioned above, the farmer shall be responsible for compensation to the company equivalent to potato weight multiplied by purchasing price per kilogram plus 1.50 percent per month *(one baht and five satang)* interest until the farmer settles all the compensation."

## Sweet Corn Contracts

### Std. Agreement used by RKI (Appendix 8.4)

"**Section 3.** As soon as the buyer accepts the produce stated in Section 2 and checks that everything is correct, the buyer shall pay the seller right away in line with the terms of payment in No. 1 of Appendix 3 attached to the Agreement.

In case the buyer does not pay the seller at once as stated in the first paragraph, the buyer shall issue an evidence of acceptance of the produce from the seller. The said evidence shall at least feature the name of the produce, seller's name, buyer's name, quantity and weight, size, quality, price, amount of money, date of delivery and date of payment by the buyer. The buyer shall sign and affix the company seal on the said evidence that the seller can use to receive payment from the buyer later in line with details in No. 2 of Appendix 3 attached to the Agreement.

**Section 4.** If a force majeure or uncontrollable incident specified in Appendix 4 takes place, and the seller is unable to deliver the produce by the schedule and at the point of delivery stated in Section 2, or the buyer cannot accept part of or the entire produce, the party affected shall notify the other party in writing of the force majeure at once. Once the force majeure is over, both parties shall discuss and reach an agreement as specified in Appendix 5 attached to the Agreement, and both parties shall resume compliance with the said agreement.

Section 4 - Fair for both like in case of Nijjer in India

"**Section 5.** In case the seller delivers the produce less than what's specified in Section 1 by .............. percent (....................), the buyer may not accept the produce. But, if the buyer accepts the produce, the price will be calculated proportionally and the buyer is entitled to fine the seller for the missing quantity at Bt............. (.............................) per kilogram."

DDC with government representatives

These contract clauses are very similar to the contracts of Thai Farming Company in Chiang Mai in the 1970s (see Laramee, 1975).

But, this standard contract, surprisingly, has no clause on input supply and payment for inputs or other conditions regarding them, which are so crucial in contract farming arrangements. It is more of a buying and selling of produce agreement between two parties.

### KC Chiang Mai Food (Appendix 8.5)

If default on delivery, legal action by company, but nothing specified in case of company not buying from farmer.

**Saha Farm Broiler Chicken Contract Agreement**

**Saha Farms**

It is one of the largest fully vertically intergratede/ co-ordinated chickn businesses and the with largest chinken products exporter in Thailand. It started with 500 chickens per week in 1969. It has GP stock farm, parent stock farms, silos and feed mills, company ownedboriler farms, contract broiler growers, and processing plants and besides its own logistics like transport. It sells in both domestic and export markets. Corn bought from farmers directly goes into two silos after moisture reduction, with capacity of 200, 000 tonnes per year besides the during capacity of 100 tonners of corn and 60 tonnes of soyabean per hour. It has two feed mills with minimum capacity of 500,000 tonnes per year. Its grand parent stock is imported from US (Cobb breed) and the farms, parent stock farms are composed of Thailand and have production capacity of hatching 145 million eggs per year with its three hatcheries. Its broiler farms can produce 120000 chicken per day. Besides, there are 5000 contract growers who are given 100% credit along with feed, midicines, waccine and other inputs (Appendix 8). The processing plants have capacity of 450 000 chicken per day. Its products have traceability, and the plants are HACCP and GMP certified. The processed chieken products range from cooked to grilled, and are sold in different brand names like saha farms, HF, ZAAB, ALEEP, SADAB, Esan, Kai Thai, Farm and Health. In 2000, out of the total exports of 246,666, 000 kgs, which is more than 20% of total (Saha frams brochure).

The chicken contract farming agreements of the company is highly one sided, biased against the grower and protect only the company interest (Appendix 10.6.) The paragraphs below illustrate this aspect:

**Appendix 8.1**

# Potato Production Facility and Potato Sales Agreement, Lot No. ......../...

The Agreement is made on .................... between ................................., by ..................................., authorized person, located at ................................., hereinafter called, "company" on one party and ..............................................., residing at ......................................................................................., hereinafter called, "farmer" on the other party.

Whereas, the company is involved in the production and distribution of potato chips and distribution of reproducible potatoes and potato production facilities and the farmer wishes to cultivate potatoes to sell to the company, both parties have agreed as follows:

**Section 1.** The farmer agrees to cultivate potatoes, hereinafter called, "produce" in the plantation agreed with the company in order to sell the produce to the company in the month of ................. The company will procure and sell reproducible potatoes, hereinafter called, "reproducible potatoes" and potato production facilities as agreed upon in the appendix to the farmer to grow in the plantation agreed upon.

**Section 2.** The farmer and company shall jointly plan for potato cultivation and harvest to sell to the company and the farmer agrees to cultivate and harvest potatoes according to the said plan. Potato cultivation and harvest plant shall be considered part of this Agreement.

**Section 3.** The farmer agrees not to transfer his/her rights and duties under this Agreement to other persons or allow other persons to exercise the rights and duties under this Agreement without written consent from the company.

**Section 4.** The company agrees to sell .......... kilograms of reproducible potatoes to the farmer at Bt.......... per kilogram, totaling Bt.......................

**Section 5.** The farmer agrees to pay for the reproducible potatoes and potato production facilities procured by the company on the date the company buys the produce from the farmer or in ....... days from the date the company delivers the reproducible potatoes and/or potato production facilities to the farmer, whichever comes first. When the farmer sells the produce to the company, the company will deduct the cost of reproducible potatoes and potato production facilities from the produce price payable to the farmer. If the produce price is less than the cost of reproducible potatoes and potato production facilities, the farmer shall pay the missing cost of reproducible potatoes and potato production facilities to the company in 15 days upon receiving a notice from the company. Late payment will be subject to a fine of ....... percent or Bt....... (..............) per day on the amount due.

**Section 6.** For efficient cultivation and good quality and quantity of the produce, the company may appoint an agricultural consultant to offer advice for the cultivation, maintenance, harvest and transportation of the produce. The farmer agrees to comply with the agricultural consultant's advice.

**Section 7.** After the harvest, the farmer agrees to sell the produce and deliver it to the company at .......................... at the schedule specified in the potato cultivation and harvest plan in Section 2. The farmer shall bear produce transportation expenses to the company's point of purchase. The produce shall feature the following qualities:

7.1 Diameter of not less than ....... Centimeters.

7.2 Specific gravity of not less than ................, equivalent to ............. of not less than .................

7.3 No defects as follows: - small earth worms - cuts from the harvest

- green peels - severe contusion
- abnormal shape - rotten, dry or wet rotten

In accepting the produce, the company will check potato quality at random. If bad-quality potatoes are in the produce, the ratio of bad potatoes will be calculated to deduct from the weight of the produce delivered.

**Section 8.** The company shall purchase the produce meeting the specifications from the farmer at Bt......... (..................) per kilogram.

**Section 9.** The company shall pay for the produce to the farmer in .......... days from the date the farmer delivers the produce to the company.

**Section 10.** The farmer agrees to sell the produce grown from the company's reproducible potatoes to the company only. If the farmer distributes, sells, transfers or does anything with the produce grown from the company's reproducible potatoes to other persons, the farmer agrees to compensate the company at ...... times of the produce price distributed, sold or transferred to other persons.

**Section 11.** In case a party breaks a section in the Agreement, the other party is entitled to cancel the Agreement and demand compensation for damage at the actual cost of damage.

Appendices to this Agreement shall be considered part of this Agreement.

The Agreement is made in two identical copies for each party to retain one. Both parties have understood the terms and conditions in the Agreement and thereby sign their names as evidence in the presence of witnesses:

Signature ...........................Company, Signature............................ Farmer

(............................) (............................)

Signature ............................ Witness, Signature............................Witness

(............................) (............................)

Appendix No. ..............

Both parties jointly agree on the procurement and sale of production facilities specified in Section 1 as follows:

1. The company agrees to procure and sell the following production facilities to the farmer:
   - 1.1 Reproducible potatoes
   - 1.2 .........................
   - 1.3 .........................

2. The farmer agrees to let the company fix the quantity and prices of each item of production facilities.
3. The farmer agrees to let the company deduct the cost of production facilities from the produce price payable to the farmer in line with the criteria specified in Section 5.

As evidence hereof, both parties sign their names in the presence of witnesses:

Signature ................................ Company

(..............................)

Signature ................................ Farmer

(..............................)

Signature ................................ Witness

(..............................)

Signature ................................ Witness

(..............................)

## Appendix 8.2

## Agreement No. ......

# Potato Production Facility and Potato Sales Agreement, Lot No. ......../...

The Agreement is made on ..................... between Pepsi-Cola (Thai) Trading Co., Ltd., by Miss Patraporn Satirasilapin, authorized person, located at No. 18, Siam Commercial Park, Plaza West, Building 2, 6th-7th floors, Ratchadaphisek Road, Lat Yao Sub-district, Chatuchak District, Bangkok, hereinafter called, "company" on one party and ............. ....................................., residing at ... ... ... ... ... ... ... ... ... ... ... ... ... ... ... ... ... ... ... ..........................................., hereinafter called, "farmer" on the other party.

Whereas, the company is involved in the production and distribution of potato chips and distribution of reproducible potatoes and potato production facilities and the farmer wishes to cultivate potatoes to sell to the company, both parties have agreed as follows:

**Section 1.** The farmer agrees to cultivate potatoes, hereinafter called, "produce" in the plantation agreed with the company in order to sell the produce to the company in March 2002. The company will procure and sell reproducible potatoes, hereinafter called, "reproducible potatoes" and potato production facilities as agreed upon in the appendix to the farmer to grow in the plantation agreed upon.

**Section 2.** The farmer and company shall jointly plan for potato cultivation and harvest to sell to the company and the farmer agrees to cultivate and harvest potatoes according to the said plan. Potato cultivation and harvest plan shall be considered part of this Agreement.

**Section 3.** The farmer agrees not to transfer his/her rights and duties under this Agreement to other persons or allow other persons to exercise the rights and duties under this Agreement without written consent from the company.

**Section 4.** The company agrees to sell 26,000 kilograms of reproducible potatoes to the farmer at Bt30 per kilogram, totaling Bt780,000 (seven hundred and eighty thousand Baht only). The quantity of reproductible potatoes may be more or less and the cost will be calculated based on the actual quantity received by the farmer.

**Section 5.** The farmer agrees to pay for the reproducible potatoes and potato production facilities procured by the company on the date the company buys the produce from the farmer or in 110 days from the date the company delivers the reproducible potatoes and/or potato production facilities to the farmer, whichever comes first. In case the farmer sells the produce to the company, the company will deduct the cost of reproducible potatoes and potato production facilities from the produce price payable to the farmer. If the produce price is less than the cost of reproducible potatoes and potato production facilities, the farmer shall pay the missing cost of reproducible potatoes and potato production facilities to the company in 15 days upon receiving a notice from the company. Late payment will be subject to a fine of 0.05 percent *(five satang)* per day on the amount due.

**Section 6.** For efficient cultivation and good quality and quantity of the produce, the company may appoint an agricultural consultant to offer advice for the cultivation, maintenance, harvest and transportation of the produce. The farmer agrees to comply with the agricultural consultant's advice.

**Section 7.** After the harvest, the farmer agrees to sell the produce and deliver it to the company at its point of purchase at the schedule specified in the potato cultivation and harvest plan in Section 2. The farmer shall bear produce transportation expenses to the company's point of purchase. The produce shall feature the following qualities:

7.1 Diameter of not less than 4.5 Centimeters.

7.2 No defects as follows:

- small earth worms
- cuts from the harvest
- green peels
- severe contusion
- abnormal shape
- rotten, dry or wet rotten

In accepting the produce, the company will check potato quality at random. If bad-quality potatoes are in the produce, the ratio of bad potatoes will be calculated to deduct from the weight of the produce delivered.

**Section 8.** The company shall purchase the produce meeting the specifications from the farmer at Bt......... (..................) per kilogram.

**Section 9.** The company shall pay for the produce to the farmer in 15 days from the date the farmer delivers the produce to the company.

**Section 10.** The farmer agrees to sell the produce grown from the company's reproducible potatoes to the company only. If the farmer distributes, sells, transfers or does anything with the produce grown from the company's reproducible potatoes to other persons, the farmer agrees to compensate the company at 3 times of the produce price distributed, sold or transferred to other persons.

**Section 11.** In case a party breaks a section in the Agreement, the other party is entitled to cancel the Agreement and demand compensation for damage at the actual cost of damage.

Appendices to this Agreement shall be considered part of this Agreement.

The Agreement is made in two identical copies for each party to retain one. Both parties have understood the terms and conditions in the Agreement and thereby sign their names as evidence in the presence of witnesses:

Signature ........................... Company

(Miss Patraporn Satirasilapin)

Signature ........................... Farmer

(...........................)

Signature ........................... Witness

(..............................)

Signature .............................. Witness

(..............................)

**Appendix No. ..............**

Both parties jointly agree on the procurement and sale of production facilities specified in Section 1 as follows:

1. The company agrees to procure and sell the following production facilities to the farmer:
   1.1 Reproducible potatoes
   1.2 ..........................
   1.3 ..........................
   1.4 ..........................
2. The farmer agrees to let the company fix the quantity and prices of each item of production facilities.
3. The farmer agrees to let the company deduct the cost of production facilities from the produce price payable to the farmer in line with the criteria specified in Section 5.

As evidence hereof, both parties sign their names in the presence of witnesses:

Signature ................................ Company

(Miss Patraporn Satirasilapin)

Signature ................................ Farmer

(................................)

Signature ................................ Witness

(................................)

Signature ................................ Witness

(................................)

**Memorandum of Additional Agreement, Agreement No. ...........**

With reference to Pepsi-Cola (Thai) Trading Co., Ltd., "company, and ............................, "farmer", signing Agreement No. ...................., the farmer agrees to sell all his/her produce to the company and not sell his/her produce to another person or farmer in order to sell it to the company and not accept produce of other persons to sell to the company in the name of the farmer. If the farmer does any of the above, the farmer is well aware that he/she shall be held liable to civil and criminal charges and the farmer agrees to let the company take potatoes that another person consigns to him/her in his/her name without payment for those potatoes.

As evidence hereof, both parties sign their names in the presence of witnesses on ................

Signature ............................... Company

(Miss Patraporn Satirasilapin)

Signature ............................... Farmer

(..............................)

Signature ............................... Witness

(..............................)

Signature ............................... Witness

(..............................)

| *Delivery Schedule* | *Standard (class/quality/size)* | *Quantity (Kg)* | *Price (Bt/kg)* | *Amount (Bt)* | *Remarks* |
|---|---|---|---|---|---|
| ........... | ........... | ........... | ........... | ........... | ........... |
| ........... | ........... | ........... | ........... | ........... | ........... |
| .......... | .......... | .......... | .......... | .......... | .......... |
| ........... | ........... | ........... | ........... | ........... | ........... |
| .......... | .......... | .......... | .......... | .......... | .......... |
| ........... | ........... | ........... | ........... | ........... | ........... |
| ........... | ........... | ........... | ........... | ........... | ........... |
| .......... | ........... | .......... | .......... | .......... | .......... |
| ........... | ........... | ........... | ........... | ........... | ........... |
| ........... | ........... | ........... | ........... | ........... | ........... |
| .......... | ........... | .......... | .......... | .......... | .......... |

Appendix 8.3

# Potato Cultivation Agreement
# Berli Juker Foods Co., Ltd.
# Category: Direct Promotion

Lot of ................................

Made at Berli Juker Foods Co., Ltd.

225/10, Village No. 1, Thepharak Road,

Bang Sao Thong Sub-district,

Bang Sao Thong Minor District,

Samut Prakan Province

Date: ......................................

This Agreement is made between Berli Juker Foods Co., Ltd., by ........................, person authorized to act for the company, located at No. 225/10, Village No. 1, Thepharak Road, Bang Sao Tong, Samut Prakan Province, hereinafter called, "company" on one party and ........ ........................, aged ........... years, holding Identity Card No. ................................., residing at House No. ........, Village No. ..........., ...................... Road, ................... Sub-district, ........................ District, .................... Province, hereinafter called, "farmer" on the other party.

Both parties have agreed as follows :

**Section 1.** The company owns reproducible potatoes, hereinafter called, "reproducible potatoes" and agrees to hand over ......... kilograms of reproducible potatoes of the Atlantic species to the farmer at the price of Bt30 per kilogram, totaling Bt.......... (.....................) and the farmer has received the reproducible potatoes at the weight specified above on the Agreement signing date.

**Section 2.** As soon as the farmer receives the reproducible potatoes from the company, the farmers shall plant them according to the details notified to the company as follows:

2.1 Date of cultivation
- cultivating from ............. to ............... date of ...................., ........ on ......... *rai*
- cultivating from ............. to ............... date of ...................., ........ on ......... *rai* - cultivating from ............. to ............... date of ...................., ........ on ......... *rai* - cultivating from ............. to ............... date of ...................., ........ on ......... *rai*

2.2 Date of harvest
- harvesting from ............. to ............... date of ...................., ........ for ......... tons
- harvesting from ............. to ............... date of ...................., ........ for ......... tons - harvesting from ............. to ............... date of ...................., ........ for ......... tons - harvesting from ............. to ............... date of ...................., ........ for ......... tons

2.3 Estimated productivity .................... tons

2.4 Plantation in
Village No. ...., .............. Sub-district, ........... District, ............ Province, on ....... *rai*
Village No. ...., .............. Sub-district, ........... District, ............ Province, on ....... *rai* Village No. ...., .............. Sub-district, ........... District, ............ Province, on ....... *rai* Village No. ...., .............. Sub-district, ........... District, ............ Province, on ....... *rai*

**Section 3.** The farmer agrees not to distribute, sell or transfer the reproducible potatoes received from the company to another person to cultivate or do anything with them.

If the farmer does otherwise, the farmer shall be held liable to the compensation for the price and damage to the reproducible potatoes to the company without conditions.

**Section 4.** The farmer agrees not to transfer his/her rights and duties from this Agreement to any other person or allow other persons to succeed his/her rights and duties without written consent from the company.

**Section 5.** The farmer shall bear all expenses incurred in the cultivation of the reproducible potatoes until the harvest.

**Section 6.** If the reproducible potatoes that the farmer receives from the company to cultivate are damaged due to the farmer's defects and/or faults to the point that there is no produce, hereinafter called, potatoes to be delivered to the company, the farmer shall be responsible for compensation to the company equivalent to cost of reproducible potatoes that the farmer receives from the company.

**Section 7.** The farmer shall plant the reproducible potatoes according to the schedule that the company specifies in its regulation and harvest the produce at the schedule that the company specifies in its regulation. The farmer shall bear expenses incurred from potato harvesting.

**Section 8.** During the cultivation, the farmer shall take good care of the reproducible potatoes and potatoes in line with the recommendations of the company's agricultural promotion officers.

The farmer shall strictly comply with cultivation conditions until the harvest in line with the regulation on cultivation and purchase of potatoes as shown in the appendices.

**Section 9.** After harvesting, the farmers shall deliver the potatoes to the company as agreed upon and the company shall buy potatoes at Bt......... per kilogram.

**Section 10.** The company or its employee or agent is entitled to inspect the farmer's plantation and the farmer shall facilitate their inspection at any time. If the company or its employee or agent notifies the farmer that the farmer, or his/her agent or dependant does not comply with the cultivation regulation or offers advice on the care of the reproducible potatoes and/or potatoes, the farmer shall comply with the advice right away.

**Section 11.** The farmer shall not distribute, sell or transfer or does anything with potatoes grown from the company's reproducible potatoes to anyone. Such act is an offense against civil and criminal law.

If the farmer does as mentioned above, the farmer shall be responsible for compensation to the company equivalent to potato weight multiplied by purchasing price per kilogram plus 1.50 percent per month *(one baht and five satang)* interest until the farmer settles all the compensation.

The Agreement is made in two identical copies for each party to retain one. Both parties have understood the terms and conditions in the Agreement and thereby sign their names as evidence in the presence of witnesses:

Signature .............................. Company Signature.............................. Farmer

(Mr. Rawin Prathummet) (..............................)

Signature .............................. Company Signature .......................... Witness

(Mr. Sanchai Chungan) (..............................)

Signature............................ Witness

(.............................)

**Appendix 8.4**

# (Official Emblem)
# Standard Agreement

## Documents and evidences required for Agreement making

**Juristic Entity**

1. Company, partnership
   1.1 a photocopy of Identity Card
   1.2 a photocopy of House Registration
   1.3 in case of a proxy, a Letter of Authorization and a photocopy of the proxy's Identity Card and House Registration
   1.4 a certificate issued by Corporation/Partnership Registration Office (not more than 6 months)
2. Cooperative/cooperative community
   2.1 a photocopy of Identity Card
   2.2 a photocopy of House Registration
   2.3 in case of a proxy, a Letter of Authorization and a photocopy of the proxy's Identity Card and House Registration
   2.4 a photocopy of cooperative/cooperative community registration
   2.5 minutes of a meeting or rules and regulations of the cooperative/cooperative community (with a list of authorities to oblige the cooperative/cooperative community)
3. Farmer group

3.1 a photocopy of Identity Card

3.2 a photocopy of House Registration

3.3 in case of a proxy, a Letter of Authorization and a photocopy of the proxy's Identity Card and House Registration

3.4 a photocopy of farmer group establishment registration

3.5 minutes of a meeting or rules and regulations of the farmer group (with a list of authorities to oblige the farmer group)

**Ordinary Person**

1. a photocopy of Identity Card/Government Official Card/State Enterprise Employee Card
2. a photocopy of House Registration

......... **(produce)** ......... Sales Agreement

This Agreement is made at ..................................................., at No. ..........., Village No. ...., ........................ Road, ........................ Sub-district, ........................ District, ............................. Province on .................................... between ........... (name/company/partnership/cooperative/farmer group/etc.) ....., located at No. ........., Village No. .......,

................................ Road, ........................ Sub-district, ........................ District, ................. Province, by ........... (name)............., authorized to oblige the juristic entity as shown in ................ (a certificate issued by Corporation/Partnership Registration Office/minutes of a cooperative meeting/etc. ..........), dated ...................., attached to this Agreement, hereinafter called, "buyer" on one party and ........ (name/company/partnership/cooperative/farmer group/etc.) ......... located at No. ........., Village No. ......., ........................ Road, ................... Sub-district, ........................ District, ................. Province, by ........... (name) ............, authorized to oblige the juristic entity as shown in ................ (a certificate issued by Corporation/Partnership Registration Office/minutes of a cooperative meeting/etc. .................), dated ...................., attached to this Agreement, hereinafter called, "seller" on the other party.

Both parties have agreed as follows:

**Section 1.** The seller agrees to sell ..............(produce) ............, hereinafter called, "produce", and the buyer agrees to buy the produce that the seller grows in accordance with the details, quality, standard, quantity, price and delivery schedule in Appendix 1 attached to the Agreement.

**Section 2.** The seller agrees to deliver the produce in Section 1 at the produce standard specified in Appendix 2 of the Agreement, at the schedule and point of delivery.

**Section 3.** As soon as the buyer accepts the produce stated in Section 2 and checks that everything is correct, the buyer shall pay the seller right away in line with the terms of payment in No. 1 of Appendix 3 attached to the Agreement.

In case the buyer does not pay the seller at once stated in the first paragraph, the buyer shall issue an evidence of acceptance of the produce from the seller. The said evidence shall at least feature the name of the produce, seller's name, buyer's name, quantity and weight, size, quality, price, amount of money, date of delivery and date of payment by the buyer. The buyer shall sign and affix the company seal on the said evidence that the seller can use to receive payment from the buyer later in line with details in No. 2 of Appendix 3 attached to the Agreement.

**Section 4.** If a force majeure or uncontrollable incident specified in Appendix 4 takes place, and the seller is unable to deliver the produce by the schedule and at the point of delivery stated in Section 2, or the buyer cannot accept part of or the entire produce, the party affected shall notify the other party in writing of the force majeure at once. Once the force majeure is over, both parties shall discuss and reach an agreement as specified in Appendix 5 attached to the Agreement, and both parties shall resume compliance with the said agreement.

**Section 5.** In case the seller delivers the produce less than what's specified in Section 1 by ............. percent (...................), the buyer may not accept the produce. But if the buyer accepts the produce, the price will be calculated proportionally and the buyer is entitled to fine the seller for the missing quantity at Bt............ (...........................) per kilogram.

**Section 6.** In case the seller delivers the produce agreed in Section 1 mixed with low-quality or sub-standard produce, the buyer shall buy only the produce agreed upon and refuse to buy the remainder or refuse to buy the entire produce, except the produce delivered features not less than ............ percent (................) of the quantity specified in Section 1 which the buyer must accept the quantity actually delivered.

**Section 7.** If the seller delivers the produce at the quantity specified in Section 1 and the buyer accepts less than what's specified in Section 1, the seller is entitled to fine the buyer for the quantity denied at Bt.......... (..................) per kilogram.

**Section 8.** If a party claims that the other party does not comply with the Agreement or breaches the Agreement, the party that claims so shall propose his claim to the dispute determining committee, comprising the buyer, the seller or an agent of the buyer or seller, whichever the case may be and three officers from government agency involved according to the list of names in Appendix 6 attached to the Agreement to determine. Decision of the dispute determining committee shall be considered final and both parties have to comply with the decision. If either party does not comply with the decision, the other party is entitled to cancel the Agreement at once and fine that party on the produce agreed upon in Section 1 at Bt.......... (...................) per kilogram.

**Section 9.** The following appendices shall be considered part of the Agreement.

9.1 Appendix 1 Details, quality, standard, quantity, price and delivery schedule, .... pages

9.2 Appendix 2 Delivery schedule and point of delivery, ......... pages

9.3 Appendix 3 Terms of payment, ........... pages

9.4 Appendix 4 Details of force majeure, ........... pages

9.5 Appendix 5 Procedures in case of force majeure, ........... pages

9.6 Appendix 6 List of persons in the dispute determining committee ....... pages

9.7 ...................... etc. ..................

If any statements in the appendices contradict with those in the Agreement, the ones in the Agreement shall supersede. But if statements in the appendices contradict each other, both parties shall comply with determination of the dispute determining committee.

The Agreement is made in three identical copies. Both parties have read and understood the terms and conditions in the Agreement and thereby sign their names and have seal (if any) affixed as evidence in the presence of witnesses. Each party retains one copy and hands over one copy to the Department of Internal Trade:

Signature ................................ Buyer

(..............................)

Signature ................................ Seller

(..............................)

Signature ................................ Witness

(..............................)

Signature ................................ Witness

(..............................)

**Form Sor.Phor. 1**

**Appendix 1**

# Details on quality, standard, quantity, price and deal schedule

No. 1 Quality and standard of the produce

..................................................................................

..................................................................................

..................................................................................

..................................................................................

..................................................................................

**No. 2 Both parties agree to sell and buy the produce in Section 1 as follows:**

| *Equipment* | *Standard* | *Required* | *Rate/ Unit* | *Total Amount* | *Paid* | *Balance* | *Remarks* |
|---|---|---|---|---|---|---|---|
| Chick Drinker | | | | | | | |
| Chick Feeder | | | | | | | |
| Jumbo Drinker | | | | | | | |
| Adult Feeder | | | | | | | |

Both parties agree to adjust the selling/buying prices of the farm produce by increasing to the market price as of the delivery date at the rate of not more than ......... percent on theprice stated in Section 1.

Form Sor.Phor. 2

Appendix 2

# Delivery schedule and point of delivery according to the standard of produce

| *Delivery Schedule* | *Standard (class/quality/size)* | *Quantity (kg)* | *Point of Delivery* | *Remarks* |
|---|---|---|---|---|
| ............... | ............... | ............... | ............... | ............... |
| ............... | ............... | ............... | ............... | ............... |
| ... | ... | ... | ... | ... |
| ............... | ............... | ............... | ............... | ............... |
| ............... | ............... | ............... | ............... | ............... |
| ............... | ............... | ............... | ............... | ............... |
| ............... | ............... | ............... | ............... | ............... |
| ............... | ............... | ............... | ............... | ............... |
| ............... | ............... | ............... | ............... | ............... |
| ............... | ............... | ............... | ............... | ............... |
| ............... | ............... | ............... | ............... | ............... |
| ............... | ............... | ............... | ............... | ............... |
| ............... | ............... | ............... | ............... | ............... |
| ............... | ............... | ............... | ............... | ............... |
| ............... | ............... | ............... | ............... | ............... |
| ............... | ............... | ............... | ............... | ............... |
| ............... | ............... | ............... | ............... | ............... |

**Form Sor.Phor. 3**

**Appendix 3**

# Terms of Payment for the Farm Produce

- 1. Payment made right at the delivery
- 2. Payment made after delivery as follows:

### 2.1. Terms of Payment

| *Delivery Schedule* | *Terms of Payment* |
|---|---|
| 1) From .............. to .................. | 1.1) First installment of Bt........................ by the ............. date of ................................ |
| | 1.2) Second installment of Bt.................. by the ............. date of ................................ |
| | 1.3) Third installment of Bt.................... by the ............. date of ................................ |
| 2) From .............. to .................. | 2.1) First installment of Bt........................ by the ............. date of ................................ |
| | 2.2) Second installment of Bt.................. by the ............. date of ................................ |
| | 2.3) Third installment of Bt.................... by the ............. date of ................................ |

### 2.2. Payment Procedures

1. The buyer shall transfer the price of the farm produce into the seller's bank account as notified to the buyer. If the seller is an agricultural institution, the buyer shall transfer the money into that institution's bank account.
2. In case the buyer transfers money into the agricultural institution's bank account, the institution officer shall be responsible for payment to each farmer.
3. If the buyer does not transfer the price of the farm produce into a bank account to settle the debts or transfers less

than the actual price of the farm produce beyond the payment schedule in 2.1, the buyer agrees to pay interest to seller at ......... percent per annum on the overdue amount until the buyer pays the seller in full.

Appendix 4

# Details of Force Majeure

**Force majeure in Section 4 of the Agreement is as follows**

1. A war, fighting, rebellion, revolution, protesting or overthrowing the government or public riot
2. Floods, windstorm disaster, fire or other natural disasters
3. Severe plant epidemic
4. Weather, environmental or production condition changes that directly or indirectly affect the cultivation
5. Factory closure or labor strike by a cause stated in Labor Protection Law
6. Other force majeure or uncontrollable causes, eg. robbery, transportation

**Form Sor. Phor. 5**

**Appendix 5**

# Procedures in Case of Force Majeure

In case of force majeure taken place before scheduled delivery or during delivery or after scheduled delivery, the following procedures shall be observed:

**Case No. 1:** Force majeure taken place with the seller: The seller shall deliver the produce at the quantity produced and the buyer shall accept the produce at the quantity delivered by the seller at the price specified in Section 1 of the Agreement and other legal requirements agreed upon by both parties.

**Case No. 2:** Force majeure taken place with the buyer: The buyer shall accept the quantity of produce that he can take and the seller shall deliver the produce in the quantity acceptable by the buyer at the price specified in Section 1 of the Agreement and other legal requirements agreed upon by both parties.

**Details that the Buyer and Seller Agree Upon are as Follows**

| *Delivery/ Acceptance Schedule* | *Standard of Farm Produce (class/quality/size)* | *Estimated Quantity Delivered/Accepted (kg)* | *Price (kg/Bt)* | *Estimated Total Price for the Farm Produce (Bt)* | *Point of delivery/acceptance* | *Payment* |
|---|---|---|---|---|---|---|
| From | .............. | .............. | ........ | | .............. | 1st installment |
| ......... | .............. | .............. | ........ | | .............. | of |
| ...... to | .............. | .............. | ........ | | .............. | Bt............ |
| ......... | .............. | .............. | ........ | | .............. | by the ....... |
| ......... | .............. | .............. | ........ | | .............. | date of |
| .... | .............. | .............. | ........ | | .............. | ............ |
| | .............. | .............. | ........ | | .............. | 2nd installment |
| | .............. | .............. | ........ | | .............. | of |
| | .............. | .............. | ........ | | .............. | Bt............ |
| | .............. | .............. | ........ | | .............. | by the ....... |
| | .............. | .............. | ........ | | .............. | date of |
| | ... | .............. | ........ | | .............. | ............ |
| | | .............. | ........ | | .............. | 3rd installment |
| | | .............. ... | | | .............. | of |
| | | ...... | | | ...... | Bt............ |
| | | | | | | by the ....... |
| | | | | | | date of |
| | | | | | | ............ |

Mode of Payment: Mode of payment shall be in line with the criteria and procedures in Section 3 of the Agreement.

**Appendix 6**

# List of persons in the Dispute Determining Committee

Both parties agree to the list of the following persons as members of the Dispute Determining Committee to determine disputes concerning this Agreement and decision of the said committee is considered final.

1. ......................(Mr./Mrs./Miss/Rank) .........................
Seller/Agent

2. ......................(Mr./Mrs./Miss/Rank) .........................
Buyer/Agent

3. ..........................................................Government Agency Rep.)

   (provincial public prosecutor/provincial agricultural and cooperative officer, provincial commercial officer/provincial or district agricultural officer/provincial or district cooperative officer/internal trade chief in the province) ...................

   Government Agency: ................................

4. ..........................................................Government Agency Rep.)

   (provincial public prosecutor/provincial agricultural and cooperative officer, provincial commercial officer/provincial or district agricultural officer/provincial or district cooperative officer/internal trade chief in the province) ...................

   Government Agency: ................................

5. ..........................................................Government Agency Rep.)

(provincial public prosecutor/provincial agricultural and cooperative officer, provincial commercial officer/ provincial or district agricultural officer/provincial or district cooperative officer/internal trade chief in the province) ...................

Government Agency: ..............................

..........................

**Note:** The persons in 3-5 should be government agency representatives, ex-officio.

# (Official Emblem)
# Department of Internal Trade's Regulation On Promotion of Farm Commodity Marketing Agreement B.E. 2542 (1999)

Whereas, it's appropriate to promote and support farm commodity marketing agreement between farmers, farmer groups, cooperatives or other traders and processing plants, exporters or buyers of other farm commodities using the standard agreement prepared by the Department of Internal Trade to reach a farm commodity marketing agreement, fair for both parties and farmers can plan for their production, have new options to sell their produce and guarantee their income from the sale of their produce while the processing plants and exporters can have an efficient marketing plan, and the government authorities can promote and support equal bargaining power and compromise for the benefits of parties concerned,

The Department of Internal Trade hereby promulgates a regulation on Promotion of Farm Commodity Marketing Agreement B.E. 2542 (1999) as follows:

**Section 1.** This regulation is called, "Regulation on Promotion of Farm Commodity Marketing Agreement B.E. 2542 (1999).

**Section 2.** The regulation shall go into effect on the date after its announcement date.

**Section 3.** In this regulation:

"marketing agreement" refers to a farm commodity deal between farmers, farmer groups or cooperatives established under specific law or other traders as the seller on one party and processing plants, exporters or other buyers as the buyer on the other party, with a written agreement that features terms and conditions on the farm commodity production and marketing according to the standard agreement form designed by the Department of Internal Trade.

"standard agreement" refers to an agreement form designed by the Department of Internal Trade and checked and approved by the Office of the Attorney-General, attached to this regulation.

"farm commodities" refers to farm produce and processed products made from farm produce.

"processing plants" refers to a plant that process farm commodities.

"exporters" refers to an exporter of farm commodities and also refers to exporters' agents.

**Section 4.** Farmers, farmer groups, cooperatives or other traders and processing plants, exporters or other buyers, who wish to make a farm commodity sales agreement with each other or a new agreement reached by both parties in the standard agreement form attached to this regulation, are required to notify the Department of Internal Trade or an internal trade office in the province where the agreement will be made so that it may proceed accordingly.

**Section 5.** To make an agreement according to the standard agreement form in Section 4, the Market Promotion and Development Division and/or the Provincial Internal Trade Office shall arrange for both parties to meet each other to discuss the details of the agreement and facilitate both parties to assure fairness and recognition to parties concerned.

**Section 6.** To make a standard agreement, both parties shall set up a Dispute Determining Committee, comprising the seller or his agent, the buyer or his agent, and three officers from government agency involved to determine a dispute arising from the agreement. Decision of the Dispute Determining Committee shall be considered final.

**Section 7.** The Market Promotion and Development Division and/or the Provincial Internal Trade Office shall regulate the compliance to the standard agreement, offer advice and counseling and useful information to both parties, or coordinate with a financial institution to offer financial support as well as initially compromise a dispute.

**Section 8.** Director of the Market Promotion and Development Division shall supervise this regulation.

Announced on August 18, 1999.

Lt. ...........Signed ............

(Suchai Chaowisit)

Director-General, Department of Internal Trade

**Appendix 8.5**

# KC Sweet Corn Contract Agreement

(as noted down from the original contract document)

Contract No.:

**Contract Between Company and Farmer by Name**

1. Seasonal contract (1 April –30 April) and quantity to be delivered 10 tonnes per day plus/minus 10%
2. Quality standard:
   - 2.1 harvest within 70-75 days
   - 2.2 harvest within 24 hours before transporting to factory, 7-day advance harvest schedule notice before harvest
   - 2.3 not too young or too old corn
   - 2.4 not mixed with other varieties, corn should be 4.5 to 6.5 cm long only, diameter should be 10 cm minimum, not more than 4 corn in one kg.
   - 2.5 sampling; 100 kg sample for quantity of less than 1 tonne; 200kg. for 3-6 tonne quantity; and 300 kg. sample for more than 6 tonne quantity
   - 2.6 insect and disease affected corn not to exceed 5%
   - 2.7 price 3 baht per kg.
3. Std. Quality price 3 baht per kg.
   - 3.1 extra quota quantity to be bought at 0.10 baht per kg.
   - 3.2 lower quantity deduction at 0.10 baht per kg from price per kg.
   - 3.3 if quantity is 80% or more, no deduction for 0.10 baht per kg.
4. monthly contract

5. seed variety to be supplied specified by name (74 or A-2), payment for seed supply within 90 days by farmers
6. price of seed 500 baht per kg and supply of seed only 200 kg. for broker (particular one)
7. no liability of company for crop failure or damage unless it is due to seed failure
8. broker/farmer to follow company advice on crop practices
9. payment by company within 7 days after delivery
10. farmer to transport produce to factory at his own cost
11. if default on delivery, legal action by company,
12. collateral to be taken by company (of driving license or ID card or land card)

Contract copy for company and farmer each and signed by both in presence of two witnesses.

## Appendix 8.6

# Planning Department Saha Farm Co., Ltd. F-CF-PD 301/R

**Chicken Farming Agreement**

Membership No. .......... Made at Saha Farm Co., Ltd.

Date: ..............................

This Agreement is made between Saha Farm Co., Ltd. by Mrs. Manunsri Chotithewan and Mrs. Worawan Pornrojanakun, Authorized Directors, office located at No. 44/4, Nawamin Road, Khan Na Yao Sub-district, Khan Na Yao District, Bangkok Metropolis, hereinafter called, "owner" on one party and ........................................., aged ......... years, residing at No. ...

.................................................................................................,
hereinafter called, "farmer" on the other party. Both parties have thereby agreed as follows:

**Chapter 1: General Provisions**

**Section 1.** The owner agrees to let the farmer raise the chickens and the farmer agrees to raise the chickens. The farmer shall have chicken houses, farming equipment and such utilities as water, electricity, driveways to the chicken houses, personnel to look after the chickens and others facilitating the farming under this Agreement.

**Section 2.** The owner has authority and sole right to prohibit anyone including the farmer and his/her dependants under this Agreement from entering into the chicken houses or farm areas under the lease right of the chicken houses. (See Chapter 4 of this Agreement)

**Section 3.** To raise chickens under this Agreement, the farmer shall be an ordinary member of the Chicken Farming for Export Association and pass the pre-qualifications as a chicken farmer.

**Section 4.** If the farmer breaks a section in this Agreement, the farmer shall agree that the owner may cancel the Agreement right away.

**Section 5.** In case this Agreement is terminated under any circumstances before the scheduled completion of each batch of chickens in Section 7 or some chickens still remain in the chicken houses, both parties agree that this Agreement shall continue to remain effective until all the grown-up fowls are caught and taken from the chicken houses.

**Section 6.** This Agreement shall remain effective from ...................... to ................

**-1-**

## Planning Department Saha Farm Co., Ltd. F-CF-PD 301/R

## Chicken Farming Agreement

### Chapter 2: Chicken raising

**Section 7.** The owner shall hand over chicks, chicken feed, medicine and vaccines to the farmer with the aim of consigning the farmer to raise the chicks to grown-up fowls and return them to the owner. The raising period is about 45-54 days with the average weight of a chicken of 1.6-2.5 kilograms/batch. Chicken raising will be no more than 5 batches a year. (One batch of raising chickens starts from chick hand-over to catching the grown-up fowls from the chicken houses.)

**Section 8.** The farmer's duties are to check and keep clean and hygienic the chicken houses and farming equipment as well as the farm area and surrounding areas of at least 20 meters, considered a restricted area prohibiting anyone from entering the said areas asides from the contractual parties and their dependants. No one is allowed to bring anything, chicks, chicken feed or anything considered as chicken feed as well as medicine not belonged or given by the owner into the said areas without prior written approval from the owner.

**Section 9.** Before handing over the items stated in Section 7 to the farmer, the owner is entitled to enter and inspect the chicken houses, farming equipment and others to make sure the chicken house conditions are well prepared and believed not to cause any damage to the owner.

**Section 10.** The items in Section 7 that the farmer receives from the owner at the volume and quantity shown in the document acknowledged by the farmer or his/her dependant are deemed deposited with the farmer. The farmer shall raise the chicks according to the procedures specified by the owner, and raise them with chicken feeds, medicine and vaccines provided by the owner to ensure that the chicks will grow up to the owner's specifications. Otherwise, if any damage occurs, the farmer shall be held liable for the damage actually incurred. During farming, no one is allowed to move the said items or property as well as grown-up fowls out of the farm without prior written approval from the owner.

**Section 11.** The farmer shall return to the owner grown-up fowls of at least 95% of the chicks provided on the date of consignment (additional chicks not included). If the number of grown-up fowls returned is less than 95% without sufficient reason and reliable evidences, the farmer shall let the owner fine at Bt100 per chicken lost (one hundred Baht).

**Section 12.** The farmer agrees that in raising chickens, receiving chicks, chicken feed, medicine, vaccines and others from the owner, the farmer shall handle with care and prevent any possible damage, deliberately or unintentionally or carelessly, by himself, his dependants or anyone. The farmer agrees to be liable to any damage whatsoever, and the said act or damage shall be deemed caused by the farmer himself.

-2-

**Planning Department Saha Farm Co., Ltd. F-CF-PD 301/R**

## Chicken Farming Agreement

### Chapter 3: Remuneration

**Section 13.** Both parties have appraised the following items to calculate the benefits:

**13.1 Chicks**

Male, big A, Bt...../chick
Male, small A Bt...../chick
Female, big A, Bt...../chick
Female, small A, Bt...../chick
Both sexes, big A, Bt...../chick
Both sexes, small A, Bt...../chick

**13.2 Poultry feed**

Poultry feed for the first stage, Bt....../bag of 30 kg.

Poultry feed for the second stage, Bt....../bag of 30 kg.

Poultry feed for the third stage, Bt....../bag of 30 kg.

**13.3 Medicine and vaccines for the chickens according to the program specified by the company.**

**13.4 Grown-up fowls according to the conditions in Section 15 at Bt........../kilogram.**

**Section 14**. The owner reserves the rights to change the value and details in Section 13 to suit conditions changed after Agreement making. However, the owner shall notify the farmer in writing before delivering the next batch of chicks.

**Section 15.** As the chicks grow up as specified in Section 7, if the owner wants to catch the grown-up fowls on any date, the farmer shall catch them at the owner's written order. The owner shall count the number of chickens or weigh them right at the chicken farm. The owner shall calculate the farmer's remuneration from the net weight and conditions specified in Section 16 of the Agreement. The said principles shall be applicable to healthy grown-up fowls, free from diseases and such leftover chemicals as pesticides or antibiotics. If the grown-up fowls are not healthy or sick, the owner shall adjust the remuneration as deemed appropriate by the owner.

**Section 16.** As the value of grown-up fowls returned to the owner according to Section 15 is arrived, the owner shall calculate the value of small chicks, chicken feed, medicine and vaccines, considered the farmer's benefits. But if same is missing, the farmer shall compensate the loss to the owner in 15 days upon receiving an invoice or from the date of catching the grown-up fowls, or allow the owner to deduct them from the remuneration due to the farmer for the following batch if the owner agrees to let the farm raise the next batch.

**-3-**

## Planning Department Saha Farm Co., Ltd. F-CF-PD 301/R

## Chicken Farming Agreement

### Chapter 4: Renting the chicken houses

**Section 17.** The farmer agrees to let the owner rent .......... chicken houses and farming equipment, located at No. ..................................., with total space of .................... square meters, able to accommodate ..................... chicks. The details of chicken houses and farming equipment are as follows:

**Chicken House No.**

Lessor's Name: Age: years

House Size: Area: square meters

Road to the chicken house: ( ) earth, ( ) laterite, ( ) small stones, ( ) others Water sources ( ) digging a pond, ( ) artesian well, ( ) a canal, ( ) water supplied by authorities, ( ) other water sources

Electricity ( ) Yes, ( ) No, Size of Transformer: amps

Floods ( ) Yes, ( ) No

Roof ( ) Thatched, ( ) Zinc, ( ) Tiles, ( ) others

Gable ( ) Single tier, ( ) Double tier, ( ) side windows

Floor ( ) Earth, ( ) Concrete, ( ) others

Structure

Ventilation

Environment

Farming equipment (leased along with the chicken house)

1. ........... spades 6. ........... water tanks
2. ........... canteens/flasks 7. ........... side curtains
3. ........... feed troughs 8. ........... lamps or gas nozzles

4. ............ drinking troughs 9. ............ others

5. ............ feed buckets

-4-

## Planning Department Saha Farm Co., Ltd. F-CF-PD 301/R

## Chicken Farming Agreement

Reported by ................................

Date: ............................................

-5-

## Planning Department Saha Farm Co., Ltd. F-CF-PD 301/R

## Chicken Farming Agreement

**Section 18.** Both parties agree that the rent shall be paid for each batch of chicks, starting on the date the owner hands over the chicks until the grown-up fowls are caught. The rent of chicken house is Bt........./batch or Bt........../chicken of the chicks delivered on the hand-over date (extra chicks not included), and the rent shall be paid.......

**Section 19.** The farmer shall keep the chicken houses and necessary farming equipment in ready and hygienic conditions and the chicken house environment in efficient farming conditions. If the owner feels that the conditions are not well prepared, the owner is entitled to withhold the hand-over of chicks for that batch and the farmer has no rights to receive the rent specified in Section 18. However, withholding of the chick hand-over shall not affect the owner's rights throughout the period of this Agreement.

**Section 20.** The farmer shall be responsible for household taxes, land taxes and other expenses on the chicken houses during the lease period.

**Section 21.** Under any circumstances, the owner shall not be held responsible for any damage to the chicken houses due to a normal cause or force majeure, except the damage caused by the owner's fault.

**Section 22.** The farmer agrees that the owner may terminate the chicken house lease agreement if the chicken houses are no more in the conditions to continue to raise the chicks or the farmer breaks a section of this Agreement.

**Section 23.** Both parties agree that if this Agreement is terminated while the chicken raising period for a particular batch is not yet completed, or there are still some grown-up fowls on the termination date, the Agreement shall be automatically extended until all the grown-up fowls are caught.

**Section 24.** The owner reserves the rights to take a civil and criminal case against violators of the chicken house lease rights under this lease agreement.

**Section 25.** The owner has legitimate rights to rent the chicken houses and surrounding areas of at least 20 meters as well as the entrance/exit ways, considered restricted areas where no one is allowed to enter without prior written approval from the owner because they may carry an epidemic or anything unsafe into the farm.

**Section 26.** If a party breaches a section of this Agreement, the other party is entitled to terminate the Agreement right away and demand compensation for the damage actually incurred.

**-6-**

**Planning Department Saha Farm Co., Ltd. F-CF-PD 301/R**

## Chicken Farming Agreement

### Chapter 5: Environmental conservation and law compliance

**Section 27.** The farmer agrees that to build or prepare a chicken house or to comply with the chicken farming agreement, the farmer shall not fell trees or encroach a forest reserve or public area without permission from the authorities.

**Section 28.** The farmer shall raise the chicks in line with the terms and conditions in the Agreement. To prevent any environmental pollution or deterioration, the farmer shall collect and clean litters, dung and other farming materials in 4 days after catching the fowls.

**Section 29.** The farmer shall comply with municipal, sanitary or local regulations including regulations of Sub-district administrative organizations and Provincial administrative organizations, as well as local officers' advice for peace and orderliness in terms of sanitary, hygienic and safety aspects.

**Section 30.** If the farmer does not comply with the principles in this Chapter, it'll be deemed that the farmer is uncooperative and the farmer breaks the Agreement.

The Agreement is made in two identical copies for each party to retain one. Both parties have read and understood all the statements therein and sign their names in the presence of witnesses:

Signature .................................. Owner

(Mrs. Manunsri Chotithewan and Mrs. Worawan Pornrojanakun)

Signature ................................ Farmer

Signature ................................ Witness

Signature ................................ Witness

## Guarantee Agreement

Made at Saha Farm Co., Ltd.

Date: ................................

This Agreement is made between Saha Farm Co., Ltd. by Mrs. Manunsri Chotithewan and Mrs. Worawan Pornrojanakun, Authorized Directors, office located at No. 44/4, Village No. 11, Nawamin Road, Khan Na Yao Sub-district, Khan Na Yao District, Bangkok Metropolis, hereinafter called, "owner" on one party and ......................................, aged ......... years,

Aged .......... years,

Aged .......... years,

Aged .......... years,

hereinafter called, "guarantors" on the other party. Both parties have thereby agreed as follows:

**Section 1.** The "owner" and .................................., aged ........... years, have signed Chicken Farming Agreement No. ..........., dated ...................................... detailed in the Agreement.

**Section 2.** The "guarantors" agree that if the "farmer" breaks a section, the "guarantors" are willing to be liable jointly with the "farmer" without any conditions as if they were a contractual party of the Chicken Farming Agreement.

**Section 3.** The "guarantors" agree to jointly be responsible for any debts, unlimited, that the "farmer" owes the "owner" as if joint debtors.

**Section 4.** If the "owner" signs another Agreement with the "farmer" asides from the Agreement in Section 1, or agrees to extend debt repayment period to the "farmer", it shall be considered that the "guarantors" also agree with all those cases even without prior notice to the guarantors.

**Section 5.** If a "guarantor" becomes a contractual party for chicken farming with the "owner", the "guarantor" agrees to let the "owner" deduct, cut or hold an amount of the profit from chicken farming, or a deposit as well as property placed with the "owner" in payment for debts that the "farmer" owes the "owner" without prior notice to the guarantor.

**-1-**

**Planning Department Saha Farm Co., Ltd. F-CF-PD 302/R2**

**Guarantee Agreement**

Both parties agree that if a dispute arises from this Agreement, the party concerned shall take legal action at the Civil Court of Bangkok. Both parties have read and understood all the statements and provisions, and sign their names in the presence of witnesses:

Signature ................................ Owner

(Mrs. Manunsri Chotithewan and Mrs. Worawan Pornrojanakun)

Signature ................................ Guarantor

Signature ................................ Guarantor

Signature ................................ Guarantor

Signature ................................ Guarantor

Signature ................................ Witness

Signature ................................ Witness

**-2-**

## Memorandum of Agreement Appended to the Chicken Farming Agreement

Made at Saha Farm Co., Ltd.

Date: ..............................

This Memorandum of Agreement is made between Saha Farm Co., Ltd. by ............. ................................., Authorized Directors, hereinafter called, "owner" on one party and ...................................., Identity Card No. ..................., hereinafter called, "farmer" on the other party. Both parties have thereby agreed to make this Memorandum of Agreement No. ..........., dated ........................., between ................................. and .........................as follows:

**Section 1.** Whereas the owner is a farming contractual party with the farmer and has experience and has been certified under poultry farming standard of Thailand, the owner therefore agrees to act as a consultant and coordinator with the Department of Livestock or other public and private organizations. The owner agrees to bear expenses with the farmer's consent to proceed and get the farmer's chicken farm certified with the poultry farming standard of Thailand.

**Section 2.** Once the owner has proceeded as in Section 1 and the farmer has been certified with the poultry farming standard of Thailand, in return to the owner, the farmer agrees and certifies that he will continue to do chicken farming under the Chicken Farming Agreement for a period of .................. from the date of certification by the poultry farming standard of Thailand.

**Section 3.** Both parties agree that the terms in Section 2 of this Memorandum shall become effective without affecting the schedule in the Chicken Farming Agreement and chicken house lease period. If the period on the same matter in the Chicken Farming Agreement or an appendix to the Agreement contradicts with that in Section 2 of this Memorandum, the one in the Memorandum shall supercede.

**Section 4.** Other terms and conditions in the Chicken Farming Agreement, not changed by this Memorandum, shall continue to remain effective.

**Section 5.** If the farmer cancels the Chicken Farming Agreement before the schedule in Section 2 of this Memorandum, it'll be deemed that the farmer breaches this agreement and agrees to let the owner hold or confiscate property, bond or guarantee deposit placed with the owner until completing the schedule in Section 2 of this Memorandum. And the owner agrees that he'll refund the said money without interest or any other benefit to the farmer as soon as the schedule is completed.

**-1-**

Both parties have acknowledged and understood all the statements in the Memorandum and sign their names in the presence of witnesses:

Signature ..............................Owner (...................................)

Signature ..............................Farmer (...................................)

Signature ..............................Witness (...................................)

Signature ..............................Witness (...................................)

## Rights of Contract Farming Sponsor

**Section 2:** 'The owner has authority and sole right to prohibit anyone including the farmer and his/her dependants under this Agreement from entering into the chicken houses or farm areas under the lease right of the chicken houses'.

**Section 3:** 'To raise chickens under this Agreement, the farmer shall be an ordinary member of the Chicken Farming for Export Association and pass the pre-qualifications as a chicken farmer'.

**Section 7:** 'The owner shall hand over chicks, chicken feed, medicine and vaccines to the farmer with the aim of consigning the farmer to raise the chicks to grown-up fowls and return them to the owner. The raising period is about 45-54 days with the average weight of a chicken of 1.6-2.5 kilograms/batch. Raising will be no more than 5 batches a year. (One batch of raising chickens starts from chick hand-over to catching the grown-up fowls from the chicken houses.)'

## Pricing

## Chapter 3: Remuneration

**Section 13.** Both parties have appraised the following items to calculate the benefits:

### 13.1 Chicks

Male, big A, Bt...../chick

Male, small A Bt...../chick

Female, big A, Bt...../chick

Female, small A, Bt...../chick

Both sexes, big A, Bt...../chick

Both sexes, small A, Bt...../chick

### 13.2 Poutry Feed

Poultry feed for the first stage, Bt....../bag of 30 kg.

Poultry feed for the second stage, Bt....../bag of 30 kg.

Poultry feed for the third stage, Bt....../bag of 30 kg.

**13.3 Medicine and vaccines for the chickens according to the program specified by the company.**

**13.4 Grown-up fowls according to the conditions in Section 15 at Bt........../kilogram.**

**Section 14:** 'The owner reserves the rights to change the value and details in Section 13 to suit conditions changed after Agreement making. However, the owner shall notify the farmer in writing before delivering the next batch of chicks.'

**Section 18:** 'Both parties agree that the rent shall be paid for each batch of chicks, starting on the date the owner hands over the chicks until the grown-up fowls are caught. The rent of chicken house is Bt........./batch or Bt.........../chicken of the chicks delivered on the hand-over date (extra chicks not included), and the rent shall be paid.......'

**Section 19:** 'If the owner feels that the conditions are not well prepared, the owner is entitled to withhold the hand-over of chicks for that batch and the farmer has no rights to receive the rent specified in Section 18. However, withholding of the chick hand-over shall not affect the owner's rights throughout the period of this Agreement.'

### Production Standards and Liabilities

**Section 10:** 'The items in Section 7 that the farmer receives from the owner at the volume and quantity shown in the document acknowledged by the farmer or his/her dependant are deemed deposited with the farmer. The farmer shall raise the chicks according to the procedures specified by the owner, and raise them with chicken feeds, medicine and vaccines provided by the owner to ensure that the chicks will grow up to the owner's specifications. Otherwise, if any damage occurs, the farmer shall be held liable for the damage actually incurred.'

**Section 16:** 'As the value of grown-up fowls returned to the owner according to Section 15 is arrived, the owner shall calculate the value of small chicks, chicken feed, medicine and vaccines, considered the farmer's benefits. But if same is missing, the farmer shall compensate the loss to the owner in 15 days upon receiving an invoice or from the date of catching the grown-up fowls, or allow the owner to deduct them from the remuneration due to the farmer for the following batch if the owner agrees to let the farm raise the next batch'.

**Section 1.** 'Whereas the owner is a farming contractual party with the farmer and has experience and has been certified under poultry farming standard of Thailand, the owner therefore agrees to act as a consultant and coordinator with the Department of Livestock or other public and private organizations. The owner agrees to bear expenses with the farmer's consent to proceed and get the farmer's chicken farm certified with the poultry farming standard of Thailand'.

**Section 2.** 'Once the owner has proceeded as in Section 1 and the farmer has been certified with the poultry farming standard of Thailand, in return to the owner, the farmer agrees and certifies that he will continue to do chicken farming under the Chicken Farming Agreement for a period of .................. from the date of certification by the poultry farming standard of Thailand'.

**Section 3.** 'Both parties agree that the terms in Section 2 of this Memorandum shall become effective without affecting the schedule in the Chicken Farming Agreement and chicken house lease period. Or if the period on the same matter in the Chicken Farming Agreement or an appendix to the Agreement contradicts with that in Section 2 of this Memorandum, the one in the Memorandum shall supercede.'

## Performance Standards

**Section 11:** 'The farmer shall return to the owner grown-up fowls of at least 95% of the chicks provided on the date of consignment (additional chicks not included). If the number of grown-up fowls returned is less than 95% without sufficient reason and reliable evidences, the farmer shall let the owner fine at Bt100 per chicken lost (one hundred Baht)'.

This is not very different from chicken farming agreements being practiced in India (Appendix 8.6).

# 9
# State and Contract Farming

Though contract farming in Thailand was initiated, in most of the cases, by the private sector, but the state soon came to play a major role in terms of both setting broad policy directions for diversification as well as in underwriting private sector activity in a variety of ways through various institutions like the Board of Investment (BOI), National Economic and Social Development Board (NESDB), and Agricultural Land Reform Office (ALRO). Though BOI, set up in 1954 and in present form since 1977, had no particular brief to promote contract farming, it has been an inevitable by-product of its activities, given its involvement in sectors which use contract farming (Burch, 1994, p. 167-168). Besides, there are two other wings of the state (MOAC and MOF) which promote contract farming through their own agencies i.e. DOAE and BAAC respectively. The very first case of state support to contract farming was in the case of Thai Farming Company wherein a public agency assisted with demonstration plots (Goldsmith, 1987). The role of the state in contract farming can be visualized as shown in figure 9.1. This tri-angular relationship shapes local informal and formal institutions and gets mediated by them, besides the resources and technology, which determine contract farming performance (Ornberg, 2003).

**Fig: 9.1**

**State, companies and farmers in contract farming in Thailand (from Ornberg, 2003)**

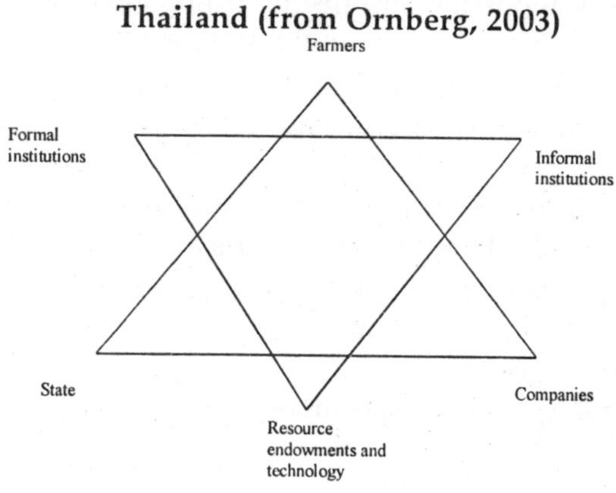

It was in the fifth plan for the first time that the NESDB accorded high priority to agribusiness, but only in sixth plan, a lead role was given to the private agribusiness, including contract farming system (Goss and Burch, 2001). Analysing the production and sale of agricultural products, the Sixth plan notes and recommends, "Contract Farming has proved viable and should be further promoted, on condition that the provisions of such agreements are amended to be more effective and beneficial to all parties concerned" (NESDB, The Sixth National Economic and Social Development Plan, 1987-91, p. 218).

Under the guidelines for agro-industries, it states:

1. Develop and support agro-industries that have high potential for exports or for import substitution,....
2. Expand the production base into new agro-industries which have high market potential from - surpluses of such raw materials as rice, maize, cassava, and rubber in the agricultural sector, and - goods with development potential such as processed food from vegetables and fruit, forest products, pharmaceutical products and health food from medicinal plants, species and aromatics.
3. Promote co-operation in integrating and developing production, marketing, research and development, technology transfer, management and co-ordinated interests and investments of the public and private sectors, which should join forces systematically in a full cycle of development plans and projects, information systems and joint public/private sector consultative committee.
4. Encourage farmers to formulate production plans focusing on quality and to join groups for producing raw materials that are required by agro-industrial plants
5. Encourage agro-industrial plants to use appropriate systems for procuring raw material and transferring technology to farmers
6. Encourage the development of agro-industries in rural localities, based on the needs of the market (pp. 227-28).

Though it does not mention contract farming per se, the use of term 'appropriate systems for procuring raw materials and transferring technology to farmers effectively' points to contract farming. Manarrungsan and Suwanjindar (1992) also conclude that these guidelines were in many respects similar to contract farming (Wiboonpoongse et al, 1998).

The academic input for the plan came from two studies, one by the Asian Institute of Technology (AIT) and the other by the Chulalongkorn University's Social Research Institute (CUSRI). The AIT study commissioned by the NESBD and the World Bank (Tang, 1984) listed only the advantages of contract farming and then went on to discuss various types of contract farming system like limited management contract and full management contract, and within latter various options like independent farmers, open account plan, guaranteed price system, guaranteed income system and guaranteed market system, besides looking at the then current practice of contract farming in Thailand in chicken raising only. It then dwells on various models (4) of organizing contract production in terms of provision of land, capital and labour wherein government was to provide land free or for price to developer who would sell it to contract farmers in parcels, or land use rights to farmers or co-operatives by the state and the developer or firm would provide or arrange funds and market for the produce. Another (third) variant of the model was an enterprise organized jointly by government, farmers and the company. But, the study recommended a model (fourth) wherein only farmers and company will be partners in an enterprise and government will only provide land, as it thought it was the most realistic one (Tang, 1984; Burch, 1994).

The Chulalongkorn study sponsored by the NESDB and the Ministry of Commerce (MOC), and funded by the World Bank (CUSRI, 1984) also perceived no inherent problems in contract farming system for farmers though it listed advantages and disadvantages of the system. While noting problems in the system in particular sectors like palm oil, and pineapple, it went on to suggest policy changes for rectifying those problems, like a specific law for agricultural contracts, group contracts, and intermediation by government officials in case of dispute (CUSRI, 1984), and recommended extension of contracting into new crops like soyabeans, cotton, lychee and longan (Burch, 1994).

To strengthen the above guidelines, the MOAC formulated, and the Cabinet approved in 1987, a 'four-sector co-operation plan (or four pronged project) to develop agriculture and agro-industry' under which agro-industrial firms, farmers, financial institutions (mainly BAAC), and government agencies (MOAC) were to work together to improve agricultural production system in terms of reducing price risk, market uncertainty, and improving farmers' technical knowledge. The idea for this project originated in the Joint public-private consultative committee to solve economic problems (JPPCC) set up in 1981 and chaired by the Prime Minister. This committee is regarded as a formal linkage between the private and the public sectors and extends upto provincial level (Paopongsakorn et. al., 1995). Under the program, the agribusiness firms and the Department of Agricultural Extension (DOAE) of the MOAC, were to help farmers in new technology adoption, the firms were to also provide an assured market and price to the farmers, DOAE was to train farmers in contract farming practice, and the BAAC was to provide low cost loans (at 8.5% in stead of normal rate of 12% charged by the BAAC) to the participating farmers. Besides extension services, the government reallocated 250 million baht deposit in BAAC from the Farmers' Aid Fund (which despite its name obtained revenue from export taxes on agricultural goods), the capital gain from which was used as interest compensation for farmer participants in the program at the rate of 3.5 per cent per annum. This was used as an incentive to encourage farmer participation. Formal contracts were to be signed between firms and farmers. Government was also to provide other necessary support e.g. irrigation. But, since the choice of farmers was left to firms, they picked up only those who really did not need help (Siamwalla, et. al, n.d.; Wiboonpoongse et. al., 1998).

A committee on co-ordinating the co-operation between public and private sectors for agricultural development was set up under the MOAC to supervise the implementation of this project. A sub-committee each for each commodity was also established to set up guidelines and to oversee the implementation of each approved project. The actual co-ordinating task was performed by a co-ordinating center for agricultural development within the Office of Agricultural Economics (OAE). The sequence of project planning and implementation was as follows: The private company was to initiate the project idea and prepare a feasibility study and submit it for consideration to the Project Committee. The co-ordinating center, OAE or BAAC appraised the project and submitted it to the committee for approval. A memorandum of understanding was signed among MOAC, BAAC or any other financial institution, and the firm. The committee helped to select appropriate area and farmers to start the project, with the help of concerned agencies. Then came the signing of contract agreement between the firm and the farmers. Then, the committee helped farmers in seeking credit from BAAC, commercial bank or agricultural co-operatives and reimbursed the interest rates (3.5%) paid by farmers by depositing the funds with the BAAC. During 1987/88 and 1989/90, 12 projects were approved under this plan (six export-oriented and six import substituting), but only seven projects had survived upto 1993 which included castor bean, basmati rice, sunflower, wheat, barley, hybrid corn and sorghum and cashew nut. Two (eucalyptus and hog) did not operate at all, three (asparagus, bamboo and ramie) ceased after one year (Burch, 1994; Wiboonpoongse et al, 1998). In a matter of 2-3 years, the Plan covered over 1,00,000 farmers and some 877,000 rai of land (Burch, 1994). About 97% of total credit under the program was provided by the BAAC (Paopongsakorn, et. al., 1995).

The OAE which monitored the Plan concluded that it was not successful and attributed the failure to factors like too much reliance on government support, rigid contract terms, new technology crops for farmers, and poor extension service. In 1993, after its evaluation, the MOAC proposed an adjustment plan which provided for low interest rate loans instead of interest rate compensation and revision of the terms of the contracts made between firms and farmers. Eight projects were approved in 1994 which included trees for pulp, sunflower, maize, eucalyptus, teak and dairy production In fact, the subcommittee for improving government-private sector co-operation concluded in 1995 that it was not necessary for every farmer to participate in contract farming and that government agencies should not get involved directly into contract between farmers and companies. It suggested that contract farming expansion should take place without perpetual government support. It emphasized that contracts should be fair and there should be risk guarantee for farmers, firms and financial institutions. The sub committee consented in 1995 itself to support only those projects under the Plan which met three conditions: ability to reduce production risk, ability to reduce marketing risk and ability to identify potential area and farmers. Finally, it improved the targeting of the 4 - sector plan by specifying commodity groups which were:

agricultural produce with high export potential i.e. rice, fruit, flower, fresh water and coastal fish; and industrial crops i.e. vegetables, sunflower, maize and fast growing trees. Farmers participating in these projects were given low interest loans (5 per cent per annum). (Wiboonpoongse et al, 1998).

The Seventh Plan carried this policy on contract farming further by making an explicit mention of it and seeking its promotion. It stated under the Guidelines for agricultural development, "Expand scope of agricultural credit and encourage contract farming business by using the following measures:

— — — (4) Encourage agribusinesses, with the government as co-ordinator among various agricultural groups to co-operate with entrepreneurs in agriculture-related businesses to have opportunities for contract farming arrangements, and to have joint investment to expand and increase the types of products of agro-industries.

(5) Supervise contract arrangements between agricultural institutions and business entrepreneurs to ensure fairness to all parties" (NESDB, The Seventh Economic and Social Development Plan, 1992-1996, p.36).

Under the heading of Guidelines for Agricultural Restructuring, it stated again, "(4) Co-ordinate and promote mutuality of benefits between farmers' groups and modern agribusinesses to ensure fairness for farmers in jointly conducting agribusinesses in the form of 'contract farming' between agricultural workers and entrepreneurs to jointly share profits and risks in the business. Measures in this regard are as follows:

(4.1) Support agribusinesses with the public sector as co-ordinator in promoting contract farming and joint investment in agro-industry between farmers' groups and entrepreneurs in agribusinesses. The joint effort should be geared towards expansion of agribusinesses to wider categories of products.

(4.2) Supervise arrangements of contracts and agreements between farmers and the private entrepreneurs to ensure prudence and justice for all parties concerned.

(4.3) Promote research on crop varieties and new culturing practice for interested private enterprises who want to carry out agribusiness on the basis of 'contract farming', but lack technical capability to realize the opportunities and to promote varieties of activities." (NESDB, The Seventh Economic and Social Development Plan, 1992-1996, p. 117)

The only departure of the Seventh plan from the Sixth seemed to be its emphasis on group contracting as against individual farmer contracts. But, in the Eighth and the Ninth plans, there is no mention of anything about or related to contract farming. That is a big change all of a sudden in policy papers, though on the ground, many things are happening which reflect on the role of the state in contract farming or rather on the lack of its role.

In the early 1990s, the contract system was organized as follows in terms of role of various parties in the system: The firms initiated the contract farming project and sought the permission of the Provincial government which approved the starting of operations in its area. Then, the district level administration, especially agricultural officers, was informed of the operations of the firm and it (firm) set up the operations and made initial contracts. After the contract, the farmers got credit either from the bank (BAAC, Co-operative or commercial, but mostly BAAC) or from the firm itself. Once the production started, the district administration would provide necessary help in extension at the farmers level through agricultural extension workers and village level staff. In some cases like cashew nuts, the state at the provincial level was active participant in contract farming as it was trying to alter the cropping pattern, and therefore, helped the company to organize, and train farmers for the project. Similarly, BAAC had a more direct role in selection of farmers for contracting in this crop besides providing credit (Padmanabha, 1995) (Fig. 9.2).

## ALRO and Contract Farming

ALRO, set up in 1975 to redistribute land among landless, had distributed, by 1989, 1.5 million rai land to more than 76000 families. Burch (1994) writes, " Significantly, much of this land was specifically targeted for contract farming" (p. 172). ALRO saw contract system as an acceptable compromise between agribusiness promotion and its mandate to preserve smallholder owner operations. Also, contract farming schemes were targeted to land reform areas. Further, agribusiness companies used incentives from multiple agencies of the government under contract farming projects like MBK cashew project using BOI privileges, and land from ALRO in land reform areas (Burch, 1994) and even bank loan for growers from BAAC.

By the early 1990s, the state had become more directly interventionist, and on occasions, even considered making contract production mandatory, as reflected in the proposal to set up National Agricultural Council (NAC)). It is a different story that the proposal has not materialized even now. To sum up, so far the state has been only used by the agribusiness companies, and it has protected their interest as against or even at the cost of those of the farmers. Most of the institutions meant for farmers or for agricultural and rural development did not even have farmer representatives on them (Burch, 1994).

Though there is no explicit mention of contract farming in the National Plans, but individual departments are still implementing it on the ground. For example, a 1999 order of the Department of Internal Trade which issues a standard contract farming agreement for companies and farmers, not only says that this agreement should be used but also specifies that it will regulate contract compliance. It is a different matter that the standard agreement designed by it is used only by a couple of companies even in 2002.

## MOAC and Contract Farming

The MOAC through its DOAE still carries out training in contract farming for farmers and local officials which includes aspects like guidelines for contract farming implementation, i.e. types of products suitable for certain kind of contracting arrangement, familiarity with the system of contract farming, supervision of contract arrangements, special financial assistance to companies undertaking contract farming, and process of implementation of the contract farming project in terms of co-ordination between public and private sectors and choice of relevant area and farmers.

It even specifies requirements before a contract farming projects is undertaken which are: farmer willingness and exposure to the concept of contract farming, feasible standards of quality of produce, price flexibility, and production and marketing plan. Discussing factors in success of contract farming project, it emphasizes on clear understanding of the concept of contract farming among participants, and a felt need for it among them, besides physical proximity between producing and processing areas, strict adherence to quality standards and honesty and sincerity of all parties involved. It assigns specific role and responsibility to farmers, farmer groups, companies, and government agencies in terms of dealing with each other for the project. It finally recommends suitable types of systems of contract farming for different types of commodities and advocates contract farming with farmer organisations instead of individual farmers. It even goes on to advise in terms of having multiple outlets for produce, both contract and non-contract, in term of different grades of produce from the same group of farmers (MOAC, 2002, see Appendix 9.1).

## BAAC and Contract Farming

On the role of BAAC in four sector co-operation plan, an EU funded project on development and extension of fruit and vegetable production in the north-east, has this to say, "The loans are provided (to farmers in this EU project) through the Bank for Agriculture and Agricultural Co-operatives, a state enterprise bank. However, the BAAC's interest rates were thought to be too high to encourage investments in horticulture, so project funds were used to repay a portion of the interest for farmers whose plantations meet basic technical standards. ...... Groups were also necessary to meet the BAAC's requirements for joint liability loan security...... Nevertheless, the progress has been slower than had been hoped, partly because of difficulties in arranging loans. The BAAC takes many factors into consideration when reviewing loan applications, and some farmers who have wanted to join the project have failed to pass the bank's scrutiny" (EU and MOAC, n.d.).

About the role of BAAC during the early 1990s, Manarungsan and Suwanjidar write "Joining a private firm to make market contract with farmers helps BAAC reduce its business risk, as the firm deducts the loan and interest from farmers' sale receipts. At the same time, the firm does not have to extend input credit itself, and farmers are able to obtain credit they need. All three parties are made more secure in this way. The BAAC gives credit, both in cash and in kind, to farmers participating in a contract agreement with the firm, but farmers who actually join the project, receive special privileges. Those who join a contract-farming project, are able to borrow double the amount (60,000 baht in 1991) available ordinarily (30,000 baht), and that too without collateral" (Manarungsan and Suwanjidar, 1992).

Since 1993, BAAC has no contract farming projects as part of the 4-sector plan but contract farmers take loans from bank as individual or group guarantee loans. The CF project was operated only for 4-5 years. In fact, bank has abolished its agribusiness section and has a new social and environment section. BAAC has four grades of farmers - AAA (highest), AA, A and B (lowest) - since last 3 years. The interest charged is lower the higher the farmer grade and varies from 8% for AAA to 11% for B with 9% and 10% for AA and A grades. The grades are based on farmer repayment performance in the past. It is 3 years no dues performance for AAA, 2 years for AA, and 1 year for A, with only restructuring of a normal loan into a due loan the previous year or a new client altogether for B grade. BAAC has group guarantee or individual guarantee for most loans. Its farmer association loans are very little (<1%) and co-operative loans about 15% of total, with 85% going to individual farmers directly or through groups. More than 90% of farm families had access to BAAC credit with 70% of them directly and another 30% through more than 3000 agricultural co-operatives (BAAC Annual Report, 2000-2001). Besides, there were 800 produce/ commodity specific farmer associations which accounted for only three per cent of total farm families in 1997 (Saenjan, 1998).

BAAC started the contract farming system in the early 1980s with CP group in which other commercial banks also participated. The CP group only guaranteed the purchase of produce from which the bank recovered its loans to growers. In 1988, BAAC was so instrumental in promoting contract farming that it recorded what it perceived to be success stories in contract farming in Thailand. The fist of these was of Adams International in tobacco for their village inspectors system who were local experienced farmers selected by the company for dealing with farmers. The second was the case of cashew nuts contract farming by MBK group under a land reform program where the company contracted with the settlers. Its unique feature was the creation of a buffer fund from the seedlings sales proceeds of the company of which 20% was contributed to this fund with 80% going to the company. This fund was used to take care of natural calamities and for providing technical advice to growers. The third was that of the CP group's contracting in pig raising wherein the company had a 7- year contract with pig raisers, and upon meeting contract terms, the land, the pigstry and the house, which were provided by the company to the growers, were transferred to them permanently (Kusakabe and Higuchi, 1992).

In 2002, more than 50% of BAAC loans are group loans for which only group guarantee is required whereas for individual loans, land papers are also required besides individual guarantee. There are 2,80,000 groups now and each group has about 15 members. The members further divide the loan among themselves. A farmer can get a maximum of 1,20,000 baht, 60,000 as group member and 60,000 as individual farmer. For individual loans, the farmer needs to give a guarantee by another member of the group. Eve landless can be part of the group if they have land to cultivate, on lease or share cropped. Under the new policy since August, 2002, the group can be any community group with maximum of 25 members and can get 5 lakh baht as loan with about 20,000 for each member (Interview with a BAAC official).

### Potatoes and the Thai State

Potatoes is one of the rare crops in Thailand where the producers benefit most from the state's policy. The crop is not subject to any kind of price support, but the outcome of the policy, nevertheless, is that prices are kept high as produced quantity is limited and consumers pay a relatively high price to the benefit of producers (Ornberg, 1996).

"For potatoes, the state is directly involved in three ways: all import of seed is controlled, import of fresh potatoes (not seed) is restricted, and the cooperative is given monopoly rights to import seed for fresh consumption" (Ornberg, 1996, p.12). "One could say that the demand for import certificate is a means for the state to control the contract farming system, as all companies need a list of farmers to get the certificate, but it is of no importance for the existence of the system as such. If seed was available on the Thai market, farmers would be able to grow potatoes without a contract with a company. But it is not obvious that they would choose to grow the varieties for processing under such circumstances as they would lose the benefit of input on credit, as well as the stable price and the secure market. The leaders of the cooperative would perhaps object to unregulated import of seed, as they might fear that it could affect the market for fresh potatoes, but for the companies it would save much time and paperwork. Anyway, it is not likely that free import of seed will lead to anything more serious than more flexibility, and it will not affect the system of contract farming as such". .... "Following the WTO agreement, Thailand must open it border for import of potatoes equivalent to 3% of domestic consumption. The quota for 1995 is 288 tons, which could be imported at a tariff of 27% of CIF (over the quota, the tariff is 139%). In 2004, the quota will be increased to 3.2 tons, and the tariff outside the quota will be 125% of CIF.43 In comparison with the quantities imported for seed every year (more than 1000 tons) this "opening up" has no real effect on the contract farming system of potatoes for production (unless they want to pay a tariff of 139%). The restricted import of fresh potatoes helps to maintain the high domestic price of potatoes for fresh consumption, but for companies processing potatoes it makes it economically untenable to maintain a year-round production of potato snacks by using imported potatoes. Some of the companies have solved this problem by producing other goods, such as biscuits, when the stock of potatoes is finished" (Ornberg, 1996, p. 13). "The kind of state measure which has benefited potato growers most (at least some of them) is the Cooperative's monopoly on the import of seed for fresh potatoes. Before the Potato Growers Cooperative existed, farmers could apply individually to PWO for a quota, with oversupply and depressed prices as a result" (Ornberg, 1996, p.14).

## Effectiveness and Problems of State Promotion of Contract Farming

So far as the role of the state in monitoring and regulating contract farming is concerned, it was reported in 1995 that "..... the government regulation of the firm is minimal. The provincial officers and the district official interviewed in this aspect of the government regulation were unaware of the specific regulations concerning the contract farming approvals. In addition, since the contracting agencies trying to create a formal infrastructure are large firms, they have approval from the central government, which the provincial government just acknowledges. Thus, the provincial control and regulation, though exists, is minimal" (Padmanabha, 1995, p. 66).

Analysing potato contract farming in north Thailand, Ornberg (1996) also writes "The Thai state is, at least on paper, engaged in the promotion of contract farming to speed up commercialization of the agricultural sector, but, in general, the companies and the farmers do the job themselves" (p. 2). The district office of agricultural extension had a very active role as a co-ordinator during the first years of contract farming expansion in San Sai district. Its role has diminished with entrance of new companies and when PepsiCo bought NS Farm in 1995, the extension offices lost all control of the potato groups. When new companies arrived in San Sai, they started farmer-groups of their own (without the help of officials) or took over the groups formed by NS Farm (Ornberg, 1999).

On the policy response to the Thai agricultural crisis of the 1980s, Siamwalla (1996) observes that the agricultural problem was defined as one of oversupply of some commodities and, implicitly, that there were profitable opportunities in other areas. It attributes the planning mechanism approach to managing Thai agriculture to contract farming practice as one of the two intellectual origins, and states, "There were some spectacularly successful examples of this practice, notably in poultry, but there were also many failures. Impressed more by the successes than the failures, the government initiated in 1987 a four-pronged program to promote a co-operative effort between the agribusiness and the farming sectors. It is not difficult to demonstrate the futility of this planning approach nor to adduce reasons for it. That various Thai governments had to resort to this approach for agriculture (of all sectors) in the late 1980s and early 1990s (of all periods in history) showed the helplessness if not the desperation with which they tackled the problems of agriculture" (pp. 8-9).

Specifically on the effectiveness of contract farming for agricultural development, Siamwalla (1996) states, "The priority for an agricultural sector policy will have to be in the development of technology that will allow Thai farmers to reduce their costs to compete effectively in the world market without lowering their standard of living. In the past, the government has relied too much on the private sector to provide the new technology through contract farming. This can be successful in some cases but not in all. In the long run, the only proven way that this can be achieved is through public sector research, and this has been the proven path in all countries with advanced agriculture, even in the United States" (p. 10).

On the effectiveness of various policies including contract farming, Paopongsakorn et. al. (1995) observes: "There is still little interaction between poor and small farmers and government officers. This is due mainly to the fact that this group of people has very limited resources (land and capital) and very little education. Therefore, it is quite difficult, if not impossible, to upgrade the poor and small farmers through existing policies. Some farmers who have been participating in many projects are not quite sure why they were involved in such a project." (p. 70).

It is the involvement and commitment of private firms right from the initial stages of the project, which is crucial, though not sufficient, to guarantee a success of the contract farming project. This commitment implies the stake of the company in the project, leads to closer contacts with farmers required for careful selection of farmers, and its commitment to buy produce from these farmers forces it to monitor farmers closely. On the other hand, if the only interest of the company is to sell seedlings (cashew nuts case in Thailand), then it would not be interested in bearing future production risk (Paopongsakorn et. al., 1995, pp. 159-160). And, this (involvement and commitment) is what is missing in most of the cases.

Commenting on the failure of the MBK Sirichai Cashewnut Co. Ltd.'s cashewnut contract farming project, Paopongsakorn et al (1995) write on the role of the government in this failure "The government who is supposed to protect the small farmers' interest, does not do its job. ....(after farmer protests) The government in early February 1995, agreed to reschedule their (farmers') debts" (p. 165). This was a factor in failure in addition to lack of commitment of the company and absence of risk assessment to the crop in the project area by the company or the government department.

On the performance of the four-sector co-operation plan, Burch (1996) concludes "The Thai farmers' experience of contract farming has been very mixed, even where the state has been involved and committed to improving farmers' incomes by linking peasant producers to agri-food companies" (p. 334). In some commodities, some farmers have prospered, though there is considerable evidence to show that in general benefits have not been sustainable, farmers have been indebted and worse off due to contract farming project failures, like in baby corn and cashew nuts, and many social and environmental consequences have been particularly serious e.g. in prawn aquaculture. Though

Thai owned companies have become strong and global players because of the state incentives and promotion of agribusiness, the farmers have not benefited, and in some cases, even lost (Burch, 1996).

### Why Such a Role of the State

There could be many possible explanations of the role played by the state in contract farming so far, though studies of contract farming, with the exception of Burch (1994), have not attempted to look at this issue. One, there has been a domination by agribusiness in the policy making arena in Thailand especially in agriculture as it has been an agro-exporting country for quite some time. There is also found to be a gap between intent and practice of policies and programmes by the state agencies. This is further reinforced by a lack of effective farmer organizations which can exert pressure on policy and also monitor policy implementation and agribusiness operations on the ground in terms of effective implementation. Finally, there is lack of commitment from agribusiness companies for rural development.

## References

Burch, David (1994): "Agribusiness, Peasant Agriculture and the State: The Case of Contract Farming in Thailand", in Tim Lloyd and Oliver Morrissey (eds.): Poverty, Inequality and Rural Development – Case Studies in Economic Development, Vol. 3, St. Martin's Press, London.

CUSRI (Chulalongkorn University Social Research Institute) (1984): Project on the Improvement of the Agricultural Marketing System in Thailand – The Southern Region, submitted to the department of business economics, Ministry of Commerce, Royal Thai Government, CUSRI, Bangkok, September.

Goldsmith, A (1985): "The private sector and rural development: Can agribusiness help the small farmer?", World Development, 13(11/12), 1125-1138.

MOAC (Ministry of Agriculture and Co-operatives) (2002): Approach paper for the Workshop 'Linking Production and Marketing under Contracts' (Contract Farming) held on Friday, February 8, MOAC (translated from Thai).

Ornberg, L (2003): "Farmers' Choice: Contract Farming, Agricultural Change, and Modernisation in Northern Thailand", paper presented at the 3rd International Convention of Asia Scholars (ICAS 3), Singapore, August 19-22.

Paopongsakorn, Nipon, et al (1995): Agricultural Diversification/ Restructuring of Agricultural Production System in Thailand, A report for FAO, TDRI Foundation, Bangkok, August.

Siamwalla, Ammar (1996):"Thai Agriculture: From Engine of Growth to Sunset Status", TDRI Quarterly Review, 11(4), December, pp. 3-10.

Siamwalla, Ammar, D Patamasiriwat, and Suthad Setboonsarng (n.d.): Public Policies Towards Agricultural Diversification in Thailand, TDRI Foundation, Bangkok.

Tang, John C S (1984): Contractual Farming – Role of Government and The Private Sector, Asian Institute of Technology (AIT), Bangkok. May.

Appendix 9.1

# Provisions of the DIT Standard Contract Farming Agreement, 1999

### General aspects

1. Documents like ID card/ house registration/certificate of registration of the relevant party (farmer/group/co-operative/company) required for signing the agreement
2. Name and address of the buyer and the seller specified in the agreement.
3. Agreement is between buyer (company) and seller (farmer). Both parties agree to as follows:

**Sections 1 and 2:** Both parties agree to respect agreement in terms of buying and selling agreed quantity produce of agreed quality at agreed price, and specified delivery schedule at specified delivery point.

**Section 3:** Payment to be made immediately on delivery after checking all produce details as in agreement. If not immediate payment, buyer to give seller the receipt of delivery and a note of payment with seal of buyer for later use, and the payment will be made in seller's bank account. In case of an agricultural institution like a co-operative, the responsibility of further disbursing the payment to the farmers is that of the institution. If payment is not made within specified time or in full amount, interest is to be paid to the seller at specified agreed rate.

**Section 4:** In-case of force majeure like natural calamity, political trouble, crop failure, factory closure, labour strike, or other unforeseen reasons on either side, each to inform the other and discuss details of solution of the problem after the force majeure is over.

**Section 5:** If produce is less than agreed quantity (beyond certain percentage), the buyer not to buy or may discount and penalize the seller for missing quantity at some agreed rate.

**Section 6:** Lower quality produce (beyond certain percentage) may not be bought by the buyer.

**Section 7:** If buyer does not buy agreed quantity fully, the buyer to compensate seller at the specific rate.

**Section 8:** Claim on violation of contract to be reported to Dispute Determination Committee (DDC which will have three govt. agency ex-officio nominees besides farmer and company. representatives) whose decision will be final and binding on both the parties. If either party does not respect it, other party can cancel the contract and fine other party for the agreed quantity at some specified rate.

**Section 9:** Main agreement to supersede the appendices in case of conflict of clause/s. Three copies of the agreement are to be signed in the presence of witnesses and one copy to be retained by each party and one for the Department of Internal Trade.

**Fig. 9.2**

**Contract Farming System in Thailand**

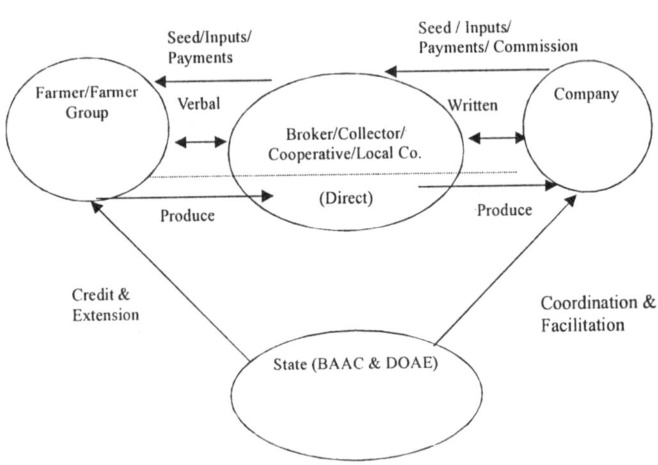

# 10

# Contract Farming in Thailand: Summary and Conclusions

## Role of Middlemen in Thai Contract Farming

Right from its inception, the Thai contract farming system has been dominated by middlemen who work between companies and farmers. It is in evidence everywhere today as found by the case studies reported in the earlier section, and documented by many other recent studies (Ornberg, 1996, and 1999; Thavornyutikarn, 1998). In the early nineties, it was noted, "The middleman system in Thailand is very strong. Many middlemen are owners of commodity shops. Some own trucks, allowing them to buy produce at the farm gate. The more roads are developed, the more easily these middlemen can drive their light trucks to buy produce from farmers......In order to consolidate patron-client relationship with their farmer clients, local middlemen visit them regularly, bringing gifts, providing occasional interest fee loans (generally not exceeding 5000 baht), etc. This type of relationship increasingly becomes an obstacle to the promotion of a more formal CF relationship between firms and farmers" (Manarungsan and Suwanjindar, 1992, p. 58)

In sugar contract farming as well, the system of middlemen, known as 'quota men' has been prevalent for long. Sugar factories make contracts only with quota men who in turn contract with sugar cane growers for the required quantity. By making contracts with "quota men" instead of having a contract with every grower, the mills can avoid high enforcement costs and a delivery schedule can be made (Ornberg, 1996). The sugar cane growers can not practically grow sugarcane if they have not been allocated quota by the quota man as sugar factory is the only buyer of cane in an area. It is also perhaps only in sugar industry that quota men have been able to organise themselves to bargain with the sugar mills (Thavornyutikarn, 1998).

In potato as well, in north Thailand, some companies prefer to employ a broker instead of working with farmer groups. The term "broker" is used by companies rather than "middleman", but there is little difference between a broker and a traditional middleman, apart from the fact that a broker usually works with only one of the companies. He is more like an employee than an independent entrepreneur. The broker, who is often a former member of the Potato Growers' Cooperative (and a skilled potato farmer), is the only contact between farmers and company, and like the traditional middleman, he may give credit to the farmers. Some companies have chosen to deal exclusively with brokers. Many Agricultural Ministry Officials are attracted to contract farming because it allegedly eliminates the role of the middlemen who are traditionally viewed as agents who exploit farmers. Obviously, they are still present, despite the contract farming arrangement, but in San Sai there is little room for exploitation of farmers. Competition between middlemen is high and information about prices is spread among the farmers (Ornberg, 1996, p. 9; Ornberg, 1999, p. 9).

Another very recent study also reports presence of local brokers and assemblers in the case of a local canning factory in north Thailand, and observes that it is good as local small business interests are involved in the vertical integration process. In fact, it comments on the four way relationship in contract farming on the ground, where roles of the four actors (farmers, companies, state, and small business interests (middlemen or brokers)) are negotiated and contested, though they fluctuate through time and space (Rigg and Nattapoolwat, 2001, p.951).

It is also a common knowledge that companies work only with middlemen or brokers not really farmers as a manager, of one of the companies studied here, acknowledges "First, we have to find out who actually signs the contract with the factory. Are they really farmers? In fact, only a few contracts feature real farmers. Most of the contractual parties are produce compilers. This leaves a gap - communication gap - between the produce buyers and the farmers" (Chunhawong, n.d).

## Environmental Impact of CF

Commenting on the non-rational chemicalisation of production techniques, Trebuil (1995) writes about the environmental damage contract farming brings, "Contract production of cash crops - usually tacit in the local fashion rather than formalized - has led small farmers to use increasing quantities of inputs in a system dictated by the demands and advice of village intermediaries who work for commercial companies. Thus, a typical input 'kit' composed with total disregard for the environment or any serious technical reference, supplied to illiterate (in Thai) Mon and Karen cotton farmers in Kanchanaburi province in 1991, included seeds from high potential varieties, but susceptible to the main insect pests; a product for dry dusting treatment (half of which does not adhere to the seeds and is lost to the environment); smart bottles for insecticides in small half litre packs (consumption of 10-20 litres per hectare), with active ingredients that are usually highly toxic yet of doubtful effectiveness, given the resistance that pests have acquired over recent years, expensive compound fertilizers in granule form, even for leaf applications (beneficial effects not proven); and herbicides. Some packs also include hormones and growth regulators" (pp. 79-80).

In north Thailand also, contract farming is leading to higher levels of chemical and pesticide use in contract crops as Ornberg writes "Potato growers in San Sai are not only facing competition from farmers in other areas, soil degradation has also made it harder and more expensive to grow high quality potatoes in this district. In the long run, it will be necessary to use more organic fertiliser (instead of chemical), to maintain and improve the structure of the soil" (Ornberg, 1996, p. 12).

But, it is not that contract farming per se led to environmental degradation in Thai agriculture, it only contributed to it as it also adopted the GR production processes prevalent in the sector. But, it can now come handy to rectify the situation as export oriented firms which need chemical free raw materials due to international market pressure, can make contract growers switch to less environmentally harmful/more environmental friendly production processes as they have the resources, including technologies and markets, to promote this kind of farming. It makes both business as well as development sense (my own observation). These firms can also help farmers adopt Good Agricultural/Farm Practice (GAP/GFP) similar to the concept of GMP in industry as the international market is increasingly demanding this kind of system in agro products now.

## Farmer Organisations

The Royal Project report (IMC, 1996) states "Collective negotiations and arrangements through farmers' organizations have not been effective nor practical, for the majority of the farmers either do not take the organizations seriously, or did not recognize the organizations as their representative. In many cases, farmers regard farmers' organizations or co-operatives as a channel to request for or to receive assistance from the government or local MPs. This is perhaps due to the fact that, most of the time, ideas of forming an organization or co-operative have been initiated by government officials rather than arising from their needs as seen by farmers" (p. 15).

## Role of CF in development/poverty reduction

There have been many warning notes on the role of contract farming in agricultural and rural development, or even poverty reduction (Goldsmith, 1985; Glover, 1987). In the context of Thailand, it was noted during the early 1990s: "It should be kept in mind that contract farming is only a means of ensuring the supply of raw materials of the firms; it is not an end in itself. There are several other means that can be used and that may even be better than contract farming. Contract farming is not a means to solve the poverty problem of rural farmers in developing countries who are used to traditional staple crops. It works well with only certain farm products and only in certain areas. Farmers with potential can benefit from contract farming, but they are not necessarily poor. .... Contract farming is contradictory to farmer organizations in that it tends to reduce entrepreneurship of farmers; what they gain is more production specialization; participating farmers pay no attention to accounting systems or the markets of both inputs and outputs..... farmers cannot apply their knowledge to other types of agricultural production. ... The government should not promote contract farming across the board (as being done by the Ministry of Commerce and Ministry of Agriculture). CF should be promoted only for specific crops with appropriate qualities" (Manarungsan and Suwanjindar, 1992, p. 58-59).

## Sustainability of Contract farming

A manager of one of the firms studied here, acknowledges that prices offered by contracting firms are not good enough for farmers to stick on with the companies as he says "normally the factory buying prices are lower than the market prices. This is a weak point of buying raw materials by factories. Most farmers try to sell their produce to the market instead of the factories since they get higher prices and are not required to comply with the conditions specified by factories" (Chunhawong, n.d.).

On the problem of quality standards in contract procurement, the Royal Project report states "This (quality standards) problem is seen so frequently in contract farming in Thailand that it has discouraged many investors from investing in agro-industry and has also disheartened farmers from entering into contract farming programs with factories" (p. 16).

Ornberg (1996) observes in the context of potato contracting, "In Thailand, it is common that an early success of contract farming is diminished, mainly because of the highly competitive market. Companies and farmers have multiple potential partners, products, and non-agricultural income sources. Broiler chickens is often referred to as the most successful case of contract farming in Thailand: shifting costs are high and the delicacy of the product makes vertical coordination essential. Sugar is another example of a crop where a functioning system of contract farming has evolved" (p.3). ... When pineapple-canning started in Thailand, the companies tried to copy the method of the sugar mills, but with meager results. The canning industry had to face competition from the table pineapple market, and for growers it was very easy to shift from the canning market to the table market. In recent years, the pineapple canning industry has started to rely more on purchases in the open market. Another case where companies have adjusted to the presence of an alternative market is tomatoes, which started as a contract farming system, but has gradually evolved to something more like a free market system. If the price of fresh market tomatoes is high, farmer do not deliver to the company and the company does not expect a supply. Companies processing tomatoes have diversified into other kinds of vegetables and fruit, and buy the farmers' tomatoes only in the peak season (p.3).

## Conclusions

There is no doubt that even small and marginal or even landless farmers are participating in contract farming of potato and sweet corn, thus making the process all inclusive. And, the farmers are, by and large, happy with the system as it prevails today. But, the long terms consequences of this system for local economy is something which has remained less explored. This is supported by another recent study of the crop and its contract system which states, "The fact that the farmers are organized into groups and/or co-operative, in combination with a supportive policy, has enabled them to use the growing domestic market for potatoes and potato products to their advantage. Moreover, being organized in groups has helped the farmers, who are growing potatoes on a contract, to gain a strong bargaining position with the companies, especially in San Sai district in Chiang Mai province, since the potato growers is this district have been outstanding when it comes to sustained and efficient organization" (Ornberg, 1999, p.1).

The state intervention has helped the farm sector and its farmers only to the extent that it has promoted competition that has been beneficial for growers like in potato in northern Thailand, and has also led to pumping of capital in farm sector through BAAC loans for contract growers. But, on most other counts, like making the system fair for farmers in terms of nature of contracts, or helping farmer organizations, in processing or marketing or even in collective selling to companies, to emerge, it has not really been effective. Rather, it has only helped companies as they could rely on state money to fund farmers in contract farming projects.

The lessons for promotion of contract farming among others include: i) whether there is enough rationale for contract farming in terms of market failure for the crop/variety/quality ii) the unique crop technology, iii) ensuring the market for the produce/product, iv) ensuring farmer benefits (yields/incomes), v) selection of farmers to avoid adverse selection problem, and vi) building trust with farmers to avoid moral hazard problem. The role of the government should be enabling and developmental in nature. Finally, it is important to remember that contract farming is situation/context specific and is a self-liquidating process as market conditions improve. In terms of research issues, the following aspects of contracting in Thailand have not been addressed at all in studies of the system so far and they need to be examined carefully to make an exhaustive assessment of the various implications of contract farming in Thailand and to incorporate them into policy for making better use of contract farming as a tool for agricultural and rural development:

1. Labour aspects of contract farming - conditions, wages, work place life, relative exploitation, gender aspects, child labour etc.
2. Intra-household aspect of contract farming like wages and gender impact within household, sharing of contract income -conflict and co-operation within the family.
3. Policy statement on contract farming (national plans) versus actual practice - gap, dynamics and reasons.

## References

Glover, D (1987): "Increasing the Benefits to Smallholders from Contract Farming: Problems for Farmers' Organisations and Policy Makers", *World Development*, 15(4), 441-448.

Goldsmith, A (1985): "The private sector and rural development: Can agribusiness help the small farmer?", *World Development*, 13(11/12), 1125-1138.

# 11

# Crisis and Diversification in Agriculture and Contract Farming in Punjab– Role of State and Agribusiness

## 1. Introduction

The green revolution in Indian agriculture has been a subject of intense debate among scholars and policy makers in terms of its implications for the rural economy and society and the sustainability of agricultural development process. There is once again a renewed interest in this subject due to the crisis in farming in the green revolution regions of the country in recent years. There have been even suicides by farmers in the green revolution belt of North India i.e. in the states of Punjab, Haryana and Uttar Pradesh; and in the Southern states of Andhra Pradesh, Karnataka and Maharashtra. There is no doubt that green revolution in Punjab agriculture brought about significant reduction in rural poverty in terms of both absolute number and percentage of poor and ultra poor population in total rural population right from the early 1970s. In 1990-91, only 3.45 percent of the total rural population, which numbered 4.86 lakh, was poor, and only 69,000 people, accounting for 0.49 per cent of rural population, were ultra-poor (those whose monthly per capita expenditure was less than 80 per cent of the poverty line expenditure (Shergill and Singh, 1995). But, more recent studies and reports show that the gains from the green revolution are not being sustained and the farm sector is in crisis for some

*. This paper was earlier published (without appendices) in Economic and Political Weekly, December 25, 2004.

time now (Sidhu, 2002; Singh and Singh, 2002; Singh, 2000; Iyer and Manick, 2000; and Chand, 1999). This chapter examines the nature and magnitude of crisis in the farm sector in Punjab during the post-green revolution period in next section, and goes on to analyse various diversification strategies recommended and adopted so far, especially the contract farming practice, in the third section. It discusses the emerging model of contract farming in section four, and concludes by discussing some general strategies as ways to tackle the farm sector crisis in a sustainable manner in the last section.

## 2. Dimensions and Magnitude of Crisis

The primary sector (mainly agriculture and livestock) accounts for 41 per cent of the Gross State Domestic Product (GSDP) in Punjab (Singh and Singh, 2002). In 1997-98, food grains comprising of cereals and pulses accounted for 74.6 per cent of the gross cropped area (GCA) of the state. The only other crop, which accounted for a significant percentage of the GCA, was cotton (9.2 per cent). By the late 1990s, 96 per cent of the gross sown area was irrigated, and 100 percent of wheat area and 94 per cent of rice area was under High Yielding Varieties (HYVs). The state had more than nine lakh tube wells and about four lakh tractors (Rangi and Sidhu, 2000). Further, 87 per cent of the paddy area and 52 per cent of the wheat area in the state was being harvested by combine harvesters. More than 80 per cent of the paddy straw and about 50 per cent of the wheat straw was being burnt by the farmers (Sidhu et al, 1998). There is an over capitalization in the agricultural sector of the State. The capital assets are grossly under utilized due to low and decreasing size of the farms. For example, in case of tractors, the average annual use is only 400 hours compared with the minimum viable use of 1000 hours. Due to this, the fixed cost component in crop cultivation cost has increased. This has hit hard the profitability of the farm enterprise especially of small and marginal farmers who over-invested in farm equipment (Gandhi, 1997). From the market side, these high costs have led to the wheat and rice production in Punjab becoming either only marginally competitive or non-competitive in the international market (Gill and Brar, 1996). In fact, wheat cultivation in Punjab had become unviable in the mid 1980s itself when a farmer in MP was able to earn higher net profits by spending less on modern inputs than a farmer in Punjab (Singh, 2000).

Water has been used highly inefficiently in Punjab agriculture. In the mid 1980s, there was wastage of water to the extent of 30 per cent (Bhatia, 1987). In Punjab, water table is falling by up to one meter per year. (Lester R Brown, 2003, www.earth-policy.org). Already 90 per cent of the 138 blocks of the state have been declared black in terms of water table falling at an alarming rate in these areas (Sidhu, 2002). It is found that 93 per cent of the paddy farmers had tube wells and 44 per cent of them had been affected adversely due to the decline in water table. These farmers had to sometimes deepen their tube wells or place the pump sets at a lower place ore in the well itself. This meant an extra cost of Rs. 2000/- for deepening the tube well during the early 1990s and Rs. 4000/- during the late 1990s compared to that during the 1980s (Singh and Kalra, 2002). The policy of free power supply to tubewells seems to have exacerbated the problem between 1997 and 2002. The zero pricing of canal water was a disincentive to farmers to conserve water. The southwestern districts face the problems of water logging and salinity, created by excessive use of water. Cotton was, thus, replaced by rice. A recent study of 100 farmers of different categories (both diesel pump owners and electric pump owners) in two districts of Punjab (Ludhiana and Bathinda) revealed that for nine months, farmers pay higher price of electricity because of flat rate system than they would have to pay under the meter system. The farmers of all types were giving as many as 27-30 irrigations to paddy and five and six irrigations to wheat and cotton respectively. But, water productivity in terms of produce per acre per cubic meter of water was lower in Punjab compared to that in UP for both paddy and wheat (Batra and Singh, 2003). Also, the over extension of rice cultivation led to increase in insect and pest attack with 57 per cent farmers reporting this problem (Singh and Kalra, 2002).

The other indictor of crisis in the farm sector in the 1990s has been the emergence of second hand tractor markets where farmers sell old and new tractors to meet other requirements of funds. There are more than a dozen daily, weekly, and fortnightly markets for the sale and purchase of second hand as well as new tractors in various market towns in the Malwa (southern Punjab) region and more specifically the cotton belt of the state where thousands of farmers participate and sell or buy tractors (Singh, 1999; Rangi and Sidhu, 2000). In a state which today has more than 3.87 lakh tractors accounting for 1/4th of the total population of tractors in the country with just 2.5 per cent of cultivated area, this phenomenon is disturbing. With only about 11.17 lakh operational holdings in the state, it means that every third holding in the state is equipped with a tractor. Added to this is the fact that more than 70 per cent of the farms are below 10 acres each. Even at the aggregate economy level, the growth rates of Net State Domestic Product (NSDP) from agriculture, total NSDP and the per capita income during the 1990s have been lower than that for the country as a whole (Chand, 1999) The growth rate of NSDP was only 2.72 per cent per annum during this period compared with 3.42 per cent during the 1980s and one of the lowest among Indian states and lower than the national average (4.02 per cent). In fact, SDP from agriculture grew at just 0.37 per cent during the 1990s and the whole of the primary sector growth was accounted for by livestock sector which grew at more than five per cent per annum during this period. Though the state is next only to Kerala in overall HDI, it ranks seventh in literacy. The development expenditure in the state as proportion of NSDP has stagnated in the 1990s (Singh and Singh, 2002). A part of the problems of the state's farm sector can be traced to the agro processing sector. A study of primary food processing units (paddy milling and oilseeds milling) in the early 1990s revealed that neither were they dependent on the local economy for labour nor for investible surpluses in a direct way (Singh, 1999a). As regards raw materials, the industry was more a consequence than a cause of the cropping pattern in the State.

Thus, the main problems of the farm sector include declining growth rate of farm production, declining capacity of the agricultural sector to absorb labour because the employment elasticity with respect to output in agriculture has come down to 0.2 per cent, monoculture of wheat and paddy which account for more than 76 per cent of GCA of the state and over capitalization of the farm sector. But, agriculture is the primary engine of growth without which Punjab will neither be able to accelerate growth nor achieve fiscal sustainability. As is clear from the above discussion, the economic condition of a vast majority of farmers, especially marginal and small, can not be improved unless there are changes in the cropping pattern and the technology of production. Diversification within agriculture is intended to stabilise incomes and employment in the farming sector. This diversification can either be in terms of variety of crops grown or technologies used for the same set of crops.

### 3. Diversification Attempts

It is only an irony that the Johl committee had to recommend as strategy for diversification in 2002 what it had recommended 16 years ago (in 1986) for the first time. The diversification strategy suggested by the second Johl committee report is that 10 lakh hectares of rice and wheat cultivation should be replaced with high value crops such as oilseeds and pulses. It proposes a crop adjustment programme to compensate farmers who make the switch. This amount comes to Rs.1280 crore which is less than the cost incurred on procuring and storing 80 lakh tonnes of rice and wheat i.e. Rs. 7000 crore for procurement and Rs. 2000 crore for handling storage and transport including wastage losses. In fact, about 3/4th of the paddy farmers reported no preference or willingness to reduce area under paddy by even 10 percent. Only 12, 7 and 5 per cent each of the paddy farmers thought of cotton, maize and sugar cane as alternatives (Singh and Kalra, 2002). In this context, some of the diversification attempts are analysed below:

Sunflower, a minor crop in the early 1980s, turned out be a major oilseed crop of the state by the early 1990s accounting for more than 50 per cent of area under oilseeds and more than 60 per cent of the total oilseed production of the state. But, soon it declined due to the lower returns compared with that from wheat, lack of quality seed, high water requirement, weather sensitivity, and adverse effect on next season crop (Singh et. al., 1997). Similarly, floriculture suffered from high risk of production, lack of weed control, high incidence of insects and pests, non-availability of good quality planting material and problems of seed collection (Garg and Sharma, 1999). It was also recognised quite early that it is important to move farmers with investible surpluses from the green revolution to the industrial sector (Gill, 1988). But, that was never attempted. On the other hand, private agribusiness firms were thought to be harbingers of change since the late 1980s. The economic logic behind the promotion of processing and marketing activities was that to bring dynamism to the agricultural sector, either cost of cultivation has to be lowered by raising productivity or cutting costs directly, or returns to the producers are to be raised by value addition or diversification. The contract farming arrangement with the growers by the private processing interests was to achieve both these objectives by providing them better seeds and other inputs and better markets and prices. Contract farming can be defined as a system for the production and supply of agricultural produce by the growers under advance contracts, the essence of such contracts being a commitment to provide an agricultural commodity of a type, at a time and a price, and in the quantity required by a known buyer (agribusiness firm). It basically involves four things - pre-agreed price, quality, quantity or acreage (minimum/maximum) and time (Singh, 2000; Fig. 11.1).

**Fig. 11.1**

**Bi-partite Contract Farming Model**

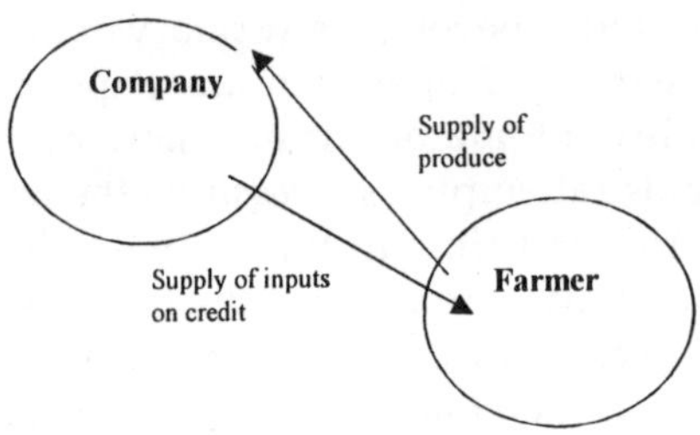


*The Pepsi-led Contract Farming System*

The Pepsi project, approved in 1988 by the Government of India, was to initiate a second agricultural revolution in Punjab where the first green revolution had reached a plateau in terms of yield levels of major crops. The Project, a joint venture among Pesico, Voltas, and the Punjab Agro Industries Corporation (PAIC) was to bring in horticultural revolution by moving the Punjab farmers away from wheat and paddy cultivation to that of horticultural crops like fruits and vegetables of various kinds. It was argued that Pepsi project was of utmost importance for Punjab (Bhatia, 1987; Singh, 1988). The project was intended to double the production of fruit and vegetables in the State which was also recommended by the first expert committee on diversification of Punjab agriculture, set up by the state government, in its report submitted in May, 1986. It had recommended that the area under horticultural crops to be increased from less than two per cent of the total at that time to about six per cent by 2000 A.D. which would have resulted in doubling the farm income. In fact, the committee had also recommended that private investments should be tapped to build horticultural processing and marketing infrastructure in the state.

Since Pepsi found the local varieties of fruit and vegetables unfit for processing, it wanted to promote new varieties and hence, the proposal for an agro-research center with an outlay of Rs. 20 million. Pepsi used contract farming system to procure the raw materials (Appendix 11.1 and 11.1A for contract agreement and manual for potato production). It is not that Punjab had not seen contract farming before. It was very widely practiced in seed and timber production during the 1980s and even in perishables like mustard leaves wherein Markfed had been procuring mustard from growers for processing into 'sarson ka saag' for export. But, it never got any policy or research attention. Within three years of its operation, the Pepsi project was able to raise the yields of tomatoes from a mere 7.5 tonnes per acre to 20 tonnes. It also attempted successfully the winter cultivation of tomato for the first time in Punjab with the help of green house technology dissemination at the farmers' level. Further, the harvesting season for tomatoes was extended from 25 days to 70 days due to the company's efforts. In fact, despite the huge losses made by the company in tomato procurement and processing, growers made good money. The company (Pepsi) introduced new technology of deep chiselling, and new methods of transplantation like shovel technique and bed head planting besides introducing new seed varieties. The new seed variety and the mechanisation of most of the farm operations led to increased productivity and reduced cost of production.

Contract farming in Punjab which was in place by the early 1990s with the entry of Pepsi Foods - an MNC (Pepsico) subsidiary - into tomato, and chillies, and a local firm - Nijjer Agro Foods Ltd. - into tomato, got further rooted with the selling off of its tomato facility by Pepsi to Hindustan Lever Limited (HLL– a Unilever (Multi-National Corporation (MNC)) subsidiary which processes 1/10th of world tomato production and is the largest food processing and marketing company in India) in 1995, and Pepsi's entry into potato contracting by the late 1990s.

The HLL plant in Punjab (set up by Pepsi) was the biggest tomato paste plant in Asia with a capacity to process 650 tonnes of tomatoes a day. HLL worked with about 400 contract growers during the late 1990s. Pepsi which had been working with hundreds of tomato and chilly farmers until 1997, later worked with only about a few dozen in chillies and potatoes each. Its potato contracts accounted for only about 10 per cent of its total procurement. Nijjer Agro Foods' tomato paste plant capacity is half that of HLL plant's and the company worked with about 400 contract tomato farmers in late 1990s (Singh, 2002). See Nijjer contract in Appendix 11.2.

## The Other Side of the Contract Farming Project

The Pepsi project had already disillusioned a large number of stakeholders like the Akali Dal, Punjab Agro Industries Corporation (PAIC), Voltas, and the Bhartiya Kissan Union (BKU). It is also argued that the soft drink component of the project was to lead to the setting up of seven bottling plants in Punjab. But only one such plant has been set up in the State. Therefore, even the more influential locals could not benefit in business terms (Gill and Gill, 1990). But how can a soft drink company ignore the considerations of the market which dictate the location of such plants? A perusal of the contract agreement which the company (and other companies) signed with the growers suggested that there was hardly any incentive for the growers to stay with the company as the entire risk was of the growers and all the insurance against risk in the contract was that of the company. Other than the supply of seedlings and the procurement of only specified quantity of certain quality produce at a pre-fixed time and price, the company's contract offered nothing to the growers. Whereas the contract gave the right of refusal to pick up contracted produce to the company, the growers were liable to be penalized if they defaulted from their commitment under the contract. And in the case of company not buying their produce even if it met all specifications, they were to agree to sell that produce in the open market. Can this kind of a contract, loaded against the growers, promote partnership between the growers and the company which was the very purpose of this project? The company also started subcontracting out its procurement to the large growers in each area who procured from the small growers on behalf of the company. Does this fit into modern agribusiness culture? How can this type of arrangement benefit those growers who really need to be integrated into modern processing systems? The growers defaulted from contract supply to the company and sold their produce in the open market due to high prices there. But, it was not that only farmers defaulted. Even companies had not been able to procure from the farmers many times, especially when they had over-contracted acreage and the yields were good. Then, either they did not give quota slips in time for entire produce or became strict on quality (Singh, 2002).

The companies (HLL, Pepsi and Nijjer) preferred large growers for contract production, perhaps to avoid problems of dealing with too many small growers, which has been the practice of all agribusiness corporations as evident from earlier studies of such companies (Glover and Kusterer, 1990). In fact, more than 1/3rd of Pepsi's contract growers had as much as or more than 10 acres of their land each under tomato cultivation. However, given the nature of these growers, they were the more frequent defaulters to the company as they could afford to do so. This led the company's tomato project into trouble. The company sold off its tomato processing plant at Zahura in Hoshiarpur to Unilever in 1995, as mentioned earlier. The average size of the operational holding of the MNC (Pepsi and HLL) growers was 72 acres, and of the local firm growers 22 acres, with the average for all growers being 61 acres. Even under Pepsi ownership earlier, most of the tomato contract growers were medium or large farmers. There was no MNC grower with less than 15 acres of operational land holding which is much above the average size of the operational holding in the state (8.9 acres) (Singh, 2002). Another study of contract farming system of the two tomato processing firms (HLL and Nijjer) in the state also found that 96 per cent of the contract growers owned tractors, with some having more than one tractor, and 82 per cent had tubewells for irrigation (Rangi and Sidhu, 2000a). These farmers have been the major beneficiaries of Green Revolution in Punjab agriculture in the 1970s or have foreign remittances from family members based abroad. Even the average acreage under contract for MNC (14.3 acres) as well as all contract growers (12.33 acres) was much above the average operational holding in the state. In fact, there have been growers of tomato in the past (under Pepsi) who put their entire land (as much as 45 hectares) under tomato (in 1995) and as much as 13 hectares under chillies (in 1996) (Singh, 2002).

The HLL contract growers did not appreciate the company selling seedlings to the non-contract farmers when it had surplus seedlings, just for the commercial consideration of making money out of additional seedling production. But, perhaps, the company wanted to create a larger base for procurement and contracts in the longer term and also surplus in the market to keep down the market prices, by doing this. The farmers were generally happy with contracting, though they did face some day-to-day problems in this system which had implications for their incomes and livelihoods. The farmers found the multinational company better than the local one so far as farmer treatment was concerned and many of them had experienced with more than one company each. The Pepsi farmers found the potato seed supplied by the company generally less than adequate for the acreage to be sown under contract and the pesticides recommended by the company as poor and costly. Two-third of the HLL farmers, 3/4th of the Nijjer growers and about half of the Pepsi potato growers reported lower yields as a case of crop failure, with another 12 per cent of HLL and 7 per cent of Nijjer growers reporting total crop failure. Some of the Pepsi growers also reported poor quality of produce. The farmers reported problems like poor co-ordination of activities, poor technical assistance, delayed payments, outright cheating in dealings, and manipulation of norms by the firms. Contract production of tomato has brought a big employment boom in these areas as the mechanization of sowing and harvesting operations of paddy and wheat crops had reduced manual work in these major crops of the region to negligible. That contracting has led to more and better employment opportunities for labor, especially women, was acknowledged by the labor (Singh, 2002).

The area under the contract crop (tomato) increased in all pockets of the region wherever there was practice of contract farming. Each pocket had a few hundred acres under tomato, which, in some areas, was not grown at all earlier. In all, the area under tomato in Punjab in 1999 was reported to be 15,000 acres and the total production of the crop 93,000 tonnes which increased to be 2.5 lakh tonnes in 2001. But, at the same time, no increase in area under horticultural crops was evident, as the production increase under contracting had come largely from yield factor and not from expansion of area. In fact, the area under fruit and vegetable crops in the state still remained less than two per cent. Also, there might have been area shift within fruit and vegetable crops due to contracting There might have been only a marginal shift from paddy, wheat and cotton to tomato partly because of better economics of tomato crop under contract which was explained to the prospective contract growers by the company officials, and partly because of the constant failure of cotton in some of these regions in the past few years (Singh, 2002).

Though many studies recommend contract farming promotion for Punjab agriculture (Rangi and Sidhu, 2000a; Sidhu, 2002), it is likely to solve the state's farming crisis only partly and as a short term measure as it is leading to higher incomes but also high chemical input intensity and water use (Singh, 2002) which are at the root of the sustainability crisis in the state's farming sector. Of the four firms operating in the state, two are multinational subsidiaries and, are therefore, globally oriented in their operations. Both are expanding their operations in food sector as part of their global strategies, and therefore are likely to stay in this business but may not restrict themselves to Punjab alone as it is already evident in HLL's move into Haryana and Rajasthan for its procurement. Also, Pepsi Foods' limited procurement of potato (10 per cent of total requirement) from contract growers leaves much to be desired. But more recently, the HLL tomato processing plant in Punjab has been shut down for the last one year. Similarly, Pepsi has given up tomato, and chillies and even potato contract farming by and large. But, it has moved into basmati paddy, groundnut and garlic contract farming since 1998 (Prabhu, 2004). It has acquired a paddy processing plant in Haryana which only means perpetuation of paddy cultivation in the region (Punjab and Haryana) to prevent which the MNC was granted entry into Punjab. On the other hand, the locally emerged and locally oriented firms (Nijjer and Markfed) are small in their operations and finding it difficult to grow on their own. Nijjer has already become a subcontractor to Nestle so far as contract production of tomato and processing of tomato into paste is concerned. It procures from farmers, processes the tomatoes into paste and supplies in bulk to Nestle. Thus, it is operating as an intermediary between the farmers and the MNC. By doing so, it not only avoids the risk of farm production by contracting but also the market risk by selling in bulk to Nestle. Thus, practically, it is operating as a subsidiary of a MNC and, therefore, all the benefits for the local economy are being reduced to that extent. The co-operative firm (Markfed) is very tradition-bound, non-aggressive and only a procurement agency. It has not really shown any major dynamism in the field of processing and marketing for the last three decades. The contracts of all the firms were anti-farmer, short-term, and costly to meet and perpetuate the existing problems of the farm sector like high chemical input intensity, and social differentiation, though contracting led to higher farm incomes and more employment for labour which, again, were not likely to sustain due to various reasons which are inherent in the nature of the contract system itself. There seemed an inherent contradiction in the objectives of the contracting parties and that of the local economy (Singh, 2002).

## State and Contract Farming

The contract-farming programme launched by the Punjab Government in October 2002 (for the rabi season) was aimed at taking away 10 lakh hectares from the wheat-paddy rotation over the next five years. In 2002-03, a total of 29,000 acres was covered under the programme, of which 20,000 acres was brought under hybrid rapeseed mustard (hyola), 7,000 acres under maize, 1,000 under barley and another 1,000 under various vegetables. The programme was being implemented jointly by the Department of Agriculture, Punjab Agro Foodgrains Corporation (PAFC- a subsidiary of the para-statal PAIC) and the private companies. The PAFC not only provided seeds purchased from reputed seed companies like Adventa India and Pro-Agro, and extension to the contract growers, but also promised to buy back the entire produce at pre-agreed prices through a tri-partite agreement involving PAFC, seed company through its dealer, and the farmer (Figure 11.2).

The tri-partite agreement specified the fixed price and bonus to be paid by the PAFC to farmer for the produce (bonus only if the PAFC was able to sell the produce at a higher price), type and quantity of seed to be supplied by the seed company at a given price for given acreage, farmer's responsibility of delivering the quality produce (produced by making use of recommended inputs bought from outlets prescribed by the PAFC) at a specified place, payment by PAFC within two days after delivery, and PAFC being the sole decider of weight of produce and the sole and only arbitrator in case of dishonouring of the contract terms by any of the parties. The contract was signed by all the three parties in the presence of two witnesses for the farmer (Appendix 11.3).

**Fig. 11.2**

**State-led Contract Farming System in Punjab (Tri-partite Agreement Among Farmer, Seed Company/Dealer and PAFC).**

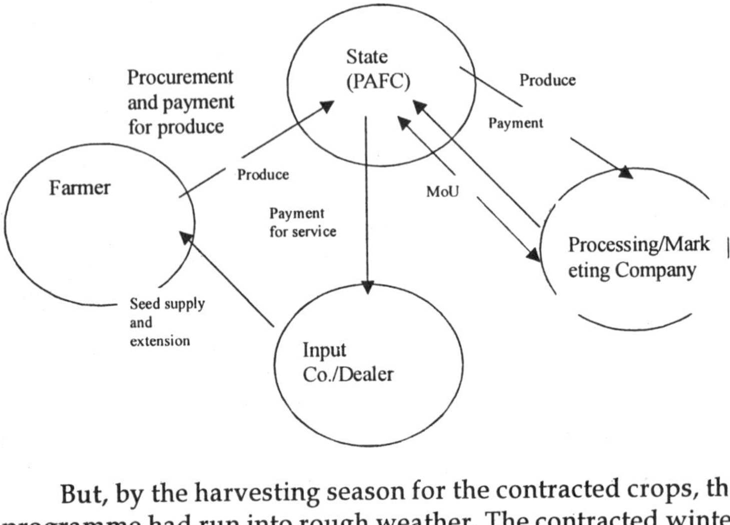


But, by the harvesting season for the contracted crops, the programme had run into rough weather. The contracted winter maize crop completely failed due to inclement weather. The contract green peas growers were forced to dump their produce in open market, after being rejected by the PAIC on quality ground as per the contract specification, as there was fungus infection due to inclement weather which was marked by heavy rains in winter season and then sudden rise in temperature. An area of 500 acres under contract production of green peas in Patiala and Fatehgarh Sahib districts had been affected. Some farmers found fault with the fungicide supplied by the contracted company. The dumping of contract-produced crop in open market led to fall in local market prices and was sold at Rs. 3 per kg. as against a promised price of Rs. 5 per kg. by the PAFC (Singh, 2003). The program could not achieve its state area goal in most crops and areas. Not only it fell short in terms of actual contracted area being less than that stated by the agency, the farmers did not plant the contract crops in the entire contracted area. The gap was much larger in latter case and even as high as 50 per cent in winter maize in Ludhiana and 20 per cent in hyola in both the districts. The seed companies only provided seed and no other extension service. Finally, none of the companies procured the produce. Instead, they advised the farmers to sell in the open market either because open market prices were higher than contract price or quality was not as desired by the companies. Except the oilseed crops (hyola and sunflower), the net returns from contract crops were found to be lower than what farmers would have got from wheat crop. Most of the problems farmers faced related to production and quality (like quality of seed and extension) and not marketing of produce (except peas) as open market could take care of contract produce. Due to this experience, a large majority (60 per cent) were not willing to enter into contract farming arrangement again ((Singh, et al 2003). Though contract farming has existed in the state for more than a decade now, it was for the first time that the state government took it up as intermediary between companies and farmers. It was part of a larger project on crop adjustment (diversification) to be implemented during 2002-2007. It was rather surprising that the state undertook contract farming as a Pepsi to the contract with the growers. Nowhere in the world has state undertaken this kind of effort for diversification. Long term and sustainable alternative of cooperatives or self-help groups signing contracts with agribusiness companies were given a go by. More recently, the state has withdrawn to the role of a facilitator of contract farming.

## 4. The New Face of Contract Farming

More recently, several agribusiness companies have made forays into the farm service sector which is being seen as private sector participation in agricultural development. One such model is that of Mahindra ShubhLabh Services Limited (MSSL) which has an agreement with the Government of Punjab to facilitate contract farming for diversification. The company offers extension services to farmers for a fee but ensures a certain level of yield. If farmers get lower than the assured level of yield then they need not pay the fee. This experiment of the company in Madurai in Tamil Nadu where farmers had to pay Rs. 500 per acre achieved assured yield in 75 per cent of the cases in first year which increased to 80 percent in the second season despite drought conditions (Naik, 2002). In Punjab, the company provides farmers quality seeds, fertilizers, pesticides, farm equipment and extension services to raise yields. It also plays a facilitating role to link farmers with processors and banks for market and credit respectively (Fig. 3). The MSSL plays the role of an integrated farming solutions provider. The company is leveraging its present network for better performance.

This is similar to what has been already implemented by Rallis India in M.P., Maharashtra, Karnataka and Haryana. The company provides all the inputs, technical support and finance to the registered growers for a specific crop and facilitates the sale of produce at reasonable price. The company follows a consortium approach. It has tied up with banks like ICICI and SBI and with buyers of produce like HLL, Picric and Cargill. The system is run through a network of 10 Rallis Kissan Kendras (RKKs) across the country. For example, in Panipat, the RKK sells inputs like seeds and fertilizers, ICICI extends credit to member farmers and Picric picks up the basmati for retailing in the UK. The farmers are enrolled with the RKK and can avail of loans upto Rs.6500 per acre (cost of basmati cultivation in Panipat) for a 6- month period at 13 per cent rate of interest. In addition, every member farmer has accident insurance coverage of Rs.1 lakh. The RKK has trained farmers to harvest basmati when moisture levels are at 16 per cent as harvesting at lower levels can lead to more broken basmati grains during milling. The farmers are paid prevailing market prices. The Rallis and the ICICI deduct the cost of inputs and the loan amount from the proceeds before paying the farmer on the spot (Karunakaran, 2002). In Hoshangabad district of Madhya Pradesh, Rallis operates in wheat. It started with a 1000-acre project and had grown to a 5000- acre project in 2002. Encouraged by this project, the company has set up new projects in fruits at Bangalore, vegetables at Nasik and basmati rice at Panipat. The ICICI collaborated with the company as they benefited from the rural penetration of Rallis, and the HLL gained as it could get good quality wheat for processing it into wheat flour (Subramaniam, 2002).

The ICICI Bank lays down pre-set criteria for farmer selection and informs input companies. The input companies/bank officials do the documentation, Input companies supply the inputs and send detailed accounts to the Bank which debits farmer account and credits input company account. At the time of harvest, the processing/marketing company collects produce and pays the bank its dues and rest to the farmer. The bank credits the farmer's account and the account is closed. An MoU among the bank, the input company and the output company is signed for the above arrangement. An undertaking from the farmer to supply produce under this scheme to the output company is taken by the bank. The ICICI Bank prefers four sector projects as against tri- partite projects as it considers inputs service very crucial for cost reduction and quality enhancement leading to better value realization for the farmer. The bank provided a total of Rs.180 crore as loans for various contract farming projects during 2002-2003. The bank-funded project has a 'credit plus' approach which involves not only credit and input supply but also extension service and marketing support. The bank also funded projects in basmati rice, chillies, potato and cotton besides wheat. It aims at raising prices of agriculture produce and lowering cost to make farming viable for the growers (Sabarinath, 2003). The Rallis' joint venture project with the Government of Madhya Pradesh, in which ICICI Bank is involved, started three years ago with 250 acres of wheat with 50 farmers. Now, there are 15000 acres under wheat cultivation.

**Fig. 11.3**

**The Quad-partite Contract Farming Model**

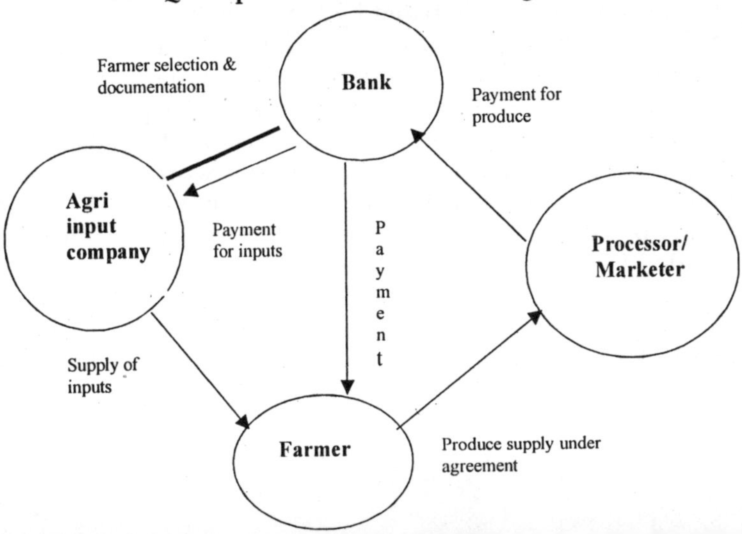

These are 'new banias' with knowledge and resources and strategy for growth through partnership. They will make money while helping others (farmers, banks and processors) make money. Their strategies involve bundling of inputs and linking up of credit with input supply which is the agribusiness of 21st century. It is interlocking of factor markets coming back in another form. But, what is wrong with it if it can provide what state and co-operatives have not been able to provide for so long i.e. timely and cost effective supply of quality inputs and finance and even tractors, and combine harvesters etc. on hire basis? Theses agribusiness services focus on more efficient use of modern inputs with a two pronged strategy i.e. yield increase or cost cutting through inputs and value addition through market improvement. This is must for competitiveness whether domestic or international. However, it remains to be seen how far they will continue with these arrangements as it seems a marriage of convenience among banks, input companies and processors/marketers all of whom look at contract farming as a way to over come their market difficulties. They are able to share their risk of working with the farmer, but the farmer's risk is not being shared by any other agency or organization.

## 5. Conclusions

One of the major issues in Punjab's agribusiness is how to create outlets for the investible surpluses available with relatively rich farmers who had already tried their hand at transport and primary agro-processing. Both these sectors are now saturated. Therefore, the best option is to make farmers partners in agribusiness projects initiated by the State and the MNCs. In this, Pepsio, Punjab Agro, and Voltas, failed. Rather, they did not attempt to involve farmers and local capital at all. Pepsi could not even retain modern farmers in its procurement operations as the contracts, as pointed out earlier, treated farmers only as supplier parties. Pepsi only chose to work with farmers under a contract because that makes best sense in agribusiness today. By contracting raw material production, the company avoided large fixed costs and hassles of getting into primary production. The farmers are unable to directly participate in agribusiness due to lack of expertise and attitude for this activity and lack of participative links with the trading and business networks. It is here that the cooperative form of organization can play some role. Therefore, what is required is not so much of multinational enterprises but a variety of enterprises which can ensure the participation of farmers in agro-industrial development as equal and active partners. Further, since the present system of cooperatives in the state does not work efficiently to cater to the business needs of such farmers, the New Generation Cooperatives (NGCs) can be given a try. This can also help mobilize some of the capital surpluses available with these farmers for the cooperative structure which is must for cooperatives in processing and marketing which are high tech and high cost activities. An NGC has restricted or limited membership, links product delivery rights to producer member equity, raises capital through tradable equity shares among membership, enforces contractual delivery of produce by members, distributes returns based on patronage, goes for value addition through processing or marketing, and makes use of information efficiently throughout the vertical system. However, it retains one member- one vote principle for major policy decisions. This kind of restructuring helps co-operatives to tackle problems of free riding by membership, of horizon which is at the root of financial constraint, and that of opportunism, both of the members as well as of the co-operative. This arrangement by co-operatives has helped them become economically efficient, financially viable, and obtain member loyalty wherever it has been tried. Additionally, non-member procurement and quantity or acreage contracts have been also used by co-operatives to tackle supply side problems (Singh, 2000a). Some of the co-operatives in India have also attempted quality based grading and pooling system to achieve better business performance (Singh, 1997).

It is important to realise that the solutions lie in the institutional plane. Unfortunately, the NGOs and other local level community institutions are missing from the state altogether. In fact, that was one of the reasons that the farmer suicides in the state could not be prevented. The lack of NGOs in the state for economic as well as social purposes has also been noted by others recently (Sidhu, 2002; Iyer and Manick, 2000; Singh, 2000). Not only that there are no NGOs in the state, the picture is no different for farmer's organizations. In fact, there are only state sponsored co-operatives for the distribution of inputs and procurement of produce, many of whom are also in red financially and not member- based. There is also a role for farmer associations in promotion of organic farming as an alternative. The state agencies, farmers' organisations, and the NGOs should intervene in contract farming situations as intermediaries to protect the farmer and broader local community interests. The NGOs can also play a role in information provision, and in monitoring and regulating the working of contracts. It is also important to realise that contracting need not be promoted for all crops, farmers and regions, and the state should play more of a regulatory role rather than a promotional role. Farmers' organisations should be promoted by governmental and non-governmental developmental agencies to deal effectively with contracting companies. Public or co-operative provision of costly inputs like tractors and combine harvesters should be made so that small and marginal farmers can custom hire these machines. What is must for making a way out of the crisis is the institutional and organisational innovations in the state's rural sector.

Agricultural diversification will work only if the current system of procurement based on Minimum Support Price (MSP) is changed in favour of new crops because it provides a powerful economic incentive to prolong the wheat paddy rotation. This has to be further coupled with user charges for power and irrigation and shifting to meter-billing. In fact, diversification should also be more than crop diversification including other allied and non-farm activities in rural areas.

## References

Batra, S and A Singh (2003): Evolving Proactive Power Supply Regime for Agricultural Power Supply, Management Traineeship Segment (MTS) Report No. 1562, Institute of Rural Management, Anand.

Bhatia, B M (1987): Towards a Solution of Punjab Problem-Restructuring and Diversification of State Economy, Centre for Policy Research, New Delhi.

Chand, R (1999):"Emerging Crisis in Punjab Agriculture –Severity and Options for Future", Economic and Political Weekly, 34(13), March 27, A2-A10.

Gandhi, V P (1997):"Technology, Cost Reduction, and Returns in Agriculture: A Study of Wheat and Rice in Punjab", Vikalpa, 22 (2), April-June, 35-48.

Garg, R and J L Sharma (1999):"Technological Constraints in Floricultural Farming in Punjab", Agricultural Situation in India, 56 (8), 471 – 473.

Gill, K K and S S Gill (1990):"Agricultural Development and Industrialization in Punjab - Some Issues Related to the Party Model", Economic and Political Weekly, 25(45), November 10, 2507-2509.

Gill, S S (1988):"Contradictions of Punjab Model of Growth and Search for an Alternative", Economic and Political Weekly, 23(42), October 15, 2167-2173.

Gill, S S and J S Brar (1996):"Global Market and Competitiveness of Indian Agriculture– Some Issues", Economic and Political Weekly, 31(32), August 10, 2167-2177.

Iyer, K G and M S Manick (2000): Indebtedness, Impoverishment and Suicides in Rural Punjab, India Publishers and Distributors, New Delhi.

Karunakaran, N (2002):"Money Grows on Trees ...", Intelligent Investor, August 31 (obtained through ISAPindia@yahoogroups.com)

Naik, G (2002):"Enhancing Food Security through Market Reforms", Productivity, 43 (1) April-June, 60-66.

Prabhu C (2004):Managing Contract Farming in Agro Industry, FPM Thesis, IIM, Ahmedabad, March.

Rangi, P S and M S Sidhu (2000):"Problems and Prospects of Agriculture in Punjab" in RS Bawa and P.S Raikhy (eds.): Punjab Economy – Emerging Issues, Guru Nanak Dev University, Amritsar.

Rangi, P S and M S Sidhu (2000a):"Study of Contract Farming of Tomato in Punjab", Agricultural Marketing, 42(4), 15-23.

Shergill, H S and G Singh (1995):"Poverty in Rural Punjab – Trend over Green Revolution Decades", Economic and Political Weekly, 30(25), June 24, A-80-A83.

Sidhu, B S, O P Rupela, V Beri and P K Joshi (1998):"Sustainability Implications of Burning Rice and Wheat Straw in Punjab" Economic and Political Weekly, 33 (39) September 26, A163-A168.

Sidhu, H S (2002):"Crisis in Agrarian Economy in Punjab – Some Urgent Steps", Economic and Political Weekly, 37 (30) July 27, 3132-3138.

Singh, A (1988):"Party Project –Vital for Punjab's Future", Business India, Feb. 22- March 6.

Singh, B, J Kaur and N K Arora (1997):"Techno-Economic Constraints in the Cultivation of Sunflower with special reference to Punjab", Journal of Agricultural Development and Policy, 9(2), 92-101.

Singh, J (2003):"Contracted green peas dumped in open market", The Tribune, Chandigarh. March 28, 15.

Singh, J et al (2003): Evaluation of Contact Farming Scheme in the Punjab State, Department of Economics, Punjab Agricultural University, Ludhiana.

Singh, K and S Kalra (2002):"Rice Production in Punjab – Systems, Varietal Diversity, Growth and Sustainability", Economic and Political Weekly, 37 (30) July 27, 3139-3148.

Singh, L and S Singh (2002):"Deceleration of Economic Growth in Punjab – Evidence, Explanation and A Way Out", Economic and Political Weekly, 37 (6), Feb. 9, 579 – 586.

Singh, S (1997):"Managing Marketing: Co-operatives in Horticultural Business in South Gujarat", Indian Journal of Agricultural Marketing, 11 (1&2), 73-82.

Singh, S (1999):"Institutional Innovations in Indian Agriculture: A Case of Input Markets", Institutional Development, 6(2), November, 3-10.

Singh, S (1999a):"Green Revolution and Agro Industrialization: A Case Study of Primary Food Processing Industries in the Indian Punjab", International Journal of Punjab Studies, 6 (1), 55-83.

Singh, S (2000):"Crisis in Punjab Agriculture", Economic and Political Weekly, 35 (23), June 3, 1889-1892.

Singh, S (2000a):"Co-operative as Contractor: A case study of contract farming by a co-operative marketing federation in the Indian Punjab", Co-operative Perspective, 35(2), July –September.

Singh, S (2002):"Contracting Out Solutions: Political Economy of Contract Farming in the Indian Punjab", World Development, 30(9), September, 1621-1638.

Subramaniam, A (2002):"Field Day in Store for Farmers", in http:// www.tata.com/rallis_ india/articles /2002060_ farming. htm.

## Appendix 11.1

# Agreement for Chip Grade Multiplication

This agreement executed at New Delhi on the 15th September, 199 between Pepsi Foods Limited, a company, incorporated under the Companies Act, 1956, having its corporate office at 3-B, DLF Corporate Park, S Block, Qutab Enclave, Phase III, Gurgaon-122002, Haryana and Registered Office at Vill. Channo, Dist. Sangrur (hereinafter referred as 'PFL'), which expression shall include its successors and assigns of the one Part one _______________(hereinafter referred to as "GROWER") which expression shall include his legal representatives and successors in interest and permitted assigns on the other part:

**AND WHEREAS PFL** requires graded chip sock potatoes, to be grown exclusively from input bags of parent seed given by it for this purpose.

**AND WHEREAS** the **GROWER** is engaged in the production of potatoes in the area of ___ acres and is the owner in title and possession of land which is available for the exclusive use of PFL under this agreement.

**AND WHEREAS** the **GROWER** has agreed to supply graded chip stock potatoes under a scheme hereinafter called the "PFL Contract GROWER Programme" in which seed potatoes shall be cultivated and grown on the land made available for this purpose, on the terms and conditions contained hereunder:

### Now Therefore, the Parties Hereto have Agreed as follows:

1. Parent seed of a certain variety which is the exclusive property of PFL shall be provided by PFL at the time of sowing to the grower @Rs. 460/bag of 81.Kg. inclusive of bag of 'A' and 'B' grade and Rs.370/-bag of 81 Kg. inclusive of bag

of 'C' grade for multiplication under in accordance with the terms of this agreement. The 25% amount will be deposited by the farmers at the time of seed booking and balance 75% will be colleted at the time of delivery of seed.

Grade A 1" - 1.5" in diameter

Grade B 1.5" - 2.0" in diameter

Grade C 2" - 3" in diameter

2. The potato grown from the parent seeds provided by PFL will be purchased from the GROWER, at the Channo factory and price of different grades will be as follows:
    1. Seed size between 48mm - 90mm, Rs.3.15/Kg. F.O.R. PFL Channo.
    2. *Potato size between 26mm - 47mm, Rs.2.60/Kg. with bag Ex farm or common place as decided by PFL representative.

Size less or more than described specification, misshaped, Green, Cut & very small size potato seed will not be purchased.

*This grade will be purchased by PFL, maximum 10% of the Chip grade.

If the GROWER achieves net multiplication ratio of 1:8 or more for chip size potatoes, he will be given an incentive of Rs.10 per quintal on chip size potatoes.

3. The price per Kg. bag specified above is exclusive of gunny bag, farmer will supply potato packed in gunny bags which will be returned to them on unloading of potato. Potato price is F.O.R. PFL factory at Channo and any rejection on deviation from enclosed specifications will be at farmer's risk & cost. For grade No.2, bags will not be returned.

4. All farm operations such as land preparation, planting, inter culture/spraying and all other operations including harvesting, storing, grading, bagging and loading will be the responsibility of the GROWER and the cost will be borne by him, provided always, however, that the GROWER shall at all time follow such instructions as may be given by PFL from time to time on any matter in connection with this agreement.

5. It is agreed between the parties that the total potato produced by the GROWER shall always be the property of PFL. Further provided that the seeds, the plants sprouting from he seeds

and all part of the plant will remain the exclusive property of PFL and shall only be disposed/sold, if so desired by PFL, as per PFL's instructions.

6. Potato planting/harvest is to be started in presence of a PFL representative or PFL has given written instruction for such operations to be started.
7. The GROWER shall render all the cooperation and assistance to PFL and its representatives in conducting field inspections of the potato crop at any time/stage and shall carry out instructions issued by PFl experts on raising/handling of crop.
8. The GROWER shall not sell or transfer to anyone else the produce meant for delivery to PFL. In case of default, the GROWER shall be liable to pay to PFL the damages for the shortfall on this account and in such an event PFL reserves the right to forthwith terminate the contract.
9. PFL shall make payment by Draft/Cheque on the receipt of and acceptance of potatoes within two weeks thereof.
10. The agreement will be operative from 15.09.199 to 31.03.199 unless extended by mutual consent of PFL & GROWER.
11. Notwithstanding, the place where this agreement is to be implemented, it is mutually understood and agreed by and between parties hereto that the contract shall be deemed to have been entered into at New Delhi and Courts of Law in New Delhi alone shall have jurisdiction to adjudicate thereon.

for *PEPSI FOODS LIMITED*

**Witnesses**

for *GROWER*

## Appendix 11.1A

# Manual for Potato Production

### 1. Field Selection

Sandy loam to loam soils with pH 7.0 to 8.0 are most suitable for this crop. The field should be level and well drained. The soil should be deep and free from soil borne diseases like black scarf and seabe.

### 2. Field Preparation

Plough the filed thrice with Mould Board plough or Disc Plough, followed by three tillage with tiller to the depth of 30 cm. Planking the field after each ploughing or tillage is must to break clods and conserve soil moisture. Remove the up-rooted weeds after each ploughing. In heavy texture soil care should be taken to plough the field at optimum soil moisture to avoid clod formation. Most of the soils of the state have developed hard pan at the depth of 15 to 20 cm. So, it is necessary to break it by chiseling before potato planting, for proper development of root system and tuber formation. The field should be well prepared before potato planting.

### 3. Potato Varieties

Recommended potato varieties for seed and table purpose are Kufri Jyoti, Kufri Badshah, Kufri Chandramukhi, Kufri Sutlej, Kufri Jawhar, Kufri Ashoka. For processing purpose Kufri Chandramukhi is an early variety, which can be planted in the middle of September and harvested in the middle of November in Haldipur and Jaldipur Districts. It can also be grown in other districts in end of September of first week of October and harvested in first fortnight of December. Kufri Lavkar and Kufri Jyoti are for spring crop. The varieties and hybrids imported by Pepsi Foods Limited from U.K. are most suitable for processing because of their very low reducible sugar content and high dry matter content.

## 4. Source of Seed Potato

Agriculture Department Tinjab, Union Potato Research Station Jaldipur and Pepsi Foods Limited; Channo, Dist. Sangrur.

## 5. Seed Preparation

Take out the seed tubers from cold store 10 to 12 days before planting. Keep it in pre-cooling chamber of the cold store for 24 hours. Treat the seed tubers with organic mercurial compound – Emisan – 6 solution of 0.25 per cent for 10 minutes to control the surface borne diseases. The solution for the treatment can be used 20 times if the tubers are clean.

## 6. Caution

Do not use metal containers for this solution.

Alternatively seed tubers can be treated with 3 per cent boric acid solution for 15 minutes. After treatment, the tubers are dried properly in shade.

## 7. Pre Sprouting

Seed tubers are brought from cold stores 10 to 12 days before planting. Spread the seed tubers in thin layer in a ventilated store in diffused light for multiple 5-6 mm long healthy sprouts within 10 to 12 days. Sort-out the blind, hairy sprouted rotten and disease tubers. Transfer the well sprouted tubers in the trays to the field fro planting while transplanting care should be taken to avoid damage to the sprout. This ensures quick plant emergence, uniform stand, faster bulking and early maturity of crop. The multiple sprouts increase the number of main stem per m2 and also number of seed size tubers as well potato yield.

## 8. Planting Time

Potato is grown in Tinjab under short day condition i.e. during September-October to January-February as autumn crop. The crop is planted at different times depending upon suitability of weather condition and marketing economy. Optimum planting time for the main crop is period having maximum temperature 320 c and minimum temperature 180 c. This is usually obtained in the first fortnight of October. To catch early market ware potato crop could be planted in the second fortnight of September. Kufri Chandramukhi as mentioned earlier can be planted in middle or end of September for processing purpose. The spring crop is planted in January and harvested in April end or beginning of May.

## 9. Manuring

Potato crop has sparce root system and requires sufficient nutrition to complete its life cycle within 80 to 100 days and give good yields. The fertilizer requirements are 250 Kg. N, 150 Kg. $P_2O_5$ and 150 kg. $K_2O$ and about 10 tonnes of farmyard manure per/ha. per acre basis the fertilizer dose is 100 Kg. N, 60 Kg. $P_2O_5$ and 60 Kg. $K_2$ O along with 4 tonnes of farmyard manure.

Full dose of phosphorus and potassium and half dose of nitrogen is applied at planting preferably in furrows. The remaining half dose of nitrogen is applied in furrows before second and final earthing i.e. 25-30 days after planting. In very sandy soils the nitrogen dose can be applied at planting, second earthing up and foliar spray. The potassium dose can also be split i.e. half at planting and half at earthing up.

The sources of nitrogen are Ammonium sulphate, Calcium ammonium nitrate and urea. Phosphorus is supplied through super-phosphate and diammonium phosphate. The source of potassium is muriate of potash. The first dose of nitrogen is applied through ammonium sulphate or calcium ammonium nitrate. The second dose of nitrogen is applied through urea. It should be applied in furrows before earthing up after weeding and hoeing. Urea should not fall on the leaves, because it burns the leaves. Zinc sulphate at the rate of 20 kg./ha. may be applied along with NPK fertilizer before planting if the soil is deficient in this nutrient. FYM at the rate of 10 tonnes/ha. should be applied before last ploughing. The availability of the fertilizers is an important factor. Generally farmers are using diammonium phosphate i.e. DAP. The fertilizer dose at planting is 150 bags diammonium phosphate, 100 kg. urea and 100 kg. muriate of potash per acre. 100 kg. of urea in two splits may be applied in second and third dose.

## 10. Seed Size and Spacing

Seed tubers of different sizes can be used by adjusting inter-row and intra-row spacing. The best size tubers are 30-40 gms which are planted at 60 cm X 20 cm spacing i.e. 60 cm inter row and 20 cm intra-row spacing. Large size seed tubers can be planted at 60 cm x 25 cm spacing or 75 cm X 20 cm spacing, smaller size seed tubers can be planted at 60 cm X 15 cm or 60 cm X 10 cm spacing. By adopting different spacing seed rate can b maintained within economical limits.

### 11. Irrigation

Per-sown irrigation is beneficial for proper plant emergence and uniform plant growth. First irrigation should be given at 25% plant emergence i.e. 8-10 days after planting. The subsequent irrigation's are given at 7-10 days interval depending upon the need. Avoid flooding over the ridges while irrigating, frequent light irrigation are preferred. Water level should not go beyond half the height of the ridge. Irrigation should preferably given in the morning and ev3ning. In total 8-12 irrigation's are needed for this crop. In case pre-sown irrigation is omitted at the time of field preparation than irrigate the crop immediately after planting. Stop irrigation 10 to 15 days before harvesting. He weeding, hoeing and earthing up should be done after 25-30 days when moisture conditions are optimum for these operations.

### 12. Weed Management

Keep the fields free from weeds either manually or through the use of herbicides. Generally weeds emerge before the potato plant. The spray of the following pre-emergence herbicides after dissolving in 1000 litres of water for one hectare or 2.5 acres within 3 to 5 days after planting can effectively control the weeds.

Sencor 1kg/ha, Goal 600 ml/ha and Lasso 3 kg/ha in 1000 litres of water as pre-emergence herbicides are most effective when applied at sufficient moisture in soil. Therefore, apply after first irrigation as soon as it is possible to enter the field. In case the pre-emergence herbicides re not used. Spray the potato field with Gramaxone 2.0 litres/ha in 800-1000 litres of water at 5 to 10 per cent plant immergence, provided sufficient weeds have appeared because it kills the emerged weeds.

### 13. Interculture

Weeding and hoeing is done when potato plants are 10 to 15 cm height i.e. after 25 to 30 days after planting. The final earthing up should be done immediately after weeding and hoeing.

### 14. Plant Protection

It involves two aspects i.e. damage due to insects and pests and damage due to disease.

### 15. Insects and Pests

Spray the crop with Endosulfan 35 EC at 1.5 litres/ha or Carbaryl 30% WP at 2.5 kg/ha in 1000 litres of water if any damage is noticed at any stage of the crop due to leaf eating caterpillar or other insects. In case of damage by cutworms, drench the ridges with Chlorpyifos 20 EC at 2.5 litres/ha in 1000 litres of water.

### 16. Diseases

Late blight is the most common disease which damages the crop to a great extent in certain years. It is recommended ht varieties having resistance to the disease like Kufri Jyoti, Kufri Badsha, Kufri Sutlej, Kufri Jawhar may grown for seed and table purposes. However, for processing the recommended varieties and hybrids are to be grown. In Punjab late blight appear in epidemic from once in 4 to 5 years. However, the control measures are to be adopted every year.

Late blight is favoured by high humidity i.e. 80 per cent or more and moderate temperatures i.e. 10 to 200c. These conditions are usually found in mid-November in this region. To control late blight, prophylactic spray of Macozeb i.e. Dithane M-45 at 2.0 kg in 1000 litres o water/ha is given in the second week of November. A sticker, Triton AE may be added to the fungicide solution at 1 litre/1000 litres of water so that fungicide is not washed out by rain. While spraying ensure hat the lower surface of the foliage is thoroughly drenched with fungicide solution, Dithane M-45 sprayed with 2 per cent urea also checks the developing loof spots caused by phoma and alterneria i.e. early blight. The spray of Dithane M-45 & may be repeated by the end of November. In case late blight has already appeared in the crop, a spray of Redomil MZ 72 WP at 1 to 2 kg/ha in 1000 liter of water should be given immediately. The haulms of severely late blight affected crop should be cut immediately to check or reduce tuber rottage due to late blight infection.

## 17. Harvesting, Grading and Marketing

Harvest the crop when skin of the tubers has become firm, which reduces bruising of skin during mechanical or manual digging operation. Harvesting should be done at proper soil moisture condition, so that digging is easy and no soil sticks to the tubers. The surface of harvested tubers should be dried. The cut, damaged, disease and rotten tubers should be sorted out. Grade the tubers into three sizes i.e. small, medium and large. The harvested potatoes are packed in to gunny bags according to heir size and marked on the bag. The product is sent to the market for selling or stored. The potatoes meant for processing should be sent to the factory immediately. Store the bags in cool and shaded place to avoid greening of the tubers till the product is sent to the cold store. Green tubers are not fit for consumption because these are bitter in taste, difficult to cook and can be toxic due to glycoalkolids.

## Appendix 11.2

# Contract Agreement

This contract agreement is between M/s. Nijjer Agro Foods Ltd., Village Meharbanpura, GT Road, Tehsil and District Amritsar (which will be referred to as Party No. 1 hereafter) and the Producer named ........... (who will grow tomatoes and will be referred to as Party No.2 hereafter). The Party No.2 will supply tomatoes to Party No.1 as per conditions given below:

1. Party No.1 will supply healthy, disease free, hybrid tomato seedlings at the rate of Rs. 150/- per 1000 to Party No. 2. The amount for this supply of seedlings will be deducted from the payment for tomatoes supplied by Party No. 2 to Party No. 1. Party No. 2 is bound to sell to Party No.1, ripened, red colour, disease free tomatoes without sunscolt at the rate of Rs. ..... per quintal.
2. Party No. 1 will provide all the technical knowledge from sowing to harvesting of tomatoes, through its agricultural staff.
3. Tomatoes will be weighed on the weighbridge at the premises of Party No.1.
4. The quality inspection of tomatoes which will be sold by Party No. 2 to Party No. 1 will be carried out by the quality control department of Party No.1.
5. Party No.2 is obliged to sell to Party No. 1 only, all the healthy tomato produce from the seedlings supplied by Party No.1.
6. Party No. 2 will grow ....... Acres of tomato crop. If the crop grown by Party No.2 is damaged du to any natural calamity like hailstorm, flood or any other reason beyond human control, then Party No. 2 will inform Party No. 1 within 7 days in writing about it. Party No. 2 will not be liable to compensate Party No. 1 in such a situation. On

the other hand, if the factory of Party No. 1 is out of order, there is power failure, or any such reason which is outside the control of Party No. 1, it will not be liable for any loss to Party No. 2 in such a situation.

7. In case of any dispute about the above agreement between the two parties, Shri RP Jain, C.A., Amritsar will be the arbitrator and his decision will be final. That decision can only be valid in a court within the jurisdiction of Amritsar district. No other court will have the jurisdiction on this matter.

The agreement has been accepted by both the parties after careful reading and listening. Both the parties are bound by the agreement. It is signed by both the parties.

Producer (Party No. 2) Nijjer Agro Foods Ltd. (Party No.1)

Witness:

1.

2.

**Appendix 11.3**

# Punjab Agro Foodgrains Corporation Ltd. 2A – Sector 28A, Madhya Marg, Chandigarh.

**Tripartite Contact Farming Agreement for Sunflower/Maize/Basmati (Strike whichever is not applicable).**

This tripartite agreement among,

1. Authorized signatory of the Punjab Agro Foodgrains Corporation Ltd., 2A - Sector 28A, Madhyamarg, Chandigarh (hereafter written as PAFC).
2. Shri. ______________________ S/o ______________________ , Resident (full address) (Hereafter written as farmer).
3. The seed company through its licensed dealer, is carried out as per the following terms and conditions.
   A. The farmer agrees to sell sunflower/Maze/Basmati at the rate of Rs. ___ per quintal plus bonus.
   B. The seed company/PAFC is supplying good quality hybrid seeds as follows.

| *Seed Variety* | *Qty. (Kg.)* | *Price (Rs. per Kg.)* | *Total Price* | *For_ Acres* |
|---|---|---|---|---|
| | | | | |

   C. The seed company/PAFC will work closely with the farmer and provide all the information about crop production and storage of produce to the farmer. The farmer will buy recommended weedicides and pesticides from the place approved by PAFC in order to avoid curious pesticides.
   D. The farmer will arrange to reach the produce in pure and dry form at the place specified by the PAFC and

will be responsible for transport, quantity and quality loss to the produce. The crop should be free from any decease and foreign matter. The produce will be wed at the weight bridge provided by the PAFC at the place of purchase only.

E. If the produce meets the above conditions/ specifications, PAFC will accept the produce at the rate of Rs. ____ per quintal plus bonus. The bonus will be paid only if PAFC is able to sell the crop to the buyers, consumers above the rate of Rs. _____ per quintal.

F. PAFC will make payment within two days of purchase of produce.

G. PAFC alone will be the Arbitrator if there is any violation of terms of the contract and its decision will be final.

H. Any dispute will be resolved in the courts in Chandigarh only and the jurisdiction will also be Chandigarh only.

Signatures

1. Farmer 2. Seed Company/Dealer 3. For, PAFC (with Seal)

Place:

Date:

Witnesses

1. ____________________. 2____________________

# 12

# Co-operative as Contractor: A Case Study of Contract Farming by Markfed in Punjab*

## 1. Introduction

Co-operatives are different from other forms of organisations not in terms of business functions they perform, but in terms of the manner and philosophy with which these functions are performed. The traditional co-operative form of organisation has suffered from various constraints which has had negative effect on the day-to-day operations and performance of co-operatives. These constraints, which originate in the very nature and principles of co-operative form of organisation, include commitment to buy the entire produce from all members, lack of financial and managerial resources, lack of market orientation, and small size of operations. As a solution to this problem of the co-operatives, a new variant called New Generation Co-operatives (NGCs) have come up and evolved overtime in various parts of the world like USA, Canada, and India. A New Generation Co-operative is one which has restricted or limited membership, links product delivery rights to producer member equity, raises capital through tradable equity shares among membership, enforces contractual delivery of produce by members, distributes returns based on patronage, goes for value addition through processing or marketing, and makes use of information efficiently throughout the vertical system. However, it retains one member- one vote principle for major policy decisions. This kind of restructuring helps co-operatives to tackle problems; of free riding by membership, of horizon which is at the root of

* Earlier published under the same title in 'Co-operative Perspective', 35(2), 2000. Also, part of the case studies in the book 'Political Economy of Contract Farming in India', Allied, New Delhi, 2005.

financial constraint, and that of opportunism, both of the members as well as of the co-operative. This arrangement by co-operatives has helped them become economically efficient, financially viable, and obtain member loyalty wherever it has been tried (Harris et.al., 1996).

Additionally, non-member procurement and quantity or acreage contracts have been also used by co-operatives to tackle supply side problems (Hinman and Ricks, 1993). Some of the co-operatives have also attempted quality based grading and pooling system to achieve better business performance (Singh, 1997).

On the other hand, the private business entities have, for long, used contract farming system to tackle problems of quantity, quality, timeliness and cost of raw materials, especially perishable produce for further processing and marketing. Contract farming can be defined in terms of a system for the production and supply of agricultural and horticultural produce under forward contracts, the essence of such arrangements being a commitment to provide an agricultural commodity of a type (quality), at a time and a price, and in the quantity required by a known buyer. In fact, contract farming can be described as a halfway house between independent farm production and corporate/captive farming. It basically involves four things - pre-agreed price, quality, quantity or acreage (minimum/maximum) produce and time.

Due to the various ill-effects of contracting on producers, it is argued that vigorous bargaining co-operatives, or other agricultural producer organisations are needed to negotiate equitable contracts. This kind of organisations have been able to secure the standardisation of contracts and their scrutiny by a government agency in the past in the US (Wilson, 1986). There are cases of farmer groups or co-operatives collectively working under contracts with private or public companies (Singh, 1999; Coulter et.al., 1999). Further, some others argue that the ill-effects of contract farming would be lessened if more of the 'contractors' were agricultural co-operatives or other producer oriented organisations. However, it has to be recognised that agricultural co-operatives may be deterred from attempting to integrate forwards into processing and distribution both by financial constraints and by the managerial problem of making a success of unfamiliar activities in the face of strong competition (Hill and Ingersent, 1982). It is in this context that this chapter looks at the case of a traditional (para-statal) apex co-operative which, like a new generation co-operative, practices contract farming within and outside its membership. This paper examines its contracts, their practice, and farmer perception of the working of the contract system.

### 1.2 Context and Methodology

This study looks at the practice and performance of contract farming by a co-operative entity in the Indian Punjab in order to draw some lessons for the emerging scenario in Indian agribusiness and the co-operatives. The Indian Punjab is the most grown region of India agriculturally. There are no studies on this aspect of the agrarian economy of the State (In fact, there has no study of this system so far in India too) which is experiencing serious problems in its farm sector in the recent years due to the tapering off of the green revolution growth momentum. The case study is based on an interview survey of contract farmers with the help of an interview schedule prepared for the purpose, and discussions with the co-operative officials. The crop (Mustard) being procured under contracts is being processed into value added food product (saag i.e. curried mustard leaves) for domestic and export markets. The primary survey of contract growers was conducted in the district of Jalandhar which was chosen due to the prevalence of the contract system of the co-operative there. A complete lists of growers was obtained from the co-operative and 12 contract growers of the co-operative out of a total of 40, were interviewed.

## 2. Profile of Markfed, its Canneries, and Contracts

Markfed, the Punjab State Co-operative Marketing Federation, a para-statal body created in 1954 to promote agriculture and agro-industries in the state, has 22 units for the processing and manufacture of various agro-products like cooking mediums, chemicals, canned food, animal feed, paddy and cotton. It also provides many other services to the farmers like supply of fertilisers, and trades in major agricultural commodities of the state. It has about 3000 co-operative marketing and processing societies as its members, but most of the share capital is provided by the state government. It claims to be the largest co-operative business in Asia with an annual turnover of Rs. 3500 crore (US $ 1.1 billion).

Set up in 1968 by the Markfed, the Markfed Canneries, Jalandhar produces for export and military supply, products like Sarson-ka-Saag (cooked mustard leaves), canned peas, and dehydrated vegetables which are marketed under the brand name of 'Sohna', the Markfed brand. The saag is mainly meant for export to the first world i.e. America, Canada, the Europe, and the gulf countries where Indians live in significant numbers, and for supply to the Indian Army. Every year, 1.2 million packs of 450 gm. each, worth Rs. 2 crore are produced and sold. The Canneries has a capacity to process 10,000 cans of saag per shift but generally operates at 60-80 per cent of its capacity. It employs 92 regular staff, and has 40 contract workers in the plant which is operated for 4 months in an year (November - February) due to the seasonality of the crop. The product is cooked farm fresh leaves of mustard and spinach garnished with onions, garlic, green chillies, condiments and a dash of maize flour. Only traditional ingredients go into its making. The crop is cut right upto root, with sickle and delivered to the factory. Then, pulping is done at the factory after cutting and washing. The product is ready to serve and has two-year shelf life.

## 2.1 The Contract:

The farmers are supposed to grow mustard organically without using any pesticides or fertilizers. The contracts with the farmers are formal, written and are invited through tenders in newspapers. They specify not only acreage to be planted with the contract crop but also the right of quantity being with the company. The grower is given a copy of the contract. The crop is procured at the rate of Rs. 0.70 per kg. in different lots as processing capacity is limited. No inputs are provided. The seed required is only one kg. and costs only Rs. 20-30 per acre. Farmers bring produce to the cannery at their own cost. Upto 10 per cent of quality defect in the produce is allowed. Beyond that, a penalty is imposed, and any lot with more than 20 per cent spoilage is rejected. The payment for the produce is made at the end of delivery of all supplies which is generally within a week of last delivery. A detailed picture of the contract is given in Appendices 12.1 and 12.2.

## 2.2 Management of Contracts

The crops of spinach and fenugreek, the essential ingredients of saag, are procured from only one farmer each under contract.

Until 1991, some other crops like peas, and tomato were also procured under contract arrangement which are now procured from the open market depending on the orders from the market. For mustard, the organisation works with only about 40 farmers every year. Generally, about 140 acres are planted every year with each farmer planting 3-5 acres. In the month of June, farmer meetings are held to convey to them the mustard acreage required by the canneries. The sowing of the crop starts in September-October and is harvested in November-December. The delivery schedules are given along with acreage contract. Earlier, the farmers were given seeds and fertilizers by the organisation. It was discontinued in 1975 because of farmer default. The number of farmers has remained more or less the same since beginning. Every year, more than 80 per cent of the farmers are new. Most of the farmers are located within 36 km. radius of the canneries. In order to prevent default, the company has gone in for interior area farmers so that they cannot sell the crop in open market. But, the co-operative does not face any major default from farmers as there is no market alternative for the farmer for the crop except fodder market, which is attractive only for a few days. The crop is procured from non-contract farmers only if contract crop is not adequate or is unfit in quality. Markfed is of the view that bringing in variety in crop production is must so that phased sowing and thus extended harvesting schedule can be achieved. It plans to introduce differential rate for different varieties so that farmers have incentive to go for a different variety.

## 2.3 Profile of Markfed Growers

The farmers working with Markfed were largely secondary level literate (75 per cent) with some being college/university educated. But, they were mostly small and medium land holders as 2/3 of them had land between 10-20 acres and the other 8 per cent only less than 10 acres each, thus making 75 per cent of them with less than or just 20 acre land each. The average size of owned holding was 21 acres. Some of them leased in land to the extent of 10-20 or 20-30 acres (1/3 of all), with others leasing only less than 10 acres each and about 40 per cent none at all. Thus, the average size of operational holdings was 29 acres and they were in the range of 10-20 acres for 42 per cent, 20-30 and 30-50 acres each for another 25 per cent each, and more than 50 acres in case of only one farmer (table 12.1).

### 2.4 Experience of Contracting and Acreage under Contracts

A significant percentage of growers (33 per cent) had 6 years or more of experience of working with the co-operative, another 42 per cent between 3-5 years and 25 per cent less than or just 2 years each (table 12.1). It was a new crop for 2/3 of the farmers as the area is not known for this crop traditionally which has been grown more in the southern Punjab region. Half of them had less than or just 5 acres each under contract crop and the other half 6-10 acres each, the average being 6 acres (table 12.1). Contract production was in owned land for all of them except one who used leased in land.

### 2.5 Farmer Logic of Contracting

Farmers are interested in this crop as it is only a two-month and an in-between (paddy and wheat) crop. It gives an output of 10 tonnes per acre valued at Rs. 7,000/- at Markfed price (Rs.0.7 per kg.) which proves very remunerative without much expense incurred. The crop may give similar returns from sale of oilseeds if allowed to ripen but it takes 6 months and that makes the farmer lose one crop season. Therefore, there is no attraction for this alternative. The farmer gets a net return of Rs. 2-4000 per acre after meeting all expenses including lease cost. The produce has no alternative market except the fodder market which is not very attractive in terms of price. So, farmers prefer to let the crop ripen if not taken by the Markfed due to factory closure, over-production, or lack of processing capacity.

## 3. Performance of Contracts

### 3.1 Farmer Defaults and Crop Failures

Almost all the farmers (92 per cent) claimed that they had met the contract terms always. The contracts have been smooth for both the parties and the defaults are almost absent due the fact that there is no attractive alternative outlet for the crop. Since the crop is to be grown organically, it sometimes leads to disease and pest attack on the crop. There was a serious crop failure reported by only two farmers and partial by one, making up for ¼ of all farmers, due to the seed failure and pest attacks (tables 12.2 and 12.3), but there was no compensation given by the co-operative. This is despite the fact that contracts have been biased against the growers as is evident from Annexure 12.2. For example, there is no mention of co-operative's liability for failure to pick up produce. There is no compensation for crop failure and even the payment period is not specified.

### 3.2 Problems and Remedies

The farmers were generally happy with the organisation and wanted to continue contracting, as it gives better and reliable income. But, some of them have filed cases against the organisation in the past for various aspects of the contract not being met by the organisation due to various reasons. The cases are still pending in courts. This has happened as it is basically a para –statal co-operative organisation and seen as a government organisation by the farmers. It is generally easy to fight a bureaucratic agency especially when there is support from within the organisation for such cases as organisational interest is not paramount or some people see the real purpose of the organisation being better served by such measures.

An indication of farmer happiness or satisfaction is that 2/3 of them had no complaints and other 1/3 had problems like delayed payments, poor co-ordination of activities, and manipulation of norms by the firm. They also did not see any role for the government in contract system but wanted the co-operative to pick up the entire acreage produce from the field with grading done at the field level itself.

## 4. Conclusion

Markfed contracts are no different from other agribusiness firm contracts with growers of different crops. Infact, they are only procurement or marketing contracts as against production contracts practiced by other firms wherein they provide inputs as well. The contracts of the co-operative have been relatively trouble-free for both the parties due to the nature of the crop involved and the nature of the organisation to a large extent. The mustard crop is risk free crop, does not require heavy use of costly inputs like pesticides, fertilisers and even irrigation in general, and under contracts in particular, as the crop is to be grown organically. Therefore, the farmer risk is low as sunk costs are low, and the cost to the farmers is land rent only as the opportunity to grow another crop is not lost due to the fact that it is a two-month in between crop. The organisation is para-statal, though co-operative by name, which means that it is not very commercial and profit hungry and is supposed to represent the farmer interest. Thus, the profit pressure on the organisation is not very high, at least from the procurement side. The member relations with the co-operative are very commercial and specific as the co-operative is not really member or user controlled and owned.

From the producers' point of view, specific points to be considered in negotiating the contract terms include the method of determining the producers' price, adjustments for quality differentials, allowance for climatic variations, credit terms, provisions for renewal and termination of contracts and for arbitration (Hill and Ingersent, 1982). A legal protection to contract growers as a group is must to protect them from ill-effects of contracting (Wilson, 1986). There is legal protection given to subcontracting industries in Japan in their relations with large firms. This set of laws specify the duties (to have a written clear terms contract with the subcontractor) and forbidden acts for the large parent firm. The forbidden acts include refusal to receive delivery of commissioned goods, delaying the payment beyond agreed period, discounting of payment, returning commissioned goods without good reason, forced price reduction, compulsory purchase by subcontractors of parental firm's products, and forcing subcontractors to pay in advance for materials supplied by the parent firm. And, these provisions are monitored by the Fair Trade Commission. Interestingly, most of the violations by parent firms were on the written form of contracts and clear terms of the contracts (Sako, 1992). Similarly, tobacco laws were amended in Uganda to protect the grower and the company interests under contracts (Coulter et. al., 1999). If contract farming is nothing but the flexible production systems prevalent in industry applied to farm production, then it is only logical to extend the legal provisions with necessary modifications to farming contracts.

The co-operative has been entangled in legal cases with the contract growers and this has led to lack of genuine partnership between the co-operative and the growers. As an alternative to legal battles, there can be a quasi-judicial system at the local level (panchayat, district administration) to monitor the contracts and resolve any conflict with appropriate penalties to any of the defaulting parties. There has to be a general code of conduct for both the parties in order to avoid conflicts and breaking down of contracts. There should also be incentives for better quality, timing and care of the crop. At the co-operative level, it is often desirable to plan and provide inputs across a wide range of activities and not just for the raw material needed. Given small land holdings, it is all the more important that the farmer benefits on a scale that motivates him to do better. This is achieved through a combination of technology, service and networking. Technology involves providing the best inputs and proper harvest and post-harvest conditions. Service ensures that the resources are made available in time and the post-harvest off take is efficient. Networking assures government support, infrastructure, banking facilities, etc. (Datta, 1996). Profit sharing with farmers through certain other arrangements can also be useful step to ensure better contracting. Farmer training and participation in management are some of the other ways of managing contracts better.

## References

Coulter, Jonathan, Andrew Goodland, Anne Tallontire and Rachel Stringfellow: "Marrying Farmer Cooperation and Contract Farming for Service Provision in a Liberalising Sub-Saharan Africa", *Natural Resource Perspectives, ODI*, No. 48, November, 1999.

Datta, SM: "Linkages with Agriculture - The Experience of the Food Processing Industry", *The Economic Times*, June 26, 1996, Ahmedabad.

Harris, Andrea, Brenda Stefanson, and Murray Fultaon: "New Generation Co-operatives and Co-operative Theory", *Journal of Cooperatives*, Volume II, 1996.

Hinman L. Donald, Donald J. Ricks: "Co-operatives, Marketing Orders and the Coordination of Supply and Demand for Perennial Crops in the U.S.", in Csaba Csaki and Yoan Kislev (eds.) *Agricultural Co-operatives in Transition*, Westview Press, Boulder, U.S.A., 1993.

Konings, Piet: "Unilever, Contract Farmers and Co-operatives in Cameroon: Crisis and Response", *The Journal of Peasant Studies*, 26 (1) October, 1998.

Singh, Sukhpal: "Managing Marketing: Co-operatives in Horticultural Business in South Gujarat", *Indian Journal of Agricultural Marketing*, 11 (1&2), 1997.

Singh, Sukhpal: "Managing Farming Contracts: Concept, Problems and Strategies", *Paradigm*, 2(2), January, 1999.

## Table 12.1

## Average and Range of Schooling (years), of Land Owned, of Land Leased, of Land Operated, of Land Under Contract (all in Acres), and of Experience of Contracting (years) of Markfed Contract Growers

| *Parameter* | *Average* |
|---|---|
| Years of schooling | 12.08 (10-17) |
| Land owned | 21.33 (0-70) |
| Land leased | 7.75 (0-25) |
| Land Operated | 29.08 (10-95) |
| Land under Contract | 6.08 (3-10) |
| Years under Contract | 6.42 (1-23) |

*Note:* The figures in parentheses are the range (minimum and maximum) for each parameter.

*Source:* (tables 12.1-12.3): Primary survey

## Table 12.2

## Distribution of Growers by Type of Crop Failure

| *Type of crop Failure* | *No. of farmers* | *Per cent* |
|---|---|---|
| Lower Yield | 1 | 8.3 |
| Total Failure | 2 | 16.7 |
| No problem | 9 | 75 |
| All | 12 | 100 |

## Table 12.3

## Distribution of Growers by Reasons for Crop Failure

| *Reasons for crop failure* | *No. of farmers* | *Per cent* |
|---|---|---|
| Disease/Pest | 1 | 8.3 |
| Seed Failure | 2 | 16.7 |
| No | 9 | 75 |
| All | 12 | 100 |

## Appendix –12.1

# Profile of Farming Contract of Markfed

| | *Contract Feature* | *Specification* |
|---|---|---|
| 1. | Type of Contract | Quantity, right to change quantity with company |
| 2. | Quality | Specified crop variety, colour, not too ripe, disease free, soft stem, no flowers and roots, quality check, quality cut beyond 10% spoilage, company decision on quality final, quality based price, rejected produce to be taken back by farmer at own cost, or company removes it at farmer cost, no payment for rejected produce |
| 3. | Delivery terms | Specified upto a date, supplies per day specified, right to change quantity with company, market fee to be borne by company |
| 4. | Price | Yes |
| 5. | Inputs on credit | No input supply |
| 6. | Technical support free of cost | Yes |
| 7. | Sales only to company | Not specified |
| 8. | Weighment only on company weighbridge | Yes |
| 9. | Compensation | No |
| 10. | Company liability for failure to buy | Not mentioned |
| 11. | Farmer default | Not specified |
| 12. | Payment | Not specified |
| 13. | Period of contract | Not specified |
| 14. | Farmer incentive | No |
| 15. | Arbitration | Company M.D. or his representative, his decision final for both parties |
| 16. | Signatures on contract form | Both the parties |
| 17. | Copy of the contract form with the grower | Yes |

*Source:* Contract agreement of Markfed (in local language).

## Appendix 12.2

# Markfed Canneries, Jalandhar No: Mk/purchase

Name:

Sir,

With reference to the meeting held on (date) ....... Markfed Canneries give you a contract to supply ......... (MT) of Saag by (date) ........ which will be purchased at Rs. .... per quintal at the canneries. Markfed canneries will pay the market fee for that.

1. Mustard Saag should be of Rai or Gobhi variety. It should be soft and green. It should be free from yellow leaves, damaged colour or any other foreign elements like grass. The leaves should not be infected with insects, pests or any other disease or attack. It should not be too ripe and be without roots and flowers. It should be harvested in such a manner that the roots and stems should be removed.
2. The acceptable material should be of such quality that atleast 90% of it should be usable. The poor quality produce beyond 10% limit will be penalised with quality cut.
3. Immediately after the Saag reaches the canneries, the Markfed canneries representative, in front of the farmer, will check the quality of produce. His decision will be acceptable to both the canneries and the farmer. Based on this quality assessment, the price will be determined.
4. The damaged or rejected produce will have to be taken back by the farmer at his own cost. If the farmer does not take that produce, the cannery will arrange to get the produce removed at the farmer's cost, recover the cost from the farmer and the farmer will not be paid any money for that produce.

5. The produce will be weighed on the weighbridge of the canneries.
6. The farmer has to supply the produce on the date given in the purchase agreement and that will be 6,000 kgs. per day. The supply of produce before or after the date will not be acceptable.
7. Markfed canneries has the right to increase or decrease the quantity of produce.
8. Any dispute arising out of the agreement will be put before the M.D., Markfed or his representative, who will be arbitrator and whose decision will be binding on both the parties.

I accept the above given conditions.

Signature of farmer Manager
Markfed Canneries
Jalandhar

# 13

# Contract Farming of Seed in India: A Study of Private and Public Sector Performance*

## 1. Introduction

The commercial seed sector in India grew considerably in the late 1980s and the early 1990s, both in the private and the public sectors, though Indian seed business accounts for only two percent of global seed business (*Spice* 2002). But, by the end of 1990s, the value of seed market in India was estimated to be close to US$ one billion which was only half this size in the early 1990s (Ramaswami 2002). The private seed sector growth was induced by the policy changes undertaken during the late 1980s which included allowing import of commercial seed, parent seed, and germplasm for vegetables, coarse grains and oilseeds; allowing formal access to public lines by private companies wherein they could buy breeder's seeds from public research institutes; and relaxation of private investments in seed sector in terms of joint ventures, technical collaboration, and entry of large domestic firms and Multi-National Corporations (MNCs). This led to more than 100 new cotton hybrid varieties being released in 1996 alone, and the share of the private sector in total seed business went up significantly though the volume of the private seed trade grew much less than its growth in value terms (Gisselquist *et al.* 2002). This is due to the fact that the private sector sells more of high value hybrids (Ramaswami 2002). Much of this growth has stemmed from either foreign investments or spin-offs from previous Indian private companies, with technical and marketing personnel branching off to start

---

* Earlier published under the same title in the Indian Journal of Agricultural Marketing, 18(1), 2004, without appendices.

their own seed enterprises. For example, one seed company - Mahyco - which is the largest private sector company in India with 200 hybrid seed varieties of 30 crops and works with 10 lakh contract growers, has given birth to at least 8 additional companies (Basant 1995; Mahyco website).

Presently, there are more than 200 seed firms in India of which 30 percent have global partners (*Spice* 2002) and there are more than one lakh dealers and distributors of seeds across the country. About 30 of these firms are Multi-National Corporations (MNCs) and domestic corporate firms, and the rest small companies and seed production organisers and traders. In fact, the three national

seed associations have more than 300 members, with a large number of them being individual seedproducers, and many small seed companies are not members of these associations (Gisselquist *et al.* 2002). Besides this, there are state level associations of seed companies. There are a few co-operatives as well in some states which produce seed. There has also been some growth of seed business in terms of seed producers growing into seed traders, traders/dealers becoming seed organisers and seed producers, and even seed organisers setting up small seed companies or becoming traders of seed (Tripp and Pal 2001).

The public sector, consisting mainly of National Seeds Corporation (NSC) and 13 State Seeds Corporations (SSCs), and accounting for 35-40 percent of total turnover of seed industry, is mostly engaged in production and distribution of seeds of cereal, pulse, and oilseed crops. The private sector on the other hand is mainly involved in the business of hybrid seeds of maize, jowar, bajra, cotton, and high value crops like vegetables. It accounts for about 60-65 percent of the total turnover of the seed industry. The SSCs also buy seeds from private sector. For example, Andhra Pradesh State Seed Development Corporation (APSSDC) buys 20 per cent of its seeds from the private sector (Shiva and Crompton 1998). This means that a significant amount of public sector sales is attributable to the private sector. Within the private sector, there are MNCs, large domestic firms, small seed companies and producer-traders accounting for 30 percent, 50 percent and 20 percent of total private sector seed business respectively. But, yet, for the main crops, i.e., paddy and wheat, it is the seed saved from the previous harvest which accounts for a very large part (60-90 per cent) of the seed requirements of these crops (Sidhu 1999; Ramaswami 2002; Pal and Tripp 2002).

Profitability being the major consideration for private sector firms, they provide only those types of seed for which there is effective demand and adequate profits. This means varieties which need to be replaced by farmers every season and which are popular with farmers. These are also varieties with high multiplication rates and controlled breeding systems. Thus, private seed companies deal with a limited number of varieties and seed is sold in standard pack sizes for targeted categories of farmers. These companies also keep changing their markets and products more often than the public sector (Cromwell 1996). The private industry also plays a leading role in the development of planting material through bio-technology and tissue culture (Chauhan 1997). Major competition among the organised sector players is in the crops of cotton, maize, sorghum, pearl millet, sunflower, flowers, and vegetables.

Seed firms, whether in the public or the private sector, contract out the seed production to the independent growers who are supplied foundation seed to produce commercial seed. The seed industry is one of the earliest examples of contract farming in India. It is a very well entrenched system of production in this industry and relatively more successful and stable as compared to that in many other sectors like milk or horticulture crops where it is of more recent origin. This chapter examines the seed production arrangements, in particular, contract farming in seed sector across types of firms and draws lessons for suitable production system for the industry for its all round development. The second section explains the concept and logic of contract farming. A general picture of contract farming system in the seed sector is drawn in the third section. The agencies whose performance is studied in this paper are profiled in the fourth section. A comparative assessment of their contracts and performance is made in the fifth section. The final section concludes the paper with lessons from the experiences of the private and public sectors in contract production of seed.

### 3. Seed Production Systems in India

Given the Land Ceiling Act in India, the seed firms cannot own and cultivate land for seed production. Therefore, the only options for agribusiness firms to procure desired quality seeds are to grow seeds on leased land or have contractual arrangements with the primary producers. Under the lease system, the entire expenses of production are borne by the company and the output from the leased land is processed and packed at company's cost. When a company introduces new varieties, the grower may not be willing to undertake certified seed production as the new varieties are not tested. In those cases, companies tend to undertake certified seed production through lease system. Proagro follows this system (Singh and Asokan 1997).

Contract farming of seed in India is currently being practised by multinational firms like Pepsi, Cargill, Sandoz, and Advanta India, domestic corporates like Rallis India, Indo-American Hybrid Seeds (IAHS), Mahyco, Navbharat Seeds, Nath Seeds, Ankur Seeds, and Namdhari Seeds, and various statal and para-statal corporations, with varying degrees of success. The seed companies and seed corporations have been able to use the contract system successfully as they work with a few farmers over a smaller area, and the small costs incurred by the companies are recovered more easily. The National Seeds Corporation (NSC) still works with 7,000 farmers under contracts despite its role being superseded by the SSCs which also practice contract farming. The NSC produces about 100 open pollinated varieties of vegetable seeds over an area of 9 lakh hectares compared to 15 lakh hectares by the entire private seed sector in India, besides dealing in 75 crops and 420 varieties (*Spice* 2002).

Two alternative approaches are in vogue under the contract system. One, growers are selected from a number of villages scattered over a large area as is the case with many small seed companies and the SSCs. Secondly, a few villages are selected for intensive coverage of farmers as in the case of Advanta India Ltd (formerly ITC Zeneca). which offers a seed village scheme under which 5000 farmers produce seeds from the parental line seeds supplied by the company.

The seed enterprises enter into a contract with the growers for production and supply of quality seed of some specified acreage. The growers bear all costs including cost of parent/ foundation seed, cost of cultivation, quality monitoring cost, transporting seed to the processing plant, and wastages and losses at the farm, and in transit, grading and packaging. They also bear all risks like low germination, reduced yield, poor quality, and rejections. They are paid a pre-agreed price only after the quality of seed is tested and for only the quantity that passes those tests. Normally, it takes about 60 days to get payment. The companies take care of their risk of crop failure by planning 10-20 per cent more acreage than required (Singh and Asokan 1997). Sometimes, companies give incentive for better germination rate and better quality of seed production. The default rates of contract growers have been low as they are assured grain price for seed crop at least and yields are better than grain crops (Shiva and Crompton 1998). Further, there are two systems for contract production of seeds:

(i) Subcontracted Procurement: Under this arrangement, certified seed is produced by the seed growers under contracts to 'small companies' or 'seed production organisers'. J K Agrigenetics in Secunderabad is one of the seed companies that follow this system. They have collaboration with Raasi Seeds of Tamil Nadu for procuring the raw seed. Raasi Seeds procures the raw seed from the seed growers. Processing of the raw seed is done in a custom processing plant which is close to the production area. The packaged seed is marketed by JK Agrigenetics under its brand name. Sandoz also contracts out seed procurement to local seed company and does not enter into written contracts with farmers or guarantee a price. The MNCs like Unilever and Cargill source certified seeds from India through a network of seed production organisers who pass on the inputs supplied by the company to the contract growers and collect seeds, conduct tests and give them to the MNCs. This is quite common in Andhra Pradesh in cotton, sunflower and jowar seed sectors (IGS 1997). The seed production organisers identify growers and secure their area commitment for seed production during the season. They also guide the growers in the proper use of input and, sometimes, extend credit for seed crop. The minimum procurement price and commission to be paid to the organisers is decided at the annual meeting conducted between the representatives of the Seedmen Association (a representative body of various seed companies) and the seed production organisers. The services, financial and non-financial, provided by the company to the grower and by the organiser to the grower vary across companies and from time to time. The organisers, who undertake seed production in an area of more than 500 acres, generally employ a sub-organiser under them so as to facilitate better monitoring and implementation of the programme.

The organiser arranges for required number of technical staff to conduct periodic field inspections at various stages of growth of seed crop. It is the duty of the organiser to ensure completion of the required number of field inspections by the seed certification staff at proper growth stages. The organiser arranges for the completion of all formalities and conditions for getting the seed certified from the concerned agency and informs the progress to the company. He supplies the requisite number of sample bags, slips for packing, packing seals, marking ink etc. and the cost, thereof, is borne by the organiser. The organiser bears the expenses pertaining to cost of tags, field test charges and all other incidental expenses to be incurred for the purpose of getting seed certified by the State Seed Certification Agency (SSCA). The organiser informs the company about the details of the mechanised processing facilities along with intake capacity and storage space prior to processing season. The organiser supplies the certified seeds in standard pack sizes. The company supplies printed cloth bags and truthful labels for packing of the certified seed at its cost. However, for transporting the raw seed from the grower's field to the processing plant, gunny bags are supplied by the organiser/company. The expenses of processing are borne either by the organiser or the grower. There is no standard trade practice in this regard. If the organiser bears the processing expenses, then he gets a higher commission from the company. In the case of large and medium seed companies, the processing operation is undertaken under the close supervision of the company's representatives. Some of the statal agencies, like the Gujarat State Seed Corporation, organise seed production and procure seeds through Primary Agricultural Co-operative Societies (PACS) at the village level, and there are contract agreements with both individual farmers as well as the society (Singh and Asokan 1997).

(ii) Direct Contract Farming: Under this arrangement, a seed company enters into an agreement with the seed growers directly for procuring the raw seed. The NSC, SSCs and private companies follow this system. Most of the farmers put small acreage under contract which is as low as 0.25 acres in cotton in the case of small companies as it is labour intensive production. Cargil guarantees a fixed price but farmers have to follow strict practices prescribed by the company. The MNC prices for seed have been higher than those offered by the local seed companies. The contract growers are registered with the seed certification agencies as subgrowers. The cost of foundation seed in the case of private companies is deducted while disbursing the payment for the raw seed. However, in the case of NSC or SSC, foundation seed is supplied on cash and carry basis. Any subsidy given by the government is passed on to the growers. Generally, the grower arranges at his expense all operations and is required to follow the seed production practices prescribed by the company from time to time. The national and state seed corporations do not supply fertilisers or pesticides to the grower but may render reasonable assistance to the growers in securing the necessary credit from the cooperative/commercial banks nominated by the corporation against terms and conditions laid down by the lending bank. However, some private companies supply pesticides and fertilisers to the farmers on credit and lend money to the growers when the crop requires very high investment, e.g, cottonseed. This amount and the interest (18–24 percent) are recovered from the growers at the time of making payment for the raw seed. Generally, it is the grower who arranges to transport the raw seed to the processing plant of the company at his own cost in the gunny bags provided by the company after harvesting the crop. However, in some cases, the company provides transportation cost to the grower.

The seed lots are tested for germination, genetic purity, physical purity, disease incidence, moisture content, and inert matter at the companies' quality control laboratories or at the Government Seed Testing Laboratory. The lots indicating variation over and above tolerance limits prescribed are subjected to retesting. If the seed is rejected at the quality test, the loss is borne mainly by the grower. If the seed is found rain damaged or the container is found damaged or torn and unsealed during the transit, the grower is not entitled for any payment for such rejected/damaged seeds. The rejected seeds can be used for food/feed or for sale to other agencies for edible/non-edible purposes. The minimum procurement price for the seed crop in most of the states is decided by the representatives of the industry, e.g., in Andhra Pradesh, the AP Seedsmen Association (which has

147 seed companies as members), seed production organisers, and the growers decide the prices. However, this rate varies and is dependent on the demand and supply factors to a larger extent, and each company may have its own rate with the growers. But, generally the seed price is higher than the price of the crop output in the grain/agricultural produce market. The contract growers are to supply the entire produce of seeds to the company under contract at the agreed price and time. Though there is generally a clause in the contract for penalty for default, it is rarely implemented due to practical difficulties. The SSCs and companies pay about 80 percent of the price at the time of seed procurement and the remaining 20 percent after the seed passes the final quality test (Kumar and Barua 1998).

## 4. Profiles of Seed Agencies

(i) Tarai Development Corporation (TDC): It was established at Pantnagar in Uttar Pradesh in 1969 with assistance of the World Bank. Functioning under the name of Uttar Pradesh Seeds and Tarai Development Corporation (UPS&TDC) since its restructuring in 1973, it has enormously increased the infrastructure and diversified its production. It became a model for other state seed corporations established in the 1970s and the 1980s (Ramaswami, 2002). At present, it produces 161 varieties of 52 crops including 51 varieties of 28 vegetables and has 14 seed processing plants and its own seed-testing laboratory. The corporation is an autonomous institution. The farmers contribute about 33% of the total share capital (Shiva *et.al.* 2000).

(ii) Andhra Pradesh State Seed Development Corporation (APSSDC): Set up in 1976, it produces and markets seeds of more than 15 crops, though rice accounts for 80 per cent of its total seed production (Tripp and Pal 2001). It provides 20-25 per cent of the total seed requirements of the state, of which 40 percent is hybrid and mainly procured from private sector. The remaining seed is produced by some 6000 farmers (Shiva and Crompton 1998). About 2/3 of these farmers are shareholders in the corporation. It has 17 processing centres in the state (Tripp and Pal 2001).

(iii) Gujarat State Seed Corporation (GSSC): Set up in 1975 to produce and market certified seed, the GSSC has inherited and retained the earlier system of organizing seed production through the primary agricultural credit societies at the village level. It produces a wide range of crops, the major ones being cotton, castor, bajra, paddy and wheat. It has 15 branch offices and staff strength of 232 comprising mainly seed officers, seed supervisors and production specialists besides managerial staff at the head office and branch levels. It worked with about 10,000 registered growers in the mid 90s with an average seed plot of a grower being 0.9 hectares varying from 0.1 hectare in the case of cotton to as much as 5.8 hectares in mustard. It harvested 38 per cent of the total area offered ranging from 96 per cent in wheat to as low as 28 per cent in sesamum in 1993-94. The co-operative link gives the GSSC the advantage of farmer commitment to supply seed, better co-ordinated procurement and transport and resolves the problem of isolation for seed production which helps it meet the procurement targets (Singh and Asokan 1997).

(iv) Navbharat Seeds Pvt. Limited: It. is a small seed company set up in 1982. by a former employee of Mahyco. Its turnover is Rs. 11 crore and it owns a seed processing plant. It produces seeds of cotton, bajra, mustard, guar, castor and okra. It organizes seed production in the states of Andhra Pradesh, Karnataka, Gujarat and Maharashtra under written contracts with 2000 seed growers. The company has seed testing facilities in Gujarat and Maharashtra. It is a member of the Gujarat Seed Producers' Association which has 65 members and which determines seed procurement price. The contract default rate varies from nil to 20 percent depending on the crop condition. The company has about 30% of the seed lines based on its own research, except cotton, where it is only 10%.

(v) Pepsi Foods Limited: It is a subsidiary of the US MNC Pepsico which has a large network of operations in India. Frito-Lay, Pepsi's salty snack company which was formed in 1961 and owns Pepsi Foods in India, now accounts for 2/3$^{rd}$ of its revenues, 50 per cent of the US market for salty snacks, and is the largest salty snacks company in the world (Usborne 1999). It has the experience of contract farming and potato processing from countries of Mexico, Egypt and China. In fact, its successful entry into Mexico is a classic example of a company beating the stringent local laws wherein it used the routes of Non Profit Organisation (NPO) to import seed and of partnership with farmers to produce seeds of potato and improve the raw material for its chips plants in Mexico (Singh 1997). The contract farming in seed potato in India by Pepsi started in 1997-98 for the first time with 5 imported varieties from USA through the Central Potato Research Institute (CPRI), Shimla, which were later multiplied locally and at the company's 12-acre farm. The contract seed producers are very few in number (10-12).

## 5. A Comparative Assessment of Contracts and Performance

The contract systems adopted by different seed companies differ in their provisions so far as the relationship with farmer is concerned (Shiva and Crompton 1998). These are procurement and input contracts, under which the companies not only agree to pick up the contracted quality and quantity/acreage produce at a pre-agreed price and time, but also provide inputs like seed on part credit, and technical advice on planting, crop care, and harvesting. The grower is to bear all costs and risks of seed production. The contracts of public and private agencies are, by and large, similar in nature so far as bias against the grower is concerned (Appendix 15.1). This bias reflects the asymmetry in the relationship between the two parties. But, the APSSDC contract is very detailed and in conventional legal language (Appendix 15.2). On the other hand, the contracts of private agencies are brief thereby providing scope for disputes (Appendix 15.3 and 15.4). Similarly, while in the case of APSSDC, there is penalty for defaults by the firm, the Pepsi and Navbharat contracts do not even mention this aspect. Further, the public agency contracts are of longer duration and have more stringent acreage conditions. But, they also offer more benefits to the farmers in terms of input provision and service orientation. As against this, the private contracts offer more differentiated, quality based prices, incentives and faster payment. They are quicker in dealing with issues like lifting of rejected seed from the processing plant.

The TDC provides 20 percent of the total requirement of certified seed in India and 80 per cent of that of the state of U.P. It has also won National Productivity Award five times (Shiva *et.al.* 2000). The TDC's emergence as a powerful seed certifying and seed distribution agency in the Tarai is well recognized. Similarly, the APSSDC is one of the better-managed seed corporations in India (Tripp and Pal 2001). It paid 8 per cent dividend to the farmer shareholders in 1996-97 (Shiva and Crompton 1998). Whereas Navbharat is doing well in terms of expanding its seed production base, Pepsi Foods is working only with a handful of farmers and despite the fact that it has a potato chips plant, it is not expanding its procurement base or seed production base.

## 6. Conclusions

That vertically integrated co-operatives or co-operative like structures are very relevant for development of seed industry is shown by the experiences of the Dutch and the Northern Ireland seed potato industries which were at two extremes of the vertical integration spectrum - the former being a totally vertically integrated and the latter not integrated at all. The former was able to grow and sustain in market due to its vertical structure largely, wherein its marketing effectiveness was facilitated greatly by its vertically integrated system (Lamont 1992). The TDC example signifies that with the help of farmer participation, an agency can achieve remarkable success. By lending the farmers the necessary technical support, the corporation has earned the goodwill of the local people. The farmers being the producers as wel1 as consumers of seeds are at the centre of all decisions. The Corporation, thus, is run with the motto of "an organisation of the farmers, for the farmers and by the farmers". The bond is so strong that the farmers see TDC as the only reliable source of seed in the Tarai region. The public or co-operative agencies have been found to be as good in quality as the private seed companies, and benefit farmers directly as they are shareholders in these agencies (Tripp and Pal 2001). Also, they provide fair competition in the market in the absence of which private sector could take the farmers for a ride. Therefore, there is a need to maintain and encourage vertically co-ordinated structures, with protection of contract grower interest, in contract seed production in India.

## References

Basant, Rakesh (1995) "Seed Industry in India- Issues Arising from GATT", *Vikalpa*, 20 (40), pp.21-41.

Chauhan, K. K. S. (1997) "Input Demand and Supply Scenario in Indian Agriculture", *Agricultural Economics Research Review*, 10(2), pp. 139-161.

Cromwell, E. (1996) *Governments, Farmers and Seeds in a Changing Africa*. Wallingford (U.K.): CAB International.

Gisselquist, D., John Nash, and Carl Pray (2002) "Deregulating the Transfer of Agricultural Technology: Lessons from Bangladesh, India, Turkey, and Zimbabwe", *The World Bank Research Observer*, 17(2), Fall 2002, pp. 237-265.

http://www.mahyco.com

IGS (India Grameen Services) (1997): *Sub-Sector Profile: Agricultural Inputs and Services*. Hyderbad: IGS, Basix.

Kumar, D.L. Raghava and Suparna Barua (1998) "Study of Production, Logistics and Marketing System of the Seed Industry in A.P", MTS Report No. 1239, Anand: Institute of Rural Management (IRMA).

Lamont, J. T. J. (1992) "Agricultural Marketing Systems: Horizontal and Vertical Integration in the Seed Potato Industry", *British Food Journal*, 94(8), pp. 3-15.

Pal, Suresh and Robert Tripp (2002) "India's Seed Industry Reforms: Prospects and Issues", *Indian Journal of Agricultural Economics*, 57(3), July-September, pp. 443-458.

Ramaswami, Bharat (2002) "Understanding the Seed Industry: Contemporary Trends and Analytical Issues", *Indian Journal of Agricultural Economics*, 57(3), July-September, pp. 417-429.

Shiva, Vandana, Afsar H Jafri, Ashok Emani and Manish Pande (2000): *Seeds of Suicide – The Ecological and Human Costs of Globalisation of Agriculture*. New Delhi: Research Foundation for Science, Technology and Ecology, December.

Sidhu, M. S. (1999) "Impact of Intellectual Property Rights on the Indian Seed Industry", *Indian Journal of Agricultural Economics*, 54 (3), July-September, pp. 370-379.

Singh, Gurdev and S. R. Asokan (1997) *Management of Seed Production Activity*. New Delhi: Oxford &IBH.

Singh, Sukhpal (1997) "Multinational Enterprises and Agribusiness Sector in Developing Economies – A Case Study of Pepsi in India" in K J Azam (ed.): *Economic Liberalisation in India-Implications for Indo-US Relations*. Hyderabad:Delta.

Singh, Sukhpal (2000) "Theory and Practice of Contract Farming: A Review", *Journal of Social and Economic Development*, 2(2), pp. 228-246.

*Spice* (2002) "Seed Business: Indian Scenario", 1(2), November.

Tripp, R. and Suresh Pal (2001) "The Private Delivery of Public Crop Varieties: Rice in Andhra Pradesh", *World Development*, 29 (1), pp. 103-117.

Usborne, D. (1999) "The Pepsi regeneration" *The Independent*, London, July 21, Business review, p. 3.

Welsh, Rick (1997) "Vertical Co-ordination, Producer Response, and the Locus of Control over Agricultural Production Decisions", *Rural Sociology*, 62(4), pp. 491-507.

## Appendix 13.1

# A Comparative Profile of Contracts of Public and Private Sector Seed Agencies

| *Aspect of Contract* | *APSSDC* | *GSSC* | *TDC* | *Navbharat Seeds (Castor)* | *Pepsi Foods (Potato)* |
|---|---|---|---|---|---|
| Status of growers | Shareholders | Sub-growers | Shareholders | Growers and sub-growers | Growers |
| Nature and duration of contract | Two contracts (Principal and seasonal), 3 years with 3 month notice to withdraw | Seasonal | Seasonal | Seasonal | Seasonal for 8 months |
| Acreage and other growing conditions | Acreage proportionate to shares held; good quality land in compact area within 3 km radius; if area below managerial limits, company right to reject area; single crop raising; isolation requirement to be met | Specified reserved acreage | Acreage specified by the company | Acreage specified by the company; No other crop upto 150 meters in the surrounding of contract crop; collection of seed by grower at own cost from company godown | Specified acreage, ownership and possession of land must; exclusive use of land for contract seed production |
| Farm operations and grower obligations | Seed to be sown within 10 days of purchase; all expenses by grower, grower to follow all prescribed practices; To extend all facilities to company/inspection agency for notified/ un-notified varieties | Entire cost of seed production by growers: only specified number of plants in field | To follow all instructions | One month specified sowing time; to follow all instructions; to follow all recommended practices; distribution of seeds to the sub-growers by main grower, seeds to be kept ready for sampling | All farm operation costs to be borne by grower; to follow all instructions as per company manual; planting and harvesting at company instance; grower to give all cooperation to company |

| Aspect of Contract | APSSDC | GSSC | TDC | Navbharat Seeds (Castor) | Pepsi Foods (Potato) |
|---|---|---|---|---|---|
| Product delivery and default | Entire produce to be delivered to the company in processed and packaged form meeting quality standards, damage liability for defaults | Transport cost to be borne by growers | Not specified | Farmer to deliver seeds at company godown within 2 days of sampling; seed to be kept ready for sampling during specified 10 days; sample to be given free of cost by grower | Transport cost from farm to cold store to be borne by company, default to be made good by grower and may lead to contract termination |
| Price | Only minimum guaranteed price specified in seasonal contracts | Specified | Based on opportunity cost of seed production | As fixed by the Gujarat State Seeds Corporation | Grade- wise specified price |
| Payment | All at Hyderabad within 45 days after procurement or 90 days of arrival of unprocessed seed at processing centre whichever is later, interest to be paid for delayed payment | Through PACSs within 40 days of seed test results | Within a week from the date of delivery of seed at regional offices | Within 30 days after clearing of seed by certification agency | Payment to be made by cheque / draft within two weeks of receipt of seed |
| Rejected seed | To be lifted within 15 days at own cost, otherwise company can dispose off to recover dues | To be removed by grower at his cost | Not specified | To be cleared by the main grower within 7 days, otherwise sold by company as commercial crop and costs recovered | Company right to buy rejected seed at market price |
| Other support; Advance against procurement | Company help to get credit from banks and to give dues directly to bank if required by agreement between grower and bank; advance to be repaid within 15 days of notice | Supply of parent seed through PACSs | Transport rebate for bringing seed to the processing centres; sometimes advance given | Company to give bags at specified time | Supply of parent seed |

| Aspect of Contract | APSSDC | GSSC | TDC | Navbharat Seeds (Castor) | Pepsi Foods (Potato) |
|---|---|---|---|---|---|
| Contract cancellation | Company free to withdraw from contract if finds farmer has committed serious breach but given a chance to explain | Not specified | Not specified | Not specified | On default to deliver |
| Nomination | Payment to nominee in case of death | Not specified | No | No | No |
| Registration and certification of growers and inspection fees | Grower to apply for with fees at the time of seed purchase; To be paid in advance and un-refundable | Certification and test fees to be paid by grower | Company help in the registration of growers with certification agencies | Grower to pay all specified charges of regn. inspection, certification and testing at the time of agreement | Not specified |
| Seed purchase & payment, and Dues recovery | Only from company, payment in advance, non-refundable except if quality is defective and reported within 20 days of sowing; due recovery from price payment; Seed cannot be transferred to other growers and to be sown only in reserved area unless permitted otherwise, use of carry over seeds only with permission but no company liability | Only from GSSC, all dues recovered from final payment, seed not to be sold to anyone or market. | Only from company, first instalment of payment immediately on delivery, final payment after processing and quality test, through DD at par free of charge | Only from company, payment to be made after purchase and weighing at company godown within 30 days of clearing of seeds; collective responsibility of all village growers to pay dues | Only from company |
| Delivery of seeds | At grower cost in his gunny bags | At grower cost in new bags | At collection centres, free gunny bag to growers by company | Not specified | At grower cost in his gunny bags |

| Aspect of Contract | APSSDC | GSSC | TDC | Navbharat Seeds (Castor) | Pepsi Foods (Potato) |
|---|---|---|---|---|---|
| Quality maintenance obligation | No company liability for deterioration until finally processed | Farmer obligation to maintain quality of seed | Not specified | Seed purchase only after germination and grow out test, poor grading penalty of Rs. 1/- per kg., decision of the company on seed quality final | Quality aspects specified, if variation exceeds 5 per cent, seed to be rejected |
| Reprocessing and retesting | At grower expenses and only once | Allowed at cost only once | Not specified | No retesting | Not specified |
| Quality | Colour, insect free, raw, damage free, physical appearance and foreign matter | GSSC decision final | Not specified | Company right to retain rejected seed at Rs. 10/- per kg. less within a week of intimation of rejection | Decision on grading at discretion of company |
| Other conditions | Grower to use certification tags and seals supplied by company/ certification agency | Free samples to be supplied at grower cost; grower to abide by any terms and conditions introduced by GSSC from time to time | Not specified | Main producer liable for sub-producers | Potato seed produced and other related material on the farm exclusive property of the company and to be disposed off only with the permission of the company |
| Incentives | Nil | Nil | Nil | Early sample lots given bonus | Incentive for higher multiplication rate |
| Final decision | Not specified | GSSC and binding | Not specified | Company M.D. | Not specified |
| Jurisdiction | Hyderabad | Not specified | Lucknow | Ahmedabad | Delhi |
| Signing of agreement | Company representative, grower/shareholder, witnesses | By grower and PACSs representatives only | Grower and Company representative | Growers and sub-growers, and the Company representatives | Grower, Company with witnesses |

*Source*: Contract agreements of companies/agencies.

## Appendix 13.2

# Principal Agreement

Agreement between the APSSDC Ltd. and the Grower Shareholder

This agreement is made this...... day of ....... One thousand nine hundred and ninety...... between the APSSDC Ltd. (herein after called 'The Corporation' which expression shall unless excluded by or repugnant to the subject or context, be deemed to include its successors and assigns) of the one part and Shri/ Kumari/Shrimathi .......... S/o. w/o. d/o ......... village ..........P.O. ......... District ...........

(herein after called the "Grower shareholder" which organisation shall, unless excluded by or repugnant to the subject or context, be deemed to include his successors and assigns) of the other part.

Whereas the parties have agreed to undertake production of seeds of the hybrids/varieties. And whereas for this purpose the corporation has been set up with the objects as stated in its Memorandum of association:

And whereas the Grower shareholder has purchased ...... equity shares of the corporation.

Now it is mutually agreed and witnessed as follows:

1. The Grower shareholder shall undertake to participate in the seed production programme of the corporation in proportion to the shares held by him. Provided that in the exigencies of the seed production programme the corporation is at liberty to exclude any grower shareholder from the said programme for any specified season or seasons during the subsistence of the agreement.
2. (a) The grower shareholder shall reserve ....... Acres of land in compact area selected for the purpose, out of his agricultural holding situated in ..... Village ....... Taluk ........

district bearing S. Nos. ......... with and in accordance with the directions of the corporation. The reserved area for seed production should be of levelled, fertile, neutral or nearly neutral and well drained land with facilities for clean and healthy seed production.

(b) The seed project envisages compact approach for facilitating economy, supervision, field inspection etc., in order to ensure quality seed production. It is therefore necessary that the compact area of production should be within a radius of three kilometres. The corporation will decide the size of the seed programme for each crop. In case the area falls below the managerial limits, the corporation will have the right to reject the area.

(c) The reserved area shall be so located that the seed crop in that area will conform to the isolation requirements prescribed in the Indian minimum seed certification standards, March 1971 as amended from time to time (unless otherwise specified in the annexure, if any) failing which the seed crop shall be liable to be rejected in part or full as may be necessary.

(d) The Grower shareholder shall raise the crop as single crop and not as mixed crop, intercrop or companion crop. Nor shall the seed crop be raised as a ratton crop without corporation's prior approval.

(e) The Grower shareholder shall arrange at his expense all operations such as land preparation, sowing, irrigation, interculture, manuring, plant protection, roughing, detasseling (in case of maize) removing pollen shedders (sorghum and bajra), harvesting, shelling/threshing and any other farm operation connected with the raising of the seed crop and shall strictly follow the seed production practices prescribed by the corporation from time to time.

3.(a) The entire produce, as estimated on the basis of crop condition indicated in the final field inspection report from the reserved area and conforming to the prescribed standards shall be offered to the corporation by the grower shareholder who shall not sell or transfer to any one else, the produce eligible for procurement by the corporation. In case of default, the grower shareholder shall be liable to pay the corporation damages amounting to the difference between the corporation's minimum guaranteed price and the sale price fixed by the Corporation for the quantity less offered to the Corporation for procurement than the estimated quantity based on the crop condition or yield of the crop indicated in the final field inspection report.

(b) The corporation shall procure processed and packed seed conforming to the standards referred to in 8 (d) at the minimum guaranteed price as notified by the corporation from time to time, if seed is processed in Corporation's plant or in a plant designated by it.

(c) The minimum guaranteed price is deemed to be all inclusive price and no other claim including taxes if any leviable, shall be entertained. The Corporation shall be entitled to recover the amount due from the grower shareholder from the amount payable to the grower shareholder.

(d) In case, where the corporation allows any advance payment to a grower shareholder against the procurement and in the event the seed lot not finally having been accepted for procurement, the grower shareholder will pay back the advance in full within 15 days of the intimation. Further, if the rejected seed lot is not lifted within 15 days of intimation, the corporation fully reserves the right to dispose off the rejected seed lot at its own discretion and recover the amount advanced as also incidental charges incurred if any for disposal from the defaulting party.

(e) The Corporation shall arrange payment to the grower shareholder within 45 days from the date of procurement or within 90 days from the date of the arrival of the unprocessed seed at the processing centre whichever is later. If the Corporation defaults in payment within the said period, then it shall allow interest at the rates prescribed for term deposit by the schedule banks.

(f) In case of the death of the shareholder, the Corporation shall make the payment of amount due to him, to his nominee Shri .............

Relationship with the Grower:

Address:

4. For seed production of notified varieties/hybrids, the grower shareholder shall submit an application to the Corporation amended for registration for certification as prescribed in the seed rules, 1968 as from the time to time and remit

prescribed fees ....... by cash/DD per application as application fee at the time of the purchase of the foundation seed. The application fee is not refundable.

5. a) Seed to be used for sowing in the reserved area shall be obtained from the corporation only.

(b) The grower shareholder shall pay to the corporation, the seed cost, plus sales tax if applicable, in advance at the rates prescribed, ex-corporation godown(s) and the packing and forwarding charges. The cost of the seed is not refundable except under the provision contained in (5) d.

(c) The grower shareholder shall not sell or transfer the foundation seed obtained from the corporation, in turn to any one for seed production under Corporation's grower shareholder programme and the corporation shall neither be responsible to the receiver of such seed for its quality nor is obliged to entertain such production under its grower shareholder programme. The grower shareholder shall not use the foundation seed obtained from the corporation for sowing, for seed production on areas other than over and above the reserved area without the corporation's prior approval.

(d) The corporation will not take back the seed supplied by it unless the quality of the seed is found to be defective and the same is proved to the corporation's satisfaction and provided further that suitable information to the corporation is made within ten days of receipt of consignment or within 20 days of sowing as the case may be. In such a case either the seed cost (excluding sale tax) may be refunded if the grower shareholder so desires or the defective seed replaced depending on the situation. The corporation is not liable for any defect in the foundation seed if the sowing is not done within ten days from the date of purchase.

(e) Use of carry over seed if any with the grower shareholder for sowing in the reserved areas is permitted provided such seed is intact and unopened in the corporation's original sealed container and provided further that the corporation's prior approval is obtained for its use. The corporation will not be responsible for the germination of the carry over seed. When use of carry-over seed with the grower shareholder is permitted, a fresh seasonal agreement has to be entered into even though the seed might relate to an earlier agreement. Also a fresh application for certification shall be submitted.

6. The grower shareholder shall pay in advance to the corporation, prescribed field inspection fee per acre or part thereof before the seed is supplied by the corporation. The inspection fee shall not be refundable under any circumstance. If the seed obtained from the corporation is sown in different locations separated by 50 metres or more between them, prescribed inspection fees shall be charged for each location and any additional amount which will thus become due should be paid before the first inspection. For sowings made with the corporation's prior approval on areas other than or over and above the reserved area, the prescribed inspection fee should be paid before the first inspection. If use of carry over seed with the grower shareholder is permitted under (5) (e) the grower shareholder shall remit the inspection fee at the prescribed rate before executing the seasonal agreement or before the first inspection.

7. a) The grower shareholder producing seeds of notified kinds/ varieties/hybrids shall render all facilities to both the corporation and the state seed certification agency concerned, for conducting field inspections of the seed crop at any time and at any stage. A seed crop of notified kind/hybrid/ variety found by either the corporation or the State agency or both as not conforming to the standards referred to in 2 (c) shall be liable for rejection by the corporation for the purpose of this agreement.

(b) For seed production of un-notified varieties/hybrids, the grower shareholder shall render all facilities to the corporation for conducting field inspections of the seed crop at any time and at any stage. A seed crop found by the corporation as not conforming to the standards referred to in 2 (c) or any other standards specified by the corporation shall be liable for rejection.

8.( a) The grower shareholder shall arrange to transport at his own cost in his gunny bags the harvested and threshed seed material to the processing plant assigned by the corporation.

(b) Seed only from that part of the reserved area conforming to the standards referred to in 2 (c) shall be processed.

(c) For seed production involving parental lines, the corporation will not process or procure the produce of the male parent.

(d) If after processing in the manner prescribed by the corporation, the seed lot does not conform to the seed standards prescribed in the minimum seed certification standards, March, 1971 as amended from time to time, seed lot will be rejected.

(e) The corporation shall make all possible efforts to expedite processing on the first com-first processed basis. The corporation shall not be responsible for any deterioration in the produce till it is finally procured.

(9. Reprocessing at the grower shareholder's expenses at the rate of Rs. 10/- per quintal or at such other high rates as may be determined by the corporation from time to time is permissible if, according to the first test:

(a) The germination percentage is not less than the standard by more than 10% and/or

(b) The pure seed percentage is less than the standard by not more than 0.50% as the case may be. Re-processing at the corporation's expenses will be done if the pure seed percentage is less than the standard by 0.50% or less. Reprocessing even at the grower shareholder's expenses for any other reason will require the prior approval of the corporation. Reprocessing is permissible only once for a lot and does not, however, guarantee conformity of the reprocessed seed lot to the prescribed standards.

10.( a) Representative random sample of the cleaned and graded seed shall be drawn and analysed before or after chemical treatment depending on the grower shareholder's choice or a person authorised by him. However, if the grower shareholder chooses to have the sample drawn and analysed after processing and treatment, an undertaking in the prescribed proforma will be taken from him to this effect. If, after treatment, a seed lot is found as not conforming to the prescribed standards, the seed lot will be rejected.

(b) The sample shall be drawn and analysed by:

(i) the corporation and the state certification agency, for seeds of notified

kinds/varieties/hybrids

(ii) The corporation for seeds of non-notified varieties

(c) In case of non-conformity of seed lots to the standard referred to in 8 (d) when analysed by the corporation, re-testing of another freshly drawn seed sample is permitted, provided the grower shareholder requests for it and bears the re-testing charge in full and provided further that the germination percentage in the first test, is not less than standard by more than 10%. Such re-testing does not however, guarantee conformity of the seed lot to the prescribed standards and is permissible only once for a lot.

11. The grower shareholder shall use the certification tags supplied by the state certification agency and the seals and thread supplied by the state certifying agency or the corporation with the approval of the state certification agency and the labels, leaflets and containers supplied by the corporation. The grower shareholder producing seed of unnotified varieties shall use the labels, containers, leaflets, seals, thread etc., supplied by the corporation.

12. For the purpose of this agreement:

    (a) The seed lot of notified kind/varieties/hybrid to be eligible for procurement by the corporation should conform to the seed standards referred to in 8 (d) as verified by both the corporation and the state seed certification agency. The seed lot would not be eligible for procurement by the corporation if it is found by either the corporation or the state seed certification agency or both as not conforming to the said standards.

    (b) For unnotified varieties, the seed lot to be eligible for procurement by the corporation should conform to the standards referred to in 8 (d) or any other standards prescribed by the corporation.

    (c) In addition to conforming to the standards referred to in 8 (d) seed lots to be eligible for procurement shall not be discoloured, insect damaged, rain damaged or damaged in any other way in physical appearance.

    (d) The seed lots to be eligible for procurement by corporation when verified by the corporation, shall not contain seeds of other distinguishable varieties (in percentage by number) in excess of the maximum permissible levels prescribed for off-types (in the field stage) in the standards referred to in (a) and (b) above.

13. The grower shareholder shall take at this expenses from the processing plant, the rejected wastes, seed discards, under sized seeds, empty cobs etc., after cleaning and grading and seed lots rejected on the basis of test reports, within 15 days from the date of intimation to the grower shareholder, failing which the corporation reserves the right to dispose off the produce in the manner deemed fit, after expiry of the prescribed period and recover the money and other incidental charges incurred and credit the balance if any to the grower shareholder's account. Further, the corporation will not be responsible for any damage to the material during the period.

14. With a view to meet the bonafide requirements of the grower shareholder for inputs and other expenses for seed production, the corporation shall render reasonable assistance to the grower shareholder in securing the necessary credit from the co-operative/commercial banks nominated by the corporation against terms and conditions laid down by the lending bank.

15. If an agreement to the effect exists between the grower shareholder and the co-operative/commercial bank nominated by the corporation, any amount due to the grower shareholder from the commercial bank for his seed will be paid directly to his account with the concerned bank.

16. The corporation shall have the power to exclude the grower shareholder in whole or part from receiving any facilities or inputs or foundation seed, if he, in the opinion of the corporation, had acted to the detriment of the objectives corporation or has committed a serious breach of any other terms of the agreement. Before any action is taken under this clause, the grower shareholder shall be given a fair chance to explain his position.

17. a) The parties agree that this agreement shall be binding on them for a period of three years from the date of its execution. After the expiry of the aforesaid period of three years, the agreement shall remain in force until it is terminated by either party by issuing a notice in writing (registered post and acknowledgement due) of not less than 3 months. Provided that this agreement becomes void if

the grower shareholder incurs any disqualification as per provisions of the articles of association of the company.

b) A separate seasonal agreement will be executed between the grower shareholder and the corporation with reference to the area under seed production crop/hybrid/variety and the minimum guaranteed price for procurement of the processed seeds as referred to in 3 (b).

18. All disputes between the parties as to the interpretation, meaning and effect or any terms of this agreement and all other disputes arising directly or indirectly, out of and in connection with or concerning the agreement or its implementation shall be referred to an arbitrator to be appointed by the Board of directors. The provisions of the Indian Arbitration Act, 1940 and the rules made thereunder shall apply to the said arbitration proceedings.

19. All powers and discretion of the corporation under this agreement are to be executed by the Board of Directors or any other officer authorised by the board.

In witness whereof the parties have executed this agreement on the day, month, and year mentioned above and in the presence of witnesses. Stamped agreement has been retained by the corporation and a true copy thereof duly signed by the parties has been delivered to the grower shareholder.

For APSSDC Ltd.

Managing Director

Witnesses:

1.

2.

# Seasonal Agreement Agreement between the APSSDC Ltd and Seeds Grower Shareholder

(Executed as per 17 (b) of principal agreement)

This agreement is made this .................. Day of ............... One thousand nine hundred and ninety seven between the APSSDC Ltd (hereinafter called 'The Corporation' which expression shall unless excluded by or repugnant to the subject of context, be deemed to include its successors and assigns) of the one part and Shri/Kumari/Shrimathi .......... S/o., W/o, D/o ......... Village ......... P.O. ........ District ............

Herein after called Grower shareholder which expression shall unless excluded by or repugnant to the subject or context be deemed to include his/her heirs, legal representatives, administrators and assigns of the other part.

Whereas the parties have already entered into an agreement (principal agreement) dated .......... to undertake production of seeds of the kinds, hybrids/varieties.

And whereas the Corporation and the Grower shareholder have agreed to a programme for the production of certified/ pedigreed category of seeds of (crop/crops .... on ...... acres during Kharif/Rabi/Summer of (Year) .......... at the minimum guaranteed price per quintal of processed and packed seed as stated below:

S.No. Crop Variety/Hybrid Rate per quintal of processed and packed seed

Now this agreement witnessed:

1. That the terms and conditions as incorporated in the principal agreement between the corporation and the grower shareholder dated ....... shall be binding on the parties and their relationship is governed by the same.
2. All the payment payable or claimable under this agreement shall be paid and claimed at Hyderabad. Neither of the parties shall be entitled to pay or claim the payments of

the amounts due at any place other than Hyderabad, though the same may be paid or accepted at any other place with mutual consent of the parties in each case of payment.

3. Notwithstanding the place where this agreement is to be implemented, it is mutually understood and agreed between the parties concerned at Hyderabad that the courts of law in Hyderabad alone shall have jurisdiction thereon.

In witness where of the parties have set their hands on the day, month and year mentioned above.

-----------------------------------

Signature of Grower Shareholder For APSSDC

Witnesses (name, address and signature):

1.

2.

## Appendix 13.3

# Contract Agreement for Hybrid Castor Seed Production

Acceptor

Shri :

Age :

Occupation :

Village :

Post :

District :

Pincode :

Phone :

**Proposer :** Navbharat Seeds Pvt. Ltd., Vasukanan, First Floor, Nr. Lotus Colony

Opp. Gujarat Vidyapith, Ashram Road, Ahmedabad - 380 014.

I, the undersigned, on this date and day at Ahmedabad city agree to abide by the following:

1. The proposer has declared a programme for production of – – – (variety) hybrid castor seed. This programme is accepted by me/us as per the conditions listed below.
2. The rules, regulation and condition of the proposer for production program of – – (variety) hybrid castor seeds are acceptable to me/us.
3. I/we will be considered main producer under the programme and other farmers (persons) participating in the programme will be considered as sub-producers. All the decisions taken by the proposer under the programme

and all the actions taken under the same will be acceptable and binding on me/us and other farmers covered under the programme.

4. I/we and sub-producers will grow foundation seeds provided by the proposer. I/we will take care that no other castor crop in the surrounding of the contract crop farms to the extent of 150 mtrs. (500 ft.) is cultivated.
5. The sowing will be between 15th July and 15th August.
6. I/we will undertake necessary actions like...roging, cutting, thrashing, grading, measurements, sealing etc. under the Indian Minimum Seed Certification Standard Act. 1988 and rules, regulations and notification there under at our cost.
7. The said foundation seeds will be procured by us at our cost from the godown of the company and will be distributed to the sub-producers as per the agreed conditions. The inspection, registration, testing and certification costs for the said foundation seed will be paid by us. Charges, to be paid at the time of agreement in cash are as follows:
   - Foundation (seed) Rs. ....... per acre (female 3kg. , male 1 kg)
   - rejected plot inspection charge Rs. 75 per acre.
   - Testing fee Rs. 230 per lot (175+50+5)
   - Agency certification charge Rs. 2.50 per kg.
   - Registration charge per producer Rs. 25.

It will be collective responsibility of all the producers of the village, if foundation (seed) amount and other charges are not paid.

8. The ready seeds will be cleaned and kept ready for sample between 1st and 10th March. Four samples of 500gm. each will be given to the company free of cost. In case of excess seed, second samples will be taken between 1 to 10th April. Sample from one producer will be taken only once. Dates for collection of sample will be decided by the certification agency.
9. Company will be purchasing stock of seed at company godown based on the grow out and germination tests conducted by the agency. All the tests conducted by company

will be acceptable and binding on me/us.

10. Bags required at the time of seed sample would be made available from the company godown in the $2^{nd}$ week of February. It will be my/our responsibility to collect the same at my/our cost. Bags required prior to this will be arranged by me/us.

11. Within two days of samples taken by the company, seeds in bags are to be sent to the company godown in good condition and proper manner at our (grower's) cost which will be stored in the company godown. Company will bear the rent.

    The foresaid seed received at company godown will be inspected and weighed at the company godown and those cleared by agency test and in good condition will be purchased thereafter. Necessary payment in this regard will be made.

12. If poor grading is noticed in the cleared seeds at the company godown, the grading expenses and deficiency will be deducted from our payment. Also, Rs. 1 per kg. will be deducted as penalty from our payment.

13. All the liabilities pertaining to sub-producers participating in the company programme will be of main producer and responsibility for final payment to them as and when received through the company will be ours. The sub-producer will be responsible to us and I/we will be responsible to you.

14. The decision of the company in respect of failed (non-acceptable) lot will be final. If the company decides to retain such lot, company will pay Rs. 10 per kg less for such lot within the week from the date of intimation of failed (non-accepted) seeds. I/we will take the material back from the company godown at our cost after settling dues to the company.

15. Company will pay to the main producers at company office within 30 days after intimation of clearing of seeds. This is to be paid to sub-producers by me/us as per their accounts.

16. Rate fixed by Gujarat State Seed Corporation for their producer for the year ..... will be acceptable and binding to me/us.

17. The main producer is required to get uncleared or failed (non-accepted) seeds within 7 days from the date of

intimation from the company godown after depositing the under mentioned charged to the company. The company will not be responsible for the goods thereafter and may sell the same as commercial castor seeds and recover the due amount i.e..

1. Rs. 230 per lot testing fee
2. Certification charge of Rs. 2.50 per kg.
3. Inspection charge for uncleared lot @ Rs. 75 per acre
4. Registration charge of Rs. 25 per producer
5. Other amount, if any.

18. Bonus: The seed certification agency may fix date in March and collect sample lots for early sample. Cleared lots will be eligible for bonus @ Rs. ........ (Rs. in words.........) per kg. over and above rates shown in clause 16.
19. The decision of the Managing Director of the company will be final, and acceptable and binding for interpretation of this agreement, any queries, any dispute and its settlement.
20. The jurisdiction for settlement of dispute under this agreement will be jurisdiction of Ahmedabad.

List of sub-producers with detail is enclosed herewith.

Sr. No. Sub-producer's Name Survey No. Acreage Sub-producer's Signature ....

1.
2.
3.
4.
5.

The above agreement with details and facts listed above is acceptable and binding on us for which I have signed.

Ahmedabad

Date:

Accepter: ............

Signature of main producer for himself

as well as a representative of sub-producers ------

Main producer who accepted the agreement for hybrid castor seed programme recommends it for other producers

General Manager (Production)

Navbharat Seeds Pvt. Ltd., Ahmedabad

**Appendix 13.4**

# Agreement for Seed Multiplication

This agreement executed at New Delhi on the 15th of September 1998 between PEPSI FOODS LIMITED, a company, incorporated under the Companies Act, 1956, having its corporate office at 3-B, DLF Corporate Park, S Block, Qutab Enclave, Phase III, Gurgaon – 122 002, Haryana and Registered Office at village Channo, District Sangrur (hereinafter referred as 'PFL'), which expression shall include its successors and assigns of the one part and

____________________________________________________

\- - - - - - - - - - - - - - - - - - - - - - - - - - - - - - - - - - - - - - - - - - - -

(hereinafter referred to as 'GROWER') which expression shall include his legal representatives and successors in interest and permitted assigns on the other part:

AND WHEREAS PFL requires bags of Graded seed stock potatoes, to be grown exclusively from the parent seeds __________ bags given by it for this purpose.

AND WHEREAS the GROWER is engaged in the production of SEED potatoes in the area of ________ acres and is the owner in title and possession of land which is available for the exclusive use of PFL under this agreement.

AND WHEREAS the GROWER has agreed to supply graded seed stock potatoes under a scheme hereinafter called the "PFL CONTRACT GROWER PROGRAMME" in which seed grade potatoes shall be cultivated and grown on the land made available for this purpose, on the terms and conditions contained thereunder:

NOW THEREFORE, THE PARTIES HERETO HAVE AGREED AS FOLLOWS:

Parent seed of a certain variety which is the exclusive property of PFL shall be provided by PFL at the time sowing to the GROWER @ Rs 460/- bag of 81 kg inclusive of bag of size A and B and Rs. 370/- bag of 81 kg inclusive of bag of size C for multiplication under in accordance with the terms of this agreement. The 25% of amount will be deposited by the farmers at the time of seed booking and balance 75% will be collected at the time of delivery of seed.

1. The Potato grown from the parent seeds provided by PFL will be purchased from the GROWER. The price of different grades will be as follows:
   - Seed size between 1.0" – 1.5" dia. Grade A Rs 280/- bag of 82 kg.
   - Seed size between 1.5" – 2.0" dia. Grade B Rs. 280/- bag of 82 kg.
   - Seed size between 2.0" – 3.0" dia. Grade C Rs 260/- bag of 82 kg inclusive of bag.

   Size less or more than described specification, Mis-shaped, Green & Cut potato will not be purchased. If grower dispatch potato different from specification by more than 5% they will be rejected at growers cost and risk, if potatoes specification variance is less than 5% than they may be accepted on grading at growers expense and risk, subject to conformation to specifications. The decision on grading will be at sole discretion of PFL. However, PFL retains the first right to buy potato seed rejected due to deviation from specifications at prevailing market price.
2. If the grower achieves net multiplication ratio of 1:7 or more for seed size potatoes and seed size potato are 95% or more of the total produce, he will be given incentive of Rs 10/- bag on seed size potatoes.
3. The price per 82 kg of seed grade specified above is inclusive of all farm and packing expenses and exclusive of gunny bag, the cost of which shall be borne by PFL. The transportation cost for seed grade and properly packed seed bags from farmers place to cold store shall be borne by PFL. For CHIP grade i.e. C grade potato, farmer has to use his own bags and bags will not be returned to the farmer.
4. All farm operations such as land preparation, planting, Inter Culture/Spraying and all other operations including harvesting, storing, grading, bagging and loading will be the responsibility of the GROWER and the cost will be

borne by him provided always however, that the GROWER shall at all time follow such instructions as may be given by PFL from time to time on any matter in connection with this agreement.

5. It is agreed between the parties that the total potato produced by the GROWER shall always be the property of PFL. Further provided that the seeds, the plants sprouting from the seeds and all part of the plant will remain the exclusive property of PFL and shall only be disposed/sold, if so desired by PFL, as per PFL's instructions.
6. Potato planting/harvest is to be started in presence of PFL representative or PFL has given written instruction for such operations to be started.
7. The GROWER shall render all the co-operation and assistance to PFL and its representatives in conducting field inspections of the potato seed crop at any time/stage and must conform to the agronomy practices issued by PFL experts on raising/handling of crop and as recommended through Frito - Lay manual for potato seed production in Punjab.
8. The GROWER shall not sell or transfer to anyone else the produce meant for delivery to PFL. In case of default, the GROWER shall be liable to pay to PFL the damages for the shortfall on this account and in such an event PFL reserves the right to forthwith terminate the contract.
9. PFL shall make payment due, after adjusting payable to PFL if any, by Draft/Cheque on the receipt of and acceptance of chip stock potatoes within two weeks thereof.
10. The agreement will be operative from 15.09.1998 to 15.05.1999 unless extended by mutual consent of PFL & GROWER.
11. Notwithstanding, the place where this agreement is to be implemented, it is mutually understood and agreed by and between parties hereto that the contract shall be deemed to have been entered into at New Delhi and Courts of Law in New Delhi alone shall have jurisdiction to adjudicate thereon.

for PEPSI FOODS LIMITED

WITNESSES ________________

for GROWER

# 14
# Contract Farming in India: Impacts on Women and Child Workers*

Globalisation and liberalisation are likely to have the greatest impact on the rural poor through their influence on the agricultural sector, terms of trade, availability and cost of inputs, and new investments in the agribusiness sector. Technological progress in farming can help the rural poor by raising farm productivity, lowering food prices, increasing employment, and reducing farming risk. But the role and influence of multinational corporations (MNCs) in food production and trade will, as an institutional mechanism, determine the exact impact of globalisation on the rural poor, who are mostly from the labouring classes. Contract farming promotes participation of domestic firms and MNCs in farming, and is seen as the 'new investment' aspect of globalisation (Ramamurthy, 2000; Killick, 2001).

Under contract farming, landowners or tenants have contracts with agribusiness marketing and/or processing firms, who specify prices, timing, quality and quantity/acreage of the produce to be delivered. The arrangement may include the supply of inputs by the agribusiness firm, who may even control and supervise farm operations in some situations. Contract farming has been practised for some time now in parts of India and there have been a few recent studies of its impacts on contracting households' incomes (Haque, 1999; Rangi and Sidhu, 2000; Singh, 2000). However, these studies rarely examine the impact of the contract farming system on labour conditions and labour relations in India. There have been only three case studies of contract

* Earlier published under the same title as IIED's Gatekeeper Series as paper no. III, 2003 and an earlier version in IJLE 2001 conference volume under a different title.

farm labour in India, including one by the author, all in the last three or four years (Ramamurthy, 2000; Venkateshwarlu and Corta, 2001; Singh, 2005).[1] However, lessons from many other developing countries are that employment in the agribusiness sector (farm production and processing/packing plants) is characterised by a lack of contracts, piece rate payment, insecure seasonal employment, gender bias, use of child labour and disregard for labour rights such as collective negotiation (Torres, 1997; Barrientos *et al.*, 1999; Barron and Rello, 2000; Saravanan, 2002).

In this chapter, cases of hybrid cottonseed production in Andhra Pradesh and vegetable farming in Punjab are analysed to examine the labour conditions in contract farming in India. It then makes suggestions for improving working conditions and terms for those working on contract farms.

## Contract Farm Labour and Women

There have been many studies of conditions for women workers and gender discrimination in export-oriented industries across the world during the past 30 years (Lim, 1990; Pearson, 1998; Barrientos *et al.*, 1999; Balakrishnan, 2002). While some (e.g., Lim, 1990) see the employment of women in such enterprises as a natural economic process driven by business dynamics and labour family needs (as demand and supply factors respectively), others view it in more gendered frameworks and have been critical of the way female labour is treated and paid in these factories. The latter studies term the whole process of industrialisation as not only *export-led,* but also *female-led* (Pearson, 1998). However, female labour conditions in the farm sector under agribusiness expansion have not yet been subjected to similar analysis.

Agriculture is becoming increasingly 'feminised' globally as men move out of the sector more quickly than women. The reasons for increasing female representation in agriculture vary from voluntary and involuntary withdrawal of men from farming, to growing wage opportunities for women in export-oriented non-traditional crops and activities. While these new labour arrangements have led to marginal increases in real income for some women workers, they have also changed relationships between workers and employers, workers and work, and led to differentiation within labour. For example, women's wages are lower and stickier (i.e. do not rise as fast) than men's, working conditions poorer and bargaining power more limited. These are, to some extent, the result of structural factors (Mehra and Gammage, 1999). Others argue that labour markets are not only bearers of gender, they also reinforce gender inequality (Elson, 1999).

Women have increasingly been employed to do more delicate work because of their supposedly feminine traits, such as docility, obedience and nimble fingers. But these are not natural or innate skills; rather they are social skills embedded during girls' upbringing as part of their socially defined subordinate position within society. In fact, the expanding employment of women in agribusiness has many parallels with female employment in industry, where women are also preferred for their so-called nimble fingers, and their work is insecure, badly paid, and flexible. In agribusiness, some of these aspects are the result of the nature of production in a sector characterised by seasonality, mono-cultivation and natural risk (Collins, 1993; Barrientos *et al.*, 1999; Elson, 1999).

Though there have been studies of gender impacts of contract farming within producer households (Carney, 1988; Bulow and Sorensen, 1993; Porter and Phillips-Howard, 1997; Jayaweera, 2002), such studies of labourers' households are more unusual. In many cases, rural women working in processing plants and related activities reported that employment had given them greater self-esteem and power within the household (Glover and Kusterer, 1990; Dunham, 1995). However, contract farming does lead to gender inequalities in the quantity and quality of work, as well as wages for women and children, who work longer hours as they are considered better workers, but are paid less (Collins, 1993; Porter and Phillips-Howard, 1997). Employment on contract farms is also temporary and sporadic. Some activities, such as pruning, spraying, thinning, pinching out, tying and harvesting of grapes, are reserved for women, and this work differentiation extends even to the processing sector (Torres, 1997; Barrientos *et al.*, 1999; Rath, 2003). Such 'gendering' of tasks is a problem as it can exclude women from activities that are better paid, less strenuous or less hazardous.

### Child Labour and Gender in India

Child labour is one of the major problems in contract farming, and this is the case throughout the developing world (Porter and Phillips-Howard, 1997; Torres, 1997; Raynolds, 2002).

However, no data on its global or regional magnitude are available because contract farming is practised in small pockets in each developing country. Similarly, there are no estimates of the magnitude of child labour in contract farming in India.

The International Labour Organisation (ILO) estimated there were 250 million working children in the world in the age group of 5-14 years in 1996 (cited in Nielsen and Dubey, 2002). The work participation rate of children between the ages of 10 and 14 years was as high as 14%, and in some parts of the world, such as central Africa, it was more than 32%. India is one of the main users of child labour in the Asian region. The 1991 Census of India reported that there were 12.6 million full time and 10.4 million marginal child workers in India, with Andhra Pradesh having the highest number of child workers (15% of the total child workers in India; cited in Kar, 2002). In the 1990s, about half the child labour in rural India was concentrated in the five states of Andhra Pradesh, Karnataka, Maharashtra, Madhya Pradesh and Tamilnadu (Lieten, 2002b).

Any kind of work by children under the age of 18 is often considered exploitation in developed countries. In India, however, the term 'child labour' applies only to children aged between 5 and 14. The *Child Labour (Prohibition and Regulation) Act, 1986* states that no child below the age of 14 shall be employed to work in any factory or mine or in any other hazardous employment (cited in Mishra, 2000).[2] The disaggregation of child labour into different occupational categories reveals that almost 80% of working children are in the agricultural sector (Gayatri and Chaudhri, 2002). Since child labour tends to be concentrated in agriculture, it may be reasonable to expect that the incidence of child labour will be higher in agriculturally less developed regions. But, that is not the case; Bihar state, usually referred to as an underdeveloped state, has one of the lowest child labour ratios in the country. On the other hand, Tamilnadu and Andhra Pradesh, more advanced agriculturally, have the highest incidences of child labour. Also, there is a significant correlation between child labour and economic participation rate, especially female participation rate. The states with the highest incidence of child labour are also the ones with a high per capita income and a much higher female work participation rate than many other states (Lieten, 2002a). This is because in contexts where there are extended labour opportunities yet a low degree of labour empowerment, poor families are tapped for additional labour power. Since adults usually have some form of alternative employment in such regions, child labour is more likely to be used (Lieten, 2002b).

A slight gender bias favouring employment of young girls can be seen across all states. In 1999-2000, the work force participation rate for rural female workers in the age group of 10-14 years was higher than for rural male workers in the same age group (96 per 1000 for rural females, compared with 91 for rural males). But the overall participation rate of rural females was much lower than for rural males (Sundaram, 2001). Employers/contractors prefer girls for a number of labour supply traits like docility, obedience and stability; a phenomenon which is well documented in the literature. Most of the girl labourers belong to the scheduled caste and scheduled tribe households, poor backward castes and other such communities. The lower status assigned to girls in Indian society, where male preference rules, further propels their employment in a number of activities. Even if parents do not wish to exploit their children, they are often trapped in a vicious cycle of indebtedness, bondage and other obligatory relations which compel them to send their daughters to work. Yet the employers or contractors of girl labour have no requirement to take care of these children; if any health problems arise, they are simply replaced with a new group. With no social security obligations, there is hardly any cost involved for the employers or contractors (Rustagi, 2002). Child labour under contracting is not subject to any legal or public disapproval.

## Case studies

The states of Andhra Pradesh and Punjab have been pioneers in contract seed production and contract vegetable production respectively in India. These case studies bring out the gender and child labour dimensions in the practice of farm labour under the contract farming system. The case studies from Andhra Pradesh, mainly drawn from Ramamurthy (2000) and Venkateshwarlu and Corta (2002), are based on intensive field research by these authors on the labour processes, conditions and households involved in hybrid cottonseed production. The Punjab case study is mainly based on my own interactions and observations in the field as part of a larger study of contract farming in the state (Singh, 2005).

## Contract cottonseed production in Andhra Pradesh

In 1999-2000 Andhra Pradesh had the highest incidence of child labour in India, with 25% of children aged between 10 and 14 in the rural areas working, compared with only 9% in India as a whole (Lieten, 2002b). This was also accompanied by the highest rural female work participation rate in the state (48%), compared with only 30% in India in 1999-2000. Furthermore, 47% of the total rural employment in Andhra Pradesh in 1993-94 was casual compared with 36% for rural India as a whole. The proportion of casual employment was much higher for female labour (53%) than male labour (43%) (Dev and Mahajan, 2001). Contract farm labour is generally casual labour, though workers may be tied by advance loans.

This sets the context for the first case study: labour in contract farming of hybrid cottonseed. Three districts of Andhra Pradesh (Kurnool, Mehboobnagar and Rangareddy) account for 70% of India's cottonseed production and 97% of the total area (28,000 acres in all) under cottonseed production in the state. About 60% of the state's seed production is destined for sale in other states of India or abroad (Venkateshwarlu and Corta, 2001).

Contract farming for hybrid cottonseed production is practised by the MNCs, as well as national and local seed companies, who arrange contracts for seed production with local farmers either directly or through middlemen called 'seed organisers'. These companies or seed organisers supply seed to the farmers, set the price of seed before harvest, and supervise the cultivation of the crop. They also advance capital to the farmers, thus linking markets for output and credit. Hybrid cottonseed production is highly labour and capital intensive. It requires four times more capital and nine times more labour per acre than ordinary cotton production. Labour accounts for 60% of the total cost of cottonseed production, and the most labour intensive operation is cross-pollination (Box 1), which has to be done manually. It involves about 90% of the total labour input and 45% of the total capital input (Venkateshwarlu and Corta, 2001).

### Box 1. Cross-pollination

Cross-pollination begins one week after flowering and involves two separate tasks: emasculation and pollination. Buds which are expected to open the next morning are gently removed by hand, and the petals removed with the thumbnail without damaging the stigma, style or ovary. The emasculated flower is covered carefully with red plastic paper bags. Pollination has to be carried out in the morning with pollen from the male parent flowers. Crossing needs to be done as soon as flowers blossom but before the female flowers bear fruit. About two months after sowing, the plants start blooming and continue growing for seven months and throughout this time the cross-pollination tasks (emasculation and pollination) need to be done each day without fail (Venkateshwarlu and Corta, 2001).

Most of the cross-pollination work is done by young girls who work daily from July to February. Cross-pollination and harvesting (picking cotton) are carried out for six months and four months each by the girls, with some overlap between the two tasks during November to February. The predominant task is cross-pollination, which takes 95% of their time. The involvement of young girls in cottonseed production is so high that it is estimated that 0.25 million girls are employed in this activity throughout Andhra Pradesh. In one case, on a 70-acre cottonseed farm dispersed over 14 different villages, 560 girls were employed and were monitored by 14 supervisors. The girls and their parents are contacted well in advance of the crop season and credit is extended to the parents who agree to assign their daughters to the cottonseed farmers for the season (July-February). This credit (cash/grain) advance, which ranged from Rs. 100-3000 in 1997-98 and was obtained by more than 90% of the girls' parents, serves to interlink the credit and child labour markets; this has become an important part of the MNCs' contract farming strategy (Venkateshwarlu and Corta, 2001).

Generally, 10-15 children are hired for 100-150 days per acre of cottonseed production. Children as young as six years old work from 8.30 am to 6-7 pm; some boys even return to the field again from 9-12 at night. The cottonseed production calendar has been standardised by companies for seed certification and marketing. This has resulted in the regimentation of children's work schedules, who are continuously employed for six to nine months a year. Children's labour is extended well beyond the standard workday (9-10 hours a day with a one hour lunch break). They are paid a piece rate of Rs. 10/- per 25 kg cotton for delinting (separating cotton from seeds), and Rs. 0.05 per pest/worm caught. Many girls also accompany their mothers for casual work. They are paid daily wages or piece rates (Ramamurthy, 2000).

Girls are preferred in cottonseed production because their wages are lower than adults', they work longer hours and more intensively, and are generally easier to control. It is reported that one girl can do the work of three adults. Though the agreement obliges these female children to work for only one season (six-nine months), in practice they tend to work for several years for the same farmer. Children are given incentives in the form of chocolates, biscuits or snacks, or prizes and bonuses like a stainless steel tiffin carrier every two years for better and faster work. They are even taken to a cinema twice a month and allowed to watch television or videos while separating cotton from seeds (an activity where children are paid on a piece rate basis). In some cases, girls are brought in from outside the local area and made to stay in the employer's house and cattlesheds throughout the season (Ramamurthy, 2000; Venkateshwarlu and Corta, 2001).

Whilst young girls are the most popular labour type on cottonseed farms, women are also employed, though for much less of the time and for fewer tasks. The most common labour arrangement for women in contract farms is daily casual work. Though this work ensures instant wage payment, in practice the wages are held back till a task is completed. There is also increased micro management of labour time and supervision of daily wage labour by landowners, who may threaten women workers with losing their jobs or withholding their wages. Labour time is controlled by the landowners in various ways, such as going to workers' homes each morning to fetch them early for work, ensuring that lunch is brief, prolonging the work day, and insisting on workers making up for any tardiness in work. Often, even the supervisors are women. In order to reduce the need for supervision and control, another labour arrangement (the piece rate system) has emerged, especially for cotton picking and weeding. The piece rate system leads to workers lengthening the workday themselves, magnifying the pace and intensity of work and even monitoring each other's performance. Daily wage labourers pick about 10-15 kg of cotton a day; those working under the piece rate system can pick as much as 20-30 kg, with some even reaching 40 kg. This leads to a change in the relationship between efficient and less efficient workers and creates a hierarchy of workers. As individual wage earnings become more uneven, average wage costs for producers are reduced (Ramamurthy, 2000).

Since the 1980s the cross-pollination work in cottonseed farms has shifted from daily adult labour to almost entirely labour by girls, who are fully bonded i.e. obliged to work only for the contract grower who advanced the loan. In fact, adult women are discouraged from cross-pollination work, and girls over 14 or those who have reached puberty at the time of agreement are not permitted to work in contract farms by the seed producers, organisers or companies. Many rumours are spread to discourage women from undertaking such work, such as that post-pubescent girls working in the fields will cause crop failure. This is no different to countries like Japan and Korea, where until the 1980s married women were prevented from working by law or strong social customs (Tzannatos, 1999).

The employment of female children in cottonseed farms has had many impacts on gender relations at the household level. For example, girls have more responsibility for household provisioning, and with more money coming in, men may withdraw from work and often resort to drinking. There are also health implications for girls involved in cottonseed work; higher levels of pesticides are used in this crop than in ordinary cotton cultivation. Girls working in cotton fields for many years have been reported to suffer menstrual problems (Venkateshwarlu and Corta, 2001).[3] Further, more and more girls are being taken out of school to do such work (Ramamurthy, 2000).

### Contract tomato and potato production in Punjab

Agricultural labour accounts for as much as 88% of the total rural labour in the state of Punjab (Gill, 2000). More than two-thirds of the agricultural labour in the state, including contract farm labour, is casual. Major reasons behind the casualisation of farm labour in the state include mechanisation of major farm operations, inflow of migrant labour, slowdown of agricultural growth, and non-viability of small and marginal holdings (Rangi *et al.*, 2001).

Women's labour participation rate in agriculture in Punjab has been extremely low (4.5% in 1991), though higher than their participation rates in the national, rural and urban workforce (2.8%, 2.2%, and 4.3% respectively). Only 1% of cultivators (farmers who own or lease land) were female in 1991 (Gill, 2001). Punjab also has had one of the lowest incidences of child labour (2.7%) in the country (Lieten, 2002a). However, Punjab has been a pioneer in India in the contract farming of perishable produce, a sector which tends to rely on women and children's labour.

Fruit and vegetables require more intensive labour than other crops. Contract farms under company supervision are little more than 'factories in the fields' from the point of view of labour. Their labour system resembles the industrial sector because of timing, quality and standardisation requirements which cannot be met by mechanical methods. This requires 'quality labour', i.e. efficient, timely and paced; 'flexible labour', that is readily available and cheap; and 'docile labour', in other words politically trouble-free labour. These conditions are met more easily by women, who are perceived to be homemakers and, therefore, low cost, sincere and more obedient workers. This amounts to manipulation of the cultural understanding of gender (Collins, 1993).

Contract farming of vegetable crops has been practised by both MNCs and local firms since the early 1990s in Punjab. The contracts specify quantity/acreage, quality, timing and price of the produce. The companies also provide seedlings on part credit and specify the production practices and inputs to be used. That contracting has led to more and better employment opportunities for labour, especially women, is true and acknowledged by the labourers (Singh, 2005). The labour intensity of vegetable crops, except potato, is much higher than for traditional crops like wheat or paddy. The labour intensity is 3,600-4,000 hours per hectare for tomatoes (depending on whether it is a summer or winter crop), compared with only 740 hours per hectare for paddy (Gill, 2001). This has created a big employment boom in the contract production areas of the state, especially as the mechanisation of sowing and harvesting operations of paddy and wheat crops has reduced manual work to almost nothing.

While employment has grown as a consequence of the labour intensive nature of the crops, accompanied by the emergence of some employment in processing, wage levels have been pushed to subsistence levels as a result of the increased competition. This has come about through in-migration and the cessation of out-migration because of the higher incomes available locally. At the same time, those in work have to deal with insecure employment and poor working conditions.

According to Gill (2001), during the mid-1990s, three-quarters of all workers employed in the state's vegetable production sector were hired labour. Further, female labour accounted for 58% of total labour hours, compared with 34% in paddy. And 49% of all those working in the vegetable production sector was hired female labour, compared with 25% in paddy. In tomato production alone, female labour accounted for almost 60% of the total labour hours. Child labour accounted for about 3-4% of the total labour hours in vegetable crops, as part of family labour. However, a woman's wage is only 75% of a male worker's wage; a child worker receives only half that of a male worker (when paid a daily wage rather than a piece rate wage).

## Labour in Tomato Fields

Women and girls mostly transplant and harvest tomatoes as such workers are more available, cost less, are more honest and better suited to picking and transplanting jobs (Singh, 2005). Mothers with infants also work in contract farms and infants and children remain on the farm throughout the day, with implications for their health and nutrition.

There is a piece rate system of wages linked to output, i.e. Rs. 2-2.5 per crate of tomatoes picked (a crate contains 20 kg of tomatoes). Thus, the more a woman or girl picks in a day, the better she gets paid. Harvesting one acre of tomatoes takes 15-20 women two days as one woman can pick only 25-30 crates a day. Wages go up when tomato harvesting competes with that of potato and wheat in some areas (Singh, 2005). But wages soon become depressed with the large seasonal inflow of migrant male labour to the state. In fact, migrant agricultural labour accounts for 25% of the total agricultural labour force in the state (Gill, 2000). The daily wage rate for female workers is only two-thirds of that received by men. In tomato harvesting, half-day wages are also common as harvesting should be completed before noon (Singh, 2005).

## Labour in Potato Fields

Potato cultivation, especially under contract, has increased women's employment; a large number of women can be seen picking and grading potatoes during harvest time, though in general, female labour accounts for only 38% of all labour used in this crop (Gill, 2001). Generally, female labour is preferred for these jobs as they require patience and care, yet women's pay amounts to only two-thirds of that received by men. A lot of child labour is also used, especially for grading. Even mothers with infants can do such work, which is generally in one place and under the shade of some tree or in a shed (Singh, 2005). Daily wages are generally paid for harvesting; usually Rs. 40/ day for women and Rs. 20/day for girls. Groups of workers may receive a fixed payment contract to harvest an entire potato field;[4] this was Rs. 500 per acre in 1999-2000. Bagging potatoes is a separate labour activity and is paid at the rate of Rs. 5-10/ bag (Singh, 2005).

In some cases, women members of the contract grower households supervise potato grading, especially when the produce is graded at the grower's farmhouse. This is preferred as most of the grading labour is female, and it is easy and more effective for a female member of the farming household to control their work.

## Conclusions

As shown in these three case studies, contract farm production is primarily carried out by female labour, and increasingly by young girls. There is a need to address the whole question of a changing agrarian production structure under contract farming from a gender perspective, especially issues associated with transfer of skills, choice of technology, organisation of labour, working conditions and terms of work.

There has been a variety of corporate responses to the problem of child labour, ranging from withdrawing operations from affected countries; dismissing child workers, thus abruptly affecting people's lives; abandoning the factory-based mode of production in favour of contracting work to home-based producers; to adopting a code of conduct for child labour; and finally, acknowledging child labour as a problem and working to eliminate its practice (Bissell *et al.*, 2002; Frenkel and Scott, 2002). Instead of banning child labour as proposed by some of the international agencies and the agribusiness players in the developed world, a better approach would be to improve conditions for working children, as such work contributes to the family income on which the child's well-being depends. A ban on child labour in Bangladesh, for example, only aggravated the problem as the children went from jobs in garment factories to much worse jobs, such as breaking bricks in the hot sun or even prostitution. Thus, a ban on child labour under pressure can be counter-productive (Kar, 2002).

Non-government organisations (NGOs) and government agencies need to monitor working conditions and wage rates in contract farming in order to prevent long hours of work, temporary employment, exposure to hazardous pesticides and below minimum wages. The employer should make provision for childcare, such as creches; and both NGOs and government should provide education and skill building facilities. If the education level of these children improves, they will be able to get out of these fields and escape poverty and exploitation. The literacy of both girls and women seems to have a bearing on the incidence of female child labour (Rustagi, 2002).

There have been many programmes at the state level to eradicate the practice of child labour. For example, there were more than a dozen such government programmes during the 1980s and 1990s in the state of Karnataka and there are also a dozen NGOs working to eliminate the practice of child labour in various districts of the state (Gayathri, 2002). The NGOs' strategies, in general, include supporting the children with health and education facilities and offering income compensation for children and their parents. But, while NGOs are doing good work at the micro level, it does not add up to a major strategy to address the huge problem of child labour. This is partly because of a piecemeal approach, lack of scale and sustainability, and high costs, as well as the dominance of donor demands and competition between NGOs. What is required is an holistic and integrated approach focusing on all the activities which involve children in a given area, followed by replication of programmes on a larger scale in a sustainable manner (Wazir, 2002).

The organisation of labour is another important measure to prevent or eliminate some of the ills of the contract farming system. For example, associations of contract farm workers could be used to monitor wage and work conditions. There have been some cases of women workers becoming empowered by women's collectives in India (Elson, 1999). Legal provisions to involve labour representatives when companies and growers/growers' groups discuss labour and wage issues would also be a step in the right direction. As a civil society intervention, codes of conduct could guide farmers' use of labour; these could be enforced by contracting agribusiness firms. These firms should also constantly work towards more ethical and humane labour standards. Such improvements would help these firms compete in the international market, especially as the international trade and labour agencies have now put labour standards higher on the agenda. Agencies like the World Trade Organisation and the International Labour Organisation could promote better labour standards and codes of conduct among agribusiness firms and farmers. It is important to realise that improving women's labour conditions and narrowing down gender differentials can increase the output and welfare of both women *and* men.

## References


Balakrishnan, R (ed.) 2002. *The Hidden Assembly Line – Gender Dynamics of Subcontracted Work in a Global Economy.* Kumarian Press, Connecticut (USA).

Bissell, SL., Chadha, SG. and Shiva Kumar, AK. 2002. Elimination of child labour: corporate options and public actions. *The Indian Journal of Labour Economics*, 45 (3): 633-640.

Bulow von, D. and Sorensen, A. 1993. Gender and contract farming: tea outgrower schemes in Kenya. *Review of African Political Economy*, 56: 38-52.

Carney, JA. 1988. Struggles over crop rights and labour within contract farming households in a Gambian irrigated rice project. *The Journal of Peasant Studies*, 15(3): 334-349.

Dev, MS. and Mahajan, V. 2001. Transforming the rural economy in Andhra Pradesh. Paper presented at the *Workshop on Rural Transformation in India – The Role of Non-Farm Sector*, organised by Planning Commission, DFID, IHD and the World Bank at Indian Habitat Centre, New Delhi, September 19-21.

Dunham, D. 1995. *Contract Farming and Export Horticulture: Can agribusiness revitalise the peasant sector in Sri Lanka?* IPS Agricultural Policy Series No. 3, Institute of Policy Studies, Colombo, February.

Elson, D. 1999. Labour markets as gendered institutions: equality, efficiency and empowerment issues. *World Development*, 27(3): 611-627.

Frenkel, SJ. and Scott, D. 2002. Compliance, collaborations and codes of labour practice: the Adidas connection. *California Management Review*, 45 (1): 29-49.

Gayathri, V. 2002. Situation analysis of child labour in Karnataka. *The Indian Journal of Labour Economics*, 45 (3): 577-600.

Gayathri, V. and Chaudhri, DP. 2002. Introduction. *The Indian Journal of Labour Economics*, 45 (3): 443-450.

Gill, KK. 2001. Diversification of agriculture and women's employment in Punjab. *The Indian Journal of Labour Economics*, 44(2): 259-267.

Gill, SS. 2000. Agrarian change and struggle of rural labour in Indian Punjab. *International Journal of Punjab Studies*, 7(1): 73-91.

Haque, T. 1999. *Contract Farming in India*. National Centre for Agricultural Economics and Policy Research, New Delhi (unpublished).

Jayaweera, S. 2002. Women subcontractor workers in Sri Lanka. In: Balakrishnan, R. (ed.) *The Hidden Assembly Line – Gender Dynamics of Subcontracted Work in a Global Economy.* Kumarian Press, Connecticut (USA).

Kar, J. 2002. The issue of child labour in Orissa: a developmental approach. *Indian Social Science Review*, 4 (1): 117-131.

Killick, T. 2001. Globalization and the rural poor. *Development Policy Review*, 19(2): 155-180.

Lieten, GK. 2002a: Child labour and poverty: the poverty of analysis. *The Indian Journal of Labour Economics*, 45 (3): 451-464.

Lieten, GK. 2002b. Child labour in India – disentangling essence and solutions. *Economic and Political Weekly*, 37 (52): December 28, 5190-5195.

Lim, LYC. 1990. Women's work in export factories: the politics of a cause. In: Tinker, I. (ed.) *Persistent Inequalities –Women and World Development.* Oxford University Press, Oxford.

Mehra, R. and Gammage, S. 1999. Trends, countertrends, and gaps in women's employment. *World Development*, 27(3), 533-550.

Mishra, L. 2000. India's stand on child labour. *Focus WTO*, 1 (5): 1-9.

Nielsen, HS. and Dubey, A. 2002: Child Labour in rural India: A Micro Economic Perspective. *The Indian Journal of Labour Economics*, 45 (3), 479-496.

Pearson, R. 1998. 'Nimble Fingers' revisited – reflections on women and Third World industrialisation in the late twentieth century. In: Jackson, C. and Pearson, R. (ed.) *Feminist Visions of Development: Gender analysis and policy.* Routledge, London.

Porter, G. and Phillips-Howard, K. 1997. Contract Farming in South Africa. *Geography*, 82(1): 38-44.

Ramamurthy, P. 2000. The cotton commodity chain, women, work and agency in India and Japan: the case for feminist agro-food systems research. *World Development*, 28(3): 551-578.

Rangi, PS. and Sidhu, MS. 2000. A study on contract farming of tomato in Punjab. *Agricultural Marketing*, 42(4): 15-23.

Rangi, PS., Sidhu, MS. and Singh, H. 2001. Casualisation of agricultural labour in Punjab. *The Indian Journal of Labour Economics*, 44(4): 957-970.

Rath, S. 2003. Grape cultivation for exports – impact on vineyard workers. *Economic and Political Weekly*, 38 (5): February 1, 480-489.

Raynolds, LT. 2002. Wages for wives: renegotiating gender and production relations in contract farming in the Dominican Republic. *World Development*, 30(5): 783-798.

Rustagi, P. 2002. Girl child labour: regional dimensions and motivations. *The Indian Journal of Labour Economics*, 45 (3): 465-477.

Saravanan, V. 2002. Women's employment and reduction of child labour – beedi workers in rural Tamilnadu. *Economic and Political Weekly*, 37 (52): December 28, 5205 – 5214.

Singh, S. 2000. Contract farming for agricultural diversification in the Indian Punjab: a study of performance and problems. *Indian Journal of Agricultural Economics*, 56 (3), 283-294.

Singh, S. 2005. *Political Economy of Contract Farming in India*. Allied, New Delhi.

Sundaram, K. 2001. Employment-unemployment situation in the nineties: some results from NSS 55th Round Survey. *Economic and Political Weekly*, 36(11): March 17, 931-940.

Tzannatos, Z. 1999. Women and labour market changes in the global economy: growth helps, inequalities hurt and public policy matters. *World Development*, 27(3): 551-569.

Venkateshwarlu, D. and Corta, LD. 2001. Transformations in the age and gender of unfree workers on hybrid cottonseed farms in Andhra Pradesh. *The Journal of Peasant Studies*, 28(3): 1-36.

Wazir, R. 2002. Eliminating child labour: do NGO interventions add up to a strategy? *The Indian Journal of Labour Economics*, 45 (3): 615-632.

## Notes

1 This paper relies heavily on these studies for analysis and insights.

2 However, agricultural work is not covered under this Act.

3 This is similar to the conditions of grape farm workers in Maharashtra; major problems faced by women grape workers

included lower backache, neck pain, headaches and menstrual problems. The women working on grape farms had the highest morbidity rate among all groups of women agricultural workers. More than 60% of the women working on grape farms reported health problems, compared with only 32% for all women workers (Rath, 2003).

4 Group labour contracts were also noted for seed cotton weeding in Andhra Pradesh (Ramamurthy, 2000).

# 15

# Leveraging Contract Farming for Agricultural Development in India: Lessons from Thailand and Beyond

## 15.1. Introduction

Agriculture in India still engages about 58% of the work force and contributes about a quarter of the GDP. A large majority of the farmers/cultivators belong to the category of small and marginal holders. The number and proportion of such holdings have been growing over time. They constituted 68.15% of the total operational holdings in 1971-72 but their proportion increased to 80.59% in 1991-92. The area cultivated by them has grown from 24.01% of the total in 1971-72 to 34.3% in 1991-92 (Singh, 2005). The share of marginal and small holdings increased to 61.6% and 18.7% respectively by 1995/96, altogether accounting for 80.3% of all holdings. On the other hand, the number of farms in the largest category declined and the average size of the largest category was falling. Further, large holdings (>4 ha) were estimated to decline to only 7% by 2000-2001 and 5% by 2010-2011 and account for only 36% and 28% of the area respectively (Jha, 2001). Given this general picture, it is not surprising that the average size of operational holding has been declining since the 1960s and was only 1.37 hectares and average size of ownership holding only 1.14 hectares in 1992. Small farmers (with holdings of <2 ha) accounted for 83.9% of all operational holdings by 2003 (Singh, 2005) Also, small farmers (including landless) had higher livestock ownership (60-80% of all livestock population) including cross-bred cattle where

12-20% small farm and landless households owned these animals compared with only 8-15% in case of larger farm households (Jha, 2001).

Small farms produce 41% of India's total grain (49% of rice, 40% of wheat, 29% of coarse cereals and 27% of pulses), and over half of total fruits and vegetables despite being in rain fed areas, resource constrained, and assuming that they are only as productive as large farms (Singh, et al, 2002; Muller and Patel, 2004). Their contribution to incremental wheat and rice production during 1971-1991 was even higher (62% and 48% respectively). The marginal holdings also had higher cropping intensity (143) compared with that of the small, medium and large farmers (129.9, 119.6, and 111.6 respectively) in the mid 1980s and higher irrigated area as percentage of net sown area with more of it being irrigated by tubewells and canals (1/3rd each) and even that with tanks being quite important (8-11%) (Agrawal, 2000; Singh, et al, 2002).

Dairying accounts for more than 50% of the household income of the landless and 30% of that of the marginal and small landholders. In fact, at the lower end of marginal and small farmer category are those who are 'near landless' i.e. they owned land between 0.002 and 0.200 ha only and accounted for more than 31% of rural households in 1991-92. These are households besides the landless (owning <0.002 ha) who accounted for 11.3% of the total rural households. The 'near landless' category has shown a steady increase since the late 1960s. Thus, more than 42% of the rural households were landless or near landless (Rao and Hanumappa, 1999).

## 15.2. Profile and Problems of Small Farmers

The average size of the operational marginal holdings was only 0.35 hectares and those of the small holdings 1.41 hectares in 1992 compared with 2.69 and 5.79 hectares respectively of the semi- medium and medium category holdings and 15.41 hectares in the case of large category holdings. The ownership holding averages for these categories were even smaller with the exception only of large category holdings which was slightly larger (Singh, 2005). In the case of rural labour households which are landless or near landless, the average size of holding varied from 0.04 hectares in Punjab to 0.74 hectares in Rajasthan in 1993-94 (ETKS, 2003). Further, small farms are highly fragmented.

Land transactions lead to further fragmentation making them non-viable in terms of resource use as well as family sustenance (Mani and Pandey, 1995). A study of a Tamil Nadu village found that of all the farmers in the village, small farmers (60% of all) who owned less than three hectares of land each, 35% had 3-5 plots and 25% had 5-10 plots and the remaining less than three plots. On the other hand, of all the farmers in the village, only 20% farmers had more than 5 plots, another 40% had 3-5 plots each and remaining less than three plots each. Thus, small farms were more fragmented. (Parikh and Nagarajan, 2004). On the other hand, in Punjab, where the average size of the operational holding was 37 and 22 acres respectively for contract and non-contract growers, compared with the state average size of operational holding of the order of about 9 acres, each holding had, on an average, 4.45 plots in case of contract growers and 2.67 plots in case of non-contract growers. The number of plots ranged from 1.36 for small farmers to 5.15 for larger farmers in CF households and 1.46 and 5.13 respectively in case of non-CF households. The larger number of plots per holding was also partly due to leased in land due to the practice of reverse tenancy in the state, especially by the contract growers (Kumar, 2005).

In India, the cropping pattern on small farms is dominated by food grains (75%) compared with that on the large farms (67%) and on medium farms (72%). But, the small farms devote more area for fruit and vegetable production (3.7%) compared to only 1.7% by large farmers and 2.4% by medium farmers, as these crops are more labour intensive (Jha, 2001). Even diversification option in terms of change of crop sequence was exercised more by small holders than that by large holders both in irrigated and non-irrigated areas (Singh, et al, 2002). Also, relatively more of the marginal and small holdings were irrigated than those of the medium or large holdings, and they used higher amount of inputs like fertilizers and farm yard manure (Singh, et al, 2002; ETKS, 2003), human labour, bullock power (Reddy, 1993; Sharma 2000), pump sets, and tractor power though not owned (Sharma and Sharma, 2000; Singh et al, 2002).

The extent of interlocking of markets was more prevalent in case of marginal and small farmers and more so in irrigated areas as irrigated agriculture has higher needs of modern inputs (Swain, 2000). The input market constraints include lack of information about markets, lack of business and negotiating experience and lack of a collective organization which deprive small farmers from interacting on equal terms with the other market participants or market intermediaries. On the other hand, prices they receive are lower than those obtained by larger farmers due to their weak bargaining power and holding capacity (Agrawal, 2000). Major problems of small and marginal farmers in India include spurious input supply, inadequate and costly institutional credit, lack of water and costly access to it, lack of extension services for commercial crops, exploitation in marketing of their produce, high health expenditures, and lack of alternative (non-farm) sources of income. The small and marginal farmers are also a bulk (more than half) of the rural poor and the under nourished (Vyas, 1996; Agrawal, 2000; Singh, et al, 20002; Muller and Patel, 2004). The employment which is the only way to raise these farmers' incomes, is low on these fields because of the low employment elasticity of output due to increasing mechanisation and the kind of crops being grown (Muller and Patel, 2004).

In Punjab, a green revolution region, a small farmer's average land holding is 0.9 hectares. In this state, there is a crisis of sustainability (economic and environmental) of farming since the late 1980s due to higher costs of cultivation. Tractors were being underutilized at a much larger scale in small farms (77%) as against only 50% and 32% in medium and large farms respectively with the overall idle tractor power being 43% for the region (Bathinda district). This indicates overcapitalisation of small farms in the state which has led to higher costs of cultivation due to fixed cost component. Even electric motors and diesel pumps which number more than 11 lakh in the state (GoP, 2005), were being grossly underutilized on small farms (16% and 84% respectively) as against over use of the electric motors to the extent of 11% on both medium and large farms and underutilization of diesel pumps to the extent of 67% and 38% respectively (Singh and Sharma, 2004). Also, the machinery costs accounted for as much as 23% of all operating costs in 1991-92 and were no different from those on large farms (Jha, 2001). In Punjab, the benefits of input subsidies are also skewed towards larger farmers. Small and marginal farmers constitute 36% of the farmers in the state and cultivate 9% of the land, but they receive only 6% of the power subsidy, 7% of the fertilizer subsidy, and 5% of the canal water subsidy. Politically, continuation of these subsidies is often justified on the inability of small and marginal farmers to pay higher user charges, but it is really the larger farmers who are obtaining most of the subsidy benefits (WB, 2003).

However, small farmers are certainly going to stay for long time in India though they are going to face a number of challenges. Therefore, what happens to small and marginal farmers has implications for the entire economy and people's livelihoods. But, they can adequately respond to these challenges only if there is right policy environment. Otherwise, they will only be losers in the process of globalisation and liberalization. It is here that we need to examine the relevance of CF for small farmers in the context of commercialization and globalisation of Indian agriculture.

### 15.3. Commercial Agriculture, Diversification, and Small Farmers

Commercial farming means risks, additional to the natural phenomena which are intrinsic risks of farming everywhere: the risk of output prices that fluctuate, of input prices that may not be commensurate with increased output, of increased vulnerability to pests and so forth (Payer, 1980). A sudden drop in international prices can drive already poor and indebted farmers off the land over the short term. So, small farmers not only lose in terms of lower price realization but also pay higher prices for inputs due to opening up of the domestic economies, in the presence of declining public investment in agriculture and high interest private sector credit (Muller and Patel, 2004). Instead of an access to lucrative markets, without proper mechanisms, they end up losing their domestic markets to imported goods. Thus, the cost of adjustment, due to globalisation and trade liberalization, to poor people becomes substantial when markets do not work very well. Market failure can happen due to many reasons like lack of basic information, dominance of the markets by a few key players, weak economic governance or poor enforcement of the law. Thus, declining viability of small farms in such situations leads small farmers to sell or lease out land to larger farmers (Payer, 1980) which is known as 'reverse tenancy' in India. CF practice has increased the incidence of reverse tenancy in India recently (Singh, 2002). The leased in area in Punjab was 19% and in Haryana, as high as 34% of the total area cultivated in 1992. In India as a whole, marginal and small farmers leased in only 35% of the total leased in area, the rest being with large farmers (43%) and medium farmers (22%). Though reverse tenancy seems to be win-win situation for both the small farmers leasing out and the large farmers leasing in as they maximize their incomes, but in agriculturally backward areas, this practice may alienate the marginal and small farmers from land altogether without alternative sources of employment (Haque, 2000). In fact, due to reverse tenancy, the number of operational holdings in Punjab declined from 13.75 lakhs in 1970-71 to 10.88 lakh in 1985-86 and were 10.93 lakh in 1995-96 (GoP, 2005). This decline in number of holdings came largely from the category of small land marginal holdings which declined by over two lakh between 1990-91 and 2000-01 and accounted for only 29.66% of the total in 2000-01 compared with 44.74 in 1990-91 (Gill, 2005).

There is plenty of distress among farmers both in agriculturally grown as well as backward regions manifested in farmer suicides. A large number of suicide cases are reported from marginal and small category of farmers. Most of the suicide cases have been reported from Andhra Pradesh, Karnataka, Maharashtra, Haryana and Punjab (Shiva et al, 2000; Iyer and Manick, 2000; Mohanty, 2001; Deshpande, 2002; Ahlawat, 2002). The areas which have achieved a greater level of modernisation and commercialisation of agriculture have also witnessed suicides by farmers and agricultural labourers (Gill, 2004). In the absence of any support, the coping costs of commercial modern farming are too high for marginal and small farmers. For example, motor burnout costs for marginal farmers were 10% of their gross farm income in Haryana and 7.7% in A.P. This figure for large farmers was only 1.6% and 2.3% in the two states respectively (WB, 2004). Further, since marginal farm households are net buyers of food, the increasing and fluctuating prices can hit them hard (Singh, et al, 2002).

The viability of the small holdings is an important issue and promoting agricultural diversification towards high value crops is argued to be one of the means through which this can be achieved (Vyas, 1996; Sen and Raju, 2005). Also, the seasonality of employment that is induced by specialization could, to a large extent, be mitigated by introducing a larger number of crops in the cropping pattern that would offer fuller employment to agricultural labour round the year (Sen and Raju, 2005). Small farmers in irrigated areas tend to specialize in few crops which is more of a forced specialization and the larger farmers in dry regions (water scarce regions) are found to be more diversified in their crop and livestock patterns. Thus, there is a positive relationship between farm size and crop or livestock diversification but negative relationship so far as employment and income diversification are concerned (Saleth, 1997).

Crop diversification can be viewed as a strategy for profit maximisation or risk minimization. The profitability would depend on yield, price and cost of cultivation (Sen and Raju, 2005). Farmers adopt or do not adopt a technology/crop depending on the economic sense it makes and other risks and environmental factors associated with it, besides awareness and persuasion which do help. But, farmers do not easily switch from field crops to horticultural or other high value crops as these are much more labour and other input intensive and require more post-harvest handling. Further, profitability is much more dependent on meeting market requirements of freshness and quality. Thus, while farmers can expect to earn more from these crops, they are required to work harder, learn new skills, and risk more capital (Benziger, 1996). Therefore, to adopt a new crop or technology, farmers need more than just the technology. Diversification towards high value crops would involve a higher level of investment per unit area, both direct and indirect. The former is in terms of higher cost of production, and the latter due to infrastructural and institutional changes required for producing and marketing many of these products that are mostly perishable or semi-perishable. Many of the high value products such as fruits, vegetables and flowers are characterized by highly volatile and speculative pricing structure due to the 'small volume' of trade. Diversification and risk are, thus, closely linked as diversification exposes producers to the greater volatility of both domestic and world prices. Risk aversion has been identified as a significant impediment to what would otherwise seem to be a rational diversification on the basis of average profitability of alternative crops which is affected by attitudes of the farmer and the nature of technology (Sen and Raju, 2005).

However, concerns have been raised about certain in-built constraints the marginal and small farmers are faced with, in particular while diversifying towards high value profitable crops.

The primary constraints to successful diversification by small farmers include non-availability of sufficient and timely irrigation, relatively higher costs of cultivation, lack of capital and credit availability, lack of knowledge about markets, lack of access to new technologies, relatively shorter shelf life of produce, price fluctuations, pests and disease proneness of improved varieties of these commodities (fruits and vegetables) and high risk (Pingali and Khwaja, 2004; Sen and Raju, 2005). However, the nature of the product/crop in favour of which diversification is taking place would to a large extent influence the motivation for diversification for small farmers. Diversification by its very nature favours large farmers (Pingali and Khwaja, 2004). Even those small farmers who can be encouraged to go for the crop switch cannot be immune from the problem of 'double exploitation; where they receive lower prices for their horticultural output but pay higher prices for food grains obtained from the open market. In fact, it is this phenomenon emerging from the existing system of agricultural marketing that explains why small farmers do not have the incentive to switch that easily to non-food crops (Sen and Raju, 2005). A study of cut flowers for Delhi market by growers in an U.P. village revealed that the net returns from flower cultivation were many times higher than those form traditional crops of sugarcane or wheat. Further, flower cultivation was dominated by large farmers, and small farmers did not take to flower cultivation as readily. Not only that, the small farmers were relatively late entrants to this crop and it seemed they could not stay in it for long due to high risk and cost of cultivation involved (Sen and Raju, 2005).

### 15.4. CF and Small Farmers

Among the various institutional mechanisms available for agricultural development, so far India has mainly relied on the state and public sector led growth and development of the farm sector with micro level operations i.e. farming per se (with or without control) being with the individual farmers. But, since most of the operators have been small and marginal farmers, the growth in farm sector was mainly determined by the role of the state – both in capital financing as well as in regulation of the activities in terms of the incentive structure created. With the liberalisation of the farm sector policy, the other two modes, of private industrial capital directly entering into the farm sector with large resources (corporate farming) which is still not legalized (for details of debate on the issue, see Singh, 1998), and the industrial capital aligning with the farming interests to bring about improvement in productivity and value addition (CF), are evolving in almost all parts of the country, especially CF, in more developed regions. In fact, CF has been seen as an institutional innovation for agricultural development in the developing world since the 1980s (Glover, 1987).

CF can be defined as a system for the production and supply of agricultural and horticultural produce by farmers/primary producers under advance contracts, the essence of such arrangements being a commitment to provide an agricultural commodity of a type, at a specified time, price, and in specified quantity to a known buyer. In fact, CF can be described as a halfway house between independent farm production and corporate/captive farming and can be a case of a step towards complete vertical integration or disintegration depending on the given context. Due to the efficiency (co-ordination and quality control in a vertical system) and equity (smallholder inclusion) benefits of this hybrid system, it has been promoted aggressively in the developing world by various agencies (Glover, 1987). It basically involves four things - pre-agreed price, quality, quantity or acreage (minimum/maximum) and time (Singh, 2002).

CF is known by different variants like centralised model which is company farmer arrangement, outgrower scheme which is run by government/public sector/joint venture, nucleus-outgrower scheme involving both captive farming and CF by the contracting agency, multi-partite arrangement involving many types of agencies, intermediary model where middlemen are involved between the company and the farmer, and satellite farming referring to any of the above models (Eaton and Shepherd, 2001; GoI, 2003). In fact, CF varies depending on the nature and type of contracting agency, technology, nature of crop/produce, and the local and national context.

The contracts could be of three types; (i) procurement contracts under which only sale and purchase conditions are specified; (ii) partial contracts wherein only some of the inputs are supplied by the contracting firm and produce is bought at pre-agreed prices; and (iii) total contracts under which the contracting firm supplies and manages all the inputs on the farm and the farmer becomes just a supplier of land and labour. The relevance and importance of each type varies from product to product and over time and these types are not mutually exclusive (Hill and Ingersent, 1987; Key and Runsten, 1999). Whereas the first type is generally referred to as marketing contracts, the other two are types of production contracts (Scott, 1984; Welsh, 1997). But, there is a systematic link between product and factor markets under the contract arrangement as contracts require definite quality of produce and, therefore, specific inputs (Scott, 1984; Little, 1994). Also, different types of production contracts allocate production and market risks between the producer and the processor in different ways. The price of the contracted produce can be growers' fixed price, residual (profit/loss) sharing by sponsor and grower, open market based price, spot market price, consignment based, two part split price, tournament price (fixed plus variable based on relative performance), base price plus quality based incentive price, or administered price.

For different reasons, both farmers and farm product processors/distributors may prefer contracts to complete vertical integration. A farmer may prefer a contract which can be terminated at reasonably short notice. Also, contracting gives access to additional sources of capital, and a more certain price by shifting part of the risk of adverse price movement to the buyer (Hill and Ingersent, 1987). Farmers also get an access to new technology and inputs, including credit, through contracts which otherwise may be outside their reach (Glover, 1987; Eaton and Shepherd, 2001). For a processor or distributor, contracts are more flexible in the face of market uncertainty, make smaller demands on scarce capital resources, and impose less of an additional burden of labour relations, ownership of land, and production activities, on management (Buch-Hansen and Marcussen, 1982; Kirk, 1987). The firm even gets an access to unpaid family labour (White, 1997) and can make use of state funds indirectly through agricultural production sector which are directed at farmers by development agencies (Clapp, 1988). Also, food processors can minimise their overhead costs per unit of production by operating their plants at or near fully capacity as contracting gives assured and stable raw material supplies from farms. The firm can also project an image of working with local producers as a partner when it undertakes CF and may even obtain statal and international agency incentives for its activities as developmental projects, instead of corporate farming (Kirk, 1987). Contracts also help improve product quality by directly introducing incentives and penalties as there are problems of adverse selection and moral hazard in any contractual arrangement resulting in underinvestment or shirking by any of the parties (Wolf et al, 2001).

At more macro economic level, contracting can help to remove market imperfections in produce, capital (credit), land, labor, information and insurance markets; facilitate better co-ordination of local production activities which often involve initial investment in processing, extension etc.; and can help in reducing transaction costs (Grosh, 1994; Key and Runsten, 1999). It has also been used in many situations as a policy step by the state to bring about crop diversification for improving farm incomes and employment (Benziger 1996; Singh, 2000). CF is also seen as a way to reduce costs of cultivation as it can provide access to better inputs and more efficient production methods. The increasing cost of cultivation was the reason for the emergence of CF in Japan and Spain in the 1950s (Asano-Tamanoi, 1988) and in the Indian Punjab in the early 1990s (Singh, 2000).

From an institutional economics perspective, the logic for CF could also come from the creation of positive externalities like employment, market development or infrastructure, if agribusiness firms create them better than the open market or the state (Key and Runsten, 1999). In other words, can CF help people other than those who have direct stakes and pay for it?. CF figures as an institutional arrangement for agricultural development in the fields of inputs, product exchange, and product upgrading, the last referring to research and innovations (Christensen, 1992).

Some others recommend CF as the only way to make small scale farming competitive as the services provided by contracting agencies can not be provided by any other agencies (Eaton and Shepherd, 2001). Contract faming also lowers transaction costs for the farmers as many of the transactions are internalised by the procuring firm (IFPRI, 2005). CF is also an alternative to corporate farming which may be costly, risky, and difficult to manage and still not viable (Payer, 1980).

But, generally, contracting agencies especially private, tend to prefer large farmers for CF because of their capacity to produce better quality crops due to the efficient and business-oriented farming methods, large volumes of produce which reduces the cost of collection for the firm, their capacity to bear risk in case of crop failure, and various services provided by these large producers like transport, storage, etc (Wilson, 1986; Winson, 1990; Burch and Pritchard, 1996; Fulton and Clark, 1996; Key and Runsten, 1999).On the other hand, small farmers are picked up by firms for contracts only when the area is dominated by them, there is government directive to do so or they are found to be low cost producers in certain areas and crops (CDC, 1989). Further, firms may work with small farmers to make use of the state support (financial and technical) to these producers under various development programmes (Glover and Kusterer, 1990) and to benefit from lower cost production on these farms as these farmers have access to cheaper family labour, and being residual claimants of their labour, work more conscientiously than hired labour (Key and Runsten, 1999).. In fact, some of them even use large growers, rural elite, and local small processors as sub-contractors to procure from the small growers for the company (Kirk, 1987). The seed companies in India use small companies as subcontractors to procure seeds produced under contracts (Shiva and Crompton, 1998). In Canada, small tomato growers were preferred as the crop required hand-picking which only small farmers do as the large ones do mechanical harvesting, especially when weather limits the use of mechanical harvesters (Winson, 1990). Similarly, in India, gherkin CF is carried out by small and marginal farmers as the crop requires plenty of labour inputs which these faming families can provide from within (Dev and Rao, 2004). Also, working with many small farmers in the case of small processors gives the required flexibility in procurement schedule helping to extend the processing season and use the equipment efficiently; and helps spread risk of supply failure as compared to working with a few large farmers.

### 15.5. Indian Experience in CF

The experience of agricultural development in India has shown that the existing systems of delivery of agricultural inputs and purchase and use of agricultural output have not been efficient in reaching the benefits of better linkages between agriculture and agro- processing industry to the farmers or the agro-industry. The timely, quality and cost effective delivery of adequate inputs still remains a dream despite the marketing attempts of the corporate sector and the developmental programmes of the state. The farmers are not able to sell their produce remuneratively. There is plenty of distress among farmers both in agriculturally grown as well as backward regions manifested in farmer suicides. Agricultural markets in India which are found to be both inefficient and imperfect, may not be able to ensure fair and reasonable returns to all the players. There are temporal and spatial variations in the markets and the producers' share in consumers' rupee has been quite low in general, except a few commodities. In fact, in some commodities like potato in some regions in India, producers end up making net losses at the same time when traders make substantial profits from the same crop (Mitra and Sarkar, 2003). In the environment liberalization and globalisation policies, the role of the state in agricultural marketing and input supply is being reduced, and an increasing space is being provided to the private sector to bring about better marketing efficiency in input and output markets. On the other hand, processors and/or marketers face problems in obtaining timely, cost effective, and adequate supply of quality raw materials.

CF has various models/variants being practiced in India at present. The bi-partite contract farming in India is currently being practised by multinational firms like Cadbury (cocoa), Pepsi (potato, chillies, groundnut), Unilever (tomato, chicory, tea, and milk), ITC Ltd. (tobacco, wood trees, and oilseeds), Cargill (seeds), domestic corporates like Ballarpur Industries Limited (BILT), JK Paper, and Wimco (in eucalyptus and poplar trees), Green Agro Pack (GAP) Ltd., VST Natural Products, Global Green, Interrgarden India, Kempscity Agro Exports, and Sterling Agro (all in gherkins), United Breweries (UB) (barley), Nijjer Agro (tomato), Tarai Foods (vegetables), A M Todd (mint in Punjab), McCain India (potato in Gujarat), (Singh, 2000a; Rangi and Sidhu 2000; Subrahmanyam, 2000; Dileep et al, 2002; Saigal and Kashyap, 2002; Grewal, 2003), Namdhari Seeds (seeds), and various government and semi-government agencies, especially in seed production and perishables like vegetables and fruits, with varying degrees of success with individual farmers. Most of the organic production is organised through bi-partite contracts (Appendix 15.4). There are many banks which provide finance for contract farming. These include NABARD, SBI, ICICI Bank and UTI Bank. Contract farming in India by the corporate sector has until a few years ago been more of a case of buy back, and input supply (Appendix 15.1, figure 15.1) and/or credit supply or linkage as depicted in Appendix 15.1, figure 15.1. See Appendix 15.5 for a bi-partite contract in mint, 15.6 in pineapple, and

Appendix 15.9 for one in gherkins.

Besides the much common bi-partite agreements between companies and farmers, there are other models of contracting as well. The tri-partite agreement among farmers, state agency (PAFC) and the extension/seed company in Punjab specified the fixed price and bonus to be paid by the PAFC to farmer for the produce (bonus only if the PAFC was able to sell the produce at a higher price), type and quantity of seed to be supplied by the seed company at a given price for given acreage, farmer's responsibility of delivering the quality produce (produced by making use of recommended inputs bought from outlets prescribed by the PAFC) at a specified place, payment by PAFC within two days after delivery, and PAFC being the sole decider of weight of produce and the sole and only arbitrator in case of dishonouring of the contract terms by any of the parties. The contract was signed by all the three parties in the presence of two witnesses for the farmer (see Appendix 13.1 in chapter 13). Though contract farming has existed in the state for more than a decade now, it was for the first time that the state government took it up as intermediary between companies and farmers. It was part of a larger project on crop adjustment (diversification) to be implemented during 2002-2007. It was rather surprising that the state undertook contract farming as a party to the contract with the growers. Nowhere in the world has state undertaken this kind of effort for diversification (Appendix 15.2, figures 15.2 and 15.2).

Recently, several agribusiness companies have made forags into the farm sevice sector which is being seen as a care of Private-Public Partenership. This has come to be known as faulitator model (see details in chapter 11).

More recently, the facilitator model has been modified with the inclusion of a local arthiya/commission agent/ input dealer as a franchisee for the agri facilitator (Appendix 15.6, Fig. 15.3; also Sulaiman et al, 2004). Franchising is a continuous relationship (long term partnership) in which a franchiser provides a licensed privilege to the franchisee to conduct business in addition to providing assistance in organising, training, and merchandizing. In return, the franchiser receives a certain amount from the franchisee as royalty. It can be product, business format or trade name franchise and is widely practiced in food, hotel and services industries. The basis ingredients of a franchise system were: obligations of both the parties, initial/later/ongoing fees and mode of payment, identified/specified territory, specified duration, termination of agreement procedures, post termination confidentiality, and procedure of arbitration.

MSSL (Mahindra ShubhLabh Services Limited) which pioneered the franchise model has 57 outlets in ten states in north, west and southern India, and only three of them are company owned and run. The rest are all run by franchisees. The crops in which the company operated are cereals like paddy including basmati, durum wheat, barley, and maize, vegetables like gherkins, potato, tomato, chilly, and garlic, fruits like grapes and pomegranates, pulses like moong, gram and peas, oilseeds like soyabean, hyola, mustard, groundnut and sunflower, spices like coriander, cumin and patchouli, and cotton. Generally, there is one franchisee in one district and it is exclusive license and business format franchising. Each franchisee has 15-25 spokes (village cluster level outlets, who are sub-franchisees and share margins with franchisees). The franchising system makes up for 2.5 per cent of the MSSL's business. Franchisees are selected based on their agricultural input business volumes and experience in local area. The initial franchise fee is Rs. three lakh per outlet (district) and varies from state to state. Further, there is also a royalty fee from farm advisory service fee (Rs. 150/acre) which is 12.5 per cent in first year and 19.5 per cent from second year onwards. For the farm advisory service, Rs. 50 is charged in cash from the farmer and the remaining (Rs. 100) in credit at the time of delivery of crop and the crops is monitored regularly by the filed staff (see format for crop monitoring and inspection in appendix). It also charges five per cent of tractor rentals and three per cent of maize harvester rentals from the franchisee and the equipment is owned by the franchisee for first two years. The franchise contract is initially for three years and extendable. The company charges a commission of 3-5 percent on sale of pesticides, fertilisers and seeds through its franchisees and 2.5 per cent on sales to output buying companies of which a large part (1.5 per cent) is passed on to the franchisee. The franchisee gets his commission as a distributor of inputs. For credit linkage, the farmers are identified by the village sarpanch and recommended to the bank by the MSSL which charges a one per cent margin on these loans which are lent to farmers at the interest rate of 12 per cent per annum. The company has a buy back agreement with the farmers which specifies a price which is prevailing market price plus small percentage as incentive say Rs. 10-15 over and above the market price (see agreement in appendix 15.7). The company also monitors farmer fields and crops for better contract performance (Appendix 15.7A).

MSSL provides support like business planning for the outlet, training, business roll out, territory manager, all input supplies, and bank linkages besides promotional support and accounting packages. The franchisee is evaluated for his performance in terms of planned and achieved targets. The franchisee is also expected to carry out some local promotional activity. The franchisee owns/leases the outlet and does not have to pay any security deposit. For franchise location and franchisee selection, an intensive business feasibility study is conducted to determine the business prospects for the district in terms of selection of crops, business planning for the centre, and business roll out and launch plan. Crop selection includes corporate involvement in the crop, nature of crop, yield improvement potential, and scalability. Selection of area for operation involves examining input usage levels. Operational aspects include agricultural marketing laws, credit issues, and government support. The franchisees are selected based on their presence in the agricultural input or/and output business in the concerned location and typically a franchisee is an arthiya or/and an agro input dealer. A franchisee employs five field staff, each one managing 100 farmers or 500 acres of a crop/s (each farmer growing at least five acres) in a village or cluster of villages, and all of them are supervised by one supervisor (written communication from Mr. Vikram Puri of MSSL, Chandigarh on January 10, 2005). In Punjab, the average acreage per farmer was 3.5 acres and there were 17000 farmers involved with MSSL system in 2004. It is more of a case of an inter locking of factor markets coming back in another form. But, this model also does not seem to be working well as there are many problems in this model in Punjab though it has worked well in some other states like Tamilnadu.

Another recent model is intermediary model of contract farming practiced by Pepsi (Appendix 15.3, Fig. 15.4, Also agreements in Appendix 15.10A, 15.10B and 15.10C) which was the hall mark of contract farming in Thailand. It has also been practicing flexible contracts interms of pricing structure which provides the growers options on pricing. Similar is the case of McCain India which also practices flexible contract price which procures 50% produce at fixed price and 50% at a minimum or maximum price (about 10% lower or higher than the fixed price) depending on the market price of the produce.

There have been some studies of the CF system in India more recently. But, most of them look at the economics of the CF system in specific crops, compared with that of the non-contract situation and/or competing traditional crops of a given region, e.g. in gherkins (hybrid cucumber) in Tamilnadu (Chidambaram, 1997) and Andhra Pradesh (Haque, 2000; Dev and Rao, 2004) tomato in Punjab (Bhalla and Singh, 1996; Haque, 2000; Rangi and Sidhu, 2000) and Haryana (Dileep et. al., 2002) and cotton in Tamilnadu (Agarwal et al, 2005). It is found that contract production gave much higher (almost three times) gross returns compared with that from the traditional crops of wheat, paddy and potato in case of tomato (Bhalla and Singh, 1996; Rangi and Sidhu, 2000), tomato and onion in the case of gherkin (Chidambaram, 1997) and cotton (Agarwal et al, 2005) due to higher yield and assured price under contracts. The studies of tomato contract production in Punjab and Haryana (Haque, 2000; Dileep et. al., 2002), of cucumber in Andhra Pradesh (Haque, 2000) and cotton in Tamilnadu (Agarwal et al, 2005) also found the net returns from these crops under contracts being much higher than those under non-contract situations though production cost in tomato was higher under the contract system (Dileep et. al, 2002). A more recent study across crops, companies and locations in Punjab also confirms this (Kumar, 2005). In case of cotton in Tamilnadu, the contract growers had lower input cost, lower interest loans, faster payment for produce, and the crop insurance facility (Agarwal et al, 2005). The studies in the states of Punjab and Haryana also reveal that contract growers faced many problems like undue quality cut on produce by firms, delayed deliveries at the factory, delayed payments, low price and pest attack on the crop (Bhalla and Singh, 1996; Singh, 2002; Rangi and Sidhu, 2000; and Dileep et. al., 2002; Satish, 2003). More recently, DSCL run input supply and CF program (Haryali Kisan Bazaar) for potato in Haryana also showed higher net returns for growers compared with non-growers due to highr yields and higher prices, though the cost of cultivation was also higher (17-24%) (Tripathi et al, 2005).

It was also found by all of the studies that most of the firms work mostly with large and medium farmers (Bhalla and Singh, 1996; Singh 2002; Haque, 2003; Dev and Rao, 2004; Singh and Asokan, 2005; Kumar, 2005; Khairnar and Yeleti, 2005) with the exception of firms in Karnataka, Tamilnadu, and Andhra Pradesh which worked with small and marginal farmers due the nature of the crops (cucumber/gherkin, and broiler chicken).

Gherkin contracting was also smooth as there was no local market for the crop, there was flexibility in contracts due to the short term nature of the crop, and farmers maintained alternative sources of income (Singh and Asokan, 2005). Similar was the case of iceberg lettuce grown for McDonalds in India which had a very thin market (Khairnar and Yeleti, 2005). This bias in favour of large/medium farmers is perpetuating the practice of reverse tenancy in regions like Punjab where these farmers lease in land from marginal and small farmers for contract production (Singh, 2002; Haque, 2003). Breach of contracts by farmers as well as firms has also been reported (Bhalla and Singh, 1996; Singh 2002; Haque, 2003). Some of these studies recommend further expansion and promotion of CF system due to its benefits (Bhalla and Singh, 1996; Chidambaram, 1997; Rangi and Sidhu, 2000; and Dileep et. al., 2002). The eligibility criteria for participation in CF projects/schemes like irrigated land, suitable land, land near main road, literacy level of the farmer are themselves discriminatory in terms of who can be a contract grower. In fact, in CF everywhere, private agribusiness firms have less interest and ability to deal with small scale farmers on an individual basis (Hazell, 2005) and promoting contract farming for small holders remains a challenge (Setboonsarng et al, 2005) .

The more recent models of CF like franchising (Appendix 15.3) being practiced by the Tatas (Tata Kisan Sansar) for wheat in states of UP, Haryana and Punjab; and by the Mahindra Shubhlabh Services Limited (Mahindra Krishi Vihar) for paddy in Tamil Nadu, Andhra Pradesh, Karnataka and basmati and maize in Punjab and Haryana are also not delivering as expected. Mahindra and Mahindra's recent involvement in Punjab agriculture has not worked to the advantage of the farmers. In fact, this model creates a monopsony where a single buyer buys produce of hundreds and thousands of farmers. This system works to the disadvantage of those farmers who lack adequate information about the market, which is termed as asymmetry of information. This model increases the buyer's power disproportionately and puts seller entirely at the buyer's mercy. Small and marginal farmers have not gained from these experiments. Wherever any gain has been reported, it is reported for the farmers in general and distinction between big/rich and small/poor farmer's gains is not reflected in any way. The interests of the poor farmers are not synonymous with those of large/ rich farmers (Gill, 2004). One of the limiting factors in performance of the contract scheme in Punjab seems to be the MSP which introduces price rigidity and acts unfavourably for the buyers and exporters. On the other hand, because Basmati is out of the purview of the MSP, its contracting performance has been quite favourable for the processors and exporters as they could discover a market price. Also, being an export crop, it enjoys a well established high value market which in turn has created a lot of comfort for the exporters. The performance of CF in Punjab has been tardy despite the fact that the state (PAFC) has been reimbursing the extension service fees to the companies, on behalf of the growers.

Further, the contracts protect company interest at all costs to the farmer and do not cover farmer's production risk e.g. crop failure, retain the right of the company to change price, and generally offer prices which are based on open market prices (Singh, 2002; Singh, 2005a; Singh and Asokan, 2005; Khairnar and Yeleti, 2005). Even organic produce buyers offer conventional produce market price based prices to their growers (Singh, 2005b). This is a serious issue as even a significant premium over market price may not help a farmer if open market prices go down significantly which is not uncommon in India. The market price based price is offered to avoid grower defaults as they can, otherwise, sell the produce in the open market due to availability of alternative market due to product symmetry. However, an important contracting agency in India offers two alternative prices to the grower: a fixed price different for different times of the season (staggered prices) plus a quality incentive based on produce quality in terms of content and defects, and a market price (preceding three days' average market price in the local mandi) linked price (which is slightly lower than prevailing market price) and a quality incentive again based on content and defects. This is quite innovative and fair system which gives the flexibility and choice to the grower and rewards quality (Fig. 7 in Appendix 15.3). There are aspects of product asymmetry and bargaining power which lead to default or monopsonistic exploitation of the grower.

The firms also manipulated provisions of the contracts in practice, e.g. in case of broiler chickens in Tamilnadu where they picked up birds before due date or delayed it depending on the demand which meant losses for contract growers. They also delayed payments upto 60 days. But, growers were locked into these contracts due to the firm specific fixed investments they had made (Singh and Asokan, 2005). Thus, many of the CF projects also failed due to either poor design of the project or default by any of the contracting parties.

Even state sponsored programme of CF did not deliver in Punjab. The contracted winter maize and hyola crops failed almost completely due to inclement weather and poor quality seeds. In case of green peas, the contract growers were forced to dump their produce in open market, after being rejected by the PAIC on quality ground as per the contract specification, as there had been fungus infection due to inclement weather which was marked by heavy rains in winter season and then sudden rise in temperature. An area of 500 acres under contract production of green peas in Patiala and Fatehgarh Sahib districts had been affected. Some farmers found fault with the fungicide supplied by the contracted company in this regard. The dumping of contract-produced crop in open market led to fall in local market prices and it was being sold at Rs. 3 per kg. now as against a promised price of Rs. 5 per kg. by the PAIC (Singh, 2003; Rangi and Sidhu, 2003). In general, across crops and regions, the CF program could not achieve the stated area goal. Not only it fell short in terms of contracted area being less than that stated by the agency, but also the farmers did not plant the entire contracted area with the contract crops. The gap was much larger in latter case and even as high as 50% in winter maize in Ludhiana and 20% in hyola in both Ludhiana and Patiala. There was a different private seed company for each crop and they only provided seed and no other extension service. Finally, none of the companies procured the produce and advised the farmers to sell in open market either because open market prices were higher than contract price or quality was not as desired. Except the oilseed crops (hyola and sunflower), the net returns from contract crops were found be lower than what farmers would have got from wheat crop. Most of the problems farmers faced related to production and quality (like quality of seed and extension) and not marketing of produce (except peas) as open market could take care of contract produce. Due to this experience, a large majority (60%) were not willing to enter into CF arrangement again (Dhaliwal et al, 2003). There have also been instances of corruption and malpractice in the PAFC run CF program due to conflicts of interest among implementing agencies and lack of monitoring (Ramachandran and Dogra, 2006; Singh, 2006).

The recent World Bank reports also point to the deficiencies in the CF program launched by the State Government of Punjab. It states that for the programme of CF to be successful, it should take into account the aspects of selection of crops for contracting, development of quick and effective contract enforcement and dispute resolution system, limiting fiscal risks to the state government, limiting the number of parties in a contractual arrangement, and developing farmers' organizations capable of contracting with sponsors, with a view to reduce transaction costs, increasing information flow, and improving farmers' negotiation position (WB, 2003; WB, 2004).

It is not incidental that most of the CF projects are in the states of Punjab, Haryana, Gujarat, Maharashtra, Karnataka and Tamilnadu which are agriculturally developed states. On the other hand, vast areas of the country such as Bihar, Jharkhand, Chhatisgarh, Orissa, West Bengal, the entire north-east India and areas of Uttaranchal, Himachal Pradesh, Kerala and Jammu and Kashmir have been bypassed by these companies. Does it mean that these areas and farmers would not benefit from commercialization and vertical integration of agriculture? These are areas with highest concentration of small and marginal farmers (Gill, 2004). This essentially means that contracting companies do not in any way encourage the participation of those who need to be helped to participate as risk preference and innovativeness require not just attitude but also resources and risk taking capability to undertake risky crops and ventures (Glover, 1987). The aspects of contracting which contribute to CF excluding small producers are: enforcement of contracts, high transaction costs, quality standards, business attitudes and ethics like non/delayed/reduced payment and high rate of product rejection, and weak bargaining power of the small growers (Kirsten and Sartorius, 2002). CF also reinforces reverse tenancy where in small and marginal farmers lease out land to large and medium farmers who are often contract growers for the companies as was the case in the Indian Punjab (Singh, 2002).

## 15.6. Ensuring Small Farmer Participation in Globalised Commercial Agriculture under CF

There are a large number of institutional arrangements to co-ordinate the small producers which should be assessed for their relevance and effectiveness in a given context, though a priori, it seems the co-operative and other similar forms of farmer organization are more relevant and sustainable, especially the New Generation Co-operatives (NGCs) which are voluntary, more market oriented, member responsive, self-governed, and avoid free riding and horizon problems as they have contractual equity based transaction with grower members (Singh, 2004; Hazell, 2005). In India, Amul has been able to successfully link up/integrate small and marginal milk producers with the national and international milk markets. It is estimated that 21% of its nine million members are landless and another 66% small and marginal farmers (Gandhi et al, 2001; Pingali and Khwaja, 2004). Some of the co-operatives like those dealing with sapota (chickoo) in south Gujarat have also attempted quality based grading and pooling system, and contractual relations with members for procurement, along with market orientation strategies like multiple outlets, and efficient use of market information to achieve better business performance (Singh, 1997). In fact, co-operative form of organization of even farm production activity by resource constrained farmers has been found to be more efficient than private farms in Romania (Sabates-Wheeler, 2002).

With right policy environment, small farms can not only survive buy can also make a developmental contribution by contributing to poverty reduction. There have been cases of success when public or private assistance to the growers in terms of technical assistance and supply of input credit was made available. In some places in Brazil, small farmers have gone in for collective tanks to meet the scale requirement though the large farmers will have an advantage as they do not face the transaction cost involved in collective use of physical assets. The dairy companies and cooperatives encourage the use of collective tanks, even by financing or facilitating credit for milk producers in some cases (Farina, 2002). Many attempts including offering differentiated contracts under CF schemes to include small farmers failed in Mexico though firms had no option but to contract with small vegetable growers. A few firms succeeded in including small farmers in their CF projects only when they also employed the farmers' family members in their processing units, used local intermediaries to supervise small growers, and/or limited the small grower contracts only to areas close to the highway, besides the other reasons like the small growers being lower cost and more efficient than the firm's own farms, their poor access to alternative outlets for produce and source of credit, and having low labour and land opportunity cost. These measures reduced the information asymmetry between the growers and the firm and the transaction cost of dealing with small growers (Warning et al, 2003).

The development agencies and projects need to internalize the fact that increasingly product markets will mean supermarkets. Therefore, market-oriented programmes and policies will indeed be supermarket oriented. If, in a given country, a few chains command majority of the food sector, then development policies and programmes need to learn how to deal with this handful of big companies. The development agencies also need to realize that small farmers and entrepreneurs have to gear up quickly to compete in the new markets that are spreading over most of the food economy. The local market niches are disappearing and the distinction between global and domestic market is getting blurred. The government and the donors will have to focus their programmes not just on exports but also on the growing market of the local supermarkets. It is important to promote good business practices that optimize retailer-supplier relations, protecting both sides. This can be initiated by establishing or improving contract regulations and business rules of practice some of which are already available in the form of legal acts in the US and Argentina. These practices can also be forced by private sector codes of practice. However, regulations do not ultimately change the economic forces under which the supermarkets operate and the changes in procurement systems are driven by these forces. These changes and the basic requirements they impose on growers are conditions which will have to be met if the growers are to be able to tap the powerful market of the supermarkets. Therefore, it is crucial that government and donor agencies help small farmers and entrepreneurs to make the investments in equipment, management, technology, commercial practice and the development of strong and efficient organizations to meet those requirements. There have been such attempts in Brazil and Guatemala (Reardon and Berdegue, 2002). In organic produce chains as well, group certification by public or development agencies can provide a chance for small farmers to take up organic cultivation.

The main requirements of small farmers in this changing environment are better access to capital and education.

Management capacity is as important as physical capital and most difficult thing to provide. Further, collective action to deal with scale requirements needs to be designed to satisfy new product and process standards or to avoid exclusion from the supply chain. Collective action through cooperatives or associations is important not only to be able to buy and sell at a better price but also to help small farmers adapt to new patterns and much greater levels of competition (Farina, 2002). The small farmers require professional training in marketing and in technical aspects of production. There is also need to strengthen small farmer organizations and provide them technical assistance to increase productivity for the cost competitive market, provide help in improving quality of produce, and to encourage them to participate more actively in the marketing of their produce in order to capture value added in the supply chain. Finally, the problem of financing the small producers needs to be tackled by finding innovative ways to provide finance (Schwentesius and Gomez, 2002).

On the other hand, regulation of super market chains to control or mitigate their market power can be an effective tool to ensure the presence of small growers in value chains as seen in the case of banana trade regime in pre-WTO period in the EU policy, single channel (monopoly) exports by producer bodies in some exporting countries like South Africa, and regulation of domestic import markets in France (Gibbon, 2003).

Though there are concerns about the ability of the small farms and firms to survive in the changing environment of agribusiness, still there are opportunities for them to exploit like in product differentiation with origin of product or organic products and other niche markets. But, the major route has to be through exploitation of other factors like external economies of scale through networking or clustering and such other alliances like CF (Kirsten and Sartorius, 2002). The experience of CF across the globe suggests that it is not the contract per se which is harmful as a system but how it is practised in a given context. If there are enough mechanisms to monitor and use the contract for developmental purposes, it can certainly lead to a betterment of all the parties involved, especially small and marginal farmers.

## 15.7. Making CF Work for Small Farmers

There have been warning notes since the 1980s about the widespread applicability of CF as a development tool (Goldsmith,

1985; Glover, 1987). Further, the hybrid nature of CF, and the often conflicting objectives it is supposed to meet, makes it difficult to either design effective public policy interventions or to organise growers (Glover, 1987). Viewed in the light of experience, the potential problems of CF point to the policy steps which are required to reduce the ill-effects of such a system like regulation and monitoring of contracts.

### 15.7.1. Legal Framework and State Support

It is difficult to police contracts due to the multiple variables involved in a farming contract like output price, input prices and supply, payments, quality standards (Glover, 1987; Wolf et al, 2001). Therefore, if the firm really wants to manipulate/ sabotage a contract, there are dozen ways to do it. Therefore, a government can not really do much to police a contract, and it should not impose contract on an unwilling firm or in an inappropriate situation. Further, the state/government may not always stand by the small growers due to the pressure from the agribusiness interests, and may suffer from the conflicting objectives of its various agencies. Since policy interventions can not really change the outcome of a fundamentally unworkable situation and the relevance of CF for small farmer development, it is better to have more realistic expectations about the policy intervention effect and define an appropriate niche for smallholder CF in terms of crops and markets. It is better to plan carefully ex ante for CF based on earlier experiences elsewhere (Glover, 1987). But, still, the state/government can play both regulatory and enabling/developmental role in CF. Legal protection to contract growers as a group must be considered to protect them from ill effects of contracting practiced by supply chains drivers. There are cases of legal protection given to subcontracting industries in Japan in their relations with large firms. These laws specify the duties (to have a written and clear terms contract with the subcontractor) and forbidden acts for the large parent firm. The latter include refusal to receive delivery of commissioned goods, delaying the payment beyond agreed period, discounting of payment, returning commissioned goods without good reason, forced price reduction, compulsory purchase by subcontractors of parental firm's products, and forcing subcontractors to pay in advance for materials supplied by the parent firm. These provisions are monitored by the Fair Trade Commission. Interestingly, most of the violations by parent firms were on the written form and clear terms of the contracts (Sako, 1992). If CF is only the flexible production systems prevalent in industry applied to farm production, then it is only logical to extend such legal provisions with necessary modifications to farming contracts. In farming sector per se, there is the Model Producer Protection Act, 2000 of Iowa State in the USA which requires contracts to be in plain language and disclose material risks, provides a three days cancellation period for the producer to review and discuss production contracts with their advisors, provides for producers to be first priority lien for payments due under a contracts in case of contracting company bankruptcy, protects against undue cancellation of contracts by companies and prohibits 'tournaments' (contracts where compensation to grower is determined by his performance relative to others) (www.flaginc.org/pubs/poultry/poultrypts.)

In India, the legal reform process is already under way with the Union Government enacting the Model Act for the state Agricultural Produce Marketing (Development and Regulation) Act, 2003 and many states (8 as suggested, and 10 partially like Gujarat, Haryana, Karnataka, Maharashtra, U.P. Delhi and Chandigarh permitting only direct marketing/CF or private/co-operative markets (only Karnataka)) carrying out the amendment in their Acts. This amended act deals with setting up of private markets, selling of produce by growers outside the APMCs (regulated markets), setting up of direct markets, specialized commodity specific markets, regulation and promotion of CF, provision for agencies and measures to promote quality, standards, and alternative markets, and public-private partnerships to facilitate more and better linkage between firms and farmers (GoI, 2004). The amended APMC Act has certain mandatory and optional provisions regarding CF wherein mandatory ones include aspects like who can undertake CF (type of sponsor and of contract grower), details about the land under contract, duration of contract, description of farm produce, other contract specifications like quantity i.e. acreage, entire crop, or fixed quantity, produce quality specifications and penalties for lower quality like rejection, or lower price, crop delivery arrangements i.e. at farm/factory gate/collection centre and transport arrangements, pricing and credit mechanisms, farmer asset/land indemnity, compulsory registration of contracts with the local authority and the procedure for dispute resolution. On the other hand, the optional features include those relating to farm practices, joint crop insurance, support services to be provided, farmer-management forum for monitoring of contract system performance, and monitoring of quality and yields. The model contract agreement is quite fair in terms of sharing of costs and risks between the sponsor and the grower (GoI, 2003). But, it leaves out many aspects of farmer interest protection like delayed payments and deliveries, contract cancellation damages if producer made firm specific heavy investments, inducement/force/intimidation to enter a contract, disclosure of material risks, competitive performance based payments, and sharing production risks. Also, there are state level variations in the amended Acts and the spirit has been diluted. For example, in Gujarat, the amended Act makes the APMC as a party in the tripartite contract stating the logic that APMCs have a useful role as facilitator as they have long standing relationship with farmers and can disseminate the CF concept and practice besides monitoring its practice. It makes the Gujarat State Agricultural Marketing Board (GSAMB) and the local APMC as the registering authority for contracts. The MD, GSAMB will examine the contract for its fairness to the farmers and can refuse to register the same if found inadequate in protection of the farmer interest. It is also the arbitrator in case of disputes. The registration costs Rs. 200 for the sponsor. Though the central model Act exempts contract procurement from market fee, the Gujarat Act makes it mandatory to pay the prescribed cess to the concerned APMC or in case of multi-location operations, to the GSAMB which will apportion it to the concerned APMCs. Though the monitoring role of APMC is desirable, but making it a party to the contract is totally unnecessary and undesirable as that is not the best way to protect the farmer interest, if that, at all, is the logic for giving the role of a party to the contract to the APMC in contracts between sponsors and the growers.

#### 15.7.1.1. Role of the State

CF will work for agricultural diversification only if the current system of procurement based on Minimum Support Price (MSP) is changed in favour of new crops because it provides a powerful economic incentive to prolong the wheat paddy rotation. The government of Punjab through PAFC has been reimbursing extension cost to the CF agencies/facilitators at the rate of Rs. 100 per acre. But, doing it irrespective of the size of holding of the contract growers defeats the purpose as it does not ensure that small and marginal farmers who can not afford to pay for extension and need to be brought into the contract system are included. Similarly, the Ministry of Food Processing industries has been providing an incentive since the beginning of the 9th Plan in the form of a reimbursement of five per cent of the value of raw materials procured through CF with farmers with a maximum ceiling of Rs. 10 lakh per year for a maximum of three years with the condition that any organization (private/ public/co-operative/Non-Government organization (NGO)/joint venture/assisted) should work with at least 25 farmers under contract for at least three years (MFPI, 1998).

In Thailand, the state not only provided coordination and support of local authorities such as agricultural extension agents, local administration officers, and the BAAC, it also reallocated 250 million Baht deposit in BAAC. The interest compensation for the farmer participants in the program (3.5 % p.a.) was made available to encourage more farmer participation and to reduce production cost. But, later, farmers could obtain only low interest rate (5% p.a.) loan instead of getting compensation for interest charge. The MOAC through its DOAE still carries out training in CF for farmers and local officials which includes aspects like guidelines for CF implementation, i.e. types of products suitable for certain kind of contracting arrangement, familiarity with the system of CF, supervision of contract arrangements, special financial assistance to companies undertaking CF, and process of implementation of the CF project in terms of co-ordination between public and private sectors and choice of relevant area and farmers. It even specifies requirements before a CF projects is undertaken which are: farmer willingness and exposure to the concept of CF, feasible standards of quality of produce, price flexibility, and production and marketing plan. Discussing factors in success of CF project, it emphasizes on clear understanding of the concept of CF and a felt need for it among project participants, besides physical proximity between producing and processing areas, strict adherence to quality standards and honesty and sincerity of all parties involved. It assigns specific roles and responsibilities to farmers, farmer groups, companies, and government agencies in terms of dealing with each other for the project. It finally recommends suitable types of systems of CF for different types of commodities and advocates CF with farmer organisations instead of individual farmers. It even goes on to advise in terms of having multiple outlets for produce, both contract and non-contract, in term of different grades of produce from the same group of farmers (MOAC, 2002). The state intervention helped the farm sector and its farmers only to the extent that it has promoted competition that has been beneficial for growers like in potato in northern Thailand, and also led to pumping of capital in farm sector through the Bank of Agriculture and Agricultural Co-operatives (BAAC) loans for contract growers. But, on most other counts, like making the system fair for farmers in terms of nature of contracts, or helping farmer organizations in processing or marketing or even in collective selling to companies, it has not really been effective. The role of the government should be enabling and developmental in nature.

### 15.7.2. Contracts and Farmer/Civil Society Organisations

Contracts need to be transparent and require frequent and independent scrutiny so that they remain competitive both with similar contracts and with open market transactions. Wide publicity of contract terms can help to stimulate competition. Secondly, vigorous bargaining co-operatives, or other agricultural producer organisations are needed to negotiate equitable contracts (Key and Runsten, 2003). These types of organisations have been able to secure the standardisation of contracts and their scrutiny by a government agency in the USA (Wilson, 1986) and the bargaining groups have negotiated input purchase and output sale collectively (Welsh, 1990). In Japan as well, farmers have managed their relationships with companies well through co-operatives (Asano-Tamanoi, 1988). Producers' organizations amplify the political voice of smallholder producers, reduce the costs of marketing of inputs and outputs, and provide a forum for members to share information, co-ordinate activities and make collective decisions. Producers' organizations create opportunities for producers to get more involved in value adding activities such as input supply, credit, processing, marketing and distribution. On the other hand, they also lower the transaction costs for the processing/marketing agencies working with growers under contracts. Thus, there is need to promote/encourage farmer groups for CF as was the case in Thailand. Group CF proves beneficial for both growers and companies (Singh, 2005e). But, there are difficulties in enforcing collective actions due to group heterogeneity, agency resistance to such actions, and making members adhere to group norms in the absence of any legal authority with such collectivities (Glover, 1987).

Besides the resources and technology which determine CF performance, it is the relationship among state, companies, and farmers, which shapes formal and informal institutions and gets mediated by them that matters (Ornberg, 2003). The practice of contracts needs to be monitored by farmer organisations or NGOs. In fact, the companies should proactively involve NGOs into their CF operations and even organise farmer co-operatives or groups for more sustainable CF programs (Mayers and Vermeulen, 2002; Pingali and Khwaja, 2004). The groups or farmers' organisations like co-operatives not only lower transaction costs of the firms but also lower input costs for the farmers and give them better bargaining power as was the case of a potato growers' co-operative in north Thailand which acted as a link between the growers and the company (Ornberg, 2003). In contract arrangements with small producers in west African countries, the cotton companies started transferring some of the operational or functional responsibilities like distribution of inputs, equipment orders, and credit repayment management, to the village associations in the 1970s itself. They provided these associations with management skills for these tasks. The companies relied on traditional village authority structures for organising the associations but limited the associations to one per village to simplify company purchasing, delivery and marketing procedures. This arrangement accounted for a significant part of each cotton company's success (Bingen et al, 2003). But, unfortunately, agribusiness companies have not been very keen to organise or support co-operatives. Rather, they have tried to fail co-operatives whenever they emerged (Konings, 1998).

### 15.7.3. Farmers and CF Agencies

In CF, both companies and growers try to improve their own positions as a negotiation which change over time (Vellema, 2004). Further, contract design is a complex task given that there is always a problem of incomplete contracts due to bounded rationality of the contracting parties (Lorenz, 1999; Tirole, 1999). Companies generally use some of the four policing mechanisms: input control, monitoring of farms/production activity, quality measurement, and revenue sharing as residual claimancy to tackle grower opportunism or 'blind spots' which arise due to information asymmetry and consequent moral hazard involved in contracting. Whereas input control can be exercised by supplying specific inputs, monitoring can be done by field staff or by new techniques like remote sensing, electronic data interchange, and precision farming which are cost effective and transparent methods. The latter two mechanisms (quality measurement and residual claimancy) are more difficult to use (Wolf et al, 2001). Therefore, it is important to consider contract design as a multi-criterion decision problem. Some basic rules of contract design include (i) co-ordinating to minimize production costs which means using price signals or instructions or both, (ii) balancing decentralization and centralisation in farm decisions which impacts problems like moral hazard and hold up, (iii) minimizing or sharing risk and uncertainty, (iv) reducing the costs of pre- and post contractual opportunism (adverse selection and moral hazard) by various mechanism of allocating contracts and monitoring them, (v) encouraging group or co-operative action among producers to lower costs and ensure better compliance, (vi) long term contracts to reduce hold up problem, (vii) balancing pros and cons of renegotiation of contracts over time, (viii) reducing direct costs of contracting, and (ix) using transparent contracts (Bogetoft and Olesen, 2002).

Finally, it is the trust between farmers and processors that is important for the realignment of the chain (Heron, 2003). Trust has been defined as the willingness to rely on an exchange partner in whom one has confidence. Trust is the function of relationship specific investments, satisfaction with product quality, prior experience, and importance of input. Trust is developed by a constant and detailed exchange of information which reduces the uncertainty of performance. In the case of farmers, a reciprocal purchase agreement has positive relationship with the farmer's trust in the buyer. Commitment is thought to be closely related to mutuality, loyalty, and the forsaking of alternatives (Batt and Rexha, 1999). Earning the farmer's trust is fundamental to success. This comes from mutuality of benefits. A host of small, timely, and regular steps help build trust. Some examples are prompt payments, being available on site, and sharing and updating best practices. The best catalyst is increasing demand from the company which improves farmers' profitability. Employing locals for extension and procurement related functions helps in facilitating better communication with growers. Growers should be allowed and encouraged to grow diversified set of crops so that risk of crop failure or contract failure can be minimised (Datta, 1996).

Developing successful backward linkages is not a short term target. The experiences show that it requires commitment, patience and perseverance. The farmer must be convinced of new technologies. Continuous demonstration is thus essential. The most successful vehicle for change is to show the benefits to farmers through demonstrations in nurseries or on the field. Upfront investment in processing is the surest way of showing the farmers the commitment of the company. If farmers can see the processing plants coming up in their area, it acts as confidence builder for them in adopting new crops and methods (Datta, 1996). Giving farmers equity shares can make them feel that they are part of the arrangement and realise that failing the firm would be failing themselves (Mishra, 1997). Establishing exacting quality standards right from the inception at every stage of the operation is an important aspect of the relationship. No efforts is too great especially in the initial period, to highlight the importance of quality. The farmer will understand that process quality is key to product quality and adopt necessary practices.

It is often desirable to plan and provide inputs across a wide range of activities and not just for the raw material needed. Given small land holdings, it is all the more important that the farmer benefits on a scale that motivates him to do better. This is achieved through a combination of technology, service and networking. Technology involves providing the best inputs and proper harvest and post-harvest conditions. Service ensures that the resources are made available in time and the post-harvest offtake is efficient. Networking assures government support, infrastructure, banking facilities, etc. (Datta, 1996). In some situations, it is not possible and easy to build immediate partnerships. Therefore, there can be a quasi-judicial system at the local level (panchayat, district administration) to monitor the contracts and resolve any conflict with appropriate penalties to any of the defaulting parties. There has to be a general code of conduct for both the parties in order to avoid conflicts and the breaking down of contracts (Datta, 1996). Partnerships with government or its agencies can help in building relations with the producers. Working with farmer co-operatives for better and more sustainable contract procurement also seems to work. This is being tried out by Marico Industries in Maharashtra in sunflower oilseeds. The company provides working capital, infrastructural facilities, managerial inputs, and job work to the co-operatives which helps these oilseed milling co-operatives to become viable.

## 15.8. Conclusions

It is important to remember that there can not be a single blue print or CF model for all situations so far as the role and nature of CF is concerned. Even for individual farmers, it is not contract per se but the relationship it represents which is crucial as the divergence between the two may prove crucial in determining the development of CF as an institution (Clapp, 1988; White, 1997). Further, it is the context of the contract which can make a whole lot of difference as there are many actors and factors in the environment which influence the working and outcome of contracts and lead to a culture of contracting which is location and community specific. The way farmers perceive CF, i.e. define their relationship with the companies, differs in each cultural context (Asano-Tamanoi, 1988; White, 1997; Ornberg, 2003). In fact, there is so much diversity in the type of firms, farmers, nature of contracts, crops, and socio-economic environment that it is better to focus on specific situation than the generic institution of CF (Little, 1994; White, 1997).

Major conditions for successful interlocking between agribusiness firms and small producers include increased competition for procurement instead of monopsony, guaranteed market for farmer produce, effective repayment mechanism, market information for farmers to effectively bargain with companies, large volumes of transactions through groups of farmers, for lowering transaction costs, co-operation among genuine agribusiness firms in the area, and no alternative source of raw material for firms (Kirsten and Sartorius, 2002). Further, for the sustainability of company-farmer partnership schemes, it is important that the company is able to successfully market its products so that farmers do not suffer from lack of market (Baumann, 2000; Haque, 2000). Building of relationships of trust with farmers through company reputation rather than marketing gimmicks is crucial. This requires mutual respect, fair and transparent negotiation process, realistic assessment of benefits, long term commitment, equitable sharing of risk, and sound business plans (Mayers and Vermeulen, 2002). Innovative pricing mechanisms like bonus at the end of the processing cycle, shares in company equity, dividends, producer's fixed price, and quality based pricing, which reward performance can help contract performance.

It is also important to note that farm sector problems like high cost of farming, lower returns, environmental sustainability require different kind of institutions (collectivities instead of individual enterprise) for which institutional innovations are a must. The legal system made available the new organizational option i.e. the Producer Companies (co-operative companies) under the Companies Act which farmers in many states have gone ahead with in various existing and new projects. There have been a large number of institutional innovations in agriculture in India at the local level recently. These include the Non-Pesticidal Management (NPM) of crops especially cotton in Punnukula village in Andhra Pradesh (CSA, 2004), producer companies for organic produce in Kerala, regulation of private tubewell water prices by village council in West Bengal as a non-market based local level institution managing a local private market driven resource (groundwater), second hand tractor markets in Punjab (Singh, 1999) and co-operative tubewells by small and marginal farmers in West Bengal which have improved efficiency (lower cost) and equity in water access, and reduced reverse tenancy (Rawal, 2002. These experiments point to the hidden local potential to create robust local institutions in such a crucial area of economy i.e. marketing. There is a need to allow and encourage such informal arrangements provided there are no irregularities and practices detrimental to the interest of the market participants. The role of the state in such situations should be supportive and somewhat supervisory in order to ensure the efficient functioning of these institutions which can deliver objectives of growth, equity, and sustainability. Another important aspect of these institutions is that they function fairly competitively, which is beneficial to the users of these markets as they get fair deal in their transactions. Some of the coping strategies/innovations adopted by farmers in CF situations include labour- water exchange, share cropping, and group leasing of land by marginal and landless farmers (Deshingkar, et. al., 2003; Singh, 2002).

Given the nature of modern farming involving tremendous amount of technological input and market orientation which require capital resources, it is but inevitable to involve private corporate business interests in agricultural development through CF system. Further, supermarket chain growth including FDI in retail, international trade and quality issues like SPS, organic trade, fair trade, and ethical trade, promotion by the central and state agencies, banking and input industry push for CF, farming crisis/non-farm growth and reverse tenancy, and failure of traditional cooperatives, will help spread of CF across crops and regions as they provide new space to this arrangement in the context of withdrawal of state from agricultural space. Even new IPR regime which encourages protection and exploitation of proprietary genetics is likely to accelerate contract farming practice (Wolf et al, 2001). Therefore, what is required is marketing extension in terms of better product planning at the farmer level, provision of market information, securing/accessing markets for farmers, provision of alternative markets and market orientation in terms of improved marketing practices at the farmer level (Patnaik, 2003). Diversification has to be beyond crops and include allied activities. Agribusiness sector is much larger than just farm production and other allied activities. This approach can help examine many possibilities in the off-farm parts of the agribusiness chains to involve poor people gainfully. This is also important from the point of view of value addition.

Though there has been plenty of successful intermediation in primary production by state and NGOs, much more of it is needed in agro-processing, credit, market access, information, and technology to enable small farmers to reap enhanced competitive benefits offered by freer market. Though land reforms are needed, the poor need access to markets as well as assets to get out of poverty. In this, land reforms should be part of overall reform agenda. Land reforms alone will not help make a dent on poverty, if not accompanied by marketing links for small farmers who are more efficient and more valuable as they are labour intensive. Intermediation is required for small farmers to link them up with global markets in processing and marketing (Lipton, 2002).

In India, due to the small farm domination of agricultural sector, the delivery systems are to be attuned to the demands and needs of small farmers which are small in scale and of sporadic nature (Vyas, 1996). Therefore, new institutional mechanism like groups, associations, co-operatives, New Generation Co-operatives (NGCs) and other collectivities or networks are needed to reach small and marginal producers more effectively. There is a role for the state agencies and the NGOs to intervene in contract situations as intermediaries to protect the farmer and broader local community interests. The

NGOs can also play a role in information provision, and in monitoring and regulating the working of contracts. Better co-operation and co-ordination between companies and co-operatives for agricultural development also needs to be encouraged.

Further, both companies and state should promote group contracts with the intermediation of local NGOs and other organisations and institutions so that contractual relationships are more durable, enforceable, and fair. An insurance component in farming interventions is must to protect the farmer interest and it is noted that some companies are already doing it. But, the most important thing is to ensure market for the farmer produce at better price under these agribusiness projects. Government should also play an enabling role by legal provisions and institutional mechanisms, like helping farmer co-operatives and groups, to facilitate smooth functioning of contract system, and not intervene in CF directly as seen in the case o. Punjab where the experiment field miserably (Kumar, 2005). On the other hand, the success and smooth functioning of the CF system in mint by AM Todd in the state (Punjab) with no involvement of the state, due to the nature of the crop, clear terms of the contract, ensured returns to growers by competitive prices by the company and the commitment of the company, corroborates the point that CF is best left to the company and the growers (Singh, 2005c). This was also the case in Thailand where the state facilitated it from outside with credit and extension (Singh, 2005d).

Also, it is important to ensure competition in CF so that farmers have choice of options. For example, CF in gherkins in Karnataka was also successful, besides the reason of lack of local market for produce, due to the fact that more than two dozen companies operated in the state. This also helps reduce exploitation of the small growers. Further, since farmers did not put entire land under contract and cultivated only 0.5 acres under gherkin contracts on an average, they were not subject to any major risk of contract failure.

Finally, there is no need to look for permanence in CF arrangements though short or medium term sustainability is desired for availing of its effects on growers and local economy. But, as market conditions for a crop/commodity change, CF can wither away as market becomes efficient. CF as a vertical co-ordination mechanism is only a response to a situation of market failure and depends on commodity/crop/sector dynamics which are liable to change anytime, especially in globalised and liberalised world. But, there are many indications that CF can continue even in the presence of competitive markets as in the developed countries or even Thailand (Ornberg, 2003). CF is only an instrument/means to agricultural and rural development, not an end in itself.

## References

Ahlawat, S R (2002):"Political Economy and the Peasant Suicide – A Case of Haryana State", Guru Nanak Journal of Sociology, 23(1), 1-17.

Agarwal, I, S Priya and S Bhuvaneswai (2005): "Contract Farming Venture in Cotton: A Case Study in Tamilnadu", Indian Journal of Agricultural Marketing, 19(2)153-161.

Agrawal, R C (2000): "Perspectives for Small Farmers in Developing Countries: Do They have a Future?", Forum zur Gartenkonferenz 2000. (http://userpage.fu.berlin/~garten/Buch/Agrawal(englisch).htm. (April 6, 2005.)

Batt, J P, and N Rexha (1999): "Building Trust in Agribusiness Supply Chains: A Conceptual Model of Buyer-Seller Relationships in the Seed Potato Industry in Asia", J. of Intl. Food & Agribusiness Marketing, 11 (1), 1-17.

Bhalla, G S and G Singh (1996): Impact of GATT on Punjab Agriculture, Ajanta Publications, Delhi.

Bingen, J, A Serrano and J Howard (2003): "Linking farmers to markets: different approaches to human capital development", Food Policy, 28, 405-419.

Bissell, S. L., S G Chadha and A.K Shiva Kumar (2002): "Elimination of Child Labour: Corporate Options and Public Actions" The Indian Journal of Labour Economics, 45 (3), 633-640.

Bogetoft, P and H B Olesen (2002): "Ten Rules of Thumb in Contract Design: lessons from Danish Agriculture", European Review of Agricultural Economics, 29(2), 185-204.

Buch-Hansen M and H S Marcussen (1982): "Contract Farming and the Peasantry: Cases from Western Kenya", Review of African Political Economy, Number 23, 9-36.

Burch, D and B Pritchard (1996): "The uneasy transition to globalisation: Restructuring of the Australian tomato processing industry" in D Burch, R E Rickson and G Lawrence (eds.): Globalisation and Agri-Food Restructuring – Perspectives from the Australasia Region, Brookfield (USA), Avebury, 107-126.

Chengappa, P G, L Achoth, K K P Rashmi, V Degga, B M R Reddy and P K Joshi (2005): "Emergence of Organised Retail Chains in India during Post Liberalisation Era", paper presented at the South Asia Regional Conference "Globalisation of Agriculture in South Asia: Has it made Difference to Rural Livelihoods?" Hyderabad, India by CESS/IFPRI/IAAE/ISAE/ISAM/ANGRAU, March 23-25, 2005.

Chidambaram, M (1997): A Study of Export Potentials for Gherkins (Hybrid Cucumber) in Tamilnadu, Department of Agricultural Economics, Centre for Agriculture and Rural Development Studies, TAU, Coimbatore (unpublished).

Clapp, R. A. J. (1988): "Representing Reciprocity, Reproducing Domination: Ideology and the Labour Process in Latin American Contract Farming", The Journal of Peasant Studies, 16(1), 5-39.

CDC (Commonwealth Development Corporation) (1989): Review of Smallholder Agricultural Programmes, Final Report, Vols. 1 (analysis, conclusions and proposals) and 2 (case studies), London, CDC, April.

CSA (Centre for Sustainable Agriculture) (2004): No Pesticides, No Pests – the remarkable story of how a village in AP rid itself of pesticides, CSA, Hyderabad, October.

Datta, S M:" Linkages with Agriculture - The Experience of the Food Processing Industry", The Economic Times, June 26, 1996, Ahmedabad.

Deshingkar, P, U Kulkarni, L Rao and S Rao (2003):"Changing Food Systems in India: Resource Sharing and Marketing Arrangements for Vegetable Production in Andhra Pradesh," Development Policy Review, 21(5-6): 627-639.

Deshpande, R S (2002): "Suicide by Farmers in Karnataka: Agrarian Distress and Possible Alleviatory Steps", Economic and Political Weekly, 37(26), 2601-2610.

Dev, S M and N C Rao (2004): "Food Processing in Andhra Pradesh – Opportunities and Challenges", CESS Working Paper No. 57, Centre for Economic and Social Studies (CESS), Hyderabad, June.

Dhaliwal, H S, M Kaur, and J Singh (2003): Evaluation of Contact Farming Scheme in the Punjab State, Department of Economics, PAU, Ludhiana.

Dileep, B K, R K Grover, and K N Rai (2002): Contract Farming in Tomato: An Economic Analysis", Indian Journal of Agricultural Economics, 57(2), 197-210.

Eaton, C and A W Shepherd (2001): Contract Farming: Partnerships for Growth, FAO, Rome.

ETKS (The Economic Times Knowledge Series) (2003): Rural Economy 2002-2003, The Economic Times, Mumbai.

Farina, E M M Q (2002): "Consolidation, Multinationalisation, and Competition in Brazil: Impacts on Horticulture and Dairy Products Systems", Development Policy Review, 20 (4): 441-457.

Frenkel, S. J. and D. Scott (2002): "Compliance, Collaborations and Codes of Labour Practice: The Adidas Connection", California Management Review, 45 (1), 29-49.

Fulton, A L A and R J Clark (1996): "Farmer decision making under contract farming in northern Tasmania" in D Burch, R E Rickson and G Lawrence (eds.): Globalisation and Agri-Food Restructuring – Perspectives from the Australasia Region, Brookfield (USA), Avebury, 219-237.

Gandhi, V, G Kumar and R Marsh (2001): "Agroindustry for Rural and Small Farmer Development: Issues and Lessons from India", International Food and Agribusiness Management Review, 2(3/4), 331-344.

Gibbon, P (2003): "Value Chain Governance, Public Regulation and Entry Barriers in the Global Fresh Fruit and Vegetable Chain into the EU", Development Policy Review, 21(5-6): 615-625.

Gill, S S (2004): "Small farmers and Markets" (a book review), Economic and Political Weekly, 39(23), 2356-2358.

Gill, S S (2005): "Diversification of Punjab Agriculture: A Faulty Design and Bureaucratic Apathy", An unpublished paper.

Glover, D. (1987): "Increasing the benefit of Small holder from Contract Farming; problems of farmers organisations and policy makers." World Development 15(4), 441-48.

GoI (Govt. of India) (2003): Contract Farming Agreement and its Model Specifications, Ministry of Agriculture, Department of Agriculture and Co-operation, Krishi Bhawan, New Delhi, September 17.

GoI (Govt. of India) (2004): Economic Survey 2003-04, Ministry of Finance, GoI, New Delhi.

GoP (Govt. of Punjab) (2005): Statistical Abstract of Punjab, 2004, Economic Adviser to Govt. of Punjab, Economic and Statistical Organisation (ESO), Publication No. 905, Chandigarh, February.

Grewal, M (2003): "Cropped by Corporates", The Indian Express, Ahmedabad, April 27, The Sunday Express Section, III.

Grosh, B (1994):"Contract Farming in Africa: an Application of the New Institutional Economics", Journal of African Economies, 3(2), 231-261.

Haque, T (2000): "Contractual Arrangements in Land and Labour Markets in Rural India", Indian Journal of Agricultural Economics, 55(3), 233-252.

Haque, T (2003): "Land Reforms and Agricultural Development: Retrospect and Prospect", in S Pal et al (eds.): Institutional Change in Indian Agriculture, NCAP, New Delhi, 267-284.

Heron, L R (2003) "Creating Food Futures: Reflections on Food Governance Issues in New Zealand's Agri-food Sector", Journal of Rural Studies, 19 (1): 111-125.

Hill B E and K A Ingersent (1987): An Economic Analysis of Agriculture, London, Heinemann.

IFPRI (2005): High Value Agriculture and Vertical Co-ordination in India –Will the Smallholders Participate?, A draft research report, IFPRI, Washington.

Iyer, K Gopal and M S Manick (2000): Indebtedness, Impoverishment and Suicides in Rural Punjab, Delhi, Indian Publishers and Distributors.

Jha, D (2001): "Agricultural Research and Small Farms", Presidential Address at the 60th Annual Convocation of the ISAE, Kalyani (WB), January 22-24.

Kar, J. (2002): "The Issue of Child Labour in Orissa: A Developmental Approach", Indian Social Science Review, 4 (1), 117-131.

Karunakaran, N (2002):"Money Grows on Trees ...", Intelligent Investor, August 31 (obtained through ISAPindia@yahoogroups.com)

Key, N and D Runsten (1999): "Contract Farming, Smallholders, and Rural Development in Latin America: The Organisation of Agroprocessing Firms and the Scale of Outgrower Production", World Development, 27 (2), 381-401.

Khairnar, S and V Yeleti (2005): "Contract Farming in India: Impact and Implications", in Ramesh Chand (ed.): India's Agricultural Challenges-Reflections on Policy, Technology and Other Issues, CENTAD, New Delhi, 105-128.

Kirk, C (1987): "Contracting Out: Plantations, Smallholders and Transnational Enterprise", IDS Bulletin, 18 (2), 45-51, April.

Kirsten, J and K Sartorius (2002): "Linking agribusiness and small-scale farmers in developing countries: is there a new role for contract farming?", Development Southern Africa, 19(4), 503-529.

Konings, P (1998): "Unilever, Contract Farmers and Co-operatives in Cameroon: Crisis and Response", The Journal of Peasant Studies, 26 (1), 112-138.

Kumar, P (2006): "Contract Framing in India. options and Implications for Small and Large farmers, TEG WP. E 267/ 06 Delhi, Insititute of Economic Growth (TEG).

Lipton, M (2002): "Access to Assets and Land in the Context of Poverty Reduction and Economic Development in Asia" Paper presented at the Global Distance Learning Course 'Reaching the Rural Poor: Strategies for Rural Development for the East Asia Region', Bangkok, June 3-6.

Little, P D and M J Watts (eds.) (1994): (eds.): Living Under Contract - Contract Farming and Agrarian Transformation in Sub-Saharan Africa, Madison, University of Wisconsin Press, 216-247.

Lorenz, E (1999):"Trust, contract and economic co-operation", Cambridge Journal of Economics, 23, 301-315.

Mani G and V K Pandey (1995): "Agrarian Structure under the New Economic Policy", Indian Journal of Agricultural Economics, 50(3), 524-530.

Mayers J and S Vermeulen (2002): Company –community forestry partnerships: From raw deals to mutual gains?, International Institute for Environment and Development (IIED), London.

MFPI (1998): Food Processing Industries, outline of assistance under schemes of the ninth plan 1997/2002, Ministry of Food Processing Industries (MFPI), Govt. of India, November.

Mishra, S N (1997):"Agricultural Liberalisation and Development Strategy in Ninth Plan", Economic and Political Weekly, 32 (13), A19-A25, March 29.

Mitra, S and A Sarkar (2003) "Relative Profitability from Production and Trade – A Study of Selected Potato Markets in West Bengal", Economic and Political Weekly, 38(44), November 1, 4694-4699.

MOAC (Ministry of Agriculture and Co-operatives) (2002): Approach paper for the Workshop 'Linking Production and Marketing under Contracts' (Contract Farming) held on February 8, MOAC (translated from Thai).

Mohanty, B B (2001): "Suicides of Farmers in Maharashtra: A Socio-economic Analysis", Review of Development and Change, 6(2), 146-189.

Muller A R and R Patel (2004): Shining India? Economic Liberalisaiton and Rural Poverty in the 1990s, Food First Policy Brief No. 10, Food First/Institute for Food and Development Policy, Oakland, May.

Naik, G (2002):"Enhancing Food Security through Market Reforms", Productivity, 43 (1) April-June, 60-66.

Ornberg, L (2003): "Farmers' Choice: Contract Farming, Agricultural Change and Modernisation in Northern Thailand", paper presented at the 3rd International Convention of Asia Scholars (ICAS3), Singapore, August 19-22.

Page, S and R Slater (2003):"Small Producer Participation in Global Food Systems: Policy Opportunities and Constraints", Development Policy Review, 21(5-6): 641-654.

Parikh, K and H K Nagarajan (2004): How Important is Land Consolidation? Land Fragmentation and Implications for Productivity: Case Study of Village Nelpathur in Tamil Nadu, NABARD Occasional Paper No. 31, NABARD, Mumbai.

Patnaik, G (2003): "Marketing, Storage, and Extension Services: State of Agriculture in India" in B Debroy and A U Khan (eds.): Enabling Agricultural Markets for the Small Indian Farmer, Bookwell, New Delhi, 81-120.

Payer, C (1980):"The World Bank and the Small Farmer", Monthly Review, 32 (6), 30-46.

Pingali, P and Y Khwaja (2004): "Globalisation of Indian Diets and the Transformation of Food Supply Systems", Indian Journal of Agricultural Marketing, 18(1), 2004, 26-49.

Ramachandran, R and C S Dogra (2006): "Punjab- Caught in A Con Tract", Outlook, January 23, 24-26.

Rangi, P. S. and M. S. Sidhu (2000): "A Study on Contract Farming of Tomato in Punjab", Agricultural Marketing, 42(4), 15-23.

Rangi, P S and M S Sidhu (2003): "Contract Farming in Punjab", Productivity, 44(3), 484-491.

Rao, V M and H G Hanumappa (1999): "Marginalisation Process in Agriculture – Indicators, Outlook and Policy Implications", Economic and Political Weekly, 34(52), A133-A138.

Rawal, V (2002): "Non-Market interventions in Water-Sharing: Case Studies from West Bengal, India" Journal of Agrarian Change, 2(4), 545-569.

Raynolds, L T (2004): "The Globalisation of Organic Agro-Food Networks", World Development, 32(5): 725-743.

Reardon, T and J A Berdegue (2002): "The Rapid Rise of Supermarkets in Latin America: Challenges and Opportunities for Development", Development Policy Review, 20 (4): 371-388.

Rustagi, P. (2002): "Girl Child Labour: Regional Dimensions and Motivations", The Indian Journal of Labour Economics, 45 (3), 465-477.

Sabarinath, M (2003): "Corp India gets agro as states sign up exec farmers", The Economic Times, Ahmedabad, April 14, 1.

Sabates-Wheeler, R (2002): "Farm Strategy, Self Selection and Productivity: Can Small Farming Groups offer Production Benefits to Farmers in Post –Socialist Romania?", World Development, 30(10), 1737-1753.

Saigal, S and D Kashyap (2002): Review of Company-farmer Partnerships for the Supply of Raw Material to Wood-based Industry, Eco-tech Services (India) Pvt. Ltd., New Delhi and International Institute for Environment and Development (IIED), London.

Sako, M (1992): Prices, quality and trust - Inter-firm relations in Britain and Japan, CUP, Cambridge.

Saleth, R M (1997): "Diversification Strategy for Small farmers and Landless: Some Evidence from Tamil Nadu", Indian Journal of Agricultural Economics, 52(1), 73-86.

Satish, P (2003): "Contract Farming as a Backward Linkage for Agro Processing – Experiences from Punjab", an unpublished paper presented at the 63rd annual conference of the ISAE held at Bhubaneswar.

Schwentesium, R and M A Gomez (2002): "Supermarkets in Mexico: Impacts on Horticulture Systems", Development Policy Review, 20 (4): 487-502.

Scott, C D (1984): "Transnational Corporations and Asymmetries in the Latin American Food System", Bulletin of Latin American Research, 3(1), 63-80, January.

Sen, S and S Raju (2005): "Globalisation and Expanding Markets for Cut-Flowers: Who Benefits?", paper presented at the South Asia Regional Conference "Globalisation of Agriculture in South Asia: Has it made Difference to Rural Livelihoods?"organised at Hyderabad, India by CESS/IFPRI/IAAE/ISAE/ISAM/ANGRAU, March 23-25, 2005.

Setboonsarng, S, P Leung and J Cai (2005): Contract Farming and Poverty Reduction: A case of Organic Rice Contract farming in Thailand, Asian Development Bank Institute (ADBI), Tokyo, November.

Shiva, V and T Crompton (1998): "Monopoly and Monoculture- Trends in Indian Seed Industry", Economic and Political Weekly, 33(39), A137-A151.

Shiva, V, A H Jafri, A Emani and M Pande (2000): Seeds of Suicide: The Ecological and Human Costs of Globalisation of Agriculture, RFST&E, New Delhi.

Singh, G and S R Asokan (2005): Contract Farming in India- Text and Cases, Oxford & IBH, New Delhi.

Singh, G (2005c): "Contract Farming of Mint in Punjab", Indian Journal of Agricultural Marketing, 19(2), 121-129.

Singh, J (2003): "Contracted green peas dumped in open market", The Tribune, Chandigarh, March 28, 15.

Singh, J P (2005): "Changing Agrarian Relations in Rural India", a Keynote Paper presented at the 65th Annual Conference of the ISAE held at PAU, Ludhiana, November 24-26.

Singh, M P (2006): Shifting Patterns of Agricultural Space: Evolution of Contract Farming in Punjab, an unpublished manuscript.

Singh, R B, P Kumar and T Woodhead (2002): Smallholder Farmers in India: Food Security and Agricultural Policy, FAO, ROAP, Bangkok, March.

Singh, S (1998): "Should Indian Farming Go Corporate?", Business India, August 24- September 6, 122-123.

Singh, S (1999):"Institutional Innovations in Indian Agriculture: A Case of Input Markets", Institutional Development, 6(2), 3-10.

Singh, S (2000): "Contract Farming for Agricultural Diversification in the Indian Punjab: A Study of Performance and Problems" Indian Journal of Agricultural Economics, 56 (3), 283-294.

Singh, S (2002): "Contracting Out Solutions: Political Economy of Contract Farming in the Indian Punjab", World Development, 30(9), 1621-1638.

Singh, S (2004): "The New Generation Co-operative: Theory, Practice and Relevance", The Co-operator, 42(5): 229-230.

Singh, S. (2005a): Political Economy of Contract Farming in India, Allied, New Delhi.

Singh, S (2005b): Organic Produce Supply Chains in India, draft report, CMA, IIM, Ahmedabad.

Singh, S (2005d): "Role of the State in Contract Farming in Thailand: Experience and Lessons", ASEAN Economic Bulletin, 22(2), August 2005, 217-228.

Singh, S (2005e): "Contract Farming System in Thailand", Economic and Political Weekly, 40(53), December 31, 5578-5586.

Singh, T and V K Sharma (2004): "Employment of Farm Resources in Punjab Agriculture", Productivity, 45(1), 140-144.

Srinivas, N N (2005): "Field test: You reap what you sow", The Economic Times, Ahmedabad, March 30, 1.

Subramaniam, A (2002):"Field Day in Store for Farmers", in http://www.tata.com/rallis_ india/articles/2002060_ farming. htm.

Subrahmanyam, K. V. (2000): Linkages Between Farm and Non-Farm Sector: Role of Processing of Horticultural Products, NABARD Occasional Paper No. 16, National Bank for Agriculture and Rural Development (NABARD), Mumbai.

Sulaiman R V, A J Hall and N Suresh (2004): "Effectiveness of Private Sector Extension in India and Lessons for the New Extension Policy Agenda" an unpublished paper presented at the workshop on 'Rural Innovations –Emphasizing the post – harvest sector', organised by CRISP, Hyderabad at ICRISAT, Hyderabad during November 22-29.

Swain, M (2000): "Agricultural Development and Interlocked Markets", Indian Journal of Agricultural Economics, 55(3), 308-3316.

Tripathi, R S, R Singh and S Singh (2005): "Contract Farming in

Potato Production: An Alternative for Managing Risk and Uncertainty", Agricultural Economics Research Review, 18 (Conference Nunmber), 47-60.

Tirole, J (1999): "Incomplete Contracts: Where Do We Stand?", Econometrica, 67(4), July, 741-781.

Vellema, S (2004): "Institutional modalities in contract farming: the case of fresh asparagus in the Philippines", paper presented at the mini-conference on Northern consumption/southern production, Copenhagen, Denmark, October 10-12. (The revised version published as "Regional cultures and global sourcing of fresh asparagus" in Fold N and B Pritchard (eds.) (2005): Cross-continental food chains: structures, actors and dynamics in global food systems, Routledge, London, 124-136.

Vyas, V S (1996):"Diversification in Agriculture: Concept, Rationale and Approaches", Indian Journal of Agricultural Economics, 51 (4), 636-643.

Warning, M, N Key and W S Hoo (2003): Small Farmer Participation in Contract Farming, a draft paper.

White, B (1997): "Agro-industry and Contract Farming in Upland Java", The Journal of Peasant Studies, 24(3), 100-136.

Wilson, J (1986): "The Political Economy of Contract Farming", Review of Radical Political Economics, 18(4), 47-70.

Winson, A (1990): "Capitalist Coordination of Agriculture: Food Processing Firms and Farming in Central Canada", Rural Sociology, 55(3), 376-394, Fall.

Wolf, S, B Hueth, and E Ligon (2001): "Policing Mechanisms in Agricultural Contracts", Rural Sociology, 66(3), 359-381.

WB (World Bank) (2003): India: Revitalising Punjab's Agriculture, Rural Development Unit, South Asia Region, The World Bank, Washington.

WB (World Bank) (2004): Resuming Punjab's Prosperity- The Opportunities and Challenges Ahead, The World Bank, Washington and New Delhi.

# Appendix 15.1

## Fig 15.1
## Tri-partite CF Model

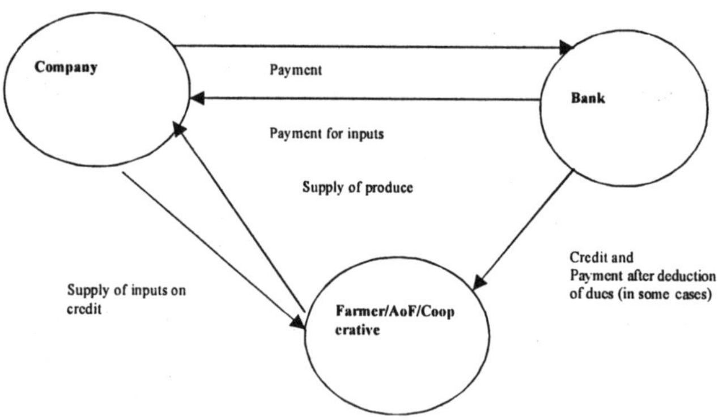

# Appendix 15.2

## Fig 15.2
## State-led Contract Farming System in Punjab
## (Revised Model)

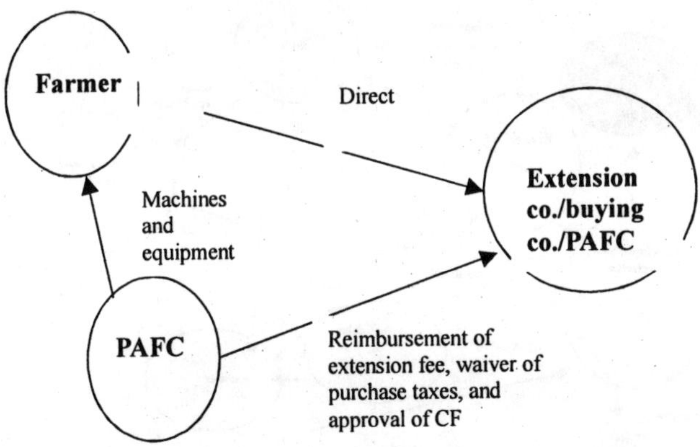

# Appendix 15.3

## Fig 15.3
## The Six-partite (Networking) CF Model

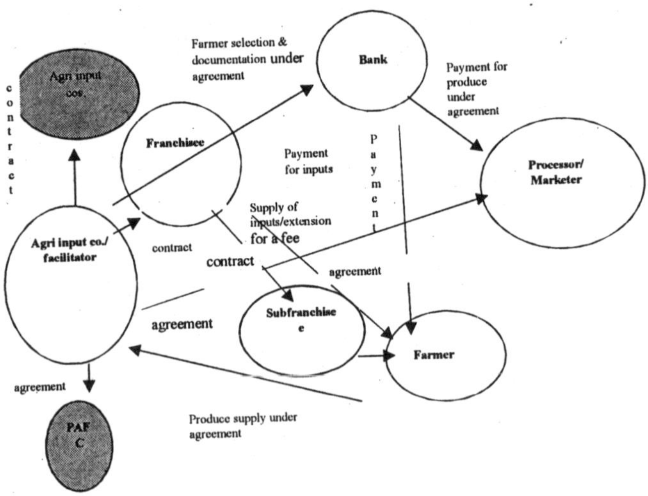

# Appendix 15.3

## Fig 15.4

## Tri-partite (Intermediary) Model of Contact Farming

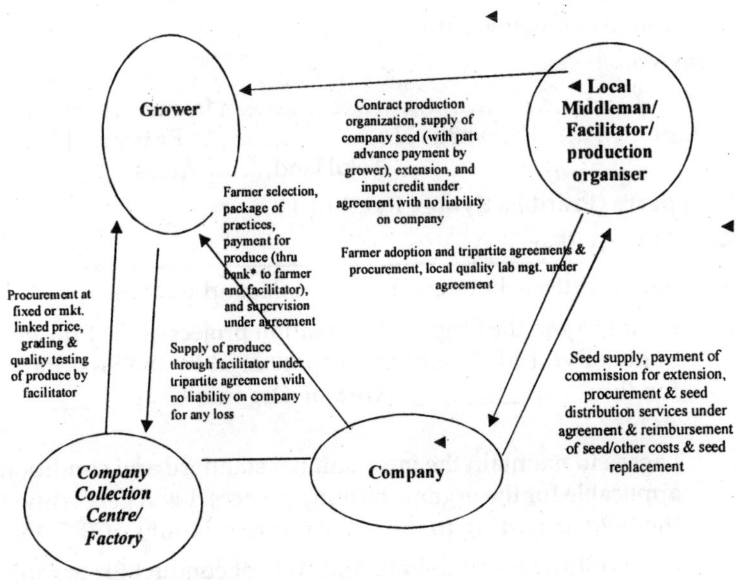


---

* Bank finances contract production @ Rs. 10,000/acre (NABARD norm is Rs. 13,000/acre for the given crop) at 7.5% rate of interest. It receives the money from the company for payment to the farmer for his produce, from which it pays the facilitator (as per authorization given by the grower), deducts its own dues, and transfers the remaining amount in the farmer's bank account.

Appendix 15.4

# Contract Agreement for Organic Production

Change in Field .................................. Year.....................
Category............

Description of Organic Farm ..............................................

Farm No.

I, ............................................ a farmer, resident of village...........Khasara No. ................ Patvari Halka No.....................................Total land.........Acres.

First party (Pratibha Syntex Pvt. Ltd.)

Second Party (Farmer)

---

Agreement is done between First and Second parties.

1. I want to join the Organic Cultivation project of the Pratibha Syntex Pvt. Ltd. (First party) sponsored by the First Party for the Year:________ Area of Organic Crop:________ Acres.
2. I agree to maintain the international standard and condition applicable for the organic farming process. I will get certified the field according to the rules and regulations of IFOAM.
3. I will follow the guidelines and code of conduct for organic farming as advised by the Consultant / Field Coordinator of the First Party.
4. I understood completely the new Organic Farming method that does not allow the use of chemical fertilizers/pesticides in crops, seeds, and on cattle.
5. I will use only certified compost inputs or alternative inputs such as green manure, rock phosphate, Deoiled Cake (DOC) as advised by the first party in order to improve the fertility of land.

6. In order to protect crop from harmful insecticides/ diseases, I will use only certified products such as Neem, natural herbs or any other organic material.
7. I will follow the crop cycle advice given by the Field Coordinator/Consultant.
8. For betterment of environment, I will plant trees around the field.
9. I will use all the waste obtained from cattle /crops to convert it into compost and give it to farms.
10. I know very well that application of chemicals or non-permissible input/s on my crop or field is not allowed. In case I use the same without prior permission from the First Party, I would not be able to sell my crop at higher rate.
11. I will inform immediately to the Field Coordinator/ technician/Company representative/Consultant if it seems necessary to breach any condition of the agreement. Field Inspector or any other representative of the first party has the right to abolish/terminate my membership as Organic Farmer without my signature with immediate effect, if I am found to use any of non permissible materials in my crop or field
12. I will keep my spray pump required for organic farming separately and will not use it for any other chemical pesticide or fertilizer. I will not give/borrow sprayer pump to any other farmers who are not practicing Organic Farming and I will provide it for testing from time to time as per the directives of the First Party.
13. During testing, if I am found guilty of using any of the non-permissible inputs, I will be the defaulter and my membership will be cancelled with immediate effect.
14. In case I can not practice organic farming in the entire land, I will keep separate the Organic field by using one meter border of any other crop (Buffer Crop) to protect Organic field /crop from the effects of chemicals used in other crops/ fields. Buffer Crop may be maize, pigeon pea, sorghum, or castor oil.
15. I will provide samples of soil, plant, leaf, or flower to the supervisor /inspector for testing purpose.
16. First Party is responsible to purchase the crop when it is certified by the representative/inspector/consultant. For certification, following information is required:

a. Proper record keeping for crops is compulsory.

b. Farmer has to keep all circulars and formats issued by First Party up to date in all respects and produce the same as and when asked by the Inspector or any other representative.

c. It is compulsory to co-operate with company representative for all the information required in organic farming about attack of insects/ diseases, soil quality, farm map, picking and harvesting details, sowing etc.

17. It is compulsory to inform Representative of the First Party about harvesting of crop so that proper arrangements for the storage of the crop may be made.

18. I am confident and will be honest for converting my farm into an Organic Farm and for this I agree to the following procedure:

    a. Annual membership of the organisation (Registration)

    b. Certification according to relevant category.

19. If I follow the rules and regulations of the Organic Farming satisfactory and fulfill all the conditions of Organic Farming, then it is clear that my entire crop /s ........will be sold to Pratibha Syntex Pvt. Ltd. (First Party) or its representative but for other Organic crops, Representative/s of First Party will make efforts to get appropriate market and accordingly it will be sold.

20. I will keep all the records of Organic Farming myself.

21. I will give organic inputs like Azedobector, P.S.B., DOC, Bone meal, Rock Phosphate as per the recommendations of Field Coordinator.

22. Use of treated (with fungal chemicals) seeds is prohibited.

23. I will use self-prepared Organic solutions/preparations from Neem leaf /Neem seed and also preparations available in market, with prior approval for the same from the First party or its representative.

24. It's compulsory for me to attend all the training and development programs for farmers.

25. I will not give any information to any News Channel / Newspaper or any other media without a written permission of the First party.

26. If I give /borrow Sprayer Pumps to/from any other farmer who is a conventional farmer or using chemicals fertilizers/ pesticides, I will be considered a defaulter.
27. Before selling of any crop, I will take written approval from the First Party or its representative.
28. Crops cultivated in the field without using any non-organic products from the last two consecutive years will be treated as Organic crops in the third year.
29. In this agreement, I agree to sell all my crops, other than Cotton, i.e. soybean, wheat and pulses to the First Party (Pratibha Green Technologies Pvt. Ltd., Indore) at reasonable rates.
30. According to the quality of cotton, the First party will pay a premium of 15% on Mandi rates to the farmers in the form of inputs like seeds, DOC, Econeem, V.T. etc.
31. If there is no border separation in the field, it is compulsory for farmer to sow at least one meter wide border crop and it must be there for at least four months and its height should be one meter.
32. I would purchase other nutrients required for the crop myself, in cash.
33. Use of Genetically modified or Terminator seeds is strictly prohibited.

Signature Signature Signature

Farmer (second party) Field Coordinator (organic) Agril. consultant (organic)

Signature (First Party) Pratibha Syntex Pvt. Ltd. (Authorized Signatory)

**Appendix 15.5**

# Mentha (Pudina)- Menthol Mint Cultivation Agreement

This agreement of _____ day _______ month ______ year is agreed between Indomint Agriproducts Private Limited, near Hotel Mayur, Ambala-Chandigarh Road, Zirkpur, Dist: Patiala (Head Office: 20, Rajmahel, 5th Floor, 84, Vir Nariman Road, Church gate, Mumbai, Phone- 022-22820462/0261, hereafter addressed as Indomint (First Party) and Shri ____________________________ son of __________________, village ________________, Post Office _____________, Dist: ____________, Punjab, hereafter addressed as farmer (Second Party), wherein the farmer has agreed to grow pudina (menthol mint) in _____ acres as per following terms and conditions:

1. Indomint will provide the roots of menthol mint to the farmer for sowing at the concessional rate of Rs. 1,000/- per acre which will be recovered at the time of crushing of oilseeds (see Sr. No.4).
2. Indomint will work closely with the farmer and will provide free technical information from selection of field, sowing, harvesting to crushing of oilseeds/uprooting of roots. This will be done personally by visiting the farmer or in writing.
3. The farmer will get the oil extracted at the plant recommended by Indomint only. If he/she fails to do so, Indomint will not be bound to pay for the oil extracted from the farmer's crop.
4. Indomint will pay for the menthol mint crop on the basis of oil recovery at the rate of Rs. 240/- per Kg. But it will deduct the root supply fee at the time of payment (to be paid within 21 days of oil extraction by bank draft) (see Sr. No.1).

5. As soon as the field is ready for sowing, the farmer will contact Indomint for pudina seeds (roots/plants).
6. The farmer will follow all the technical advice given by Indomint from time to time in writing or orally. The advice given by Indomint for higher and better quality oil from mint can be changed (increased/decreased) and the farmer is bound to follow that. The farmer will harvest mint crop once or twice and get the oil extracted as advised by Indomint.
7. The entire mint crop produced by the farmer will be the property of Indomint for which it will pay the farmer as per Sr. No.4.
8. The roots of mint left in the field after harvest will be the property of Indomint, and Indomint will instruct the farmer to keep or dispose off the roots (all or some) which the farmer is bound to comply with. If Indomint wishes, it can transfer roots to another place or another farmer for seed purposes at its own cost. Both the parties can also agree to leave a part of or whole of these roots with the farmer for next sowing. In such a situation, Indomint will provide free technical advice to the farmer to produce maximum roots. The farmer will abide by the instructions and advice of Indomint. The farmer will not sell the roots or any part of the plants in any form, at any time, to anyone without the permission of Indomint.
9. This agreement can be extended for one or more years under same or new terms and conditions depending on the mutual consent of both the parties.
10. Both the parties have signed/put thumb impression on the agreement after reading, hearing and considering the given terms and conditions.

Assistant General Manager Farmer

Indomint Agriproducts Pvt. Ltd. Name and Address

Witnesses

1. ______________________ Date: ______________

2. ______________________ Date: ______________

## Appendix 15.6

# AGREEMENT (Production-cum-Marketing Contract)

This AGREEMENT made this day of __________ between Messers Nadukkara Agro Processing Company Limited (NAPC), an existing Company under the companies Act, 1956 having its Registered Office at Nadukkara (PO) Avoly, Muvattupuzha 686 677 (Kerala), hereinafter called 'the Company'. The term 'Company' unless contrary to the context, shall include its successors and assigns of the ONE PART and

Shri__________________

Son of _________________

Residing at_____________

Here in after called the "the registered farmer" (Registration No. _________) which term unless contrary to the context, shall include his heirs, successors, assigns, legal representatives of the OTHER PART.

**Whereas**

a. The 'registered farmer' is cultivating ____________ acre of pineapple (var. Kew) in Survey No ______________ Village ________________ Panchayat _______________ Taluk ___________________ District ________________ in the State of KERALA.

b. The Company has to meet its requirements of fresh pineapple fruits (var. Kew) for use in manufacture of its products.

c. The company after satisfying itself about the ownership of the said land (Original title deed/Certificate of possession) within its command area of five panchayats viz., Avoly, Arakuzha, Manjallor, Ayavana and Kallorkadu has agreed to entrust the cultivation of pineapple (var. Kew) to the 'registered farmer' in the said land in half an acre and accept the pineapple fruits as per terms and conditions of this agreement.

d. The 'registered farmer' has offered to grow the pineapple (var. Kew) in the said land in half an acre and supply the fresh pineapple (var. Kew) to the company as per terms and conditions of this agreement.

e. The 'registered farmer' has offered to undertake the cultivation of pineapple variety 'Kew' in the said land, as per directions of the company, within a period of not exceeding 4 (four) years from the date of his registration.

f. The parties are desirous of recording the terms and conditions thereof: NOW THIS DEED WITNESSETH:

It is agreed by and between the parties that:

1. The 'registered farmer' will implement all the instructions given by the Company's officers or authorized supervising agents from time to time with regard to planting schedule, variety (Kew), plant population (6,000 plants in half acre + 20 percent), harvesting and delivery, etc. at his own cost.
2. The 'registered farmer' undertakes to deliver at his cost the stipulated quantity and quality of pineapple (var. Kew) at stipulated time to the company at their factory in Nadukkara or nearest procurement center, if opened by the Company. The range of quantity to be delivered and standard quality specifications will be separately provided by the company for reference of the 'registered farmer'. The company representative will extend necessary advice to the 'registered farmer' in this regard.
3. The 'registered farmer' undertakes to cultivate pineapple (var. Kew) in the said land mentioned above and he undertakes not to make any change in the above unless authorized by the Company in writing.
4. In the event of non-compliance of any one of the following terms and conditions the Company will be free to de-register the farmer without giving any prior notice. The conditions are:

    i. Cease to own land in one of the five panchayats mentioned above.

ii. Discontinues the cultivation of pineapple (var. Kew) during the period of agreement.

iii. Fails to supply any variety ('Kew' or 'Mauritius') during the interim period of four years a quantity of 10MT/ half acre/year + 20% for Mauritius and Kew

iv. Fails to plant 'Kew', 6000 plant + 20% in an area of half an acre within a period not exceeding four years of becoming the 'registered farmer'.

v. Fails to start supply of the specified quantity of 10 MT + 20% of 'Kew' within a period not exceeding five and half years of becoming 'registered farmer' and thereafter maintains supply of fruits every year till the contract is over.

Any loss incurred by the 'registered farmer' on 'de registration' will be on his account and responsibility. The company will not entertain any claim whatsoever in this regard.

5. Any crop failure due to natural calamities or any other reasons whatsoever will also be to 'registered farmers' account. The company will not entertain any claim whatsoever.

6. In the event of quality (including grade) of fruits being below/above the prescribed standard specifications, the company will make necessary adjustments (downward/ upward) from its declared unit price. Such price adjustment procedure will be intimated to the 'registered farmer' at the time of signing this agreement.

7. The company on its part agree that

   i. It will facilitate sourcing of suckers of 'Kew' variety to 'registered farmers' at prevailing market price.

   ii. It will extend technical guidance on package of practices to registered farmers to improve yields and reduce cost of production.

   iii. It will facilitate channelisation of government support for installation of irrigation facilities (Sprinkler/Drip) to the 'registered farmers'.

   iv. It will extend a credit package to all 'registered farmers' and link recovery of credit with sale of produce to the Company.

v. It will pay Rs. 3.50/kg. of pineapple (Mauritius with crown and Kew without crown) for the standard grade and quality delivered to the company by the 'registered farmer'. The price adjustments (downward/upward with reference to declared price) for the non-standard pineapple (in terms of grade or quality or both) will be as per the norms fixed by the Company and informed in advance to the ' registered farmer'.

vi. The company may provide for benefits to 'registered farmers' depending on the performance of the company.

vii. The company will make the payment for pineapples delivered by the 'registered farmer' and the payment will not normally be delayed beyond three days.

8. This Agreement will come into force this day of ____________________ 2000 for a period of seven years. 'Registered farmers' who are willing to continue are entitled to renew the agreement.

The parties agree to abide by the terms and conditions mentioned here in during the subsistence of the agreement. Any dispute arising out of or relating to this agreement shall be settled through the arbitration of Programme Director of Kerala Horticulture Development Programme (KHDP) or its successors.

In witness where of the parties have signed these present in Nadukkara on the date mentioned above.

'Registered Farmer' Authorised Representative

____________(Registration No.) Nadukkara Agro Processing Company (NAPC) Ltd.

Witness:

1.

2.

## Appendix 15.7

# Tri-partite Agreement (MSSL)

### Agreement

This agreement dated — — between MSSL, a company under the Companies Act 1956 with registered office at __ as the first party, henceforth addressed as 'extension company' and Mr. _ S/o _ Village _ Taluka _ Dist. _ (State) as the second party, henceforth addressed as 'farmer'.

Whereas, the farmer wants to grow alternative crops for productivity and quality improvement and wants good extension advise about new crops and crop cycles to save cost on crop care, cleaning of produce, weighment, transport, storage and marketing, in order to improve his economic condition.

Whereas, the extension company agrees to provide the farmer information about quality of produce and market demand for it. The company agrees to help the farmer in obtaining good quality seed, giving information about increasing yields, modern farming techniques and helping in marketing his produce at pre-agreed price.

For this, both the parties agree to the following:

### Terms of Agreement

1. The extension company, after examining the national and international market and buyers in these markets will have agreement with these buyers/exporters/consumers (who will henceforth be addressed as 'buyer') about the quality, quantity and price of farmer's produce.
2. The extension company will inform the PAFC about the agreement between the extension company and the buyer about quantity, quality and delivery schedule.
3. The extension company will determine quantity and quality of produce with the consent of the farmer, the price of which will be-/quintal.

4. The extension company will provide the farmer quality certified seed as per the following:

   Crop Variety Quantity (Kg.) Price (Kg.) Total Cost (Rs.) For– acres

5. The extension company will provide the farmer high quality agricultural, technical knowledge with full mutual cooperation. But, it will not be responsible for any type of loss of produce/crop before marketing of produce.

6. The farmer will buy insecticides/pesticides/weedicides from retailers recommended by the extension company only.

7. The extension company will help the farmer in obtaining bank loan for agriculture related purchases. The bank will determine the loan amount and rate of interest. The farmer will give an undertaking to the extension company to the effect that the extension company can deduct the principal and interest from the payment for the produce and deposit in the bank.

8. If the buyer for any reasons refuses to buy the produce on its arrival in the market, the extension company will inform PAFC about it immediately. PAFC will act as the following:

   a. will buy the produce at pre-determined price -Rs. - per quintal and pay within 7 days,

   b. will acquire the undertaking affidavit and other papers from the extension company which will be needed to claim damages from the buyer. The extension company will try its best to get the damages to the PAFC compensated by the buyer.

9. Any damage to crop due to natural calamities will be paid as per government decision and instructions. The extension company or the buyer will not claim any damages for non supply of produce under such conditions.

10. The farmer will be responsible for bringing clean, pure, and storable produce to the market determined by the extension company and will be solely responsible for the transport, loading and unloading of produce quantity and quality of produce. The produce should be free from any impurities. The weighment will be done only on an approved weigh bridge.

11. The farmer agrees to sell his produce to the assigned buyer as per this agreement and will not sell to any other buyer without the permission of the extension company.

12. The extension company will arrange payment for the farmer's produce from the buyer within 7 days. In this arrangement, produce bought by PAFC under 8(a) of this agreement is not included.
13. Any disputes relating to the terms of this agreement will be referred to MD, PAFC who shall have the sole right to decide on the matter and whose decision will be abided by both the parties.
14. In credit booking, buy back purchase is not certain. If PAFC increases its demand for buy-back, then produce of the farmers with credit booking will be purchased and they will be charged Rs.100 per acre.

First Party Second Party Third Party

(Extension Co. Rep. (Farmer) (PAFC Rep. with Seal)

Witness 1 Witness 2 Cash Rs.50

Credit Rs.100

*BASIS FOR QUALITY ASSESSMENT AT THE TIME OF PURCHASE*

| *Crop* | *Wheat* | *Mustard (Hyola)* | *Barley* | *Basmati* | | *Basmati* | *Maize* |
|---|---|---|---|---|---|---|---|
| Variety | PBW 274/233 | PAC 401 | PL 426 | HBC 19/Basmati 386 | | Pusa Basmati -1 | Hybrid |
| Purchase price/quintal | MSP+Rs.20 | 1360 | 500 | Grade A 1200 | Grade B 1100 | 800 | 500 |
| Moisture | | 8 % | 11% | <16% | 16-17% | <17% | <14% |
| Admixture | | 2 % | | <1.5% | 1.5-3% | <2% | |
| Brokens | | 2% | 2% | | | | <1.5% |
| Unripe/green grain | | 4% | | <5% | 5-8% | <6% | |
| Unripe grain with potash | | | | <2% | 2-3% | | |
| Small grains | | 10% | | | | | |
| Infected grains/pest affected | | 0% | 0% | | | | 0% |
| Empty Grains | | | | | | 2% | |
| Cut/colourless 52& brokens | | | | <1% | 1-2% | 0.5% | 0% |
| Other foreign matter | | | | <1% | 1-2% | | 0% |

Appendix 15.7

# MSSL Farmer Diary – Maize Kharif 2004

Farmer No. ---------------------

Name of Farmer:------------------

Father's Name:------------------

Khasra No.:--------------------

Village:------------------------

Taluka:------------------------

District:-----------------------

Phone No.:---------------------

Crop Cycle:---------------------

Type of Soil
(amount of nutrients
based on soil sample):-----------------

Crop/Variety:-------------------

Seed Lot No.:-------------------

Date of Sowing:-----------------

Date of harvesting:---------------

Name of Field Officer:------------

Name of franchisee/spoke:------------

| *First inspection* | *Date Inspection/recommendation* | *Recommendation/comment* | *Farmer signature* |
|---|---|---|---|
| Seed rate/acre | Highshell – 8 kg.<br>M-Indian – 2225, 2562 – 10 kg. | | |
| Method of sowing | By sprinkling/ in rows/on bunds/on plain field/inside of bunds/on bed<br>Distance between rows - 45 cm/60 cm/70 cm<br>Distance between plants – 20 cm/25 cm/30 cm | | |
| Use of fertilisers | DAP – 50 kg.<br>Urea – 15 kg.<br>MOP-25 kg.<br>Zinc Sulphate -5 kg. | | |
| Weed mgt. | Atragin (500gm/acre) for wideleaf weeds and /or<br>Laso (1.5 lt./acre) for grass like weed | | |
| Pest mgt. | G pest Yes/No<br>After 10-12 days: Teevra, M Cyper, Indosulfan | | |
| Second inspection (after 18-20 days) | Date | | |
| Excess plants removed | After 15-20 days | | |
| No. of plants | Needed (22000-25000/acre)<br>Actual - | | |
| Pest mgt. | G pest Yes/No<br>After 18-20 days – Teevra (500 ml.), M Cyper (200 ml.), Indosulfan (500 ml.) | | |
| Second doze of fertilisers | Urea -50 kg<br>MOP-25 kg. | | |
| Soil/weed mgt. | After 25-30 days | | |
| Third inspection (after 40-45 days) | Date | | |

| | |
|---|---|
| Use of fertilisers | Urea -25 kg. (as needed) |
| Pest mgt. | Leaf eating pests – Yes/No<br>500 ml thiodan/dusban/kumalfas |
| Diseases | Give details |
| Fourth inspection (after 60-70 days) | Date |
| Pest/insect attack seeding | Give details |
| Fifth inspection (around harvesting) | Date |
| Probable date of harvesting | |
| Estimated production | |

## Appendix 15.8

# A TRI-PARTITE AGREEMENT

This agreement is made on this 23rd day of August, 2003 by and between;

Punjab Agro Food Grain Corporation (PAFC), a company of the Punjab Govt., and registered under he Companies Act 1956, having its registered office at 2 A, Sector 28 'A', Madhya Marg, Chandigarh-160002, herein after referred to as PAFC through Mr. Kripa Shankar Saroj, IAS, Constituted Attorney, which expression shall unless repugnant to the context or meaning thereof shall include its successors in interest and permitted assigns, of the One part;

**And**

Mahindra ShubhLabh Services Ltd. (MSSL), a company registered under the Companies Act 1956, having its registered office at Mahindra Towers, Dr. G.H. Bhosale Marg, P.K. Kurne Chowk, Worli, Mumbai - 400018, Maharashtra, herein after referred to as MSSL, through Mr. Vikram Puri, Constituted Attorney, which expression shall unless repugnant to the context or meaning thereof shall include its successors in interest and permitted assigns, of the Second part;

**And**

(—), a company registered under the Companies Act 1956, having its registered office at, 201 Vipps Centre, Masjid Moth, G.K.-II, New Delhi - 110 048, herein after referred to as, through Mr. Sanjiva Rishi, General Manger - Exports, Constituted Attorney, which expression shall unless repugnant to the context or meaning thereof shall include its successors in interest and permitted assigns of the Third part;

**Where as**

As part of the overall crop diversification plan of he Govt.

of Punjab, PAFC undertakes to facilitate contract farming operations for basmati paddy hereinafter more specifically defined as 'crop' as notified by APEDA / Govt. of India and interface with Govt. of Punjab for necessary notifications for exemption / reduction of mandi tax, other taxes, levis and duties as applicable for basmati grown, stored and transported under Contract Farming, as detailed in Annexure - V of this agreement. PAFC will provide the farmers with a guarantee to buy the harvested crop at a minimum comfort price.

MSSL is capable of identifying farmers for contract farming and to provide field extension support, agri-inputs & credit to the farmers for the cropping and harvesting of the required varieties; which is a leading Rice processor and exporter, is interested in direct procurement of Basmati paddy from the farmers registered under the scheme;

Now this agreement witnesses as follows:

### 1. Effective Date

This Agreement shall become effective from the date of signing thereof and valid for one year and can be renewed on mutually agreed terms and conditions.

### 2. Location

A few districts in the State of Punjab as detailed in Annexure - I have been identified for the purpose of contract farming. The exact locations would be finalized after a detailed survey of the districts. The parties will try and cover certain acreage under Basmati in the season of Kharif beginning April 2003. Based on the initial performance, the acreage would be reviewed as per mutual agreement in the forthcoming seasons. The details regarding the identified districts and acreage are given in Annexure - I.

### 3. Identification and Registration of Farmers

MSSL will identify the farmers willing to participate and register them under the scheme of contract farming. PAFC will provide necessary support through the district agricultural offices to MSSL for propagating the scheme at the field level.

### 4. Provision of Seed

Would provide the requisite quantities of seeds of Basmati paddy to MSSL, duly certified and approved by appropriate government agencies, which would in turn sell the same to the registered farmers. The price of seed would be decided jointly by and MSSL. In the event is unable or unwilling to provide the seeds, MSSL shall procure the same from reliable sources and provide the same to the registered farmers. Money needed for the required quantity of seed will be taken in advance from and the same amount will be reimbursed after the sale of seeds to the registered farmers. As far as possible, shall be consulted about the varieties and sources of seed.

### 5. Services to Farmers

MSSL shall arrange to provide field extension support to the registered farmers, either directly or through any associated extension agency. They may employ the services of experts having in depth knowledge and practical experience of the crop under contract. MSSL will charge from the registered frames service fee for registration as well as for providing dedicated agronomic and other field extension support as below.

a. Preparing concept paper incorporating all the technical detail and package of practices required in respect of the crop.

b. Identification of suitable variety/verities of seed for the crop.

c. On farmer's request, carrying out of soil analysis of the land proposed to be cultivated by the registered farmers.

d. Technical advice to the farmers regarding agronomic practices required to be followed for optimum production and quality.

e. Provision of advice to the farmers on the correct time and procedure for harvest and on post harvest cleaning and other quality control processes.

MSSL shall endeavour to provide credit facility to the interested registered farmers through a suitable reputed bank for purchase of agri-input (fertilizer, seed and agro-chemicals). The credit can be availed only in the form of inputs and no cash disbursements would be made.

### 6. Quality specification

_ has specified the varieties of Basmati as given in Annexure-

II for cultivation and MSSL would be responsible to ensure the cultivation of the requisite variety. The quality specifications for the basmati rice to be taken up for cultivation under contract farming are enclosed in Annexure-III and from a part of this agreement. MSSL shall communicate the quality parameters to the registered farmers, so that the crop is produced accordingly.

### 7. Monitoring and intimation

MSSL will monitor the Basmati crop on an ongoing basis and shall intimate the progress to on a regular basis for any adverse features, which may affect the yield and quality of the Basmati rice.

### 8. Procurement

-will be responsible to purchase all the Basmati paddy produced by the registered farmers provided the same meets the quality specifications laid down in the Annexure-III of this agreement.

MSSL will act as a facilitator for the purchase of the produce from the farmers on behalf of__. Shall depute its experts for checking the quality of the procured material at the collection centers and the off-take and movement thereof. The final decision regarding the quality of the farmers' produce is to be taken on the spot by __ in the consultation with MSSL and in case of poor quality; the value is to be discounted as per the established norms. The ownership / responsibility of the produce is then transferred to the buyer. The registered farmers will be advised o the total value of produce, payment for which shall be made within seven days.

In case any dispute regarding he quality, the paddy shall be returned by the buyer (-) to the procurement center immediately and the farmers shall be asked to take the same back or replace the same with the paddy of acceptable quality. No complaints regarding the quality shall be entertained after two days of the receipt of the paddy in the warehouse of the buyer.

### 9. Procurement prices

– guarantees that it shall purchase the product at a fixed price (FP) as specified in annexure-II, loaded on trucks from the purchase center / collection centre of MSSL. The prices of the Crop prevailing in the reference Mandis as per annexure-IV shall be regularly monitored by MSSL. For any significant increase in price in the reference mandis, the procurement price shall be renegotiated with .

The packing material i.e. gunny bags of required capacity shall be supplied by . in addition shall bear all costs pertaining to mandi labour, bagging, stitching (including sutli), weighment, storage, stacking of bags and loading on to trucks. Out of the advances for procurement of paddy given by to MSSL. Actuals will be billed separately at the end of the season.

**10. Licenses for procurement**

MSSL will obtain the necessary permissions/licenses from the relevant State Govt. agencies to procure the basmati rice a their designated procurement centres. Alternately, PAFC would appoint MSSL as a sub-agent for procurement within PAFC's own license.

PAFC/ - will provide all necessary help to MSSL in obtaining these approvals. PAFC / would assist MSSL in complying with all regulatory requirements pertaining to mandi licensing, food control orders and sales tax/purchase tax etc. MSSL shall procure K2 form from market committee against the applicable market fee and make it available to for their records/transaction.

PAFC will arrange to declare the agreed procurement locations as approved mandies for this purpose.

PAFC shall ensure that exemption/concessions are provided by the State Govt. from the payment of mandi tax, cess or duties etc. as per details given in Annexure-V.

It is clearly understood between the parties that the aforesaid mandi and other taxes would not be borne by MSSL in any case. The same shall be borne by Ltd.

**11. Procurement Infrastructure from PAFC**

The procurement location shall be mutually agreed between PAFC & MSSL. Any expenditure incurred on creation of platforms/sheds will be borne by PAFC.

PAFC will be responsible to ensure that suitable infrastructure including Mandi yard, mechanized/motorized cleaners, wooden pallets, tarpaulin etc. are available at the procurement centres to enable the following:

i. Unloading of Paddy

ii. Cleaning
iii. Bagging
iv. Stitching
v. Stacking of Bags
vi. Weighing
vii. Handling and Loading of Trucks

PAFC will install at these centres appropriate high capacity-cleaning machines at their cost.

**12. Transport**

MSSL shall arrange to dispatch the entire quantity of paddy procured on any particular day to the designated warehouse/ location of by trucks on a "freight to pay" basis. The transportation shall be carried by a transporter designated or approved by and the cost of transportation including transit insurance will be borne by . the part truck paddy left at each centre may be moved the next day provided there is no perceived threat of rains or storm. In case of any such threat, the entire stocks may be moved to the designated location even if part truckloads are involved. MSSL shall get the trucks weighed on a standard weighbridge at the time of dispatch, in the presence of the representatives and the same shall be recorded in the LR/RR. A difference in the measured weight of up to 200 grams per quintal of Crop consigned on the truck between the weight recorded on the LR/RR and he weight recorded by the weighbridge at 's warehouses at the time of unloading of the trucks shall be ignored. However, in case the variation is more than the limit specified above, the claims if any shall be settled directly between and the transporter who has carried the crop using a mutually acceptable independent weighbridge. shall take appropriate transit insurance cover for all the crop consigned by MSSL.

**13. Insurance**

–shall be responsible for the insurance of the produce including the transit from the time of issue of 'J' form to the farmers.

**14. Remuneration**

– shall pay a commission of 2.50% of the value of total procurement to MSSL within seven days from the date of dispatch of paddy from MSSL's collection yard, for all the services rendered by MSSL against invoice to be raised by MSSL. In case of procurement by PAFC, commission of 2.0% would be paid by PAFC to MSSL within seven days.

## 15. Financial arrangements

Payment will be made by to the credit of MSSL's bank account on the seventh day from the date of LR/RR. The LR/RR date is to be used as a proof of receipt. In case of delay of payment beyond 7 days, additional three days will be given on request against a payment of additional 0.25% of the value of the contract. In case of delay in payment beyond 10 days for any reason whatsoever, the above-mentioned plus an additional interest at the rate of 18% per annum shall be paid by for the number of days of delay in payment by beyond 10 days.

In respect of the above contract purchases, shall provide a Bank Guarantee for an amount equivalent to 30% of the value of the contract from a scheduled commercial bank before commencement of procurement. The Bank Guarantee will remain valid from 1st November to 31st December (at any given time Bank Guarantee should be adequate to cover the outstanding against supplies made).

MSSL can unconditionally invoke the Bank Guarantee if the payments are not made within seven / ten days as agreed above.

## 16. Corporate guarantee

— — shall give an unequivocal corporate guarantee to MSSL that they will stand by the commitment made in this Agreement.

## 17. Termination

17.1 The Parties may terminate this Agreement forthwith in the following cases:

(a) In vency – if either party goes into liquidation either compulsory or voluntarily (save for the purposes of reconstruction or amalgamation) or if a receiver is appointed in respect of the whole or any part of its assets or if the party makes an assignment for the benefit of or composition with its creditors generally or threatens to do any of these things or any judgment is made against the party.

(b) Default – If the party is in default under this Agreement, which default is not remedied to the reasonable satisfaction of the other party within thirty(30) days after the receipt of written notice of the default.

(c) Change of management of control – if any material change occurs in the management or control of a party and in particular any substantial change of directors or shareholders of a party save in accordance with the provisions of this Agreement or with the prior written consent of the other party.

17.2 The Agreement may be terminated forthwith by mutual written consent of the parties.

17.3 Settlement of Accounts :

The parties shall, upon termination, reconcile and settle their dues immediately. The modalities for such settlement shall be mutually agreed upon in writing which writing shall form an integral part of this AGREEMENT.

## 18. Miscellaneous

**18.1 Warranty:**

Each of the parties warrants its powers to enter into this Agreement and has obtained all necessary approvals to do so.

**18.2 Force Majure:**

All parties will be released from their respective obligations in the event of national emergency, war, prohibitive governmental regulations or if any other cause beyond the reasonable control of the parties renders performance of this Agreement impossible. The parties agree that if such an even continues for a period of 60 days or more either party can opt to declare the Agreement void. The Agreement be declared void earlier by mutual consent.

**18.3 Notices:**

All notices between the parties shall be in writing, by facsimile (receipt acknowledged), by registered mail or similar communication, and shall be addressed as follows:

PAFC

Attn: Mr. Kripa Shankar Saroj, IAS

Ph. Nos. (0172) 651470, 656241, 656242, 656247

MSSL

Attn: Mr. Vikram Puri (Business Head)

Ph. Nos. (0172) 387 111, 387 100, 371 690

Attn: Mr. Sanjiva Rishi

Ph. Nos. (011) 2646 5757

All communications shall be deemed to have been given on the date of delivery or transmission if personally delivered and on the date of delivery receipt if sent by registered mail.

**18.4 Assignment:**

Neither party shall assign any of the rights and/or obligations under this Agreement to any third party without the prior consent of the other party.

**18.5 Dispute:**

1 in the vent of any dispute or disagreement between the Parties in relation to this Agreement, the parties shall in good faith use their best endeavors to resolve the dispute or disagreement.

All disputes between the parties hereto pertaining to or arising out of this Agreement shall be settled by the parties in accordance with the Arbitration and Conciliation Act 1996 as amended from time to time. The parties shall appoint an arbitrator to be appointed by a mutual consent to settle the dispute between them. The arbitration shall be conducted in Chandigarh. The award given by the arbitrator shall be final and binding on the Parties. The language of the arbitration shall be in English.

**18.6 Jurisdiction:**

It is agreed that only the Chandigarh Courts shall have jurisdiction in respect of the subject matter of this AGREEMENT.

**18.7 Confidentiality:**

1 Each party accepts and agrees to treat as confidential, the details of this Ag4remeeent and all information obtained from the other party pursuant to this Agreement and shall not divulge such information to any person (except to such party's own case on a need to know basis) without the other party's prior written consent provided that this restriction shall not extend to information which was rightfully in the possession of such party prior to the commencement of the negotiations leading to this Agreement, and /

or which is already public knowledge or becomes so at a future date (otherwise than as a result of breach of this Clause) or is disclosed by virtue of Government/ Court Order(s)/direction(s), Statues, Reserve Bank Of India or by any other competent/regulatory/investigate authority etc.

2 **Relationship:** This Agreement is on a Principal to Principal basis and any party to this Agreement shall not be deemed to be the agent of the other except and to the extent provided in this Agreement neither shall it be construed to be a joint venture. Each party shall e responsible for all its obligations towards its respective employees. No employee of any of the three parties shall claim to be employee of the other party and each party shall indemnify and keep indemnified the other party against any loss, damage or claim suffered/ made by any of its employees.

**18.8 Proprietary Rights:**

No party to this Agreement shall use the logo, trademark, trade name copyrights etc. (Proprietary rights) in any advertisement, publishing or material without the written consent of party owing such proprietary rights.

**18.9 Waiver:**

The failure by a party to enforce at any time or for any period any or more of the terms or conditions of this Agreement shall not be a waiver of them or of the right at any time subsequently to enforce all terms and conditions of this Agreement.

**18.10 Survival of Terms:**

The rights and obligations of the Parties under clauses 13,14, 15, 17.3, 18.5.1, 18.6 & 18.7 of this Agreement shall survive even after expiry or termination of this Agreement.

**18.11 Entire Agreement:**

This Agreement supersedes all prior arrangements, proposals and understandings between the parties whether written or oral in this regard and constitutes the entire arrangement between the parties in this regard.

**18.12 Severability and partial invalidity :**

1 If at any time, any provision of this Agreement becomes illegal, invalid or enforceable under the applicable law or directions/orders of any court of competent jurisdiction and/or any judicial/administrative/governmental directions, the legality, validity or enforceability of the remaining provisions of this Agreement shall not be affected or impaired thereby and the Agreement shall continue in full force and effect as if this Agreement had been executed without the illegal/invalid or unenforceable provisions or part thereof.

2 The parties shall endeavor to replace any provisions severed from this Agreement with a legal, valid and enforceable provision that closely matches the intent of the original provision.

**18.13 Attachment(s)/Amendments to form Part of the AGREEMENT :**

1 The attachment(s), writings and amendments thereto shall be deemed to be part of this Agreement as though the provisions thereof were set out therein in extension. The Agreement shall not be amended, altered or modified except by an instrument in writing and signed by the parties. Where the amendment, alteration, modification is done by e-mail or fax or any other recognized mode (whether electronic, digital or optic), the same shall be immediately thereof be reduced in writing and signed by the parties.

IN WITNESS WHEREOF the parties hereto executed these presents on the day and year hereinabove written.

SIGNED AND DMSSLIVERED by the within named

PAFC by its duly Constituted Attorneys,

________________________________________

MR. KRIPA SHANKAR SAROJ, IAS

In the presence of

SIGNED AND DELIVERED by the within named

MSSL by its duly Constituted Attorneys,

________________________________________

Mr.____________________________

In the presence of

SIGNED AND DELIVERED by the within named

By its duly Constituted Attorneys,

________________________________________

MR. SANJIVA RISHI

In the presence of

# Annexure-A

## Annexure-I

| *District* | *Blocks* | *Acreage* |
|---|---|---|
| Kapurthala | | |
| Jalandhar | | |
| Hoshiarpur | | |
| Ludhiana | | |
| Nawashehar | | |
| Ropar | | |
| Fatehgarh Sahib | | |

## Annexure-II

| *Variety* | *Acreage* | *Procurement Price (Per Qtl.)* | *Source* |
|---|---|---|---|
| HBC-19/Basmati 386 | 9000 | Rs.1350 | Picric Ltd. United Rice Land Ltd. |
| Pusa Basmati-1 | | Rs.900 | |

## Annexure-III

| *Particulars* | *HBC-19/Basmati-386* | *Allowances* |
|---|---|---|
| Moisture | 17.0% Max | |
| Admixture | 2.5% Max | |
| Green Grains | 6.0% Max | |
| Empty Grains | 2.0% Max | |
| Empty Shells | 0.5% Max | |
| Damaged, discolored & broken | | |

*Note:*

1. Higher moisture than 17% would not be accepted
2. Admixture & other points - if under reasonable deviation would be dealt under the mechanism of a quality discount or cut as/called in the industry circles.

## Annexure-IV

*Reference Mandis for monitoring of Price*

| Sr. No. | Reference Mandi |
|---|---|
| 1. | Amritsar |
| 2. | Gohana |
| 3. | Kaithal |
| 4. | Tarantaran |
| 5. | Taraori |

## Annexure-V

| *Sl. No.* | *Fee/Cess* | *Current Applicable Rate (%)* | *Proposed Rate (%)* | *Rebate for Commodities under Contract Farming (%)* |
|---|---|---|---|---|
| 1. | Market Fee | 2 | 0.25 | 1.75 |
| 2. | R.D. Cess | 2 | 0.25 | 1.75 |
| 3. | I.D. Cess | 1 | 0.25 | 0.75 |
| *Total* | | 5 | 0.75 | 4.25 |

## Appendix 15.9

# Contract Agreement Between the Company & the Farmer

This AGREEMENT is made between Intergarden India Pvt. Ltd. a company under the Companies Act, 1956 and Shri. – – – – – – – – – – – S/o Shri. – – – – – – – – – – – of – – – – – – (place) in – – – – – – – – – – – District/Block or his/her legal heir/ representative/administrator and the persons appointed by them.

The Company is a 100% export oriented registered unit and is engaged in processing of vegetables and fresh fruits in salt water and vinegar and exporting the same. For this purpose, it has established processing facilities especially for gherkin (cucumber). The company intends to have long term arrangement with the suitable farmers who are willing to sell their produce to the company.

The farmer should be owner/in possession of farm lands and should be willing to grow the above produce and willing to sell the entire produce to the company as per the terms and conditions prescribed under this arrangement:

1) The farmer has to grow gherkins or any other crop indicated by the company in half/one acre of agricultural land, taking three crops in a year, as per the norms prescribed by the company. The farmer has agreed not to grow any other crops in the above land without the permission of the company.

2) The farmer agrees to sell the entire produce grown in the above land to the company without any conditions and he will not sell the same to any other company without obtaining the prior approval of the company.

3) The farmer will be responsible for taking adequate measure for growing above crops. Further, he confirms that he will

follow the technical guidance given by the company. He agrees to follow the norms relating to use of prescribed quality of seeds type of fertilizers and chemicals for plant protection.

4) The farmer will be responsible for segregation of the produce as per the standards prescribed by the company and the farmer will be responsible from delivering the produce in the manner indicated by the Company to the specified places.

5) The company has rights under this agreement to inspect the land of the farmer and guide the farmer in growing of the above crops.

6) The company will try to ensure supply of chemical fertilizers and chemicals for plant protection, at competitive rates, to the farmer. The farmer has to use these materials only for growing of the crops specified by the company and should not use the same for any other purpose.

7) The farmer has to give a receipt for the materials received from the company. In case, the farmer is not available while distributing these materials, the same will be handed over to his relatives, wife, son, daughter and they will acknowledge the receipt of the same.

8) The farmer will have to sell the produce to the company at the rate fixed by the company for the various quality types.

9) The company will accept only the good quality produce and the proceeds will be paid by means of a crossed cheque, once in a week.

10) The farmer has to repay the loan amount along with interest to the company irrespective of whether the company purchases the produce or not. In case, he is not able to repay the loan amount within 6 months, he has to repay the same along with interest at 18%.

11) In case, the farmer does not utilize the material supplied by the company or uses improper practices for growing the crops or does not grow the crops, this agreement will be automatically terminated. But, the farmer may have to meet the losses suffered by the company in this regard.

12) This Agreement will be operative for a period of one year, but the same can be extended by one/two years under the same terms and conditions.

13) This Agreement has been executed based on mutual trust for the purpose of exporting the farm produce and as such both the parties agree to honour their respective commitments and responsibilities.

14) The company may enter into similar agreements with other farmers but the company assures this farmer that it will abide by the conditions under this agreement, more particularly regarding extension of loan, provision of fertilizers, offering guidance etc.

15) In case, both the parties of this agreement are unable to meet the conditions under this agreement due to reasons beyond the control of both the parties, unless the farmer repays the loan and cost of the materials supplied by the company, both the parties will not be responsible for breach of contract.

16) In case, the farmer does not supply continuously, during the two crop period, the produce as per the quality standards of the company, this contract will be terminated automatically.

17) In case of difference of opinion between he two parties, both the parties would try to resolve the dispute amicably and in case not being able to do so, the same will be referred to an arbitrator under the Indian Arbitration Act, 1940.

18) This Agreement will be under the jurisdiction of Bangalore City Court and resolving of disputes arising under this agreement will not come under the jurisdiction of any other court in India. Both the parties have agreed to the above conditions and has signed this agreement in front of the following witnesses:

| 1. Witness 1 | Farmer |
|---|---|
| 2. Witness 2 | Company |

*Source:* Contract farming in Gherkins under AEZ in Karnataka, study report, Jan 3-4, 2003, NABARD, Mumbai

## Appendix 15.10A

# Potato Multiplication Agreement

This agreement is made and entered into on this ____ day of ____, 2003 between FRINTO-LAY INDIA, a company incorporated under the Companies Act, 1956 with its registered office at 3B, DLF Corporate Park, Qutub Enclave-III, Gurgaon and an office at 13th Floor, Mohan Dev Building, 13 Tolstoy Marg, Connaught Place, New Delhi (hereinafter called 'FLI' which term shall unless repugnant to the context shall include its successors in interest, nominees and assigns), of the First Part.

AND

Sh. ______________________________, S/o. __________________________, R/o. ________________________________________ (hereinafter called 'GROWER' which term shall unless repugnant to the context shall include his successors in interest, nominees and assigns), of the Second Part; Whereas

1. GROWER is the owner/lessee of _______ acres of land at ________________________________________ (hereinafter called "the said land") and is desirous of undertaking the multiplication of Potato seeds for chip on the said land and
2. FLI is willing to provide FL Variety potato seeds (FLI Proprietary developed out of FLI R&D) to the GROWER for Chip multiplication, and to procure the output at a predetermined price subject to terms & conditions laid out in the agreement.

Now this Agreement Witnessth as Under:

### 1. Supply of Fl Variety Potato Seeds

1.1 FLI agrees to supply _____ Kgs. of ________________ FLI variety potato seeds valued at Rs. ______ per Kg.

amounting to Rs. ___________ (Rupees ___________________________) (hereinafter "Seed Value") to the GROWER for multiplication into chip grade potatoes by planting in the said land. FLI will deliver seeds to the Grower at a designated common place in Pune Distt.

1.2 GROWER shall pay to FLI, in advance a sum of Rs. _______ (Rupees ________________________________), being ___% of seed value. The balance ____% of the seed value amounting to Rs. _______ (Rupees ______________________) (hereinafter balance seed value) shall be adjusted from the amount payable under clause 3.2 of this agreement to the GROWER by FLI.

## 2. Multiplication of Fli Variety Potato Seeds

2.1 Grower shall be responsible for all farming activities including land preparation, irrigation, planting, plant protection measures and harvesting to maximize yield per acre and to produce quality chip grade potato as prescribed in Annexure ___.

2.2 Grower shall be responsible for providing all the required inputs including water, chemicals, fertilizers, fungicides, insecticides and labour.

2.3 Grower shall strictly follow Package of Practice as prescribed by FLI as per Annexure __. Grower shall conduct the planting and harvesting operations and the packing of the multiplied chip grade potatoes in the presence of the FLI representative or after receiving instructions from FLI to start such operations.

2.4 FLI reserves the right to supervise at all times the activities of multiplication being carried out by the GROWER and shall advise, training and consultancy including advice on use of insecticides/pesticides to the GROWER necessary for the multiplication.

2.5 GROWER shall offer the entire produce to FLI for sale at its Factory Ranjan Gaon. The produce will be graded & quality tested at the collection center. FLI basis the quality test results & the parameters set out in Annexure ___ purchase the produce or reject & return the produce entirely or partly.

2.6 GROWER shall keep the FLI variety potato seeds and the multiplied chip grade potatoes in hygienic and safe condition and ensure its safekeeping.

### 3. Delivery of Multiplied Chip Grade Potatoes

3.1 GROWER shall deliver the chip grade multiplied potatoes to FLI or its designated Party FOR at FLI Factory Ranjan Gaon as per the time schedule agreed upon between the parties and at a date not later than the date specified in clause 7 of this agreement.

3.2 "The repurchase Price" shall include the cost of planting, rouging, haulm-cutting, harvesting, sorting, grading, packing of the multiplied chip grade potatoes, cost of transporting the multiplied chip grade potatoes at FLI factory at Ranjan Gaon and inputs used in the multiplication operations, including, water, chemicals, fertilizers, fungicides, insecticides. The said Repurchase Price shall be payable within fifteen days of the receipt of the entire yield. Subject to clause 3.4 of this agreement. FLI shall pay the Repurchase Price to the grower basis either of the following.

At a fixed price of Rs. 5 per Kg. for September, October harvest and Rs. 5.50/kg. for the November 03 harvest of multiplied chip grade potatoes delivered by the GROWER to FLI plus an incentive based on the solids and TPOD basis the quality checks made by FLI as per Annexure 'B'.

OR

Under market linked pricing scheme as appended plus an incentive based on the solids and TPOD basis the quality checks made by FLI as per Annexure 'B'. (One option to be struck out & acknowledged by both parties)

3.3 FLI shall conduct a quality check immediately on delivery of the multiplied chip grad potatoes. FLI shall neither be liable to take delivery of the multiplied chip grad potatoes from the GROWER nor shall be liable to pay any consideration for the multiplied chip grade potatoes to the GROWER if the multiplied chip grade potatoes are not of the quality as is specified in Annexure 'A'.

**4. General**

4.1 GROWER shall be responsible for all taxes, levies etc. in respect of the said land and the GROWER.

4.2 GROWER agrees to indemnify and keep indemnified FLI against any loss, costs, charges and expenses that FLI may suffer or incur on account of any claim being made by any person or persons against the GROWER or FLI in respect of anything done in pursuance of this agreement or arising out of any defect in the title of the said land or in any other manner whatsoever.

4.3 GROWER represents and warrants that it shall not, during the subsistence of this agreement:

(i) sell or dispose of the FLI variety potato seeds or multiplied chip grade potatoes to any person or company other than to FLI or any party designated, in writing by FLI; or

(ii) use the FLI variety potato seeds, for any purpose, other than multiplication under the terms of this Agreement.

4.4 FLI will not be held liable or responsible for any failure in the crop or for any shortfall in the yield of the FLI variety potato seeds.

4.5 The relationship between FLI and the GROWER shall be on principal to principal basis and this agreement shall always be construed accordingly.

4.6 GROWER shall be responsible for procurement, direction and supervision of all labour utilized in carrying out of the multiplication operations. The said labour shall at no time be deemed / represented to be employees of FLI. GROWER shall be fully responsible for all actions of its workforce and deal with any suits/ legal actions, which may arise in connection with them and keep FLI indemnified in this regard.

4.7 FLI has the right to assign the right to purchase the multiplied chip grade potatoes from the GROWER to any Designated Party.

4.8 This Agreement shall become effective from the time of handing over the FLI variety potato seeds to the GROWER by FLI and would terminate upon the GROWER handing over the entire yield of multiplied chip grade potatoes to FLI, which shall not be later than __________.

4.9 Courts in New Delhi will have exclusive jurisdiction in the event of any legal/jurisdictional proceedings.

4.10 This agreement has been read out to the GROWER in vernacular in the presence of the witnesses hereunder and the GROWER represents that he fully understands the terms and conditions of this agreement.

IN WITNESS WHEREOF these presents have been executed on behalf of the parties hereto as of the day and year first above written.

For, FRITO-LAY INDIA (GROWER) Witnesses:

1. ____________
2. ____________

## Appendix A

# Market Linked Pricing Scheme

| *REFERENCE RATE* | *FLI RATE* | *REFERENCE RATE* | *FLI RATE* | *REFERENCE RATE* | *FLI RATE* |
|---|---|---|---|---|---|
| 3.00 | 2.96 | 5.30 | 5.23 | 7.70 | 7.59 |
| 3.10 | 3.06 | 5.40 | 5.32 | 7.80 | 7.69 |
| 3.20 | 3.16 | 5.50 | 5.42 | 7.90 | 7.79 |
| 3.30 | 3.25 | 5.60 | 5.52 | 8.00 | 7.89 |
| 3.40 | 3.35 | 5.70 | 5.62 | 8.10 | 7.99 |
| **3.50** | **3.45** | 5.80 | 5.72 | 8.20 | 8.09 |
| 3.60 | 3.55 | 5.90 | 5.82 | 8.30 | 8.18 |
| 3.70 | 3.65 | 6.00 | 5.92 | 8.40 | 8.28 |
| 3.80 | 3.75 | 6.10 | 6.01 | 8.50 | 8.38 |
| 3.90 | 3.85 | 6.20 | 6.11 | 8.60 | 8.48 |
| 4.00 | 3.94 | 6.30 | 6.21 | 8.70 | 8.58 |
| 4.10 | 4.04 | 6.40 | 6.31 | 8.80 | 8.68 |
| 4.20 | 4.14 | 6.50 | 6.41 | 8.90 | 8.78 |
| 4.30 | 4.24 | 6.60 | 6.51 | 9.00 | 8.87 |
| 4.40 | 4.34 | 6.70 | 6.61 | 9.10 | 8.97 |
| 4.50 | 4.44 | 6.80 | 6.70 | 9.20 | 9.07 |
| 4.60 | 4.54 | 6.90 | 6.80 | 9.30 | 9.17 |
| 4.70 | 4.63 | 7.00 | 6.90 | 9.40 | 9.27 |
| 4.80 | 4.73 | 7.10 | 7.00 | 9.50 | 9.37 |
| 4.90 | 4.83 | 7.20 | 7.10 | 9.60 | 9.47 |
| 5.00 | **4.93** | 7.30 | 7.20 | 9.70 | 9.56 |
| 5.10 | 5.03 | 7.40 | 7.30 | 9.80 | 9.66 |
| 5.20 | 5.13 | 7.50 | **7.40** | 9.90 | 9.76 |
| | | 7.60 | 7.49 | 10.00 | **9.86** |

Referemce Rate is the Average of Preceeding 3-Day Block of Published Newpapers Rates for Potato at Gultekadi Markety Ard, Pune

**Terms & Conditions for Fli Rates Are:**

1. Delivery to be Mare at Factory at Ranjangaon.
2. Rates Mentioned are for Chip Grade Potato Only.

3. Rates Are Inclusive of Transportation upto Factory.
4. Gunny Bags will be Returned if Lifted on the Same Day.
5. Under Size/ Over Size Potatoes to be Paid @ 30% of Fli Rate.
6. Rotten/Soil/Green Mechanical Damage Potato will be Returned on the Same Day.

**Annexure-B**

# Incentives for TPOD & Solid % (Amt. in Rs.)

| *SOLID* | *INCENTIVE /KG* | *FLI TPOD* | *INCENTIVE/ KG* | *TOTAL INCENTIVE/KG* |
|---|---|---|---|---|
| <15 | 0.00 | 12-15 | 0.00 | 0.00 |
| | | 8-12 | 0.05 | 0.05 |
| | | >8 | 0.10 | 0.10 |
| =15-16 | 0.10 | 12-15 | 0.00 | 0.10 |
| | | 8-12 | 0.05 | 0.15 |
| | | >8 | 0.10 | 0.20 |
| =>16 | 0.15 | 12-15 | 0.00 | 0.15 |
| | | 8-12 | 0.05 | 0.20 |
| | | >8 | 0.10 | 0.25 |

## Appendix 15.10B

# Contract Farming Administration Agreement

This agreement is made on this ____ day of _____ in the year 2003 between Frinto-Lay India, a company incorporated and registered under the Companies Act, 1956 having its registered office at 'S' Block, 3B DLF Corporate Park, Qutub Enclave - III, Gurgaon - 122 002, Haryana (hereinafter called 'FLI' which term shall unless repugnant to the context or meaning thereof, includes its successors, nominees and assigns) of the FIRST PART.

**And**

Shri ____________________________, S/o. ______________________, R/o. ________________________________________ (hereinafter called "Hundekari" (which term shall repugnant to the context or meaning thereof, includes its successors, nominees and assigns) of the SECOND PART.

**Whereas**

1. Hundekari is engaged in the activities of providing marketing services to the farmers and its activities includes providing agri inputs on credit including seeds as and when required by the farmers, organizing grading and sorting of the produce, bagging and transporting of agricultural produce on farmer's behalf to the market; and
2. FLI is involved in development, production & marketing of snack foods; and
3. Hundekari & FLI are desirous of entering into an agreement wherein Hundekari shall execute a programme in contract farming in potato with the farmers on behalf of FLI and

FLI buys the potato so produced by the specified farmers under separate tripartite agreement to be executed between the farmers, Hundekari and FLI (hereinafter "Tripartite Agreement"), subject to terms and conditions specified in this agreement.

Now therefore the Parties here in Record their Intention as Follows:

**1. Definitions**

1.1 "Specified Areas" shall mean the village ________ located in Pune, Maharashtra.

1.2 'Specified farmers' shall mean all farmers engaged in cultivation of potatoes under chip grade potato multiplication program in the specified areas and with whom a Tripartite Agreement has been entered into between the Hunderkari and FLI.

1.3 'FL' variety potato seeds shall mean a specific variety of potato seeds that are the result of research and development activities of FLI and in which all intellectual property rights vests in FLI.

1.4 'Chip Grade Potato Multiplication Program' shall mean an association between Hundekari, FLI and individual specified Farmers whereby the specified farmers multiply FL variety potato seeds into chip grade potatoes as per the package of practices and procurement of such multiplied chip grade potatoes by FLI.

**2. Obligations of Hundekari:**

2.1 Hundekari will administer chip grade potato multiplication program for FL variety potatoes seeds with the specified farmers at such commercial terms as may be agreed between the specified farmers, FLI and Hundekari as per separate tripartite Chip grade potato multiplication agreements.

2.2 Hundekari will sign up the specified farmers for the programme. Hundekari shall organize to get the tripartite Chip grade potato multiplication agreement signed.

2.3 Hundekari shall coordinate the distribution of the FL variety potato seeds to the specified farmers which has been supplied by FLI to Hundekari at such price as may be agreed in the tripartite agreement.

2.4 Hundekari shall provide to FL acknowledgement/ receipts from specified farmers for the FL seeds received.

2.5 Hundekari will work as the main link between specified farmers and FLI for the purpose of extension/ development communication and shall maintain the village boards provided by FLI.

2.6 Hundekari may take advice from FLI exports in order to maximize output & to avert crop failures.

2.7 Hundekari shall assist the specified farmers by helping specified farmers in procuring quality inputs as and when required.

2.8 Hundekari shall assist FLI in procuring the output from the specified farmers as per the harvest visa issue by local FLI representative. Hundekari shall endeavor to see that the entire produce is supplied to FLI as per the terms of the tripartite agreement.

2.9 Hundekari will also manage local quality labs for cook test and solids measurement.

2.10 Hundekari will provide loans to farmers as and when required by such farmers for procurement of agri inputs and for carrying out the multiplication operations.

2.11 In the event of the specified farmer failing to supply multiplied seeds or any part thereof to FLI for any reason whatsoever, Hundekari indemnifies FLI for the balance unpaid and unadjusted value of the seed supplied to the specified farmer by FLI.

**3. Obligations & Rights of FLI:**

3.1 FLI shall procure from the specified farmers the Chip grade potatoes so produced by specified farmers subject to certain terms & conditions as laid out in the tripartite Chip grade potato multiplication agreement.

3.2 FLI shall provide acceptable quality of FL variety seeds with respect to size and germination (__ %) minimum.

3.3 Any consideration payable to Hundekari by FLI under this agreement shall be subject to deduction of tax at source, if applicable.

3.4 FLI will deduct and pay to Hundekari amount equivalent to the seed cost and payment for any other service/input, incase "Adhikar Patra" executed by the specified farmers is provided by the Hundekari to FLI at least 7 days in advance.

3.5 FLI shall replace the rejected seed at the time of delivery in case the seed is found to be of inferior grade or of lower germination.

3.6 FLI shall replace the seeds in case the germination fails due to virus.

**4. Consideration of Hundekari:**

4.1 In consideration of the administrative services rendered by Hundekari to FLI under this agreement, FLI shall pay a commission of 10 paise per kg on the total accepted quantity of potatoes procured by FLI from the specified farmers. This payment falls due after the end of procurement of multiplied potatoes.

4.2 FLI shall also pay to Hundekari a service charge of 50 paise for every Kg. of seed supplied to specified farmers. This payment falls due after every truck is distributed by Hundekari.

4.3 FLI shall also pay to Hundekari a service charge of 5 paise per kg. on the total accepted quantity of potatoes procured by FLI from specified farmers for providing extention support including lab operation and FLI board maintenance.

**5. Confidentiality:**

5.1 Both parties shall use utmost care to maintain strict confidentiality of all technical and other information relating to this agreement. Neither party shall use such information for any purpose other than the purpose contemplated under this agreement. This obligation of confidentiality will not apply to information that is generally available to the public through no act or omission of the parties or becomes known to either party through a third party with no obligations of confidentiality, or is required to b disclosed by law, court order or request by any government regulatory authority.

**6. Termination:**

6.1 This agreement can be terminated only by FLI by providing one month's prior notice. Provided that the rights that may have accrued to the parties under this agreement shall survive and the parties shall have the right to enforce such rights.

**7. Arbitration & Jurisdiction:**

7.1 This agreement shall be subject to the exclusive jurisdiction of the courts at Delhi, India.

7.2 The parties shall make best efforts to resolve all differences and disputes arising in connection with this agreement, through cooperation and consultation. In case the differences or disputes are not settled amicably, then they shall be finally settled under the Arbitration and Conciliation Act, 1996. The award of the arbitrator(s) shall be final and binding on the parties. Arbitration proceedings shall take place in Delhi, India.

IN WITNESS WHEREOF, the parties have caused their respective duly authorized representatives to execute this Agreement the day and the year first herein above written.

For, FRITO-LAY INDIA (HUNDEKARI) Witnesses

1. ______________

2. ______________

## Appendix 15.10C

# Chip Grade Potato Multiplication Tripartite Agreement

This agreement is made and entered into on this ____ day of _____ 2005.

**Between**

PEPSICO INDIA HOLDINGS PVT. LTD. (FRITO LAY DIVISION), a company incorporated under the Companies Act, 1956 with its registered office at 3B Corporate Park, DLF Qutab Enclave, Phase-III, Gurgaon, and having an office at Mohan Dev Building, 13 Tolstoy Marg, Connaught Place, New Delhi (hereinafter called 'PIHPL' which term shall unless repugnant to the context shall include its successors in interest, nominees and assigns), of the First Part.

**And**

Sh. ______________________________, S/o. _________________________, R/o. ______________________________________________ (hereinafter called 'GROWER' which term shall unless repugnant to the context shall include his successors in interest, nominees and assigns), of the third Part;

**Whereas**

1. HUNDEKARI and PIHPL have entered into an Agreement dated ______ wherein the HUNDEKARI has agreed to facilitate chip grade potato multiplication program in village _____________ of Pune in Maharashtra state with growers and provide Farming Solutions in connection therewith.
2. PIHPL has identified the GROWER alongwith the Hundekari and Hundekari has agreed to extend loans to the growers for arranging inputs as and when required.

3. Hundekari is responsible for the payment of seed amount on behalf of the grower of PIHPL and hence Grower authorizes PIHPL to deduct amount as mentioned in Adhikar Patra to be debited to farmer's account and paid to Hundekari on its behalf.

Now this Agreement witnessth as Under:

### 1. Supply of FI Varitety Potato Seeds

1.1 PIHPL agrees to supply ____________________ Kgs of ______________ PIHPL variety to the GROWER through Hundekari ................................ for multiplication into chip grade potatoes by planting in the said land. PIHPL will deliver seeds to the Hundekari at a designated common place in Pune. Such seed shall then be forwarded to the Grower by the Hundekari.

1.2 Hundekari shall pay 50% of the FL variety of seed supplied to the farmers through the Hundekari immediately on its delivery to the Hundekari as per clause 1.1 above. Balance 50% shall be adjusted against the Repurchase price payable by PIHPL. In the event of the grower failing to supply multiplied potatoes or any part thereof to PIHPL for any reason whatsoever, Hundekari indemnifies PIHPL for the balance unpaid and unadjusted value of the seed supplied to the grower by PIHPL.

1.3 Hundekari to take post dated cheque from grower for the balance 50% as a security. It is a Hundekari obligation to provide a receipt of the cheque to the grower. This post dated cheque will be presented to recover seed cost wherein grower fails to supply multiplied potatoes or any part thereof to PIHPL by 30th November 2005.

### 2. Multiplication of Pihpl Variety Potato Seeds

2.1 Grower shall be responsible for all farming activities including land preparation, irrigation, planting, plant protection measures and harvesting to maximize yield per acre and to produce quality chip grade potato as prescribed in Annexure-A.

2.2 Grower shall be responsible for providing all the required inputs including water, chemicals, fertilizers, fungicides, insecticides and labour.

2.3 Grower shall strictly follow Package of Practices as prescribed by PIHPL as per PACKAGE OF PRACTICE BOOK provided. GROWER shall conduct the planting and harvesting operations and the packing of the multiplied chip grade potatoes in the presence of the PIHPL representative or after receiving instructions from PIHPL to start such operations.

2.4 PIHPL reserves the right to supervise at all times the activities of multiplication being carried out by the GROWER and shall advise, training and consultancy including advice on use of insecticides/pesticides to the GROWER necessary for the multiplication.

2.5 GROWER shall offer the entire produce to PIHPL for sale at its collection centre at Ranjangaon. The produce will be graded & quality tested at the collection centre. PIHPL based on the quality test results & the parameters set out in Annexure A purchase the produce or reject & return the produce entirely or partly.

2.6 GROWER shall keep the PIHPL variety potato seeds and the multiplied chip grade potatoes in hygienic and safe condition and ensure its safe keeping.

2.7 Hundekari shall ensure that the obligations of the GROWER under this agreement are complied with. Any non-compliance by the Grower shall be deemed to be non-compliance by the Hundekari.

### 3. Delivery of Multiplied Chip Grade Potatoes

3.1 GROWER shall deliver the chip grade multiplied potatoes to PIHPL or its Designated Party OR PIHPL collection center at Ranjangaon plant as per the time schedule agreed upon between the parties in line with the vendor visa issued by the authorized representative of PIHPL.

3.2 "The Repurchase Price" shall include the cost of planting, roughing, haulm-cutting, harvesting, sorting, grading, packing of the multiplied chip grade potatoes, cost of transporting the multiplied chip grade potatoes at PIHPL collection centre at Ranjangaon and inputs used in the multiplication operations, including water, chemicals, fertilizers, fungicides, insecticides. The said Repurchase Price shall be payable within fifteen days of the receipt of the entire yield of PIHPL. Subject to clause 3.4 of this agreement, PIHPL shall pay the Repurchase Price based on either of the following:

At a fixed price of Rs. 6.25/- per kg. for harvested potatoes supplied in September 05, Rs. 6.25/- per Kg. for harvested potatoes supplied in October 05 and Rs. 6.80/- per Kg. for potatoes supplied in November 05 harvest of multiplied chip grade potatoes delivered by the GROWER to PIHPL plus an incentive based on the solids and TPOD basis the quality checks made by PIHPL as per Annexure-B.

Provided that PIHPL shall deduct from the Repurchase price amount as mentioned in the Adhikar Patra, if deposited as per clause 1.2 of this agreement.

3.3 In case grower's potato multiplication ratio from the seed supplied by PIHPL exceeds 1:10 then PIHPL will have the rights to refuse to buy the potatoes in excess of 1:10 ratio. Grower should provide evidence that potatoes being offered in excess of 1:10 ratio is being multiplied from the seed supplied by PIHPL under contract.

3.4 PIHPL shall pay the repurchase price (less deduction as per clause 1.2) to the Grower in the event no Adhikar Patra is received from the Grower.

Provided that in the event PIHPL receives a Adhikar Patra signed by the Grower requesting PIHPL that the payment of Repurchase price or part thereof be paid to the Hundekari, PIHPL shall pay such amount as is mentioned in the Adhikar Patra to the Hundekari and the balance, if any to the Grower.

In either of the two cases above, PIHPL, on making payment to the Grower or to the Hundekari or both as the case may be, shall be deemed to be sufficiently discharged from its liability to pay the Repurchase Price.

3.5 PIHPL shall conduct a quality check immediately on delivery of the multiplied chip grade potatoes. PIHPL shall neither be liable to take delivery of the multiplied chip grade potatoes from the GROWER nor shall be liable to pay any consideration for the multiplied chip grade potatoes to the GROWER if the multiplied chip grade potatoes are not of the quality as is specified in Annexure-A.

**4. Limitation of Liability:**

Notwithstanding anything contained in the agreement:

4.1 PIHPL shall not in any way be deemed to be the Guarantor or Surety for the Grower for repayment of any moneys that may be due to the Hundekari from the Grower.

4.2 PIHPL shall not be responsible towards the payment of Repurchase price to the Grower or to Hundekari.

(a) In the event of a crop failure, either due to force majuere or for any reason whatsoever, or

(b) In the event of the failure on the part of the Grower or the Hundekari to deliver Multiplied Chip grade Potato to PIHPL to its satisfaction.

4.3 PIHPL shall not be liable to pay to the Grower or Hundekari any amount, which is in excess of the Repurchase Price accruing to the Grower.

4.4 In any of the events as contemplated under clauses 4.2 and 4.3, the Hundekari may recover any amount from the Grower through any civil/criminal action, to which PIHPL shall not be a necessary party.

**5. General:**

5.1 GROWER shall be responsible for all taxes, levies etc. in respect of the said land and the GROWER.

5.2 GROWER agrees to indemnify and keep indemnified PIHPL against any loss, costs, charges and expenses that PIHPL may suffer or incur on account of any claim being made by any person or persons against the GROWER or PIHPL in respect of anything done in pursuance of this agreement or arising out of any defect in the title of the said land or in any other manner whatsoever.

5.3 GROWER and Hundekari represent and warrant that they shall not, duting the subsistence of this agreement.

Sell or dispose of the PIHPL variety potato seeds or multiplied chip grade potatoes to any person or company other than to PIHPL or any party designated, in writing, by PIHPL; or use the PIHPL variety potato seeds, for any purpose, other than multiplication under the terms of this Agreement.

5.4 PIHPL will not be held liable or responsible for any failure in the crop or for any shortfall in the yield of the PIHPL variety potato seeds.

5.5 The relationship between PIHPL, Hundekari and the GROWER shall be on principal to principal basis and this agreement shall always be construed accordingly.

5.6 GROWER and Hundekari shall be responsible for procurement, direction and supervision of all labour utilized in carrying out of the multiplication operations. The said labour shall at no time be deemed/represented to be employees of PIHPL.GROWER and Hundekari shall be fully responsible for all actions of their workforce and deal with any suits/legal actions, which may arise in connection with them and keep PIHPL indemnified in this regard.

5.7 PIHPL has the right to assign the right to purchase the multiplied chip grade potatoes from the GROWER to any Designated Party.

5.8 This Agreement shall become effective from the time of handing over the PIHPL variety potato seeds to the Hundekari by PIHPL and would terminate upon the GROWER handing over the entire yield of multiplied chip grade potatoes to PIHPL, which shall not be later than ____.

5.9 Courts in New Delhi will have exclusive jurisdiction in the event of any legal/jurisdictional proceedings.

5.10 This agreement has been read out to the GROWER and the Hundekari in vernacular in the presence of the witnesses hereunder and the Hundekari and GROWER represent that they fully understand the terms and conditions of this agreement.

IN WITNESS WHEREOF these present have been executed on behalf of the parties hereto as of the day and year first above written.

For, PEPSICO INDIA HOLDINGS PVT. LTD. (GROWER) (HUNDEKARI)

Witness: 1. ______________________

2. ______________________

# Annexure-'A'

Potatoes to be Accepted if Found as per Below Quality Specification:

**1. Cook Test sample**

(a) Undesirable Color of Water (UC) : Less than 5%

(b) Total Defects of Potato Water (TPOD) : Less than 20%

(c) PIHPL Potato Solid : Less than 14%

**2. On physical sample basis**

*Details Limitation Action*

Less than 45 mm diameter Less than 3% Consignment will be accepted

More than 85 MM diameter Less than 5% Consignment will be accepted

Greening Less than 3% Consignment will be accepted

Mechanical Damage Less than 5% Consignment will be accepted

Dry Rot Less than 2% Consignment will be accepted

Scab Less than 7% Consignment will be accepted

Second Growth Less than 2% Consignment will be accepted

**Soil:** In a consignment of 10 ton of potatoes soil of 180 kg maximum adhere with potatoes will only be accepted. Any potatoes which do not comply with above specification will be returned o grower on the same day of unloading.

# Annexure-'B'

| *Particulars* | *September 2005* | *October 2005* | *November 2005* |
|---|---|---|---|
| Fixed Repurchase Rate | Rs. 6.25 per kg. | Rs. 6.25 per Kg. | Rs. 6.80 per kg. |
| Quality Incentives | | | |
| 1) PIHPL Solid | | | |
| 14% to 16.25% | Nil | Nil | Nil |
| 16.25% to 16.50% | Re.0.05 per kg. | Re.0.05 per kg. | Re.0.05 per kg. |
| 16.50% to 16.75% | Re.0.10 per kg. | Re.0.10 per kg. | Re.0.10 per kg. |
| 16.75% to 17.00% | Re.0.25 per kg. | Re.0.25 per kg. | Re.0.25 per kg. |
| More than 17% | Re.0.35 per kg. | Re.0.35 per kg. | Re.0.35 per kg. |
| 2) TPOD | | | |
| More than 15% | Nil | Nil | Nil |
| 12% to 15% | Re.0.05 per kg. | Re.0.05 per kg. | Re.0.05 per kg. |
| 8% to 12% | Re.0.10 per kg. | Re.0.10 per kg. | Re.0.10 per kg. |
| Less than 8% | Re.0.15 per kg. | Re.0.15 per kg. | Re.0.15 per kg. |
| 3) Time lines of Supplying Potatoes | | | |
| Period | September 2005 | October 2005 | November 2005 |
| 1st fortnight of the month | | | |
| 2nd fortnight of the month | | | |

# Index

## H



## I